New perspectives on community development

Mahlon Apgar, IV

Principal, McKinsey & Company, Inc.

Editor

London . New York . St Louis . San Francisco . Auckland . Düsseldorf
Johannesburg . Kuala Lumpur . Mexico . Montreal . New Delhi . Panama
Paris . São Paulo . Singapore . Sydney . Tokyo . Toronto

Published by McGRAW-HILL Book Company (UK) Limited
MAIDENHEAD . BERKSHIRE . ENGLAND

07 084475 5

Library of Congress Cataloging in Publication Data

Main entry under title:

New perspectives on community development.

   Includes bibliographical references
   1. Cities and towns—Planning—Addresses, essays, lectures. 2.
New towns—Addresses, essays, lectures. 3. Regional planning—
Addresses, essays, lectures. 4. Social policy—Addresses, essays,
lectures. 5. Community development—Addresses, essays, lectures.
I. Apgar, Mohlon. II. McKinsey and Company.

HT166.N44   309.2'62   76–3511
ISBN 0–07–084475–5

12345 JWA 79876
PRINTED AND BOUND IN GREAT BRITAIN

Contents

Forewords

Problems and prospects in community planning

RICHARD LLEWELYN-DAVIES

To create a completely new town or community by deliberate action, whether public or private, is an heroic undertaking. So it is not surprising that no continuous thread of history runs through the evolution of the idea and its practical achievement. Instead, there has been a wave series. Pressure to resolve the environmental and social problems of urban society builds up, eventually generating a burst of sustained activity aimed at the creation of new urban centres, usually during a period of economic and political confidence. Then, often in a period of recession, the wave subsides, the interest in new communities fades, and nothing more is done until the next wave begins to build up.

Britain and the US are today in the trough of the wave, while in France the new towns program is already past its peak. After a period of considerable sustained effort, with dramatic developments in both theory and practice, we have now entered a phase when few new projects are likely, at least for a year or two. It is the right moment to stand back a little and review, in a critical but constructive manner, the achievements of the past ten years. This very timely book is a major contribution to such a review.

It is certain that deliberately created new urban centres will be part of the future. No reasonable scenario for the future pattern of urban life can omit this powerful tool for change and improvement. It is now known that the creation of new communities is well within the economic and political means of many societies. What is not yet fully understood is how best to organize community development, how to maximize the benefits, or how to minimize the wastage of human and financial resources that has too often resulted from bad planning and bad management.

This book addresses, very rightly, the *process* of creating new communities, and sets out the principles that should guide future developments. It contrasts sharply with most previous books on the subject in its strong, indeed almost exclusive, emphasis on *process*—which it treats as a continuous exercise in the skilled management of the economic, financial, political and social aspects of development. Earlier writings concentrated on the broad philosophic goals of the new town

ix

enterprise and on its physical planning in terms of layout, land use and architecture, largely ignoring operational and management issues. The resulting gap in the literature of new town development reflected a gap in the theory, which has been the cause of many failures and difficulties in the practical implementation of new town plans. So this book, with its new emphasis on process, is very welcome. Using as a framework the two main divisions of traditional thinking—the purpose or goals of new communities and their physical form—I shall attempt in this foreword to relate this new emphasis to the established background of theory and practice, which it powerfully supplements.

We must not forget that the idea of the new town had its origin in that of Utopia. From Sir Thomas More to Lewis Mumford, the ills of society were identified with existing cities. The new city was both the means of creating a juster, happier society, and its principal symbol. Today, there is general scepticism about any panacea for social evils and a consciously pragmatic attitude towards most social enterprise. But a new town or a new community is still seen, both by those who sponsor it and by those who judge it, in a very different light from any other public or private undertaking. It is still expected to achieve a significant forward step across a wide spectrum of human concerns—to offer a perceptibly better life to those who come to live and work in it. This is a tremendous goal for any human enterprise. But it is this goal, more or less clearly articulated, that motivates the planners and builders and sets the standard against which their achievement will be criticized and eventually judged. The language in which we express our Utopian purposes is today rather low key: we refer to innovation rather than reform, and to communication or participation rather than freedom. But the old ideals are still there, much as they were 50 years ago.

As Mahlon Apgar argues in his introductory chapter, these fundamental goals are best made explicit. Stated vaguely or left implicit, they make for grave problems in both planning and implementation. Sometimes two desirable goals are so related that the more you have of one the less you have of the other. For example, large areas of landscaped open space are desirable; so is convenient, economic public transport. But the one militates against the other. If this conflict is faced and consideration given to the tradeoff relationship, a rational balance can be found. But if both goals are pursued without qualification there is no solution, and hopes are bound to be disappointed. Another, almost universal, goal is a balanced population with a range of characteristics reflecting, at least in some degree, those of the society as a whole. But this needs to be clearly stated in realistic, quantitative terms at the outset. Moreover, the grain of the mix has to be decided: How large a block of houses within a narrow price range will be acceptable—1,000, 100 or 10?

Another reason for making goals very clear at the outset is to bring forward the question of who will pay for what. In this book there is no lack of examples of conflict and breakdown resulting from ambiguity as to the source of funds, both for initial investment and for subsequent maintenance, required to meet the social needs of new communities. In the US, this issue usually arises between the entrepreneur who undertakes the development and one or more of the numerous government agencies at various levels that are concerned with education, health, roads, water supply, etc. In Britain, exactly the same issue arises between the new town development corporation and the external government agencies. The conflict is no less real because a British development corporation is itself a creature of central government. This underlines Mahlon Apgar's argument that the same basic problems beset both the private and the public developer. Early and clear definition of goals enables these questions to be brought into the open, debated, and decided at the beginning, greatly reducing the danger of hopes and promises going unfulfilled.

When planning began for the British new city of Milton Keynes,[1] it was decided to devote a substantial amount of the available time and human resources to study, discussion and definition of goals for the city—planned to reach a population of 250,000 in fifteen to twenty years. This effort, which formed the basis for the plan, is already proving to have been a wise investment, giving a baseline against which development can be continuously monitored, evaluated and revised as necessary.

A more advanced technique was recently used in a study concerned with the explosive population growth of Bogota, capital of Colombia.[2] This study proposed the development of several 'new-towns-in-town' on the edge of the existing city to absorb the incoming population. An attempt was made to assess how the available investment funds should be distributed among the main sectors of expenditure: housing, transport, education, health, and so on. At present, investment decisions are usually taken in each sector independently. For example, the decision whether or not to embark on a major road construction project would normally be based on a cost-benefit analysis showing the return on the proposed investment. Obviously, this sector-by-sector approach fails to take into account the fact that the total resources available for a development are usually limited. A massive investment in new roads that is fully justified by cost-benefit analysis may still be wrong in terms of the balance of investment among roads, housing, education and health. As a guide to decision-taking on investment priorities, the Bogota study sets forth the respective consequences, in terms of various alternative levels of investment in each sector. Such a presentation enables the relative cost of achieving a range of goals in a community development to be compared, and the priorities judged in relation to cost.

The first step in planning an effective development process, then, is to define the development goals as precisely as possible. These goals can then be reviewed in terms of their mutual compatibility and in terms of resource availability. Where investment from external sources will be required, this must be faced, debated and agreed. If this is not done—if goals are left Utopian and undefined—then disappointment and disillusion are inevitable, and the collapse of the project is a real possibility.

When we turn from development goals to the physical form of new communities we find a dramatic contrast. While developers have pursued goals that have too often been vague and lofty, their approach to the physical plan has commonly been highly determinate and precise. Traditionally, the planners of new communities made a leap in the dark. From the hazy notion of a garden-city Utopia they jumped to very precise conclusions. They had no trouble deciding that industry must be separated from residential areas, that there was an ideal size for new towns, that people should live in self-contained 'neighbourhood units', that vehicles should be separated from pedestrians, and so on. No train of reasoning connected these judgements with the goals, and no convincing justification for them can be found in social research. (More recently an even less rational set of concepts, based on the idea of stringing development along the line of a monorail or some other technologically advanced transit system, has become fashionable.)

The reasons why such a compact and rigid set of concepts has until very recently governed the design of new communities have been discussed at length elsewhere.[3] The single most important reason was that planners and designers had been trained to create a product, not to carry out a process. It is the main theme of this book that community development, to be successful, must be seen by all concerned in terms of the process, not the product.

Within limits, the design of a single building or the planning of a small development can be treated as a product. Architects have been generally trained to work in these terms, and the architect's viewpoint long dominated the training and attitudes of planners. Faced with the task of planning a new town, designers naturally thought in terms of the end product, the complete town, which, once built, would remain unchanged for an indefinite future. The design of the town, therefore, had to be specified in detail—even though the last stages of construction might be twenty years away. So, to invent his detailed brief, the designer had to build up a precise picture of the life many years ahead for which the town would cater, and this meant indulging in a great deal of pure guesswork as to people's future needs and wishes. Thus, the pressure for product definition produced an array of rather arbitrary planning concepts that dominated the physical form of new communities until about five years ago.

Both in Britain and in the US, the resulting highly deterministic plans ignored the need to allow for change and failed to recognize the development process as a continuous modifying input to the plan. Not surprisingly, few of these plans endured for long. Some were scrapped completely and others were heavily modified, with consequent loss of part of the earlier investment, especially where infrastructure—roads, sewers and power lines, designed to serve the final disposition of land uses—had to be altered when already half built.

The implications of treating new community development as a process subject to continuing change, as postulated in this book, present a formidable challenge to planning and design. How can physical construction be planned for an unknown or uncertain end result? At first sight this may seem impossible—but it can be done if design is approached in a new way. Oddly enough, the last few years have seen the development of a new approach to architectural design and large-scale construction that parallels and relates to the concept of planning elaborated in this book. Some architects, working on large complex projects such as universities and hospitals, have developed the idea of an 'indeterminate architecture'.[4] Realizing that these building complexes are never finished, but are in a constant state of growth and change, they have studied how to plan and build a skeleton of circulation routes and service channels around which building space can be fitted in a variety of forms and dimensions, as future needs may dictate.

This approach can be effectively applied in planning a new community. It was first used in the plan for Milton Keynes, and has been applied in various ways to several other new town plans in Britain, the US, Canada and Australia. This style of planning seeks to keep future options in the location of homes, employment, shopping, etc., as open as possible, and to postpone for as long as possible commitments on location and investment in infrastructure. As development proceeds, changes in the market and in people's life styles and preferences can be accommodated without costly changes in what has already been built. Of course, not every option can long be kept open. Every item of investment, every length of road, every sewer, every house as it is put in restricts the range of future choices. But it is possible to plan so as to keep a chosen range of options free, and to make each investment decision so as to leave as much freedom as possible for the next one. This kind of planning is, of course, very beneficial to the project's cash flow. Being also far more difficult than the traditional once-and-for-all design, it calls for sophisticated professional skill in practice. More important, it requires much closer co-operation between the designers and planners and those concerned with the social, financial and political elements of development. This is possible only with a tightly knit development team working together on the process as a whole, as proposed in this book.

Open-ended planning, responsive to change and to pressure from the public, is hard to achieve. It puts much more onus on the developer, whether public or private, than does the familiar authoritarian approach. But today long-term, large-scale development can be managed in no other way. Like it or not, the new approach must be accepted. In my view, it can be warmly welcomed.

The history of planning for physical development shows a steady increase in the scope of concern. Planning in terms both of public policy and of individual projects has tended to cover larger and larger land areas, and to extend over longer and longer time spans. Where original plans dealt with the disposition of land use and the design of transport networks, further plans now tend to cover economic, social and political development as well, and these latter considerations are seen as more basic than land use or transport. This massive enlargement of concern is clearly justified. Old-style physical plans took so little account of so many essential elements that they were very often disregarded—or, where they were enforced, proved counter-productive. But the techniques initially used for comprehensive planning were those of a small-scale, limited earlier discipline. It was not immediately perceived that enlargement in the scales of space and time rendered ideas such as the Master Plan inapplicable. The development of a project of strictly limited size, which will be completed in a short time, can be controlled by a definitive plan. But this becomes impossible when the project is the development of a new community or of an existing community over time.

The management planning approach put forward in this book is the natural counterpart to the new step-by-step physical planning techniques that are now rapidly evolving. The main principles of step-by-step planning are simple enough: a plan is developed that best meets defined goals and constraints; implementation of the plan, especially of infrastructure, is phased incrementally and constantly monitored to ensure its responsiveness to change.

But this approach, though conceptually simple, can be applied successfully only by an integrated team as part of a comprehensive, well-organized process. The nature of the process, and the methods and skills needed to manage it, are the subject of this book.

References

1. *The Plan for Milton Keynes*, Vols. I and II, Llewelyn-Davies, Weeks, Forestier-Walker and Bor for the Milton Keynes Development Corporation, March 1970.
2. *The Structure Plan for Bogota, Colombia*, Llewelyn-Davies, Weeks, Forestier-Walker and Bor, for the Republic of Colombia, the International Bank for Reconstruction and Development and the United Nations Development Program, 1973.
3. Llewelyn-Davies, R., 'Town Design', *The Town Planning Review*, **37**, 3, October 1966.
4. Weeks, J., *Indeterminate Architecture*, Transactions of the Bartlett Society, **2**, University College, London, 1964.

Progress in community development:
The Columbia experience

JAMES W. ROUSE

It is timely to report, as this book does, on the process of planning and developing communities. Awareness of the need for development at community scale has heightened as the wasteful, ugly, and inhuman results of reckless sprawl have been recognized and railed against by increasing numbers of people and public bodies. The growth of cities—subdivision by subdivision and project by project—is inefficient and irresponsible. Sprawl and clutter are the inevitable consequences. It is not possible to provide for the preservation of our environment, the conservation of energy, the building of rational communities, when the planning and development target is but a few hundred acres of land or dwelling units.

We are faced with a generation of continuing growth in the number of new households formed each year. Roughly 25,000 new dwellings will be needed each week, somewhere in America, for the next 15 years to meet this surging demand. We can splash these dwellings across the land and chase their growth with a disorderly array of schools, churches, stores, offices and factories, as we have done in the past, or we can learn from the irresponsible patterns of growth and choose for the future an alternative of new communities that provide for people and the services they need, for preservation of the land, for the conservation of energy, and for the economical use of scarce capital resources.

This alternative is no longer a matter of hypothesis or distant hope. The positive effectiveness of community development has been demonstrated in new towns built and building throughout the world. They have been developed with a variety of goals and thus achieved different results. But it is clear that through the community development process, it has been possible to set goals and work successfully toward their fulfilment. No single new town is typical of all and certainly the experience of Columbia, the new city between Baltimore and Washington, is not universal, but it provides a valid image of the contrast between scattered, formless, un-planned non-communities that have marked the random growth of the past, and the comprehensively planned new communities that are a legitimate hope for the future.

In 1963, when the assembly of land for Columbia commenced, there were 13 small housing settlements scattered east and west of a two-lane road roughly midway between Baltimore and Washington. Along the road, a few gas stations and roadside stores had emerged and one small shopping centre had been built. Two elementary schools, about five miles apart, were scheduled for construction to serve the area's growing population. Some 7,500 people lived there.

This patchwork had popped up since the Second World War, just beyond the burgeoning suburbs of two major cities only 40 miles apart. The population of the surrounding county, which had increased slowly until 1950, jumped by 57 per cent in the following decade. US Route 29, connecting the two cities, had already been widened to four lanes for much of its distance and was scheduled for widening through the Columbia area by 1969.

In nine months, 145 farms and separate land parcels were purchased to put together the 14,000 acres that have become Columbia. The site was like a piece of Swiss cheese, with the 13 existing settlements and various unacquired parcels constituting the holes in the cheese. Of the 14,000 acres, 4,300 were acquired from land speculators or developers who were poised for conventional, piecemeal development and awaited only the extension of sewer and water through the area—already a part of the County's public works plan.

Thus, the future of the Columbia area was clear. Existing settlements would grow; new settlements would come forth; completion of the two elementary schools would support the area's growth; the road widening would improve access; the first pockmarks of commercial use and commercial zoning would justify further zoning to enable the spread of service stations, stores, roadside eating places, and other business along the highway. Along with ugliness and congestion, these facilities would provide added convenience to the land behind. More growth, scattered schools, snarled roads, cutting back of front yards, pressure for more government services, rising taxes, little or no industry to support the rising call for government services.

In the course of this random disorderly growth, hills would be bulldozed into stream valleys, streams put into storm sewers, flood plains raised—a massive abuse of the land and the waterways. Developers, working separately, could not economically set aside the acreage required to sensitively protect and preserve the stream valleys and flood plains that laced the countryside. Local planning and subdivision controls would at best protect only major stream valleys.

The scattering of schools, churches and stores without relationship to each other would fracture the potential for focusing community interests and activities which these facilities have historically provided in the centres of towns and small cities throughout the world.

Each little piece of this unfolding process would be separate, so that its cumulative impact could be perceived only in hindsight. It is this hindsight perspective with which we lament the random sprawl that has marked the decade-by-decade growth of metropolitan areas. It has damaged the physical environment and generated ugliness along the highway. It has been inconvenient for its residents; negative to the growth of community among people; expensive in capital outlays, both public and private; uneconomic to local and state government. It has provided poorly for its residents and produced problems for future generations. In short, it has been physically destructive, anti-human, and inefficient.

This was the prospect for the Columbia area in 1963 and would surely have been the product—but the prospect was not fulfilled. Instead, the land was assembled and a comprehensive plan was adopted for the development of a new city. Compare the results of the sprawl that was in prospect with the community that has emerged.

Every stream valley and flood plain has been protected and preserved. The natural drainage system serves the land area. Thirty-five hundred acres have been committed to permanent open space. Three lakes have been built—waterways that give space, beauty, and recreational opportunity and act also as important sedimentation control basins to receive upstream erosion and prevent downstream spoliation. Development has been concentrated on the land best suited to development, avoiding the bulldozing of hills into flood plains; preserving the essential shape of the area. The land itself has not been defiled but dignified by the development process. The commercial uses along the highway have been largely extinguished and the highway has become a landscaped parkway instead of a victim of creeping commercial growth.

Planning and development on city scale over a large land area has provided for neighbourhoods with an elementary school, nursery school, day care centre, park, swimming pool, meeting room—all in a neighbourhood centre within easy walking distance, permitting the natural coming together, in the ordinary course of life, of families living in the neighbourhood.

Three or four neighbourhoods constitute a village at the centre of which provision is made for a middle school and high school, supermarket, small stores, bank, churches, offices, library, major recreation facilities so that the people of a village have their day-to-day community needs served at a central place which brings together parents, teachers, children, ministers, and merchants in their daily living and working.

The gathering together of community services and facilities creates a sense of place; shapes the physical community; provides a feeling of scale in human dimension; enlarges relationships among people; encourages a community of mind, purpose, expectation, action. The absence of such central places in metropolitan sprawl bleeds away the opportunity for community.

Planning and development at city scale made it possible for the County School Board to examine new potential in public education. With sites provided 15 years in advance, with neighbourhood and village schools in prospect, with school populations susceptible to close projections, the system of public education was re-examined and radically upgraded—in response to the opportunity presented by a planned new city. It has become what some observers have described as the most advanced system of public education in America.

The prospects and special opportunities of city scale development induced the Johns Hopkins Medical Institutions to bring forth a system of comprehensive health care which has established a group medical practice, hospitalization, psychiatric counselling and full emergency coverage on a prepaid volunteer plan. No comparable medical plan and facilities are available in the Baltimore–Washington region.

The Catholic, Jewish, and Protestant denominations took the initiative to join hands in the establishment of a Religious Facilities Corporation to provide religious facilities at the village centres; to save the cost of 'a church on every corner'; to bring about understanding and respect among the denominations for each other; to combine on programs while maintaining the integrity of the separate faiths.

A residents' association was established which provides recreation services, nursery schools, day care, public transportation and special programs of education, entertainment, culture and recreation.

A path system leading to neighbourhood and village centres provides an easy, convenient and pleasant route on foot or on bicycle. A low-cost bus system enables people to move from home to work, to recreation, to shop, and from village to village.

At the centre of the villages is 'downtown' where the one-of-a-kind activities that historically have aggregated at the centre of cities are brought together. Department stores and major retail facilities, restaurants, banks, offices, hotels, cinema, theatre, concert pavilion, zoo, constitute a city centre laid out to provide convenient access to and rational relationships among the various services. Downtown is bounded by a lake on one side and a park on another. It is a beautiful and efficient downtown—only possible through planning and development at city scale.

The creation through the community development process of a good environment—physically and socially—attracted business and industry which the County had not heretofore experienced. This produced an assessable base to help pay the cost of the government services that contributed to the environment that attracted the business and industry. Growth became a benefit, not a burden to the economy of local government.

Studies have shown that sensitive regard for the land—the preservation of steep hillsides, stream valleys and flood plains and the concentration of development where, for the preservation of land, it best should occur—has substantially reduced the capital outlay for streets, sewers and water and will result in large future savings in operation and maintenance costs for county and state government.

Thus, the development in Columbia of a better environment has required not greater but less capital investment; will be not more expensive but more economical to maintain. In a world in which there is increasing awareness of a shortage of capital resources to meet competing needs and yearnings, the effectiveness of community development in reconciling rising expectations with reduced outlays is important.

People and societies become habituated to patterns of the past and tend, too often, to accept that which persists as the inevitable consequence of forces beyond control or modification. Such is the case with the growth of cities. Haphazard growth is largely the product of the times when private property rights gave the owner of land an unfettered right to do with it as he pleased. Over time this sovereignty has been modified in the higher interest of the public good. Health and safety controls, zoning, planning, and more recently the controls emerging from sensitivity to abuse of the environment have bit by bit asserted the priority of the public interest and rights of the individual property owner in the use of land. Taken together, these influences and controls have transformed the capacity of society to achieve desirable objectives in the growth of cities and the use of land. The past does not necessarily foretell the future unless we choose to let it happen; and we have other choices available to us.

This book can be important to the future of city development by making planning and development at city scale a practical process available for use either as a private or public instrument for giving sensible shape to urban growth.

Of course, community development is more complex than traditional piecemeal development. It deals with problems that cannot be faced at a smaller scale. But these are the problems that are manifest in sprawl. The solutions are opportunities which require a community perspective to manage and unfold. To build and hold this necessary community perspective probably requires a new relationship between local government and the development process. The image of the developer as an adversary of the public interest encourages a reluctance on the part of public officials at local, state and national levels to provide private development with the kind of public support that is essential to the effective development of new communities.

The public interest will be best served by producing the best possible new communities. This goal should not be compromised nor its fulfilment diluted by anxieties about public actions that could result in benefits to the private developer. The public good is not served by a reluctant or distrusting attitude in government towards the developer or the development process. In many instances, it may be necessary to create local community development corporations to acquire land; plan; zone; install streets and utilities; and then market the land to home builders, commercial and industrial developers. The local community could retain the services of a private developer to manage the community development corporation for them. But the corporation itself would be under the control of the local government; would be seen as serving the interests of local government; would return profits to the local government. Such a development mechanism would not inhibit or materially change the development process necessary to perform the task. This book sheds light on the essential ingredients of that process.

State and national governments can encourage and bring about the development of new communities by acknowledging their importance to the responsible growth of the country and by giving them special emphasis and support in regular programs for public utilities, highways, public transportation, open space, education, health, human services, etc. The development of new communities is critically important, difficult yet clearly feasible. It requires the reshaping of relationships between government and the development process.

The failures and the fall-out of random growth and sprawl are clearly manifest in abuse of the land, inconvenience, congestion, ugliness, high cost and loss of community potential. The alternative of development on community scale is demonstrably constructive in respect of the land and the life of people and is economic in the use of energy and capital resources. How then—when these contrasting alternatives are before us—can we fail to come down decisively for the programs and processes that will assure the accommodation of future growth in planned communities? People will not permit the continuance of irrational growth as they see the alternative that is available. People and their governments will insist upon development processes and the relationship of government to them in such manner as will make new communities—new towns, new cities—the bright reality of future metropolitan growth.

Acknowledgements

This book owes its inspiration to the many outstanding developers with whom I have worked, and its completion to the contributors who willingly met tight deadlines amid the inevitably crowded schedules of busy professionals. My colleagues—particularly John S. Crowley, Henry M. Strage, John Griffith-Jones, Trevor MacMurray and David Thompson—have provided unflagging support as the book has taken shape, and were closely involved in the development of many of the analytic approaches that are described in Parts II and III.

A number of others have been instrumental in the complex editing and production process entailed in a volume with 15 authors travelling between four countries. Susan Starks applied her consummate skill and good humour in editing the manuscript. Roland Mann added his unique flair to six of the chapters and Robert Whiting coped gracefully with many awkward technical details. Sheldon Franklin designed the figures; Paul Savage and Steven Callman executed them. Linda Cowan efficiently supervised the typing of numerous drafts, and Irene Miller did a meticulous job of proofreading.

Mahlon Apgar, IV
London, January 1976

Introduction: Emerging issues in community development

MAHLON APGAR, IV

This book is for people concerned with the practical problems of developing planned communities and resolving the policy issues they raise. It is not an academic treatise, a technical handbook, or a pictorial essay; these already abound. Rather, it is a critical review of the aims, methods and difficulties of community development today as seen by professionals working in the field. Their perspectives, I believe, clarify the background against which decision-makers and interested laymen will be debating the issues and charting the course of future development.

The problem of definition

Community development means different things to different people. To real-estate developers and home builders it is apt to mean large-scale, mainly suburban housing projects in which superior site layouts and extensive amenities are designed to attract increasingly demanding families who are community-oriented in their interests and life styles. To political activists and social workers who see themselves as community organizers and tribunes of the underprivileged, the term embraces programs to improve deteriorating conditions in the inner city, evoking a community consciousness among residents and strengthening their local institutions in new cities and old.

With such divergent viewpoints, it is not surprising that the language and literature of this subject reflect disparate, often conflicting approaches, fraught with elusive concepts and obscure meanings. But there are common threads as well. 'Community development' by public and private interests in both growth centres and declining areas is characterized by comprehensive planning to integrate social, economic and spatial objectives and activities; by a fundamental re-examination of basic assumptions about the purpose of cities and communities and the roles of public and private institutions in them; by some recognition of the need to improve community life as

1

well as individual living conditions; and by changes in the established attitudes and procedures that have governed urban policies, construction methods, and management concepts.

The form, location and scale of community development programs are far less central than the process by which they are created. For it is the emphasis on conceiving, planning and managing development as a single integrated process that has compelled developers to think in new ways about the problems of urbanization and the means of achieving social goals.

Thus, it is with the process rather than the products of development that this book will be concerned—a process marked by five distinctive features:

1. Definition of development goals in terms of the full range of individual and community needs and demands to be met, rather than of preconceived administrative functions and technical requirements;
2. Determination of the many activities required to meet those objectives efficiently, effectively and equitably; of the links between activities; and of their proper implementation sequence;
3. Continuous program evaluation and review to identify new needs and shortcomings in current programs; develop new solutions; and manage the ensuing changes in development strategy, organization and operations;
4. Mobilization of a wide variety of public and private resources, institutions and individuals to underpin the process; and
5. A unified organization that undertakes the entire development as a single project and manages it according to a predetermined strategy embracing a physical layout; a financing, staffing and resource management plan; and a construction and marketing program.

Within this framework, the book explores the practical experience that has been gained to date in applying the development process in planned new communities. Several factors have led to this approach. First, the elements of development strategy and structure, whether undertaken by public or private sponsors, are virtually identical in new communities throughout the world, making comparisons useful. This is partly because new town theory and practice, especially since the fifties, have been consistently formulated, widely communicated, and well understood by those concerned with the problems and opportunities in urbanization. More important, however, community development addresses needs that are universal in changing societies, in a way that is relatively independent of political ideologies, planning systems and development methods. Thus, countries as diverse as the US, France, the Soviet Union and Tanzania have adapted this essentially British invention to suit their own conditions.

Another reason for highlighting experience in new communities is that their sponsors have been able to develop and test innovations in planning, finance, and administration that would have been difficult within the encrusted bureaucracies of existing cities and towns. The opportunity to meet communal and individual needs more effectively has produced remarkably creative ideas and approaches to the tasks of urban development. Moreover, the policy concepts and management techniques that have been designed to guide new community programs are particularly adaptable to the more subtle and complex development forms now emerging outside the new town context. For example, high-density, mixed-use, in-town projects present comparable problems of development economics and social planning in determining the best mix and maximizing the interaction of users, occupants and services. And today's typical planned suburban housing development, with a range of supporting services, has similarly broad social and economic objectives. Though smaller in scale than the traditional new town, it thus can benefit from the new towns' experience in resolving the balance between different uses and in organizing community programs.

Just as our definition of community development in the book can apply equally to public and private undertakings, so too do the terms we employ for the actors in the development process. For simplicity and economy, 'developer' and 'development enterprise' are used throughout to refer to public as well as private organizations engaged in community development. They are the prime movers, who originate the concept and manage planning, construction and operations. Some readers may have difficulty adjusting to the notion that terms and techniques they associate with commercial property entrepreneurs can be applied equally well to public enterprise. Yet the tasks, roles, and management styles required of community development organizations are common to both sectors.

Similarly, the term 'decision-maker' is used to embrace both those who determine development policy and those who administer it. The traditional distinction between these roles is less and less appropriate to the character of today's development process, where new needs and unforeseen events may require rapid changes in both policy and operations. These two aspects of management are now inextricably intertwined—the province of executives whose primary task is to make the important decisions that guide and control the development enterprise and projects.

Background and structure

The book had its genesis in my conviction that planned community development, despite the unevenness of its results to date, is an essential key to improving the quality of urban life. Whether it is seen as a vehicle for stimulating and guiding metropolitan and regional growth or for reversing urban decline, the fundamental goal of community development is to provide an efficient, attractive and supportive environment where people may live, work and enjoy their leisure, with maximum scope for individual choice. For the reasons given above, new communities provide a valuable case study of how this goal has been pursued, and of the problems and opportunities that have been encountered—particularly in the US, Britain and France.

The new towns program was one of Britain's earliest and most important essays in community development, sustained by a carefully conceived set of government policies, strong public corporations and a systematic approach to planning. With similar aims, France has embarked on an ambitious national program to develop larger regional cities. The concept has been implemented in the US mainly through privately developed satellite towns with no overall metropolitan or area-wide framework of objectives or planning controls. Other states in Europe, Asia and Africa are looking mainly to the British model as they fashion their own development policies and programs.

Each country has naturally adapted the planned development concept to meet its own needs and objectives. In Britain, it began as a tool of evolving social policy to improve urban conditions by containing the growth of the major cities. This meant dispersing people by providing better housing and jobs in self-contained new towns, and ultimately stimulating regional economic development. In the US, new communities were viewed originally as vehicles for channelling expected population growth and redistributing employment to avert the familiar consequences of suburban sprawl, and only later as means of achieving more fundamental economic and social policy aims. In France, they were born of the plans to decentralize population and institutions from Paris and build up the country's regional structure.

Despite several decades of experience, especially intensive in the past 10 years, little comparative evaluation has been undertaken, and realistic attempts to draw together the lessons learned have been noticeably lacking. American and French developers, like nearly everyone else, have come in droves to see the British projects. Fewer UK 'new townsmen' have done the reverse; the view prevails that there is little more to be learned. Tours by official delegations have produced histories and photographic essays but almost no core analytical studies. Yet each country could benefit a great deal from the experience of others.

This book aims to make a modest beginning toward demonstrating, on a practical level, the value of such cross-fertilization While comparative in content, it is not a multinational research study, for the contributors are working professionals whose main interest is not scholarship but practical results. In discussing some of today's important problems and opportunities in the development process, they have drawn mainly on their working experience in a number of countries.

In Part I, the key aspects of national policy and institutional frameworks for community development in Britain, the US and France are considered. These countries have a long history of and established programs for community development; each has fashioned innovations that are relevant to problems faced by others. The British program, with its effective structure for physical development, could surely benefit from American experience in community management and the French approach of design-and-build 'competitions'. Similarly the US could learn from the more realistic financial provisions and land acquisition policies of the UK and the regional development framework of the French. But as William Nicoson points out, sensible solutions to such problems and opportunities are prey to the vagaries of policy formulation—and these must be equally well understood by both decision-makers and policy analysts.

Part II presents an approach to strategic planning for community development that has been applied in a number of contexts in the US and Europe during the past few years. Designed specifically to overcome the inflexible and traditional limitations of both corporate and urban planning practice, it is likely to be of special interest to those concerned with the problems that now plague countries suffering increased pressure on their domestic resources. The response to uncertainty is largely intuitive in most development organizations, yet the scale of their operations and the level of their commitments call for a new style of analysis and new management skills. The roles of community programs and community design are explored as essential elements of the strategic approach, for they offer vast potential for meeting needs through more creative and effective use of the talents and resources employed in development.

Part III discusses important lessons from recent experience in tackling the multiple problems of community development. Because of their size and complexity, these projects are notoriously difficult to manage. Examples of inadequate financing, excessive costs, missed opportunities, and insufficient or incorrect development products to meet established needs are legion. The contributors have drawn on current experience in several countries to present a variety of operating principles and workable approaches.that are overcoming these problems and achieving better results in project planning and management.

Finally, Part IV looks to the future. Experience gleaned from new programs and projects can be applied to the increasingly complex problems of urbanization that beset both public and private decision-makers. The British development corporation has proved to be an efficient organization for the physical planning and development task. But can it be made more responsive to local wishes and priorities without losing its effectiveness? How can it be adapted to meet the special requirements of the smaller-scale projects that increasingly make up the major thrust of new urban development?

Similarly, in the rest of Europe and in all but a few areas in the US, the large 'greenfields' new city that has predominated in the past quarter-century is being overtaken by neighbourhood-scale mixed-use developments that can be planned and implemented more quickly with fewer risks and less disruption to the overall pattern of urban and regional life. Pressure for urban conservation, replacing the postwar legacy of clearance and redevelopment, focuses attention on the need for strategies that combine highly selective new building with housing rehabilitation and strengthening of community service systems.

While not all may welcome these changes, the challenge for public policy is clear. How can the original aims of the new towns concept be achieved in a larger number of smaller projects? How can the resulting proliferation of 'new neighbourhoods' be controlled and integrated into the regional structure? What combination of land-use incentives and sanctions, public infrastructure investment and community services will enable effective management of the development process under these new conditions? Part IV sets out a framework within which such issues can be explored.

Throughout the book, three themes insistently recur: the weight placed on the development process as against the development product; the changing relationship between the public and private sectors in this process; and the ever-growing need to take uncertainty and change explicitly into account at every stage. Moreover, increasing popular pressure within established new communities highlights a number of important questions of policy and operations management that still have to be resolved. Each of these deserves some discussion here.

Product and process

Most of the debate on land-use and urban development policies centres on the form and function of the development product—that is, satellite new town, central business district, planned unit development or suburban subdivision. But, crucial as physical forms and economic uses are, to concentrate on them may obscure the more fundamental goal of providing a better framework for human life and activity.

New towns in particular seem to convey to their creators specific images that are readily translated into detailed plans and designs. Yet the purposes, policies and development concepts underlying these plans often suffer from a lack of clarity and rigour because of the sheer variety of product definitions. The result, as David Thompson points out, is that the ultimate product may fall far short of its planners' ambitious aims. For example, the British program has slowly evolved from Howard's original free-standing 'social city' to embrace expanded towns and regional new cities—but its powers and organizational mechanisms are under increasing fire for their 'undemocratic' nature. The US Title VII program, which officially posited four product types, has seen only the 'satellite' town realized on any scale. And the French are experiencing considerable teething troubles in implementing their imaginative but complex 'discontinuous' new town on several sites spread through an entire sub-region.

Seen instead as a systematic approach designed to meet explicit operational objectives, the development process is distinguished by two features easily over-looked in the zealous concentration on product. First, considerable creativity in systems design and program planning is often brought to bear, with innovative arrangements of the mixed uses that are planned to meet the needs of those who live, work and shop there. Because the developer provides public open space, amenities and a wide range of community service systems (e.g., health clinic, schools, childcare) as well as the built environment, continuing analysis of needs and demands permits clear identification of gaps in current products and programs, forcing consideration of how these might be changed or adapted. This type of evaluation and review helps to minimize the inherent inflexibility of buildings, roads and other physical structures by consistently linking them to specific development objectives. It also accommo-dates shifts in demand for various building types, layouts, styles, mixes of use and other characteristics of the product that follow the fashion of the day and assump-tions of need by the architect, the politician, the financier and others who determine the built environment.

Second, the focus on process rather than product encourages innovation in reaching for the qualitative goals of community life that still seem so elusive in cities and suburbs alike. For all the aesthetic significance of the garden city tradition in new towns, major innovations have been demonstrated in other aspects, such as financing, community governance, organization and management processes, though these are not given such prominence in the literature of urban development. Local programs and professional practices have also provided important insights into possible ways of tackling other large-scale tasks with predominantly social objectives, such as renewing the inner city. The French, in particular, have drawn from the British experience the need to pay early attention to both the structure and processes of new town governance and management. Thus, the concept of *animation*—strengthening social cohesion by initiating a variety of cultural, political and economic activities, and avoiding the conflicts that underlie 'new town blues'—has been a distinctively French innovation.

Not surprisingly, new needs, coupled with innovations in development methods, have led to the creation of entirely new products under many labels. In countries as diverse as Japan and Mexico, established industrial parks are metamorphosing into new towns as residential, commercial and civic uses are grafted on to the factory and office base. The US has seen three major forms emerge recently:

1. The Planned Unit Development (PUD)—which is replacing large-scale, single-family suburban tracts with smaller-scale yet higher-density clusters of residential, commercial and light industrial uses;
2. Metropolitan growth-point development—the new suburban centres in which the regional shopping mall is embellished with apartments and offices, civic buildings, and often a range of community services; and
3. Mixed-Use Development (MUD), where the former office skyscraper is being transformed to include residential, shopping and cultural uses as well as offices in a single structure or building complex (e.g., the new Olympic Tower in New York). These new forms have their parallel in other countries, and the new city or town is today only one product—albeit the grandest—among many equally complex types.

From inception to full development, the typical development process lasts from four to five years for the PUD to the 20-year or longer period required for a complete new town or city. The developer and local government must together oversee the course of development and ensure that it is integrated with the surrounding community and sub-region. Both market and community planning benefit from this high degree of development control: the production volume of dwelling units, offices and other uses must be absorbed into the local market to sustain development pace and avoid premature saturation, while demands placed on local public services must be closely sequenced with local authority capital programs and service growth to avoid overcrowding.

The community development process thus represents a marked shift from traditional development forms. The small-scale, single-use house or office building produced by the merchant builder and the small contractor requires little formal planning. Back-of-the-envelope arithmetic, quick deals, and a make-and-sell one-off style of operation are sufficient—and indeed can respond rapidly to volatile market changes. But small-scale development is by nature entirely reactive. No attempt can be made to lead the market or to sustain the heavy front-end costs of formal planning. Moreover, no single such development is likely to have enough

7

impact to call for a conscious attempt at integration with the surrounding community by the developer or the local authority.

But equally the large-scale development process presents a daunting challenge for policymakers, managers and planners alike. Not only is the total concept complex: policy objectives are so diffuse, subjective and volatile as almost to defy specification. Along with the hard facts of costs, schedules and performance standards, program planning and evaluation must embrace more subtle issues: Which groups value and use which development products and services? Who participates in which community programs? Which institutions and groups should be encouraged to lead opinion, make or influence decisions, and gain a local power base? What role should the developer play in their formation and growth—since, by design or default, his role will be highly influential?

Compared to the concrete, product-oriented activities of physical design and construction, some crucial analytic processes are difficult for the development policymaker to grasp and control. Community planning offices are slowly being transformed from design studios relying on three-dimensional models to simulation laboratories for rapid evaluation of alternative development strategies and action programs. The techniques of large-scale operations management have become more influential than master land-use plans in practical policy and program decision-making. This, of course, explains why financial officers, to the chagrin of planners, so often dominate the content, direction and results of community development. Policy-makers can exercise control only by mastering the financial and management as well as the physical and social dimensions of development.

Then, too, since the field of inquiry is so broad, the process of creating communities accommodates a wide variety of people and institutions playing complementary roles, first to conceive, then to implement, and ultimately to live with the many products and programs that a community comprises. Some of these roles are clear cut. Design, financing, construction and management are well defined by their respective professions for all manner of development products. The rights and responsibilities of private and public sector buyers, users, providers and regulators have likewise been clarified by tradition, practice, policy and statute.

But when the dimension of 'community' is added, the sharp distinctions between public authority, private developer and professional contractor are blurred. Relationships among economic, demographic and physical factors are harder to define: while planning and building continue apace, social scientists still debate the most rudimentary connections between physical and social structures and processes.

Thus a recurring theme in the book is the need, in designing community institutions, to take relationships among objectives, participants, tasks and programs more fully into account. Like physical structures, the programs intended to meet social aims must be consciously planned, tested and evaluated before funds and talents are committed on a large scale. By focusing on people's needs and aspirations—rather than on building form and use—new towns can succeed where conventional approaches have failed in humanizing the faceless bureaucracy of public services and refining the usual rough-and-tumble results of large-scale construction. Indeed, when the historians of tomorrow assess today's new towns, they may well deal harshly with designs and technical features that are no better—and often are worse—than piecemeal developments. But they should pinpoint as a fundamental contribution the provision of buildings and services co-ordinated at the local level to meet the demands of a broad socioeconomic mix. The classic dictum of architects that 'form follows function' is being rewritten by community developers: *product follows process.*

Public or private?

An equally important lesson learned from the new towns experience is that weaving together social, economic and environmental goals, diverse constituencies and numerous programs to achieve the community development concept is a task too mammoth, and too intricate, to be entrusted to either the public or the private sector alone. Neither sector, let alone any single organization, has a monopoly of the wisdom, foresight, skills or resources required to provide for the range of human needs and activities that compose a dynamic community. The complexity of the development task and the plurality of interests to be accommodated demand the widest possible combination of perspectives and capabilities if both individuals and the community are to benefit.

In short, community development demands a combined public and private response, based on an objective assessment of the capabilities and potential contributions of each. In principle, this should be an easy aim to achieve. Enough experience has been accumulated to compare the roles and relative performance of different institutions in a variety of settings. Depending on the project and the operating environment, both public agencies and private firms have proved effective in planning, delivering and managing community products and programs. But the policy decision on which type of enterprise should be encouraged to play these roles typically rests on popular conceptions of how it will achieve results and distribute benefits. In practice each country has shaped the roles to fit national traditions and expectations. For example, the British public new town development corporation, the French *Etablissement Public d'Aménagement* and the American private new community developer, though born of different legal and political systems, pursue a similar mix of goals, perform virtually identical functions, and have very similar organization structures, operating styles and methods.

In the UK, the public development corporation has wide powers to acquire land for development, and—taking advantage of low-cost sixty-year government loans—to build, operate and maintain virtually all the facilities and programs for a functioning community. In France, the public EPAs can pre-empt land required for development and prepare the master plan for a new community, but essentially they work through private developers and contractors, who must agree to share the values created through the development process. In the US, the initiative rests mainly with the private sector, assisted in some cases by government loan guarantees and grants in return for meeting specified social criteria. Figure A compares the main features of these systems.

9

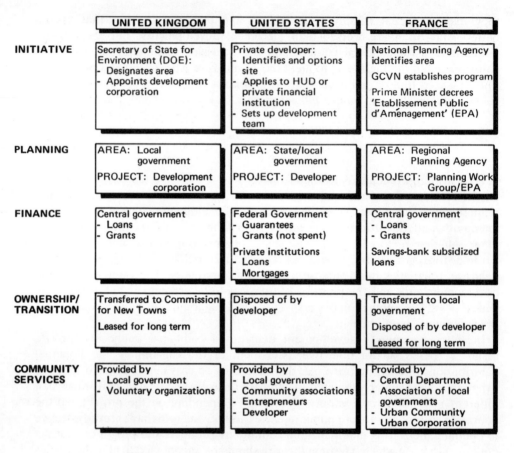

	UNITED KINGDOM	UNITED STATES	FRANCE
INITIATIVE	Secretary of State for Environment (DOE): - Designates area - Appoints development corporation	Private developer: - Identifies and options site - Applies to HUD or private financial institution - Sets up development team	National Planning Agency identifies area GCVN establishes program Prime Minister decrees 'Etablissement Public d'Aménagement' (EPA)
PLANNING	AREA: Local government PROJECT: Development corporation	AREA: State/local government PROJECT: Developer	AREA: Regional Planning Agency PROJECT: Planning Work Group/EPA
FINANCE	Central government - Loans - Grants	Federal Government - Guarantees - Grants (not spent) Private institutions - Loans - Mortgages	Central government - Loans - Grants Savings-bank subsidized loans
OWNERSHIP/ TRANSITION	Transferred to Commission for New Towns Leased for long term	Disposed of by developer	Transferred to local government Disposed of by developer Leased for long term
COMMUNITY SERVICES	Provided by - Local government - Voluntary organizations	Provided by - Local government - Community associations - Entrepreneurs - Developer	Provided by - Central Department - Association of local governments - Urban Community - Urban Corporation

Figure A   Features of new community development systems

Despite the promise of public–private partnerships in these and other countries, however, an emerging school of thought holds that community development should be entirely a public sector responsibility implemented by official agencies with broad public powers. This position is rooted partly in ideology and partly in past performance. The public purpose and the financial potential inherent in the concept of community development, so the argument goes, call for strong state initiative and control to ensure that the public interest is met. Otherwise the appeal of short-run gains will override community aims, and the private investor/developer will flourish at the public's expense. And, it is claimed, the malaise of the US new communities program, exemplified in the financial woes of most private developers today in all countries, proves that private enterprise cannot, in any case, do the job.

Unquestionably, the British development corporation has demonstrated how efficient and effective a public agency can be in the basic tasks of physical planning and building, while in France, the EPAs show promise as catalysts in the development of social, political and cultural institutions and programs.

Yet wholly public planning and development agencies and processes have shortcomings of their own—most notably, sheer bureaucratic sluggishness and a costly tolerance of woolly thinking. This reaches its apogee in the procedures required of community-scale projects, where numerous bodies of local and central government at various levels of the administrative hierarchy, each with its own criteria and interests, must be involved in 'considering' proposed developments, though in theory only a few official approvals are actually required. Each will view the project in a different context, ranging from the building site, to the city or county, to the region and even the nation.

These systems are often cumbersome, excessively demanding and time-consuming. One project I reviewed in Britain was held up for nearly two years while the growth pattern of every town and village in an 80-mile radius was evaluated by the local authority—yet its research had no practical effect on the ultimate recommendations. In another case, more than 100 sites were delayed for some 18 months in the face of high demand while the planning authority deliberated, though no new facts were discovered during that time that would alter the conclusion. Even the most basic plans for new public infrastructure, which should be completed in months, are taking years to produce. Developers have spent small fortunes on fruitless official consultation, while projects that would have met wide-ranging social and economic objectives have been curtailed, to the community's cost. It is sadly ironic that the British planning system in particular, which has been admired the world over for shaping the urban structure, should now be failing to enlist the speed, dynamism and customer/user orientation of the development entrepreneur in community-scale projects.

Beyond bureaucratic inertia, there is the arrogance of administrative power that we are apt to find wherever public control is exercised over private interests. Planning and development officials often have extraordinary authority to impose their private will on the public. As one observer puts it, 'The official's obsession (is) to make the applicant for planning permission comply in every detail with what he personally thinks to be the right use, disposition and appearance of the building being proposed.'[1] In theory, of course, elected representatives determine the policy context within which the official makes those decisions, so that the aggrieved applicant has recourse through his representatives and legal appeals. But in practice, the official's professional judgement often outweighs the protestations of the applicant—however expert or sound in logic—before a committee of the elected. Nor does the official have any serious incentive or sanction to limit the delays and costs that his actions may cause. Again, in theory, he is trained, informed and unbiased. But he has no monopoly on these qualities—nor, for that matter, does the private developer have a monopoly on wrong-headedness. The personal whims of the self-righteous official can be just as costly to the community interest as those of the self-interested citizen.

1. Powdrill, E. A., 'Opinion', *The Planner*, **61**, 4, 132, April 1975.

Checking bureaucratic excesses is, of course, only part of the issue of public or private community development. Another is the question of respective roles and competences. The ability to respond to needs efficiently and effectively is a characteristic skill of the private development entrepreneur operating in a competitive market economy. Competition disciplines him to be resourceful in designing and building, and to avoid waste through prudent compromises. Recognizing that small changes in cost, space and amenities—spread over the facilities, products and services of a community-scale project—will produce significant savings and superior values, he will place heavy emphasis on figuring out how to cut costs, simplify procedures and build in more value. Consider: $1,000 of unit costs saved in a 10,000-house project is $10 million extra in the development budget available for better amenities and services; $1,000 is lost or saved by adding or deleting just 50 square feet in a unit that costs $20 per square foot to build; in an 800-square-foot house, a saving of $1.25 per square foot of cost is worth $1,000, or $10 million in the total budget.

It is such simple yet basic trade-off analyses between product features and price that so often enable the best of the entrepreneurs to reveal unforeseen policy options and to create better developments and greater value than their public agency counterparts. Since the buyer or user must ultimately make the product/price trade-off decision, the developer must respond sensitively and objectively to changes in buyer tastes or preferences. New product concepts or features must be based on a sound understanding of market priorities; otherwise buyers simply will stay away. Eyeing the uneven results and excessive difficulties of oversized, monolithic 'greenfields' new towns, some US private developers have moved quickly to scale down and simplify new projects without sacrificing the basic principles of community development.

Finally, the rigorous analysis required of the developer leavens the planning process by introducing the user's perspective and decision criteria at each design and development stage. The compartmentalization of staff specialists in most public building agencies results in a rigidly sequential approach, from basic research and regional studies through completion of the finished product. Technical concerns predominate. In the absence of 'consumer advocacy' or competitive analysis, assumptions go unchallenged, and control and redirection of the basic plans are hampered.

Recent results in France, the US and Japan suggest that private initiative plays an essential part in pioneering the practical application of new social, economic and political concepts to meet community needs that are seldom considered in wholly public projects. A vital force in the development process, this type of innovation is not the invention of costly new ideas, but of day-to-day improvements in development products and procedures in response to operational uncertainties, such as cuts in finance, program changes, developer–resident conflicts, and unforeseen needs to be met.

In particular, innovations in community services and governance have resulted from the private developers' search for more responsive and efficient institutional forms of community management. For example, the tool of 'fiscal (rating) impact analysis', developed in the Columbia new city project to show local planning authorities how the overall benefits of community development would exceed the costs of additional public and private services, has since become a basic planning and negotiating tool in the US. Such techniques had not been necessary in the controlled economics of European new town building, yet when a leading private developer in Britain recently presented the same type of funds-flow arithmetic, it was eagerly embraced by the local authority, which saw in it an incentive for community-scale development that had not been seriously considered. Similarly, the community association originated with the support of private developers to provide those services that people can undertake through a co-operative process for their own benefit but that are unlikely to be provided by public agencies or commercial organizations.

Private developers, moreover, have even proved to be better prepared for constructive public consultation than their public authority counterparts. Their awareness of the need to 'meet the market' in project plans and products has resulted in a more objective approach to the concerns and needs of each local interest group, and to the possibilities of meeting them within the project. Indeed, the American and French community developer today will often invite public participation in various forms, not only to reduce the risks of later confrontation but also to seek guidance. He may even allocate a budget and several site options, turn over the choices—and responsibilities—to community groups, and simply serve as contractor once their decisions are made. The burden of discussion then falls on the basic practical political issues of *what* should be built in, for, and ultimately by, the community, rather than on secondary technical questions of *how* it can best be done.

This quick review of some of the relative strengths and weaknesses of public and private development organizations should suffice to highlight the importance of properly deploying the capabilities of both sectors in the quest to build better communities. The basic policy task, I suggest, is to create a framework of incentives and powers within which private initiative and resources can be coupled to public goals. With increasing pressure on public finance and growing restiveness among taxpayers, sensible policymakers will do their best to strike such a balance in meeting community development aims.

As several contributors point out, the difficulties and risks experienced in the large 'satellite' new towns have clarified the need in many growth areas for public powers to provide for banking sufficient blocks of suitable development land to be brought into future building programs at economic but non-speculative prices. This public role of 'land banker' would still leave the private developer ample scope to apply his innovative talents and problem-solving skills in managing the planning and building process, just as the institutional investor and lender have in their banking role. To date, the French EPA structure, though still largely untested and by no means free of administrative shortcomings, most closely approaches this ideal of the public–private partnership. In the US, Britain and most other countries, however, considerably more hard thinking and experimentation is needed, on a project-by-project basis, to design workable new institutional arrangements.

Some major changes clearly will be required to ensure effective working relationships. First, there must be agreement on the economic potential and the mix of objectives to eliminate the political and bureaucratic risks that have so often beset projects with a public purpose and driven capable developers from the field. Next, zoning should wherever possible provide complete flexibility in land use and sufficient income-producing space to ensure a competitive advantage over less desirable development forms. Local property taxes must be held within reason so that the price of land assembly does not become prohibitive; this means that local government's revenue base should be supported by a broader taxing authority for the extra short-term administrative and program costs entailed by community-scale development. With a sound financial base, approvals should be rapid and straightforward. In other words, the imponderables that remain should be market uncertainties—not the results of administrative impediments.

New financing criteria and instruments need to be designed with an eye to the multiplicity of aims and corresponding risks in the new towns concept. Clearly, the private developer's return should be related to the risks he assumes and the benefits he produces for those who supply development funds, as well as for the community at large. Much of the debate on private and public benefits has centred on the balance of investment in the physical product—infrastructure, common facilities and so on. Yet, in my experience, the value the developer adds, and the basis for his returns, is more a matter of program innovations, improved processes and ways of working that better respond to people's aspirations and needs.

There is also a need for popular and political expectations to be tempered by recognition of the risks in undertaking this mammoth task. Even the best developments have too often been overloaded by unrealistic expectations, and when such programs fall short of their aims, increased pressure for public sector initiative and control are inevitable. Unquestionably, it should be possible to build more attractive communities and run more effective community programs within the established rules of the game. The available knowledge about what people want and the resources required to satisfy their wants can be marshalled more successfully. The development enterprise can—and should—be expected to find new approaches to problems that are within its competence and resources.

But new town developers, public or private, cannot by themselves revise social policy, redistribute wealth, alter ingrained prejudices, or perform the multitude of other societal chores that are increasingly demanded of them. These are tasks that far exceed their competence and resources. With a more realistic outlook all round, the divisive ideological issue of public versus private development should yield to the recognition that community goals can best be met through the partnership of public *and* private interests.

The challenge of uncertainty

More than most human enterprises, the development process is burdened by the uncertainties of continuing change. Until recently, most development organizations had considerable confidence in their ability to anticipate change by predictive techniques, and to control and mange it through systems and procedures—a confidence symbolized by the development 'master plan', which was seen as a tool for controlling change over a 15- to 20-year development period. The economic upheavals of the past two years have severely undermined these assumptions, but few developers—public or private—seem to have altered their approaches accordingly. We now live in an era in which the overriding condition of planning and decision-making is change so rapid and fundamental that it affects both development strategy and day-to-day operations. Yet the concepts and procedures governing today's development process stubbornly adhere to assumptions that are no longer valid.

In fact, planning for change is impeded in several ways. First, the land-use plan, almost universally accepted as the basic tool for development control, translates single-value forecasts and assumptions about future events into rigid prescriptions for land allocation. Neither the plan itself, nor the analytic processes behind it, account explicitly for a *range* of possible outcomes or the variety of possible scenarios that would logically follow. And it is not normally accompanied by a parallel analysis of how best to allocate human and economic resources on the site—necessary as this is to accommodate the multiple objectives and uncertainties of the community concept. As is beginning to be recognized in principle, these shortcomings have resulted in massive overspending and misdirected investment. But the fixed view of the future and the single path to desired results still prevail in most new town planning practice. (The framework of urban planning systems and procedures in the US, Britain and France is summarized in Fig. B.)

A second barrier to coping with change is overreliance on statistical methodology and historical analysis, which can result in misleading assessments of social and economic forces and failure to design appropriate mechanisms to cope with them. Purely quantitative extrapolations of population data, for example, overlook the impact of changing life styles, the growing ecological consciousness, the car and the pill—all of which have become more important than birth and death rates in shaping patterns of population growth, mobility and house purchase decisions. Marshall Kaplan, a distinguished social planner turned new town manager, sums it up nicely: 'People just don't live the way the social scientists want them to.'

Since even the theorists are uncertain about the side effects of public intervention and the causal relationships between new social programs and ensuing events, it should be self-evident that any global, long-term community development approach based mainly on spatial change is bound to fail for want of attention to the social, political and economic dimensions. As David Harvey puts it: 'Any successful strategy must appreciate that spatial form and social processes are different ways of thinking about the same thing. We must harmonize our thinking or create contradictory strategies.' Yet too often in practice we still find each separate profession or academic discipline defining community problems within traditional boundaries rather than analysing their interrelationships. Failure to consider the effects of various development strategies on different customer or user groups has led to serious problems, while intervention in the market to redirect the distribution of people and jobs, housing and services, has succeeded best where the developer has carefully analysed the options available to him should economic and political events not go according to plan.

15

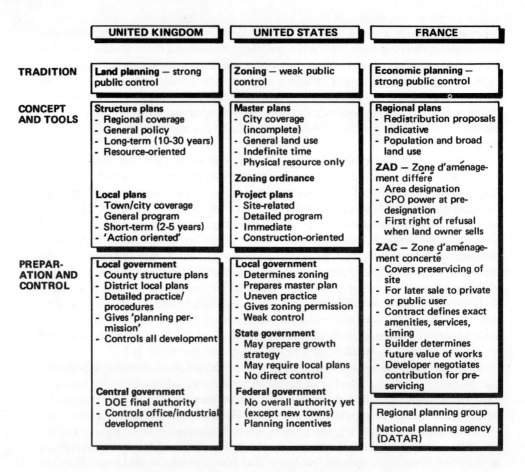

	UNITED KINGDOM	UNITED STATES	FRANCE
TRADITION	Land planning — strong public control	Zoning — weak public control	Economic planning — strong public control
CONCEPT AND TOOLS	**Structure plans** - Regional coverage - General policy - Long-term (10-30 years) - Resource-oriented	**Master plans** - City coverage (incomplete) - General land use - Indefinite time - Physical resource only **Zoning ordinance**	**Regional plans** - Redistribution proposals - Indicative - Population and broad land use **ZAD** — Zone d'aménagement differé - Area designation - CPO power at pre-designation - First right of refusal when land owner sells
	Local plans - Town/city coverage - General program - Short-term (2-5 years) - 'Action oriented'	**Project plans** - Site-related - Detailed program - Immediate - Construction-oriented	**ZAC** — Zone d'aménagement concerté - Covers preservicing of site - For later sale to private or public user - Contract defines exact amenities, services, timing - Builder determines future value of works - Developer negotiates contribution for pre-servicing
PREPAR-ATION AND CONTROL	**Local government** - County structure plans - District local plans - Detailed practice/procedures - Gives 'planning permission' - Controls all development	**Local government** - Determines zoning - Prepares master plan - Uneven practice - Gives zoning permission - Weak control **State government** - May prepare growth strategy - May require local plans - No direct control	
	Central government - DOE final authority - Controls office/industrial development	**Federal government** - No overall authority yet (except new towns) - Planning incentives	Regional planning group National planning agency (DATAR)

Figure B   Features of urban and regional planning systems

With rapid changes in the economy, in social values and in the distribution of political power, this legacy of planning tools and processes, designed to cope largely in spatial terms with a single specified course of events, is fast losing its value. Parts II and III describe new approaches to strategic planning, project evaluation and management, based on the explicit assumption of frequent change, which focuses on reducing the risks and allocating resources more effectively under conditions of uncertainty.

Although community planning may require *thinking* that everything is related to everything else, it has clearly become counterproductive to expend too much effort in working out a 'total systems framework', only to demolish it when conditions change. The new methods of planning therefore rely more on tightly structured, well-informed judgements than on exhaustive quantitative analyses; on description and explanation of existing situations and short-term opportunities rather than on excessive prescription and anticipation of the future; on evaluation of full program costs and benefits, and careful phasing of financial, staff, land and even political commitments, rather than on conceptualizing and funding grand designs; and finally, on broad strategic scenarios supported by specific analyses of selected policy issues rather than on detailed long-term plans.

Issues for the future

After three decades of intensive experience, new towns are at a watershed. Forged in the British New Towns Act of 1946 and hardened in the crucible of national programs in at least a dozen other countries, some have become mature communities while others have barely taken shape. Yet throughout the world their purpose and realization are today threatened by economic and political uncertainty.

The problems that beset new towns have received considerable attention in recent months from their critics and proponents alike. What makes them so difficult to resolve, however, is the 'community' dimension that distinguishes them from conventional urban development—namely, the planning, provision and management of both facilities and services to achieve socioeconomic mix, a higher quality of life and a more vital, attractive environment.

We have already touched on the challenge of public consultation in planning these services. Likewise unresolved are the most basic questions of identifying and capturing the economic values of efficient and effective new town development. Until recently, this shortcoming has not been crucial; the benefits of community programs have simply been assumed to outweigh their costs. But with strong pressure on resources and tighter budgeting, these tasks will be basic to community-scale investment in the future. When critics assert that new town projects are too costly, their full economic and social costs and benefits will have to be demonstrated. We shall need to find ways of converting potential future values into current cash flow and developing financing instruments that will encourage the required social investment to be made.

We shall be obliged, as well, to define and assess the overall performance of new town projects in terms of their community goals if the need for short-term financial measures of progress is to be met. A community 'balance sheet' will be an essential tool in identifying sources of investment and alternative types of return—not simply in financial terms, but also in broader economic, social and environmental terms. Rigorous evaluation will be essential to prune away the ineffective projects—i.e., those *not* creating community benefits and values—and to support a system of rewards and sanctions. A daunting task, perhaps, but vital and unquestionably feasible, as chapters 6 and 7 suggest.

Another challenge is the problem of transition facing the residents and development enterprise once the original plan has been fulfilled. Already acute in Britain, this is a rapidly emerging problem in the US and elsewhere as projects mature and plans are completed. The older new towns are having trouble in coping with the needs and aspirations of second-generation residents, who, having come as children,

17

are now leaving home and forming new households themselves. These towns are at, or are fast approaching, their original target population figures, yet they show no signs of reaching a 'natural' population limit at that level. Is the future growth of these towns to be encouraged or checked? Is their future development, like their original development, to be planned comprehensively or should they develop incrementally in the future like other, less planned communities? The issues of transition embrace not only ways of planning and organizing organic growth, but also problems specific to the community development concept, such as the need for permanent management of community services and programs that the developer or his agents have controlled throughout the building and marketing phase of the new community.

Finally, for this era of rapid change and uncertainty, the strategic task is to extend the concept itself to meet the double-edged problem created when larger conurbations begin to engulf smaller, decentralized community units. While new communities and PUDs are being scaled down to contain their risks and ease their development, they will almost surely proliferate in response to unmet demand. For public policy, then, the challenge of this change is to integrate a larger number of smaller, mixed-use projects throughout wider metropolitan regions, and at the same time reverse the decline of derelict inner city areas. For corporate management, the co-ordination and leverage of staff, materials and myriad activities over multiple situations and sites pose massive problems of program planning and control.

New institutional arrangements, new methods of policy analysis, and new machinery for planning, budgeting, operations and community management clearly are needed. But if we will only stop for a moment in the headlong rush of building to assess what has already been achieved in the new towns and in many other fields, we may find that the 'new' approaches required need not be invented anew. The British development corporation model, the American community planning process, the French 'competitions', value improvement methods, project management—all these and many more approaches developed in the past few years in several countries offer a strong foundation for the needed innovations.

The issues of preparing for the future, as I see them, are to a great extent ones of adaptation and application rather than creation. How can the established framework of legislative instruments and development concepts be better adapted to the social—as well as the physical—tasks of community building and renewal? How can the existing institutional machinery and established pratices be adapted to manage communities of stable size rather than cope with the massive growth for which they were designed? How can socioeconomic 'mix', 'balance' and urban 'vitality'—all fundamental principles of the new community concept—be injected into a wide variety of existing towns and neighbourhoods? In short, how can change be managed in smaller increments, with more subtle means but on a larger scale? As an aid to readers who are grappling with such problems, a 'checklist' of issues and hypotheses is included in the appendix.

The contributors to this book, who are themselves deeply involved in the dynamics and day-to-day workings of the community development process, explore in the chapters that follow some of these challenging issues and the most promising new ideas and methods. Should the reader be stimulated to pursue these approaches further the book will have amply served its purpose.

Part I

Community development policies and institutions

Developing whole communities to provide an efficient and attractive environment for the full range of human activities—living, working and leisure—is surely one of the most formidable challenges to which planners and entrepreneurs have addressed themselves in the past quarter-century.

How much success can we thus far claim in meeting this goal? In chapter 1, David Thompson assesses the British new towns both as instruments of national development policy and as places to live. His verdict is favourable—but with reservations.

Britain's new town program, of course, is long-established, and also firmly in the public sector. The American case is quite different. In 'The United States: the battle for Title VII', William Nicoson provides a fascinating insider's view of an abortive attempt to involve the Federal Government in new community development. Nicoson believes that the benefits of public–private partnership in the urbanization process transcend political ideologies. 'We ought,' he says, 'to do better next time.'

It is too early to attempt a verdict on the French new towns program. As we are reminded in chapter 3, these new towns are hardly out of the cradle. But the French are testing new solutions to the administrative problems specific to new towns—land assembly, relations with local administrations, financing mechanisms—and to those connected with life in any city, such as the flight to the suburbs, the segregation of urban functions, and the search for architectural quality.

Chapter 1. Britain: the new towns revisited

DAVID THOMPSON

The British new towns program has come of age. Now nearly 30 years old, its achievements are coming under close scrutiny, both from abroad (the UN Conference on New Towns was held in the UK in 1973) and from inside the country, where a House of Commons sub-committee has recently been examining new town problems and progress. The British program provides the most extensive available experience of large-scale planned community development, and is frequently cited as a model for other countries. To gain the benefits of this experience, any review must be undertaken not only from the national perspective, assessing the extent to which the program has contributed to wider social and economic policy objectives, but also from a community perspective, asking how far it has fulfilled the high expectations of its protagonists.

Policy or concept?

Attempting an assessment of such a major social experiment is a difficult task, the more so because no formal policy plan exists for the new towns program as a whole against which to measure progress. Paradoxically, new towns established to provide an ordered alternative to haphazard urban sprawl have been developed without an explicit national strategy as to how many there should be, where they should be built, and how many people they should house.

Rather than springing from an overall plan, the development of the new towns has been guided by a concept, developed largely by an obscure parliamentary clerk, Ebenezer Howard, to solve the twin problems of overcrowded cities and depopulated countryside. His ideal, enunciated in *Tomorrow: A Peaceful Path to Real Reform* (1898), was a town of about 30,000 people, providing for all the physical, social and employment needs of its population, spaciously laid out, and relying on the surrounding green belt for agricultural produce and recreation.

His struggle to realize this ideal contrasts dramatically with the subsequent success of the new towns program. Howard founded the first garden city at Letchworth, near London, in 1902. Supported entirely by private finance, the new town was plagued by problems that may sound familiar to private developers today: development was slow, heavy interest charges and operating costs were incurred before any income was produced, management and organization were weak, the business and ideological aims of the venture were in conflict.[1]

As his Letchworth venture limped ahead, Howard launched a second new town project in 1920. With Welwyn Garden City he hoped to catch the public in a post-war mood for reconstruction and achievement. But the boom in speculative building in the twenties and thirties almost brought Welwyn to grief, and the Government had to bail the company out with a loan.

These experiences did not bode well for the Garden Cities movement. Howard died in 1928 and although his close associate Frederic Osborn continued to keep the movement in the forefront of planning debate, no practical steps towards establishing new towns were taken by any government between the wars. The impetus to the program that Howard had hoped for after the 1914–18 war came only with the Second World War. Then events moved quickly.

The form that postwar reconstruction was to take became a pressing issue with the first air raids on London. In 1940, the Barlow Commission, considering the distribution of the industrial population, recommended (in an influential minority report) a new agency, to facilitate population dispersal by means of garden cities and satellite towns. In 1944, the Abercrombie Plan for Greater London also recommended setting up satellite towns to reduce congestion in Inner London. This urgent need led to the establishment in 1944 of the Reith Committee on the New Towns, which laid down the physical planning basis for the new towns and recommended that a public corporation should be the development body. The New Towns Act became law in 1946. Only a week later, Stevenage in Hertfordshire was designated the first new town.

Right from the start, the new towns have been subjects of intense interest. Their advocates and their opponents were equally impassioned. They were novel in concept, and often controversial in design and appearance.[2] Most of all, perhaps, they raised expectations that serious national problems could be tackled successfully—in particular, that they would provide a physically pleasant, economically viable solution to overcrowding in the big cities; that they would contribute to the regeneration of these cities; and that they would play a part in the economic planning of their regions. To what extent have these expectations been fulfilled?

The national perspective

In one very fundamental sense, Britain has clearly had enormous success in developing new towns. As one American observer put it, 'The British new towns are there, you can go and see them.'

There were 14 new towns in the first generation, or 'Mark I' new towns, designated between 1946 and 1950. Most were overspill towns, eight around London and one outside Glasgow. They were mainly 'greenfield', intended for populations of 25,000–60,000, and all located 25 to 30 miles from their parent city—far enough away, it was thought, to prevent significant commuting but not so far as to make people unwilling to move to them. The remaining five—two in the North-East, and one each in Wales, Scotland and the Midlands—were intended to meet specific local needs for industrial growth centres and centres of urban development.

After this initial group, designation of new towns was halted in favour of extending existing towns, with only one new town, Cumbernauld, designated between 1950 and 1961. In this period, however, the original new towns prospered. They successfully attracted both population and jobs, and by 1962 the English new towns taken as a whole were showing a surplus on their revenue accounts.

A second generation of five new towns was designated in the early sixties. These were planned to be larger than the original towns, built for larger target populations, some over the 100,000 mark, with higher densities, and located further from London. Their increased size reflected both the need for larger populations in the towns in order to support a full range of social and commercial activities, and also the role that larger towns could play in their particular regions.

In the later sixties, a third group of nine new towns was designated. In the main these were characterized by their larger size—populations ranging up to 250,000—and by the fact that most of them were based on existing large towns, such as Northampton and Peterborough.

From concept to reality

In all, Britain's new towns now house nearly two million people, including those resident before declaration, and provide jobs for some 900,000.

That the new towns have been so successfully established is largely due to the effectiveness of the development corporation machinery set up in 1946 and scarcely altered since.

The development corporation itself is a powerful and single-minded body. Its board is appointed, not elected, and thus largely free of direct political pressures. The board members are chosen for their individual qualifications, not for any representative purposes, although in fact the board usually contains people with strong local associations, often elected representatives of local authorities. The corporation's full-time professional staff of planners, architects, engineers and so on are not civil servants or local authority officers, and they form a single team free of the interdepartmental rivalries that have so often bedevilled the performance of other British governmental agencies.

Because the development corporation has access to central funds, the new towns have never been in danger of running out of money in the critical investment phase of their development. The development corporation borrows money needed for capital projects and operating funds from central government. The loans are made for a term of 60 years at a fixed rate of interest. Although the corporation cannot borrow money from any other source, it can use funds from sale and leaseback arrangements, from rents, and from the sale of sites to builders and industrial developers. Services and facilities normally provided by central and local government (the bulk of community and welfare facilities) are financed in new towns in the same way as in the rest of the country.

Another important feature of the way in which new towns are set up is the ability of the corporation to purchase land, compulsorily if necessary, in its designated area at a price that ignores any change in value caused by the designation of the new town (although compensation to the land owner takes account of other possible uses for the land for which planning permission would have been granted). With these powers the development corporation can overcome the otherwise thorny problem of land assembly, and capture all the development gain from the new town for the community.

Apart from simply being built, and attracting population and employment, the towns have done well in other ways.

The group of new towns that encircle London, the 'London Ring', nearing completion now, have achieved their aim of self-containment in employment. By and large there are slightly more jobs available in the towns than there are residents in employment. At the same time, the proportion of new town residents commuting to London appears to have been declining steadily.

Financially, too, the viability of the new towns does not seem to be in doubt. They were always regarded as long-term investments, with a considerable period elapsing before they could show an operating surplus after making interest payments on their loans. While the new towns as a whole have not yet reached that position, the more mature 'London Ring' new towns have all moved comfortably into surplus. They also have a very considerable, though imponderable, capital gain locked in their physical assets.

In its first 30 years, therefore, the British new towns program has established the new town as a viable instrument of planning policy. The physical problems of carrying out the development have been overcome, the towns have shown that they can attract population and employment in line with their targets and, eventually, make a profit for the public purse. But the physical creation of the new communities is only part, albeit a vital part, of what the new towns program is intended to achieve. What of its other objectives: its initial and continuing aim of helping the regeneration of major cities, and its more recently developed purpose of assisting in regional and economic development?

Assisting the cities

The original theory propounded by Howard and his successors was that as new towns were developed and drew population from the existing overcrowded cities, pressure on land in those cities would decline. As a consequence, land values would drop and this combination of fewer people and cheaper land would allow the cities to be redeveloped at a lower density, providing better housing, open space, and an improved environment in the old cities, as in the new towns.

26

In practice, of course, things have not worked this way. To begin with, it appears that industry has very largely expanded, rather than transferred, into new towns, so city sites have not fallen vacant. Moreover, even when industry and people have migrated, others have come to take their place. Although public authorities may technically have had the opportunity to capitalize on temporary vacancies in order to redevelop city areas or turn them into open space, in practice land values have remained so high that this has proved impossible. The existing cities have just not had enough money to take real advantage of any relief the new towns program might have afforded.

Even had the resources been available, however, the new towns would have contributed little to relieving congestion in cities. For example, although over 400,000 people have moved to the London new towns since their designation nearly 30 years ago, the 1944 Abercrombie Plan for London envisaged half a million people within 10 years moving to new towns. Further, of the 828,000 migrants from the Greater London Area in the period 1961–6, only 46,000, or just over $5\frac{1}{2}$ per cent, actually went to the new towns. It is not that the existing towns have failed to meet their population targets—most are well on the way to meeting them and some, notably Stevenage and Harlow, have shown the potential, and even the need, to grow considerably beyond them. There were simply not enough new towns declared, even with increases from their original target population, to make a major impact on London's overspill needs.

A more serious criticism of the way in which the new towns program has contributed to the relief of big city problems concerns the type, and not simply the numbers, of people who have moved to them. The new towns have a socioeconomic composition similar to that of the country at large. However, the overall percentages hide a significant under-representation of unskilled manual groups. In addition, the elderly are notably under-represented in new towns as, with the exception of Crawley, are immigrant groups. The towns have attracted the younger and the more skilled, thus, if anything, exacerbating the problems of the cities by drawing off the more economically able groups, leaving behind proportionately more of those groups in the population less capable of fending for themselves.

It has been argued that these groups have not moved to new towns because they don't want to. This may be a factor, but recent research suggests that it is not likely to be a major reason. While unskilled manual workers form only 8 per cent of the population of London, they account for 20 per cent of the applicants for jobs in new towns through a government-sponsored scheme designed to match workers wishing to migrate to new towns with employers looking for workers. The same research project also suggested that elderly people were quite happy to move to the new towns. They seemed to regard a house in the new town, with a garden and access to open space, as an acceptable retirement home. Additionally, black workers certainly did not seem to regard new towns as 'not for them'.[3]

A more important explanation seems to be the lack of knowledge about new towns. Few of the groups in question seemed to know of the existence of schemes by which they could move to new towns, and, significantly, a survey of those who had

27

moved showed that most of them had heard about the opportunity either through their friends or through an employer.

The basic cause of the problem, however, is much more fundamental. The new towns program has in fact actually discriminated against those people who are likely to suffer most from the overcrowding and stress in large cities—the poor, the elderly and the unskilled. Obviously the discrimination is not intentional. It arises because the establishment of new towns is seen as an objective separate from, although complementary to, that of improving existing cities.

The development corporation of a new town is charged only with the task of developing the new town. There is a general requirement that it provide a broad range of employment, and obtain a reasonably balanced population, but its targets are expressed in terms of people and jobs rather than of social mix or types of employment. It would be perfectly feasible for new towns to ensure that, for example, they attract a specific number or proportion of unskilled manual workers. They don't do this, however, as it would interfere with what becomes a primary goal of the new town, that of attracting adequate employment quickly.

The need to attract employment in order to ensure that the new town develops at the pace required of it makes the town reluctant to discriminate, in the early years, among the types of employers it attracts. The firms that come to new towns tend to be growth industries, probably with a strong technological base, requiring skilled or semi-skilled rather than unskilled labour, and capable of paying relatively high wages. A very high proportion of their employment is in engineering and electrical goods manufacture. About a third of the jobs are in this category, compared with some nine per cent for Britain as a whole. These industries have, compared with employment generally, a marked preponderance of skilled and semi-skilled manual workers and a corresponding lack of demand for unskilled manual workers. The employment aims of the new towns program therefore seem to militate against those people in the existing cities who might most benefit from relocation in a new town.

In addition, they are not particularly well served by the government-run scheme that helps workers to find jobs in the new towns. Despite the general lack of information about the scheme mentioned earlier, it contains a significant proportion of unskilled groups. Unfortunately, it is not a major source of new employees in the new towns, since employers find it more convenient to recruit their labour direct and only about 10 per cent of new town jobs are filled through it. (By contrast the scheme fills some three quarters of the jobs in towns carrying out officially sponsored planned expansion.) The impact of the scheme may be even smaller in the London new towns, since there only 15 per cent of the applicants are actually submitted to employers, and of those only a similar proportion are actually employed.[4]

Nor are the problems limited to employment. To cope with setting priorities among long housing waiting lists and to provide an added incentive to employers, the new towns generally have switched from a personal waiting list, which anyone who has a job in the town can join, to an industrial waiting list, to which only employers are allowed to nominate. Employers are, quite naturally, more likely to use this opportunity to secure the managerial and skilled staff they need, than to nominate less skilled employees. Consequently, unskilled and semi-skilled workers are forced to commute into the new towns where they work. The trend towards owner-occupation in the new towns also puts pressure on the lower paid, who are, by that very fact, less able to take advantage of an increase in the number of houses for sale.

The worker who successfully negotiates both the problem of obtaining a job and that of obtaining a house does not necessarily end up better off. Rents in the new town are often as high as or even higher than in the cities from which the immigrant comes, the cost of living is not significantly different, and nor are wages.

All these factors suggest that while new towns have from their own point of view been successful in attracting both a range of employers and a range of social classes, they have not significantly contributed to solving the problems of the existing cities. And in Peter Hall's blunt phrase, 'the policy has not helped the old and the poor'.[5]

While the main focus of the new towns has been on developing more attractive towns to cope with the overspill from crowded cities, increasingly they have been seen as a possible means of stimulating economic growth in their region or sub-region, and hence as a tool for remedying the regional imbalances that have been such a feature of the British economy since the thirties.

Supporting regional policies

The first new towns have had no role to play in tackling the economic problems of the weaker regions, nor in attempting to stem the flow of migration from the North and Scotland into the South-East. Most were basically concerned with overspill from existing cities. Of the remainder, all save Peterlee were intended to provide housing and social facilities to support employment already in existence or attached to one specific major project, as in the case of Glenrothes and Corby.

In retrospect this lack of emphasis on economic development and growth is rather surprising. The problem of the depressed areas had been very evident during the early thirties. Government policy had first tried to deal with it by encouraging workers to move to where the jobs were but by the late thirties this policy was seen to be ineffective. Too few people moved, and most of those who did were the younger and more enterprising workers. As early as 1935 the policy of creating centres for new industrial development using 'trading estates' had been established, and immediately after the war legislation had been passed giving the Board of Trade special responsibilities for areas of high unemployment. However, at that time physical and economic planning were little co-ordinated and so new towns were promoted simply as a means of achieving physical objectives, such as the decongestion of existing cities, without an attempt to realize their potential in meeting economic as well as physical objectives.

In the early years of the new towns program, in fact, regional policy even worked to the detriment of new towns. In the first six years after the war, the Labour Government used its powers of control over industrial development to such effect that about two thirds of the jobs of industrial firms that moved went to the less developed areas of the North, Scotland, Northern Ireland, Wales and the South-West, which between them contained only about 20 per cent of the population of the

29

UK. Meanwhile, the new towns struggled. The concept was new, the towns themselves were little known and, inevitably, in their early years not well endowed with facilities and amenities. In these circumstances it might have seemed reasonable to assist them through the application of the various controls and incentives affecting the location of industry. However, the split between the ideas of the physical planners and the aims of those responsible for economic planning and the location of industry worked against this. The ever-precarious state of the balance of payments, and the consequent need to give assistance to existing or potential exporters, overrode all locational questions when resources had to be allocated. Development areas came next, with the new towns a poor third. Even when a new town was located in a development area, it did not receive preferential treatment. Firms were, indeed, encouraged to move into the development area, and then perhaps into the new town, but would not be encouraged to move from major cities of the development area to new towns. Thus, although the central government planners were attempting to move population from the existing overcrowded cities into the new towns, they were giving no assistance in the relocation of the firms that might provide the jobs for any immigrants.

The initial group of Mark I new towns, therefore, played no role in tackling this central problem of British regional and economic development. They were not intended for that purpose, they were in the wrong places to do that job, and they were simply too few and too small.

By the time the Mark II new towns were declared in the sixties, the situation had changed radically. After a relatively promising start in the period immediately after the war, it was clear that the problem of the depressed areas was as intractable as ever. The less prosperous regions were losing population at an increasing rate, and the gap between them and the South-East was widening. As Needleman and Scott have shown, 'the four less prosperous regions, with 35 per cent of Britain's male labour force in 1952, obtained only 8 per cent of the increase in male employment over the next decade'.[6] In that decade total employment in the regions did in fact increase by 4 per cent but this compared with about 12 per cent in the rest of Britain, and only about a quarter of the increase was in jobs for men. The main tool by which the Government attempted to control the location of industry was the industrial development certificate (IDC). Unfortunately, its use was limited to the control of the location of manufacturing industry, at a time when the relative importance of manufacturing industry was declining and employment in service industries was increasing rapidly. Thus between 1950 and 1963 over three times as many jobs were created in service industries in the South-East than were created in the whole of the less prosperous areas of the North and Scotland.

Consequently, by the late fifties successive governments had attempted to supplement the control of industrial development with positive financial incentives by which they hoped to induce firms to move to development areas.

It was against this background of increasing concern at the problems of regional imbalance that the second generation of new towns was designated. As the concern for regional problems in both the more and the less prosperous areas developed, and the planning became increasingly focused at a regional and sub-regional level, the prime objectives of new towns broadened, from overspill to regional development.

The change of emphasis when it came was rapid. The early Mark II new towns, such as Skelmersdale and Runcorn, were basically still overspill towns. The fact that they were bigger, and had a substantial existing population within the designated area, was not initially a response to regional needs. Rather, it was an attempt to avoid the lack of social amenities for which the original new towns had been criticized, particularly in their early years. However, by 1967, six years after Skelmersdale was designated and four years after Runcorn, the channelling of growth in the South-East region was the primary motive for the declaration of the new towns of Milton Keynes, Peterborough and Northampton, which were between them to have a population of about three quarters of a million.

It is too early to assess how beneficial this broadening of new towns objectives will be for the regions. The new towns have the potential to attract the growing service and light industries, the lack of which has hampered the development of the outlying regions in the past. This is evident in, for instance, the prevalence of the light engineering and electrical industries in the new towns. Nor is the potential limited to the southern new towns. For example, IBM have a research centre in Peterlee, Glenrothes advertises its success in attracting electronic companies, while the National Engineering Laboratory is now in East Kilbride.

However, it is doubtful whether the full potential of the new towns in boosting regional development is being fully realized. First, the scale of new town development in the development areas is modest. There are, it is true, more new towns in development areas, relative to the total population, than in the rest of the country, with one new town per million inhabitants in the development areas compared with one new town for just under two million inhabitants in the remainder of the UK. Whether this is a sufficient differential to make a serious impact on a long-standing imbalance remains to be seen. A second and more important doubt arises from the fact that there is no overall plan in the UK for the distribution of economic growth, and the regional plans have not yet been developed for all the planning regions. As a result, the conscious use of new towns as a means of encouraging and channelling regional development varies from region to region. Although the strategy for the South-East led to three major new towns being designated, the only other region where new towns have been developed consciously as a major tool of regional planning is Central Scotland. Here, the Toothill Committee's report, the outcome of an inquiry held in 1961 to look at ways in which growth could be fostered, heavily emphasized the concept of urban growth centres as the main focus of government assistance and effort in the regions. The plans for Central Scotland that resulted from the Toothill investigations focused on the existing new towns as major potential centres, and led to the designation of Irvine and Livingstone.

Outside the South-East and Central Scotland, a more explicit use of new towns in regional development has been hampered by the less advanced state of regional planning. The North-West has, in Central Lancashire new town, the town with the largest target population—420,000. As well as facilitating urban renewal in the three major existing communities within its designated area, Central Lancashire is

31

intended to be a major centre for growth in the North-West. However, it achieved this position almost by accident. The town was originally conceived as an overspill centre for the Liverpool–Manchester area. As it became apparent that the population of these cities was declining and that another overspill town for this area would not be needed, the role of Central Lancashire changed. However, at first, far from being seen as a vital and desirable growth centre, the new town aroused considerable fears that its effect on its hinterland would be harmful.

The lack of an overall national plan or fully developed regional plan entails the risk that the very success of the newer and larger new towns in some regions will exacerbate the problems in other regions. For example, the Northern Regional Economic Planning Council has publicly complained that the designation of Milton Keynes as a major growth centre will inevitably hamper regional development in the North-East.

Thus, as a tool of regional development the new towns program is still unproven. Its potential, ignored in the first postwar years, has now been identified. However, without overall co-ordination and specific consideration of a new town's role in redressing or limiting regional imbalances, this potential could well be wasted. At worst, the very existence of a new town could intensify the regional problem.

The community perspective

The British new towns have undoubtedly been successful in creating communities in which people are happy to live. There have, of course, been complaints about the lack of facilities in the new towns, particularly in the early years, and in some areas the complaints last into the maturity of a town, but overall the available evidence is clear. Studies of residents' opinions show that the overwhelming majority think they are better off living in the new towns than in their previous locations, and objective studies confirm the view.[7]

However, the advocates of new towns have always argued the inevitable superiority of a carefully planned community over the haphazard growth of both the existing cities and the new suburbs, and the British new towns are seen as the physical proof of that belief. It is therefore fair to ask how well the new towns have used the opportunity to develop a wholly planned community on, in general, a 'greenfield' site. The question is of more than simple academic interest: many of the British new towns are still in their very early stages, while other countries are attempting to follow Britain in developing new communities.

Against the standard of 'could the new towns have been better?' two shortcomings emerge. The first is that, despite a high general level of provision of services and facilities, certain groups in the population are not well catered for. One such group are the elderly. Although not unwilling to move to new towns, they are considerably under-represented in new town populations, as initially the towns tend to attract younger, more mobile workers. Development of housing more suitable for older people tends to be delayed and, because of the financial pressure on the development corporation, is added only later. When it is built it therefore tends to be at the perimeter of the town, remote from central services. Hence, in one established town with a relatively high proportion of older residents, over 70 per cent of retired people described housing near shops as a major need.

Another group who are relatively poorly catered for, surprisingly considering the very high proportion of young families in new towns, are young married women. Given their numbers, the fact that they are probably living some considerable distance from their parents, and that very many are restricted by the need to look after young children, their needs might be thought to warrant priority attention. However, a lack of nursery school, day centre and playgroup provision is typical: in one well-established town a recent study showed that provision of nursery and pre-school places would need to increase by well over 100 per cent to meet even a conservative estimate of the town's needs. While this situation is well known, a less recognized gap is the lack of employment and social opportunities. In one new town half the women not working, representing about a quarter of the potential female work force, said they would go out to work if they had the opportunity, while a quarter felt 'cut off' from social contacts and an even higher proportion wanted some form of social club meeting during the day. For some, even the physical design of the town can appear to be against them. One ex-resident of a new town remarked to the author that 'Our Radburn layout looked lovely, but it meant that no one ever passed our house by chance. My wife felt wholly cut off.'

As the new towns mature another group is emerging whose needs are not well met. The second generation in the towns, the children of the original in-migrants, are in many cases now at the age of wanting to leave home to live independently. In many instances they are forced to leave the town altogether because of the total lack of provision in the towns of the type of housing required by single, mobile young people.

The relative failure to provide for these key groups in the population represents a clear shortcoming in the new towns when measured against the highest standards that they set for themselves. The other shortcoming has been the failure to take full advantage of the 'greenfield' nature of the new town situation. While some innovations have taken place in the physical design of new towns—such as the 'figure of eight' road system at Runcorn, or the grid network development pattern at Milton Keynes— there has not been a similar level of innovation in the provision of services. As one observer has put it: 'The only thing that is new about new towns is the buildings', while a symposium of doctors, administrators and others involved with new towns concluded: 'In new towns there has been no planning for medical care and the same old general practice is being carried on. . . This is a serious indictment of the (Health) Service as a whole but an even more serious indictment of the Health Service in new towns, where the opportunities should have been realized and seized 20 years ago.'[8]

This lack of an innovative approach has been costly, as is clearly shown by the figures when advantage has been taken of the opportunity to provide services from the beginning. In one new town the district council, the development corporation, and the local churches made contributions to the development of a dual-use comprehensive school. As a result, for a total expenditure of well under £75,000, the community is being provided with a church, a community centre, green rooms, storage space, and changing accommodation of a higher standard than the education authority could provide, as well as other benefits, in addition to the use of the normal facilities of a £1 million-plus school. Provided separately, the community facilities may well have cost nearly £500,000.

While these shortcomings do not destroy the overall judgement of the success of the new towns, they do represent a failure to utilize to the full the opportunities presented to plan and develop a wholly new community. It is therefore valuable to see why, in these areas, new town performance is poorer than it might have been.

There have been two reasons: first, the fragmented nature of the planning carried out for new towns and, second, the lack of effective evaluation of the achievements.

No single agency is responsible for the whole of the development—social, physical and economic—of a new town. The development corporation has proved an excellent instrument for planning and achieving physical development. However, the responsibility for providing services usually lies elswhere. Some, such as schools, are provided by the county council, some, for instance refuse disposal, by the local district council (which may or may not be coterminous with the new town area). Others are the responsibility of field authorities directly accountable to central government, for example, health, or of the local branches of government departments, as in the case of employment exchanges. Thus while development corporations have been responsible, on average, for about 65–70 per cent of total capital expenditure in new towns, when one looks at the current expenditure, the development corporations' share is much lower. In one new town we studied, the corporation's expenditure, net of debt charges to remove the effect of prior capital costs, was only about 20 per cent of the total public sector expenditure in the town.

Thus a wide variety of agencies can be involved in providing services. While the agencies naturally do not plan in isolation, each has its own priorities, which may or may not coincide with those of the development corporation. Particularly in the case of those agencies covering wide geographic areas—the health and water authorities, the county councils, the transport undertakings—the gap in the priority given to the new town will be considerable. Thus the Chairman of the Development Corporation Board at Milton Keynes, in many ways Britain's 'showpiece' new town, has complained publicly and bitterly about the provision of public transport and hospital facilities in the new city.[9]

In these circumstances planning tends to be, in practice, carried out on a service-by-service rather than a client group basis. For those groups, such as school children, whose main needs are provided by one particular service or agency, this provides no problem, but where the needs of a particular group are the responsibility of several agencies, or no agency in particular—as in the case of the elderly or young married women—the quality of planning and provision inevitably suffers.

The difficulties caused by the fragmented approach to the planning of the new towns may be to some extent inevitable, given the administrative and governmental framework in Britain. The fact that the development corporation cannot fully compensate for it, and avoid the subsequent shortcomings, is largely the result of the lack of clear evaluation of the performance of the new towns and the consequent physical focus of the development corporation planning. The basic cause of this lack is the brief given to the development corporation, for while it has clear and precise targets for the growth of population and employment, its social objectives are usually left in too vague a form to be of use in guiding planning and evaluating performance. As a result, as an officer of the development corporation of an earlier new town explained, 'At first, the important thing is not to fail to reach the population target. It doesn't matter what the town is like to live in.' This may be an extreme statement of the position but the development corporation's focus is directed towards the more measurable and tangible aspects of new town development, which are, in any case, its own particular responsibility, and not towards the less tangible objectives where its co-ordinating influence is required. This physical focus is compounded by the fact that the corporation's main planning mechanism, the Master Plan, is still essentially a land-use plan.

If there was a broad evaluation of new town progress—social and economic as well as financial and physical—the bias could be limited. However, the evaluation carried out tends to reinforce the bias. The annual reports to Parliament, and the management accounts required by the responsible ministry, the Department of the Environment, review in considerable detail the physical and financial progress of the towns—even down, at times, to the number of trees and shrubs planted. But little progress has been made in regularly evaluating performance in the less quantified areas, which would highlight the lack of provision for key groups or the failure to develop new ways of delivering services to take advantage of new town opportunities.

Thus, while undeniably the performance of the British new towns has been good from a community perspective, there are shortcomings that merit attention as the second and third generation of new towns are developed. Similarly, from a national perspective the concept and mechanism of new towns has been tested and vindicated, but their full potential has not yet been realized. What, then, are the future prospects for new towns in Britain?

Future prospects

The new towns program in Britain is still young. Only four of the 31 new towns in the UK are complete to the stage of being handed over to the New Towns Commission, and only four more are approaching their target population. So, while over three quarters of a million people have already moved to new towns, twice that number are planned to move to new towns already designated before they are complete. Even without further designations, the size of the new towns program, at least as measured by population growth, will increase significantly over the next two decades.

The continued growth of the existing towns seems likely to provide the main thrust of future new town activity in the UK, as it is unlikely that there will be significant new designations in the near or the middle term. One reason for this is the steady

35

decline in perceived population pressure in this country. Population projections are consistently being revised downwards. For example, in 1964, the population projection for the year 2000 was 74.7 million. However, by 1971, that projection had been reduced to 62.8 million. Indeed, the continuing fall in the birth rate in the UK has led to the suggestion that it has fallen below replacement level and that, in time, the population will actually begin to decline. At the same time, the major cities are losing population. There is thus likely to be little demand for the designation of further 'overspill' new towns to reduce the pressure on overcrowded city centres. In addition, the recent realignment of local authority boundaries in the UK, which creates strategic planning units covering each of the major conurbations and its immediate hinterland, is likely to militate against any possible proposals of this kind.

Until recently it did seem likely that two new towns would be declared, both associated with major national development proposals. However, the plans for a third London airport and a Channel tunnel have been dropped and are unlikely to be revived in the next few years. Nor does it seem likely that private developers will undertake significant new community development.

In the past the problems of land assembly, the risks and financing problems inherent in carrying out very large-scale development, and the difficulties created by the sophisticated British planning system have usually been sufficient to dissuade private developers from undertaking new community development. It is unlikely that this situation will alter significantly in the current economic climate, especially given the uncertainties surrounding the effect of the new Community Land Act. While the Act may, in time, make it easier for developers to assemble parcels of development land and lead to an increased number of 'new village' developments, it is unlikely to help developers wishing to carry out larger-scale development on, say, the American model.

However, the lack of major new development of the more traditional type of new town does not mean that the future holds nothing new. A less ambitious form of new town could, perhaps, be used to combat the persistent inner-city problems of the major British conurbations. So far no attempt has been made to use the new town, or any other comprehensive redevelopment or rehabilitation mechanism, to tackle these problems. Yet there is evidence that action along these lines could be taken. In the US the 'new town in town' is one of the four types of new town initiated under Title VII, while in this country, Central Lancashire has as a major objective the promotion of urban renewal in the three large towns within its designated area. In addition, the 'partnership new towns', such as Northampton and Peterborough, which include substantial existing population centres within their designated areas, provide experience for development corporations working very closely with large and powerful local authorities, and the latest government statement on new towns supports this type of development. While so far this cooperation has not always been smooth, their experience may help to overcome the problems of the always potentially difficult relationship between the development corporation and the local authority, which has always been a major obstacle in the past to using new town powers in existing conurbations. It could be that as their own resources, both financial and in terms of skilled manpower, are increasingly stretched, the local authorities in stress areas may be more willing to consider new approaches to the seemingly intractable problems of the inner city.

In addition, as Griffith-Jones argues in more detail in the final chapter, the new towns face the challenge of modifying the development corporations' relationship with the inhabitants of their areas, in response to the twin pressures for greater individual participation in development decisions, and for closer links between the corporation and the elected local governments. At the same time as they deepen their relationship with the inhabitants of their areas, many corporations have the opportunity to extend their relationship with private developers. To date the private developer has played little more than a contractor role in the new towns. But, following the French example, they could in future undertake development on a much more substantial scale, utilizing the full range of their entrepreneurial skills—from project conception, through design, financing and construction to marketing and ultimately community management.

In the previous pause in declarations of new towns, between 1950 and 1964, the initial new towns demonstrated the viability of the new town concept and the development corporation mechanism. Today their basic viability is no longer in doubt. The challenge of the future is to adapt the proven concept and mechanism to a new and more demanding set of requirements.

Author's Note: The author gratefully acknowledges the assistance of Mrs Susan Starks in the preparation of this chapter.

References

1. Rodwin, L., *British New Towns Policy*, Harvard University Press, Cambridge, Mass., 1953.
2. For example, see G. Cullen and J. M. Richards in *Architectural Review*, July 1953, criticizing the 'prairie planning' of the new towns.
3. Ungerson, C., *New Towns and 'Minorities'—Some Research Results*; in Second Report from the Expenditure Committee, Vol. II. HC 305, HMSO, London, 1974.
4. Ungerson, C., ibid.
5. Hall, Peter, *et al.*, *The Containment of Urban England*, Vol. 2, p. 350, Allen and Unwin, 1973.
6. Needleman, I., and B. Scott, 'Regional Problems and Location of Industry Policy in Britain', *Urban Studies*, 1, 2, 1964.
7. For example, Valerie A. Kahn, *The East Kilbride Housing Survey*, University of Birmingham, 1970, and its companion volumes on Crawley, Aycliffe and Stevenage, give resident views; and Lord Taylor and Sidney Chave, *Mental Health and Environment in a New Town*, Longmans, 1964, present an objective study.
8. *The Provision of General Medical Care in New Towns*, Office of Health Economics.
9. Milton Keynes Development Corporation Seventh Annual Report in *Reports of the Development Corporations*, 31 March 1975, p. 189, HC 317, HMSO, London, 1975.

Chapter 2.   The United States: The battle for Title VII

WILLIAM NICOSON

> We are all a little wild here with numberless projects of social reform; not a reading man but has a draft of a new community in his waistcoat pocket.—Ralph Waldo Emerson writing to Thomas Carlyle.

One version of Emerson's metaphorical new community of 1870—a catch-all instrument of countless public policy objectives—became legislative reality in 1970 with passage by Congress of the Urban Growth and New Community Development Act. Whenever a government encourages the building of entirely new communities, the objectives of public policy inevitably sweep through the full range of intractable problems encountered in existing communities. If, furthermore, the Government's jurisdiction extends beyond the new community's boundaries, other regional or national policy considerations are encountered such as locational objectives of urban growth and the geographic allocation of public resources.

The explicit policy missions of the new communities programs under the 1970 Act (known as Title VII) were formidable. It was the purpose of Congress to

> encourage the orderly development of well-planned, diversified and economically sound new communities . . . ;
> strengthen the capacity of state and local governments to deal with local problems;
> preserve and enhance both the natural and urban environment;
> increase for all persons, particularly members of minority groups, the available choices of locations for living and working, thereby providing a more just economic and social environment;
> encourage the fullest utilization of the economic potential of older central cities, smaller towns and rural communities;
> increase the capabilities of all segments of the home-building industry, including both small and large producers, to utilize improved technology in producing the large volume of well-designed, inexpensive housing needed to accommodate population growth;
> help create neighborhoods designed for easier access between the places where people live and the places where they work and find recreation; and
> encourage desirable innovation in meeting domestic problems, whether physical, economic or social.

To help implement these broad, multiple and potentially conflicting objectives, a set of carefully tailored programs offered financial and technical assistance to both public and private land developers who complied with Federal standards. The assistance was designed to overcome specific obstacles that might hinder balanced community-scale development.

First, since long-term debt financing for development was virtually impossible to obtain, Title VII authorized guarantee assistance, effectively substituting the Government's credit for the developer's credit. Guarantee assistance was made attractive for public developers by an interest subsidy, designed to encourage site selection, land assembly, master planning and infrastructure development by state or local agencies of government.

Second, in order to promote planning for innovative features in new communities, Title VII authorized grants to public and private developers for environmental, social and technological planning of special value. The legislation contemplated that such grants might be made at an early stage in the planning process, prior to approval of a project for guarantee assistance, so that innovative planning would not be stifled through the natural momentum of the planning process.

To ease the short-term fiscal impact of a new community on local government, Title VII authorized additional grants for financing public services provided to approved new communities during the first three years of their development. It also made available add-on funds, complementing the variety of existing Federal grant programs, for infrastructure development beneficial to an approved new community—public works such as water and sewer lines, treatment plants, parks, libraries, hospitals, mass transit systems, highways and airports.

Title VII was more than a catalogue of good intentions. Recognizing the obstacles to achieving its multiple policy objectives, it prescribed a number of carefully tailored programs designed to overcome them. It will never be known whether the good intentions might have been achieved, since only the two pre-existing programs—guarantee assistance and limited infrastructure grants—were ever activated by the executive branch of government, and both have since been abandoned.

The history of the struggle to enact and fund Title VII provides an illuminating study of public policy formulation in a federal system of government, such as the US, where powers and responsibilities are shared by Federal, state and local agencies of government and where power is formally separated at the Federal and most other levels among legislative, executive and judicial branches.

If the generic function of government policy formulation is to serve the public interest, the first question under such a system must be: which public? Local government and national government have vastly different public constituencies. 'Public policy' on any issue will vary with the constituency: competing public interests may be accorded conflicting priorities by different public constituencies. Local government, for example, by re-zoning for park use the proposed site of low-income housing or by requiring three-acre lots for residential development, may place environmental interests first, but state or Federal interests in equitable accommodation of growth may be judged paramount and asserted in contradiction of local public policy.

39

A second question is: who defines the public interest, and in what terms? In theory, the public policy underlying legislative programs is determined by the legislature and refined, but never disregarded, by the executive branch in the course of program administration. The courts arbitrate any conflict between legislative and executive policy and any conflict between the actions of either branch and the constitutional constraints of the system. In practice, however, fundamental policy for legislative programs in the US is determined increasingly by the executive branch, and Federal policy in the absence of legislative enactment is determined increasingly in the courts.

Until the late sixties, the only Federal initiative in support of new town development came during the depression of the thirties, and not the least of the public objectives behind Federal sponsorship of the three new towns of that period was the stimulus they provided for the economy. It is ironic, then, that the financial hazards of a general economic recession should in large part have caused the Federal Government to abandon its new community assistance programs in 1975. Obviously the public interest was perceived differently in the seventies and the thirties. Also, in the thirties the executive branch pursued the policy objectives mandated by Congress; in the seventies it did not.

Advocates of new community assistance sought Federal legislation throughout the sixties, but it was not until 1968 that the first limited but viable programs were enacted. This Congressional action became politically possible because the lobbying force of the country's mayors was converted from opposition to acceptance of the new community concept. Earlier the mayors had feared that the new communities would compete with them for available Federal resources. By 1968, however, they had become convinced that traditional piecemeal urbanization on the periphery of the cities was responsible for many of the cities' problems: homogeneous upper-income subdivisions and vast suburban shopping centres drew away the revenue base of the cities, leaving behind the problems of the poor and of deteriorating facilities and services for which a larger, not a smaller, revenue base was needed. The concept of new mixed-income suburban communities promised some relief from the pattern of increasing economic polarization between city and suburb.

In August 1968, freed from organized mayoral opposition, Congress authorized the Department of Housing and Urban Development (HUD) to assist private developers of new communities through Federal guarantees of borrowings used for land acquisition and land improvements and to increase its existing assistance to local government for infrastructure development benefiting an approved new community.

In January 1969 Richard Nixon assumed office for his first term as President of the United States. The outgoing HUD officials had not had time to set up the complex administrative machinery required for approval of plans to build an entire community. The incoming HUD officials wanted time to study the legislative mandate, and some urged that the 1968 new community programs be ignored as being too limited in resources to achieve the ambitious objectives of Congress.

In October of 1969 I was asked by HUD to study the new communities legislation and recommend a course of action. I concluded that the programs of guarantee assistance and infrastructure grants were conceptually efficient, offering substantial incentive for meeting Federal standards with minimum impact on the Federal budget. I recommended that these programs should be implemented and that HUD should request authority for additional pump-priming grants and for assistance to public development agencies. At the end of 1969 I was asked to take charge of the new community programs.

'I'm with you. We're setting up an interdepartmental task force to study proposals for new legislation.' Daniel Moynihan, then a presidential assistant, was talking to HUD representatives at a White House lunch in October 1969. By November, Moynihan was clearly not with us, but unfortunately his interdepartmental task force was.

Two major studies had influenced White House thinking on new communities: *Urban and Rural America: Policies for Future Growth* by the Advisory Commission on Intergovernmental Relations (1968) and *The New City*, containing the report of the National Committee on Urban Growth Policy (1969). Both recommended major Federal initiatives in support of new communities.

In the early days of the Nixon Administration these studies could not be safely ignored by the two White House rivals for the role of the President's principal adviser on domestic policy: Daniel Moynihan and John Ehrlichman.

Each sought initially to stake a paternity claim for any new initiatives that might eventually emerge. The rivalry ended with the 'promotion' of Moynihan to the post of 'Counsellor', effectively severing him from the policy-making machinery (staff of the Urban and Rural Affairs Councils, later the Domestic Council) over which Ehrlichman took command. As soon as this outcome became evident within the White House, Daniel Moynihan lost all interest in new community initiatives and actively encouraged the attendance of the principal academic opponent of the new community concept at several government meetings. Ehrlichman, on the other hand, became too busy with the crisis-management aspects of his new responsibilities to devote much time to new community initiatives, and the only member of his staff with any expertise in the subject matter had been inherited from Moynihan.

This left HUD Secretary George Romney, not at first an advocate of new community legislation, mired in a frustrating process of interdepartmental consultation in which he was obliged, without White House support, to champion proposals he thought had been born in the White House. These consultations took place throughout the fall and winter of 1969–70 within a committee of the Urban Affairs Council—chaired, for some reason, by the Secretary of Transportation. The Committee or its task-force staff would meet on average once every two weeks, exchange objections based almost exclusively on the parochial interests of participating departments, and decide nothing.

In the meantime, the studies recommending major new community initiatives were also being read on Capitol Hill. Congressmen visited some of the new towns under way in Europe. The large projects at Columbia, Maryland and Reston,

Virginia, influenced Congressional attitudes. The new community concept was one of the principal subjects examined in hearings of the *Ad Hoc* Subcommittee on Urban Growth (chaired by Congressman Thomas L. Ashley of Ohio). A draft bill calling for a massive $22 billion program of direct loans and grants for new community development over five years was circulated for comment to public interest groups by the Ashley staff.

Secretary Romney used this Congressional activity in support of his argument that the process of interdepartmental consultation had served its purpose and that John Ehrlichman should immediately convene the Urban Affairs Council itself to consider HUD proposals for new legislation. Ehrlichman agreed. The political rivalry with Congress, and particularly with the Democratic majority, played a role similar to the previous personal rivalry with Daniel Moynihan. Concern that someone else might take credit for a major initiative rekindled White House interest in new communities and a Council meeting was called for 26 March 1970.

The processes of legislative and executive policy formulation operated to provide mutually reinforcing incentives. When word leaked to Congress that a meeting of the Urban Affairs Council had been called, Congressman Ashley and Senator Sparkman moved quickly and on 25 March filed their draft bill. Since supporters could not at such short notice agree on the amounts to be authorized for loan and grant assistance, the authorization figures were left blank. Democratic leaders feared that Administration proposals to be approved at the Council meeting would capture the initiative from Congress unless their bill was entered first on the Congressional agenda.

There was no cause for alarm. Like the countless committee and task-force staff meetings preceding it, the Council meeting decided nothing.

The following scenario conveys the flavour of discussion at the Council meeting following a presentation by HUD of its proposals. While the dialogue is grossly simplified, it reflects general positions taken by the participants, to the best of my five-year recollection.

ROBERT FINCH (Secretary of Health, Education and Welfare): Don't you have examples of poor urban development outside California?

SPIRO AGNEW (Vice-President, presiding in the absence of the President): We need to put new cities way out there far from existing cities.

JOHN VOLPE (Secretary of Transportation): We need to improve existing cities, particularly existing transportation.

PAUL McCRACKEN (Chairman of the Council of Economic Advisers): I would not favour any initiative which flies in the face of the free market. Let the market determine where the growth occurs.

GEORGE SHULTZ (Secretary of Labour; shortly to become Director of the Office of Management and Budget): You're proposing new categorical grants, but the Administration backs revenue sharing.

JOHN EHRLICHMAN (Executive Secretary of the Council): From my Seattle law practice experience, I wonder whether we know how to build new communities. (Exits to take a phone call.)

DONALD RUMSFELD (Director of the Office of Economic Opportunity): There will be growth on the periphery of cities whatever we do. Why shouldn't we try to improve its quality?

SPIRO AGNEW: We need to put new cities way out there far from existing cities.

GEORGE ROMNEY (HUD Secretary): We're milling around in this meeting! We can decide later where to put new communities. The issue to be decided today is whether to offer more assistance in putting them *somewhere*.

SPIRO AGNEW: Columbia was a pain in the neck while I was Governor (of Maryland). I say put them out in the boondocks.

JOHN EHRLICHMAN (returning from another telephone call): We'll continue this later. I have to fly to San Clemente.

While present for only portions of the discussion, John Ehrlichman had been able to observe himself the results of interdepartmental consultation. The meeting was never continued.

Throughout discussions within the Administration on new community initiatives, Federal officials tended to become preoccupied with the question of location. The more politically oriented the official, the greater the preoccupation. For officials, sensitive to rural constituencies, new communities were potential instruments for revitalizing the declining economies of rural areas and slowing population movement to established urban centres. For officials sensitive to inner-city constituencies, new communities were potential instruments for renovating city slums and wastelands and stemming population exodus to the suburbs.

In both these cases, of course, Federal intervention would mean 'flying in the face of the market' and generally demand a far greater commitment of Federal resources than a budget-conscious Administration would contemplate. It would also require far greater and more direct state or local government involvement in the development process than a conservative Administration was prepared to encourage.

There was indeed a new community in the waistcoat pocket of every official, regardless of political persuasion, but most demanded resources that the official was unwilling to commit.

New communities undertaken directly in the path of suburban growth demanded the least public assistance, and the realistic proponents of new community legislation realized that, so long as the initiative remained with the profit-oriented private sector, any other location for a new community would be exceptional. George Romney understood that the fiscal and philosophical prejudices of the Nixon Administration made it pointless to debate the location of new communities, but he preferred to defer the debate rather than resolve it prior to action on his proposals. There was no pressing need to alienate officials oriented toward rural or inner-city concerns.

For those of us engaged in the battle for Administration support of new legislation, the tendency of policy-making officials to become preoccupied with location rather than quality of development was frustrating. But it was also inevitable and quite proper that Federal officials should focus upon the peculiarly Federal question raised

43

in any consideration of new community policy: how can a new community program influence shifts in the location of population and economic activity among regions of the country to achieve national objectives? Unlike all the other issues of public policy raised by new community development in the US, this issue may be addressed only at Federal level.

The greatest difficulty for those addressing this issue was that no one knew what our national objectives were. Throughout the sixties there had been much academic and some public interest generated in the need to formulate national growth policy; but there had been virtually no government action. Within the Nixon Administration, the issues were discussed but not resolved. No agreement could even be reached on what issues came within the scope of any national growth policy. Under these circumstances it was not surprising that, some years after promising to unveil a growth policy, the Administration should retreat to the position that we might not even need one.[1]

Early in 1970, however, the Administration was still promising a national growth policy and struggling sporadically to make good the promise. Opponents of new community initiatives could argue that HUD, in its greed for a larger slice of the Federal pie, was peddling a program before it had a policy. The absence of policy was, in fact, painfully dramatized by the recurring debates over new communities' location.

HUD's answer was that any national growth policy must embrace considerations of quality as well as location, and that the debates over location of new communities should not obscure other Federal policy objectives served by balanced land development at community scale. These quality objectives of growth policy were not viewed exclusively as Federal objectives, but as primary local public policy objectives, shared by the Federal Government. HUD referred to the opportunities for protecting air quality by bringing jobs closer to homes, by building at densities sufficient to support mass transit, and by planning neighbourhoods on a pedestrian basis; for protecting water quality by rigorous community-scale monitoring of the effects of development on both surface and ground water; for making the most efficient use of land, permitting retention of greater open space and conserving the nation's most fundamental yet finite natural resource; for improving the possibility of achieving integration of residents through a range of income levels; for improving provision of health and educational services; for reducing the costs of public infrastructure through long-term planning and economies of scale; and on and on.

This litany failed to inspire other departments of government, except to produce vague annoyance with HUD for venturing into their own special policy preserves. However, they did seize upon one invocation for their own purposes: the argument that new communities, freed from the constraints of existing communities, offered varied opportunities for physical and social innovation. Yes, replied the opponents of new initiatives, the Federal program should be experimental in nature, and HUD should confine its efforts to a few demonstration projects, abandoning any attempt to mount a large ongoing program with the potential of influencing growth patterns. There was, after all, no national growth policy.

44

Discussion inevitably then turned to the relative merits of a 'growth-centre strategy'—building new communities on the base of small rural towns—as opposed to a 'free-standing strategy'—putting them out in the boondocks.

George Romney trudged once again into the office of John Ehrlichman. Was it conceivable that still another Council meeting should be called to waste still more time? No, Ehrlichman agreed. The HUD proposals for new community legislation should be immediately submitted to the President in a memorandum he would sign. Except of course that, as was customary, the memorandum would appear to transmit recommendations from the Council.

This decision to bypass the Council, as its committee had earlier been bypassed, was made on Friday 10 April. For reasons never understood, the memorandum was required for delivery to the President aboard an afternoon flight on the following day. After six months of 'milling around', as George Romney described it, we were obliged to compose an action memorandum for the President literally overnight.

The White House provided examples of action memoranda in the style to which the President was accustomed. These consisted of a tightly organized set of tersely-stated options, with a place provided at each option for the President to check his preference. Policy arguments for and against were compressed to a sentence or two in each case. Exposition on underlying issues was rigorously excluded.

In retrospect I think it was a mistake for us to prepare a decision paper in this mould. We could give the President the crisp technical options he wanted on the variety of complex issues involved in new legislation for new communities, but we could not effectively convey the general benefits for the public interest inherent in the new community concept itself. It is likely that the President remained largely unaware of the range of social, environmental and economic objectives of public policy served by encouraging balanced development of land at community scale.

At daybreak on Saturday the draft was delivered by hand to the White House, where Mr Ehrlichman's staff spent the morning editing it still further. It emerged from this process even more desiccated and bewildering in its array of alternatives than we had managed to make it in our all-night session. Mr Ehrlichman signed it, and delivery to the President was made on schedule.

During the remainder of April and throughout May HUD waited for a response. On 1 June, while away from Washington, I was tracked down by a call from Hilbert Fefferman, HUD's veteran legislative lawyer, who throughout his career had championed new community legislation. The President had declined to approve. To approve what? Anything at all. Any option at all. The President had decided to defer the entire question for further consideration with the new budget in the fall. He had concluded that inflationary pressures in the economy were then too acute to permit the Administration to embark on a major new spending program. But, by the way, had a new program been possible the President would have preferred an active ongoing program to a limited experimental program. 'Don't take it so hard', said Hilbert Fefferman. 'Congress enacts legislation, not the President. Stick it out for a few months and you may have a new program yet.'

He was right about the legislation. But I was to discover that a new program required more than new legislation.

Inflationary pressures precluded the Administration from embarking on a major new spending program? I was outraged. Federal new community assistance did not increase total spending in the urbanization process. On the contrary, over the long term material savings resulted from land development at community scale rather than by traditional piecemeal increments. It could therefore be argued that new community assistance programs were counter-inflationary in their impact on the economy. And in no event could the modest measures we proposed be considered as major new spending programs. We wanted very limited authority for innovative planning grants and for interest advances to both public and private new community developers. We had also proposed the use of eminent domain powers to assist land assembly, with appropriate safeguards and without cost to the Government. The large-dollar program was already in place and involved guarantee assistance, simply a means of channelling private funds into projects serving public purposes, without Federal outlays or other budgetary impact.

I was naive enough to expect that Secretary Romney might be able to discuss these matters with the President. That was not President Nixon's decision-making style. He appeared to fear that face-to-face advocacy from his cabinet members would turn him from the safe path of secluded selection among paper options. This was a style to which cabinet members were forced to adjust if they chose to remain in office. Secretary Romney chose to remain throughout the four years of Mr Nixon's first term. He knew that the President's decision was final.

Congressional advocates of new community legislation, however, advanced their cause during the summer. Much to the surprise of White House observers, prospects for passage of the Ashley bill steadily improved. The HUD Under-secretary then sought Ehrlichman's permission to negotiate with the Senate and House committees for a workable new community bill—the same legislation HUD had earlier urged the President to propose. Approval was granted. Negotiations were carried on under the guise of supplying technical drafting assistance to the committee staffs. Acting as intermediary, Hilbert Fefferman shuttled between the committee offices on Capitol Hill and reluctant representatives of the Office of Management and Budget in the Executive Office Building, who privately criticized Ehrlichman for authorizing such an exercise.

Fefferman began by persuading the ranking Republican on the Housing Subcommittee in the House of Representatives, Congressman Widnall of New Jersey, to introduce a revised version of the HUD bill. He was then successful in persuading the staff of the Senate Subcommittee to prevail on Senator Sparkman and other Democratic sponsors of the initial Senate bill to accept the same HUD version. As negotiations continued in the House between Congressmen Ashley and Widnall, the Senate rapidly approved the HUD version as one title in an omnibus housing bill. Agreement also appeared imminent in the House, but collapsed when Congressman Ashley insisted on retaining a provision of his earlier bill creating within the President's office an Urban Growth Council with the continuing function of formulating and monitoring the execution of urban growth policy. The Administration strenuously opposed this provision, contending that the President's office should be organized by the President, not the Congress, and that the existing Domestic Council had already been given the growth policy mandate.

When the omnibus bill came to a vote on the House floor, the new communities title was similar to the HUD version already accepted by the Senate, except for the offensive provision creating an Urban Growth Council and a House program of public service grants for new community jurisdictions during initial years of development. Administration forces then mounted a surprise attack on the entire new communities title and, while its proponents were off the floor, succeeded in having it stricken from the bill. In the subsequent conference between House and Senate, the title was restored—without the Urban Growth Council but retaining the public service grants.

It was on New Year's Eve that I received another telephone call from Washington. The President had just signed the bill. Title VII was now law.

At the time, I had no appreciation of the loss sustained by the public interest through elimination of the Urban Growth Council from Title VII. It seemed pointless to risk a Presidential veto, and the substantive new community programs appeared far more important.

But I now see that an Urban Growth Council might have been the salvation of the new community programs. The Congressional aim was to institutionalize growth policy formulation within the White House through the UGC in much the same manner as the Council on Environmental Quality had institutionalized Federal formulation of environmental policy. A single-function policy council inevitably becomes an advocate for government programs that reinforce the policy. An advocate at the White House was precisely what the new community programs lacked.

An Urban Growth Council, with a professional staff, would have formulated a growth policy of one kind or another. The Domestic Council under President Nixon produced no policy whatever to guide national growth, and from my limited Council experience, this came as no surprise.

In optimistic anticipation of the passage of Title VII, my staff had quietly drafted a full budget presentation that called for funding of all Title VII programs in the Administration's 1972 budget to be sent to Congress at the end of January 1971. I had also made contingency plans for staffing the new programs and reorganizing the new communities office. We were thus prepared to give instant effect to our new Congressional mandate.

During January, there was every expectation that our ambitions for the new communities programs would be realized. Regulations for the guarantee and supplementary grant programs had been in place for a year. In February 1970, the first new community had been conditionally approved and in October the first HUD guarantees were issued. Developers then had a chance to evaluate the administrative machinery of the guarantee program, and they apparently concluded that it would work.

These events, combined with the substantial expansion of new community programs under Title VII, produced a groundswell of interest among builders and developers. The number of proposals submitted to HUD mounted dramatically.

The budget bureaucracy within HUD was taken aback by the voluminous submission we had drafted for the Office of Management and Budget (OMB). There were too many technical questions about these new programs. The budget people had not been consulted by the lawyers on the language of funding authorization in the bill. It would all require weeks of careful review within the HUD budget office.

At the next budget review meeting with OMB representatives, Secretary Romney handed over our draft. Although it was just a draft, he stressed that consideration was urgent in view of the schedule for budget submission to Congress. The formal HUD submission would be made when OMB was ready to act.

OMB officials, however, did not regard the funding of new community programs as an urgent priority. These were the programs that HUD had peddled to the Congress when the President had declined his sponsorship; the programs that Administration forces had then succeeded in striking from the House bill, only to see them reinstated in conference, probably with HUD connivance. They were, in short, programs for which the political opposition, conspiring with HUD officials, had managed to take all the credit.

This was not, of course, the response that OMB transmitted to Secretary Romney. HUD was told merely that there were too many technical questions in the new programs and too little time to resolve them. The President's 1972 budget was forwarded to the Congress with a brief note indicating that Title VII had been enacted too late in the session to be reflected in the budget.

We were prepared at HUD to accept the OMB assertions at face value and immediately submitted a request that the Title VII programs should be funded in a supplementary budget. On 31 March 1971 Caspar Weinberger, then Deputy Director of OMB, wrote to Secretary Romney denying the request and indicating that the new categorical grant programs in Title VII were inconsistent with the Administration's proposals for general and special revenue sharing. A small apportionment of funds for the interest loan program was approved, but was later quietly withdrawn.

This line of attack on the new communities programs had been foreshadowed a year earlier during our interdepartmental consultation on new legislation. It carried a depressing superficial logic, and gave us a much more realistic insight into how far we would be able to carry out the Congressional mandate of Title VII. Our short-lived euphoria came to an end.

The Administration's proposals for sharing Federal revenues with state and local governments were designed to replace the complex maze of narrow-purpose grant programs that Congress had authorized over the years with a general-purpose allocation of Federal funds from the Treasury (general revenue sharing) and several broad-purpose formula allocations from the domestic departments (special revenue sharing). The theory of these proposals was that state and local governments, freed from the constraints of categorical requirements, were in a better position to decide how to spend Federal monies to serve their own interests and would waste less time and effort in the process of securing Federal assistance.

This was a promising theory. Both Secretary Romney and I supported the Administration's revenue-sharing proposals. We did not believe, however, that all categorical programs should therefore be dismissed.

The purpose of revenue sharing was clearly not to encourage state and local governments to undertake specific new responsibilities serving public interests in tandem with the Federal Government, but rather to permit state and local governments to carry out existing responsibilities more efficiently.

The most desirable system of Federal assistance should therefore embrace both revenue-sharing programs and categorical programs: revenue sharing for the existing functions of government and categorical assistance for new functions requiring added incentives. Support for new community development clearly fell in the second group of functions. Our budget proposals were not inconsistent with revenue sharing; they were complementary. Furthermore, to the extent that the authorized recipients of new community grants were private developers, revenue sharing among different levels of government was scarcely relevant. In the case of innovative planning grants, for example, no alternative source of funds existed for private developers.

In the case of new community grants for local government, the political realities invariably assured that positive incentives for assistance to new communities would be replaced by disincentives when categorical grants were replaced by revenue sharing. By definition, new communities have no voting constituency at the outset when the support of local government is critical. It would require both visionary wisdom and political bravado on the part of elected local officials to pour shared revenues into unpopulated projects at the expense of existing centres of population. Yet this is precisely what the broader public interest (Federal if not local) in the urbanization process may require.

In the long term, there may be no inconsistency between Federal and local policy. But the local politician stands today for election before today's electorate. It will be a rare man who can afford to serve today the conflicting interests of the electorate 20 years hence.

In these circumstances, the Federal interest in assuring orderly urban development of high quality must be asserted. Carefully tailored pump-priming grants in the manner suggested in Title VII are the most efficient means of securing local co-operation. In terms of future benefits and savings in the urbanization process,[2] the limited Federal investment is clearly worthwhile.

Opinion was divided at HUD on the advisability of appealing the OMB budget rejection. The HUD budget bureaucrats were, of course, opposed to an appeal. They seemed to regard it as their function to reflect OMB thinking within HUD councils and consistently sought to divert and delay our funding efforts.

The Under-secretary, Richard Van Dusen, also opposed appeal. For years, he had been George Romney's close adviser both in business and in politics. He regarded it as his function to reflect White House thinking within HUD and protect George Romney from his own combative instincts in dealing with the White House. It was true that HUD under George Romney enjoyed relatively little credit with the White House under Richard Nixon. Van Dusen sought to reserve whatever credit there was for the Department's priority objectives. He regarded the funding of Title VII as a dubious priority with little chance of success. I could not differ on the chance of success. I did differ—it was in fact my duty to differ—on the issue of priority.

George Romney decided to appeal. He directed the appeal, however, not to the President but back to OMB. We would, furthermore, concentrate our efforts on the two grant programs for which we could make the most compelling case. Van Dusen was happy with this decision since it did not draw upon Presidential credit, and so was I, for I assumed Romney's relations with OMB Director George Shultz were bettter than his relations with Richard Nixon.

We decided to appeal the failure to fund interest-differential grants for public developers and special planning assistance for innovation. Our appeal was forwarded to OMB on 28 June 1971 and rejected on 15 July 1971. OMB thought it unwise to give public developers an advantage not enjoyed by private developers, and unnecessary to subsidize innovative planning that could be assured by standards of review for guarantee assistance.

The response was chilling. It had become executive policy to ignore the new programs of Title VII as unwise or unnecessary. Congress had considered these questions and found otherwise. Was it within the province of the executive branch to substitute its own policy for that of the Congress? Surely we now had no choice but to appeal to the President.

In the long battle over enactment and funding of Title VII, there was no more critical issue than the place of public development agencies in the scheme of Federal new community policy. OMB voiced sensitivity to the issue of competition with private enterprise when it dismissed interest-differential grants as providing an unfair advantage to public developers.

In financing its conduct of the people's business, state and local governments in the US do in fact enjoy a considerable advantage over commercial financing of private business. Federal law provides an income tax exemption for interest paid to the holders of bonds issued by state or local government. This provision of the tax law permits such bonds to be sold at lower interest rates than would otherwise prevail in the market.

Under Title VII, a state or local development agency seeking a new community guarantee is required to waive this indirect subsidy and issue bonds paying fully taxable interest. This was dictated by Treasury policy against guarantee of tax-exempt bonds. Interest on Treasury bonds enjoys no tax exemption, leaving them at a disadvantage if traded in the same market with Federally-backed tax-exempt bonds of state or local government. In exchange for the waiver resulting in higher interest costs, Congress intended that the agency should receive a direct grant from

HUD in the amount by which taxable interest exceeds the tax-exempt interest that would otherwise be payable.

This grant, therefore, gives a public developer no greater advantage over a private developer than that already enjoyed by virtue of the Federal tax law.

What troubled officials at OMB and the Domestic Council was not so much the issue of preference for financing of the people's business as whether new community development was properly the people's business rather than private business. They had an instinctive distrust of any government intrusion into functions traditionally reserved to the private sector. Perhaps there was little tradition of private development of balanced communities; but large-scale land development was not uncommon, and a few projects, such as Reston and Columbia, demonstrated balance both in land use and, to a certain extent, in race and income level of residents. If private developers were willing to try, these officials reasoned, why shouldn't Title VII assistance be reserved for them?

There was only one practical problem. One existing public development agency was already undertaking new community projects: the New York State Urban Development Corporation (UDC), created at the insistence of Nelson Rockefeller, a Republican governor and supporter of the Administration. HUD received a directive from the White House that no preference should be accorded either public or private projects in application processing. In theory, the OMB rejection of funding for interest-differential grants was merely furthering this policy of neutrality, whereas in fact the decision effectively discriminated against public developers by destroying any incentive to seek guarantee assistance at high taxable interest rates. The UDC accordingly declined to apply for guarantee assistance but did request HUD recognition that its new community projects complied with Federal standards, in the hope that they might some day benefit from Federal grant assistance.

Officials at the UDC contended that their experience revealed no dissatisfaction among local builders and developers. On the contrary, private builders were delighted to participate in UDC projects, since the difficult and risky phases of community-scale development—land assembly and community-wide land improvements—were assumed by the Corporation. For the private builder or developer operating at village or lesser scale, the UDC front money and master planning were seen as blessings, not competition.

For the public interest, the existence of a state development agency permitted critical site-selection decisions to be governed by considerations of regional growth policy rather than by the fortuitous factors affecting availability of land for private assembly. Long-term site-selection policy in the furtherance of regional growth objectives could become a reality.[3]

On the specific issue of the interest-differential grant, Governor Rockefeller argued that Federal fiscal policy would be served by its implementation. Studies have demonstrated that more revenue would be collected as a result of waiver of the income tax exemptions than would be expended in compensating grants. In short, here was that rarest of Federal programs: a grant that saved the Federal Government money.

51

Officials in the HUD budget office did not really follow this argument and initially refused to use it in the OMB appeal. After I produced a voluminous Brookings Institution study and Congressional research in support of Governor Rockefeller's position, they relented, and the argument was briefly stated.

It made, of course, no difference at all.

While HUD officials were debating among themselves and drafting appeals to OMB for new community funding, the budget process was proceeding on Capitol Hill. As a token of its displeasure with the Administration on the issue of new community funding, Congress appropriated $5 million for innovative planning assistance in fiscal year 1972, even though no request had been made by the Administration. For a few weeks there was renewed hope at HUD. Word then came from OMB that no plans should be made to spend the token $5 million: the funds had been impounded.

Innovation in new communities appears to be an elusive concept on the ground, but it fills both trade and academic literature. Even the most severe intellectual critic of the new community concept grants that the opportunity to do something new in building new communities may be significant for communities in general.[4]

Testing new ideas in existing communities is made difficult by physical, economic and political constraints. Existing facilities may create too many obstacles. Existing services may be too vital to interrupt. Existing attitudes of local authorities or residents may be too settled to permit change. All this may render an advance in the art of community building either prohibitively expensive or mechanically or institutionally impossible.

Many urban innovations now on the drawing boards will be effectively demonstrated only in new communities. But economic feasibility is relative. In the best of circumstances, innovation will be expensive and cannot be expected to be undertaken in the public interest without public subsidy. The financial commitments of new community development are onerous enough even without innovation. Is it sensible to insist that the profit-oriented private sector should shoulder alone not only the burden of community-scale development, but the added costs of innovation as well?

The only realistic result to be expected from OMB insistence that the Federal interest in innovation should be exhausted in the review process for guarantee assistance, was either that no new communities would be approved for Federal assistance or that in approved new communities innovation would be nominal and meaningless.

Results will vary of course with the definition of innovation. Arrangements for a particular educational component of day care may be innovative in the sense that it is novel within a metropolitan or market area though tested extensively elsewhere. Standards for guarantee assistance may serve well enough the Federal interest in wider application of newly demonstrated features, where costs are known and market acceptance may safely be predicted.

But without stronger Federal incentives there will be no absolute advances in the state of the art. It requires money as well as imagination to study the costs and benefits of a climate-controlled village under a shelter envelope or an internal circulation system of individually programmed pollution-free vehicles on computer-operated guideways. It is not the technology or the imagination we lack. It is the Federal support.

Special planning assistance under Title VII was tailored to circumvent the principal enemy of innovation in new communities: the momentum of the planning process. Before he can make arrangements for permanent financing (be it through Title VII or some other source), any private developer regards planning for innovation as a prohibitive luxury. Yet by the time these arrangements are made, early irrevocable planning decisions may have ruled out innovation.

Congress tackled this dilemma by authorizing special planning grants to be made prior to approval of a new community for guarantee assistance, thus permitting planning to benefit at an early stage from investigation of promising innovations.

Congress may create wise programs and for each program may wisely appropriate funds, but it cannot manage the programs or spend the funds. For this purpose, the Constitution created an executive branch of government.

'The President took the same oath of office as we: to execute faithfully the laws enacted by Congress. Should we not help him do his duty?'

A draft appeal from Secretary Romney to the President was the focus of discussion.

HUD budget officials were concerned that the HUD budget for fiscal year 1973 was about to be submitted to OMB. They were concerned about the effect of a pending Presidential appeal for 1972 upon the simultaneous discussions with OMB on 1973.

The HUD budget director had a solution. He would himself send the draft Presidential appeal to OMB, indicating that the Secretary planned to forward it to the President unless the issues were satisfactorily resolved during discussions on the 1973 budget.

This stratagem amounted to nothing more than still another appeal to OMB, with the sole difference that it was more offensive than the last, carrying the explicit threat of Presidential intervention. No answer was received from OMB other than the eventual refusal to permit any 1973 funding for the new grant programs of Title VII.

There was never any chance that the answer would be otherwise.

Looking back, it is tempting to rail against the President's men who, without apparent hesitation or compunction, substituted their judgement for the judgement of the people's representatives in Congress. Reality, however, is more complicated.

Some time in April or May of 1970, the President had been called to focus on new community programs. He probably gave the subject some 10 minutes of his time. Perhaps he spoke briefly with John Ehrlichman. He reacted by postponing consideration of HUD proposals owing to inflationary pressures.

This was interpreted by the President's men as a negative reaction, and that interpretation was justified. Unfortunately, the President was never again called to consider the new community programs throughout his term of office, although circumstances affecting executive policy had changed.

Whenever a policy issue touching new communities was raised with the President's men, their instinctive reaction was negative because the President's only reaction had been negative. None of these specific issues was ever deemed sufficiently important in itself to justify a return to the President. Over the years, however, the sum of these decisions constituted executive policy of significant import for the nation. And the policy was misdirected, for it followed a course charted at a time and under circumstances overtaken by events.

The President's brief attention to new communities came before Congress had enacted Title VII, at a time, indeed, when enactment was not anticipated. Bureaucratic inertia transformed the President's mood of that brief moment into the stuff of executive policy.

It is also tempting to attribute this result to the legendary isolation of Richard Nixon as President. I am not convinced. Although I know nothing about the formulation of executive policy in other administrations, I would nevertheless guess that bureacratic inertia was a powerful factor. Presidents are frustrated with the bureaucracy because they are seldom able to communicate with the people with power to make their policy work: the program managers. Program managers are equally frustrated because they can seldom communicate with the President about policy. Inertia governs.

Almost a year had elapsed since Title VII was enacted. At the end of an unrelated meeting in Secretary Romney's conference room, he himself raised with me the issue of funding for Title VII.

I noted that he had twice appealed and twice been refused and thanked him for his support. To my surprise, he replied that he might have done more. He might have taken the case personally to George Shultz, or even to the President.

I could not let the opportunity pass. 'Will you see the President?' I looked very hard at George Romney.

He took only a brief moment for reflection. 'Yes', he said.

But he did not. Perhaps a meeting could not be fitted into the President's schedule. More likely George Romney spoke next to Richard Van Dusen. It is easy to imagine the Under-secretary ticking off at least five more pressing matters that HUD was then negotiating at the White House. Surely a request for the President's time should be reserved for these more pressing matters in the event of necessity.

I could not bring myself to push George Romney further, and did not even ask why the meeting with the President never took place.

I sensed that my useful service to the Administration was rapidly drawing to an end. My advocacy of the new community programs was becoming counterproductive. I was viewed as an activist rather than a team player. The programs might have a better chance if championed by an administrator more in sympathy with the philosophy and style of the President's men.

But there was one last chance.

Among the provisions of Title VII was a requirement that the President should report to Congress every two years on the formulation and implementation of urban growth policy. The first report was due during February 1972. HUD was given the responsibility of preparing the initial draft of this report. I was asked to contribute a section on new communities.

Our draft set out a number of initiatives, including a new program of start-up grants for public development agencies and a national competition for innovative features in new communities. If we could not fund existing programs, perhaps we could achieve the same objectives by funding new programs.

These proposals were accepted by Secretary Romney, incorporated into the HUD draft and shipped to the White House in the first few days of 1972. We heard nothing more until we read the *Report on National Growth 1972* forwarded by the President to Congress on 29 February. It contained no proposals for new community initiatives. In fact it contained no proposals for initiatives of any kind. Nineteen-seventy-two was a Presidential election year. Proposals in the field of national growth policy were bound to be controversial.

After learning of the fate of our suggestions for the *Report on National Growth*, I inquired whether HUD would make further efforts to fund Title VII grant programs. In late March I received the answer: no. I could not, in all conscience, quarrel with this decision. The prospects seemed too hopeless. But neither could I, in all conscience, remain. On 7 April 1972 I resigned.

When I left HUD at the end of May, 10 new community projects had been approved for guarantee assistance; the two programs originating in the 1968 Act—guarantee assistance and supplementary grants—were active and healthy; and the morale of the small staff was good, in spite of the long hours and budget setbacks.

Operational problems, however, could be foreseen. My staffing request had been denied, and the period for application review was lengthening. The General Accounting Office had begun a new community study, which was to last for three years and exercise throughout this period a chilling effect upon the willingness of HUD officials to make hard judgements. Developers expressed increasing frustration with the HUD decision-making process. They had expected that their projects would be accorded priorities in other government programs, particularly at the Federal Housing Administration, but their expectations were consistently disappointed.

On 1 July 1973 the program of supplementary grants was terminated in line with the Administration's proposals for special revenue sharing. HUD offered no substitute, but under the Housing and Community Development Act of 1974, Congress provided a discretionary allocation for new communities in block-grant funding for community development.

Beginning in 1972, when the Administration's lack of support became clear, the flow of proposals from developers began to subside. By 1974 a campaign had been launched at HUD to 'clean out the new community pipeline'. Several worthy as well as questionable projects were driven out of the program. In the process, the active and potential political support for the new community programs on Capitol Hill was seriously impaired.

By late 1974, the severe recession in the housing and development industries had thrown a number of the approved projects into serious financial crisis. These were projects at peak debt that had invested all disposable funds at constantly inflating prices in land and land improvements, only to find that builders could not buy for lack of construction financing. It became apparent to HUD that virtually all approved projects would require refinancing, though in most cases it concluded that economic feasibility was not in doubt.

The second *Report on National Growth*, due in February 1974, was submitted to Congress by the President in December 1974. In a striking omission, the report failed even to refer to the new community programs that had been authorized by the same Title under which the report itself was required.

On 14 January 1975 HUD announced the suspension of application processing for guarantee assistance, the only surviving Title VII program. The four prospective projects then under review were turned away. HUD indicated that it intended to devote all resources to the 14 projects already approved. From the high hopes of January 1971, the new community programs had been reduced to a salvage operation in exactly four years.

There are valuable lessons as well as projects to be salvaged from the shambles of Title VII.

From the experience we have learned that

- assembly of community-scale acreage from fragmented holdings by a private developer is difficult, time-consuming and costly;
- the location of community-scale acreage available for acquisition by a private developer usually bears little or no relationship to optimum location for purposes of regional growth policy; and
- the cyclical nature of the real estate and credit markets make 20-year projections of cash flow in land-development projects virtually meaningless.

These lessons all point to the necessity of Federal encouragement for the creation of agencies of state or metropolitan government with power to

- assemble land at sufficient scale and in optimum location for purposes of growth policy;
- undertake master planning for development of the acquired acreage;
- install community-scale infrastructure; and
- dispose of the acreage in several village-scale tracts to private developers for distinct three- to five-year sub-projects, executed pursuant to the master plan.

In short, what is needed is a fruitful public–private development process in which the public sector would exercise its powers over land as well as its responsibilities over land use and the provision of services in the public interest; while the private sector would find the economic hazards of land development reduced with shortened periods of development.

The obvious question, particularly in the context of the recent default by UDC on some $100 million in notes, is whether the public sector assumes the economic hazards relinquished by the private sector. Of course it does and of course it should.

For every public benefit there are attendant public costs and risks. It is the duty of our government representatives to balance the benefits against the costs and risks as best they can, and then to secure for the public the benefits of transcendent value measured in that balance.

The benefits to be secured by direct public–private partnership in the urbanization process are transcendent: this is the process that determines the quality of the physical and social environment in which we spend our lives. It is difficult to comprehend how the US, alone of all the urbanizing nations, has with few exceptions neglected to charge the public sector with the direct participation in this process required to protect the public interest. This neglect is all the more remarkable since the desirable degree of public participation does not interfere with functions that the private sector has shown itself willing or able to perform and would in fact encourage private sector involvement by reducing the economic risks.

Should Congress at some future time care to consider once again how Federal legislative policy on land development should be asserted, I suggest the following legislative package:

1. A program of start-up grants for state or metropolitan development agencies;
2. Guarantee assitance (with interest-differential grants where taxable bonds are guaranteed) for the projects of those agencies that conform to an approved regional growth strategy;
3. Guarantee assistance (as in Title VII, but with streamlined processing) for private developers operating within such projects;
4. Innovative planning grants (as in Title VII) with implementation set-asides from community development block grants; and
5. A Federal development agency with authority to act in those states that fail to respond to these new incentives.

Although such a package will not be rushed immediately into law, the need for it is, I think, immediate.

Buried in the battles over Title VII, there may also be broader lessons about the operation of the US federal system of government. What are the standards by which we should judge Presidential performance in the execution of legislative policy? If executive policy has come to weigh too heavily in the balance against legislative policy, how can the balance be restored? Impeachment is clearly too radical a remedy for sins in the nature of those committed against Title VII. Yet we can see that the policy imbalance between executive and legislative branches in the Title VII imbroglio strained the system and damaged the public interest.

Strains of this nature may be inherent in a system of government founded on the principle of separation of powers. In a parliamentary system, no administration could

57

survive the flagrant contempt for legislative mandates demonstrated by the Nixon Administration for new community legislation. In a parliamentary system, the Prime Minister, serving in Parliament, is answerable at once to Parliament for neglect of its mandates; to stay in office he must retain the confidence of Parliament.

Under the US system founded on the separation of powers, only in the most extreme circumstances will any imbalance between executive and legislative branches be corrected by driving out the chief executive, and then only with severe national trauma. Lesser abuses must be checked by the third branch of government, the judiciary.

Executive impoundment of Congressionally appropriated funds did not originate in the Nixon Administration, but under the Nixon Administration it became a routine and irresponsible weapon of executive policy. When the balance tipped too far, the courts were called upon to order correction. As a result, the use of executive impoundment in the future will need to show a responsible consistency with Congressional objectives, a consistency that would be difficult to show in the case of the Administration's disregard for the mandate of Title VII. But correction in the courts is a lengthy process, and it requires a motivated plaintiff. There is now talk among approved new community developers of a class-action against HUD to obtain the benefits promised by Title VII, but no one is talking about a suit to open the program to new projects.

For every disfunction of the body politic there exists no certain remedy, but that may be all for the good. We have learned enough from the hope and disappointment of Title VII to become more ambitious. If Congress will lay aside past executive slights and issue a yet broader mandate, the likelihood of a positive executive response may improve. It can hardly decline.

Emerson obviously did not expect the new community of every reading man to find its way from his waistcoat pocket on to the map. It is impossible now to know to what extent full use of Title VII might have accomplished the unexpected. But since we do know much more about the sort of public participation needed to achieve the vast variety of public objectives incorporated in a new community program, we ought to be able to do better next time.

References

1. *Report on National Growth 1972*, US Government Printing Office.
2. See *The Costs of Sprawl*, US Government Printing Office, 1974.
3. See *New Communities for New York*, a report prepared by the UDC and the New York State Office for Planning Coordination, 1970.
4. See Alonzo, William 'The Mirage of New Towns', *The Public Interest*, **19**, 3, 1970.

Chapter 3.   France: The focus on innovation

JEAN-EUDES ROULLIER and MAHLON APGAR, IV

De novo settlements in France are as old as urban growth itself. Towns have been deliberately created to spur economic and political development as far back as the Middle Ages.[1] But planned communities, serving a broad range of social and cultural, as well as economic, objectives are new. Only in the past two decades have the problems of urban growth provoked widespread consideration of the need for comprehensive policies to guide and control urbanization.

Although the first regional planning studies were not launched until 1961 and the first new town development corporations until 1969, the French have made considerable strides in a relatively short time. Nine new towns have been designated and are presently under construction in the vicinity of the biggest French conurbations. More than 40,000 acres of land have been acquired, which is about half of total provisional requirements. Programs for sewer, water and road construction are under way. And a vast housing program has produced a little under 100,000 units in just five years—with a current building rate of about 23,000 units, or four to five per cent of all the new housing in France.

But it is not only the housing program that distinguishes this as the most ambitious of all national new towns policies.[2] In the next quarter-century, each of the nine new towns should build up populations ranging from 100,000 to 400,000 on sites of from 6,100 to 42,000 acres—one-third to five times the area of the city of Paris (2.3 million inhabitants). Their development form will be either continuous (Evry, Lille-Est, Le Vaudreuil), or resemble a network of interdependent settlements of 30,000 to 80,000 people, physically separated by green belts but integrated by multiple centres of living, working and leisure that are being designed to encourage close communications and more responsive institutions. Each new town is focused on the creation of a main urban centre designed to attract office and service jobs (between a quarter and one-half of total future employment).

What marks the French new towns most, however, is their focus on innovation. From preventing floods to maximizing individual choice and community cohesion, the program seeks to influence the forces that govern life and environment in an urban area by applying new concepts and tools in the community development process.

This chapter explores the ways in which innovation is being developed and applied. It is not intended as a comprehensive survey, but aims only to highlight the main thrusts of innovation with a few selected examples. Its focus is on institutional rather than technical change. For in a world fascinated by novelty and new technology, innovation is often conceived in terms of gadgets and grand experiments. It must be emphasized that the French projects are intended to improve the patterns of urban development and to tackle some of the stubborn problems of the big conurbations. Innovation, therefore, is seen not as an end in itself but as a means of meeting community needs.

We shall look first at the overall policy context within which innovation is occurring—the objectives and early gestation of the policy and the administrative difficulties that require new solutions. We shall then consider two dimensions of innovation—the concepts that foster new ideas, and the problem areas in which fresh approaches are emerging.

The policy context

Under the Sixth National Plan for 1970–75—the formative years of the French program—two main principles were agreed for the new towns.

1. *Complete integration in the existing regional structure.* The new towns were to be new urban centres with all the main—but not all the specialized—activities of a city, located on major transport axes at a 'reasonable' distance from large conurbations: not too near, to avoid becoming a suburban extension of the city, but not too far, so as to play an effective role in redistributing the activities and relieving the growth pressures in their respective regions.

2. *Comprehensive development of housing, employment, leisure activities and community services.* In common with the United States and most of Europe, France had suffered the social costs and visual blight of postwar housing developments that frequently lacked adequate commercial, social, cultural and transport facilities. The new towns were conceived to remedy this defect. In line with regional integration, they were to be centres of tertiary employment, complementing rather than competing with the mother cities' primary job base.

Underlying both these planning principles was a less explicit, though even more fundamental, purpose: the new towns should enhance the quality of urban life, not only in aesthetic terms (more open space, better architectural and urban design), but more especially by creating a fertile setting for all the hundreds of day-to-day activities (shopping, school, play) in which social relationships can be formed and reinforced. This aim pervaded discussions among politicians, experts and laymen alike as the national policy evolved, and it has spawned several concepts of social planning that may be the most important and lasting contributions of the French program, and to which we shall return later.

These principles were themselves the product of a more general movement toward regional development that began in the mid-fifties and was institutionalized in 1963 with the establishment of a central organization for regional planning (Délégation à l'Aménagement du Territoire et à l'Action Régionale), set up to study: (1) the functions and problems of development in the Paris region; (2) the balance of economic activity throughout the country; and (3) the means of regenerating development in both stable and declining regions. Two years later, the Paris regional planning agency (Institut d'Aménagement d'Urbanisme de la Région Parisienne) proposed that growth in the Paris region should be controlled by the creation of eight new towns along two main axes parallel to the Seine.

Both bodies concluded that limiting the capital's growth and strengthening the regions were complementary objectives that could be achieved by decentralizing activities from the outlying suburbs of Paris and establishing them in existing provincial cities. Because this strategy would build on the resources and infrastructure in the regions, it would not only be more economical than entirely new 'greenfields' (or freestanding) cities; it could also avoid the worst of the social problems encountered in such cities. A web of community institutions and relationships would already be in place and, though it might need strengthening, it would not have to be woven anew. The new towns policy is thus only one element, among many others, of this overall national policy.

From the dialogue that ensued between Paris and the regions, the Government eventually forged a policy balancing five new towns around Paris (Evry, Cergy-Pontoise, St Quentin, Marne-la-Vallée, and Melun-Sénart) with four situated near provincial conurbations (Le Vaudreuil, l'Isle d'Abeau near Lyons, Lille-Est outside Lille, Etang de Berre to the west of Marseilles). Conceptually, they represent two distinct types: *discontinuous,* where the new town is physically segregated from its mother city, and *continuous,* where it is not clearly separated but is simply one of many growth points in the area. Both types are the result of two possible policy options for organizing public initiative and investment. On the one hand, new centres can be created by deliberately planning, financing and building for 'a new way of life' so that people and institutions in them are influenced directly, although the future growth pattern in the region may not be. On the other hand, by installing the infrastructure along preferred axes of growth to serve existing centres, demand for new housing in a much wider area can be met while at the same time checking sprawl and concentrating development throughout the region. In both the US and the UK, for example, new centres have been created but the development of regional infrastructure has usually lagged behind, with the result that their full potential for guiding growth has not been realized. The French policy embraces both options. This has led to extensive government action (see Table 3.1) and has given the projects a unique character that derives not only from their size but also from the declared intention to meet the needs of the new population.

Even their most ardent advocates recognized that the new towns would be but one means of healing urban ills; despite their extensive housing programs, all nine will accommodate in 30 years only as many people as two years' housebuilding throughout the country. Since they were clearly not going to be a panacea, it became

61

Table 3.1

New Town	Acres	Population (000) Existing (1968)	Projected (2000)	Jobs created	Housing starts
Paris Region					
Cergy-Pontoise	29,902	50	200	9,005	8,075
Evry	12,502	20	140	7,325	7,929
Marne-la-Vallée	37,062	97	500	2,950	9,302
Melun Sénart	43,100	64	290	5,370	5,354
Saint Quentin	26,742	30	290	11,250	14,919
Others					
Berre	94,772	77	400	21,390	20,334
Lille-Est	6,250	26	105*	2,771	4,382
L'Isle d'Abeau	78,802	40	200	2,140	2,337
Le Vaudreuil	16,250	6	140	685	3,246

All figures cover 1971–4; housing starts are only for those receiving public assistance, i.e., about 95 per cent of total construction.
* Add 40,000 students not included.

widely accepted that one of their most useful functions would be as laboratories, to demonstrate new approaches to solving urban problems. The mere fact of having available, from inception, an expert, multidisciplinary planning and development team, vast areas of vacant land and building programs of between 1,000 and 5,000 dwellings a year would afford public authorities and private developers alike an exceptional testing ground for new techniques.

A second by-product of the new towns program was that it would encourage improvements to the fragmented structure and cumbersome procedures that characterize French local administration and finance. The Commission on New Towns for the Sixth National Plan confronted this key issue squarely: 'it is unreasonable to expect a new town to be built if each building program first requires 20 subsidies, 30 loans, and various other funds to be requested from different government departments and agencies.'[3] Any of the new towns would encroach on several, possibly as many as 20, rural 'communes', each responsible for the development and provision of most community facilities within its own boundaries, and already subject to the massive financial, social and political demands of rapid population growth. Naturally, each commune would respond by acting in its own interests, seeking to attract the new town's revenue-producing commercial and industrial properties, but to shift roads and other investment to its neighbours. Even where the communes adopted a more positive view, any new town wishing to build public facilities under the existing financing system could not do so without first applying for a subsidy and then obtaining a loan from a host of different authorities, who, for quite legitimate reasons, have their own problems and priorities.

Yet the prime requisite in managing community-scale development is that resources, powers and participants must be equal to the task and sufficiently well co-ordinated to enable rapid decisions and major trade-offs between all the main elements of the project concept to be made. Small wonder that in 1969 one expert observed rather caustically: 'To engage in new town building with the administrative and financial tools we have now . . . is like building Concorde with a screwdriver.'[4]

However, in such a politically charged arena, forging the tools and streamlining the machinery simply could not be done overnight. Instead, the projects had to be launched with makeshift resources so that the new organizations and processes could be set up more gradually and systematically until responsibility could ultimately be assigned at the proper level. The task, in short, was less that of preparing a grand design or securing development financing than of patiently working through hundreds of small, incremental improvements in the maze of procedures and widely scattered decision-making centres—recognizing all the time that many independent, rigid and outmoded parts of the bureaucratic machine had to continue to function.

There were encouraging precedents at the time that proved that new communities could work and that organizational problems could be surmounted. The British new towns were seen as evidence that resources could be well adapted to the objectives, with a largely autonomous public corporation responsible for comprehensive planning and development in a businesslike way; and a single, flexible and relatively inexpensive form of overall financing designed to provide considerable working capital during the long period before reaching the cash break-even point. The Languedoc–Roussillon tourist and leisure resort development program had shown that it was possible to co-ordinate financial support from various government bodies through an interdepartmental commission and a joint expenditure budget. And the organization in 1961 of the Paris Regional Government had demonstrated that a new multicommune authority could ensure a wider, more co-operative view of local problems and provide a budgetary means of taking co-ordinated action.

Thus, in a country long known for its rigid centralization and Cartesian style of problem-solving, the new towns policy has been a significant departure. France has neither a native equivalent to the 'social city' of Ebenezer Howard nor a Columbia project on which to model the program, yet the plans that have emerged show sound analysis, refreshing diversity and considerable pragmatism—the main qualities that mark successful innovation.

The dimensions of innovation

As innovation is aimed at problem-solving rather than simply the invention of new ideas for their own sake, it is only natural that the greatest innovative attention should have been devoted to the main difficulties encountered in community-scale development. In the sections that follow, we highlight examples of innovation in six problem areas: development organization, local government organization, interagency co-ordination, financial support, design and building, and community processes and functions. First, however, we must emphasize three concepts that underlie the initiatives and changes now taking place and that recur in the ensuing discussion.

1. 'Animation'. This uniquely French concept embraces nearly all the collective activities that can help to strengthen the social cohesion of new community residents and enliven the community, particularly during its early years. It is a means of

63

avoiding the anonymity and isolation that typify many urban housing projects, while attempting to humanize the 'building site' atmosphere that pervades such large construction operations. The initial emphasis on the cultural and psychological needs of the individual in an urban setting now embraces the economic, social and political institutions in which he associates with others. While spatial design is an obvious instrument of 'animation' through the grouping of specific activities (as in the neighbourhood or town centre), even more fundamental results are being achieved through special community programs in which personal relationships are established and encouraged to grow.

2. *Catalyst.* Complementing the role of 'animateur' is that of the 'community catalyst'. Since the development corporations are not empowered to build directly, the temptations of grandiose schemes are denied to them. They have the harder, but more fruitful, task of influencing others—architects, builders, employers, residents—by creating an environment and defining the framework of development. In short, they orchestrate the symphony rather than play it, marshal talents and resources rather than provide them all, and try to ensure that a wide variety of activities and institutions act in harmony to meet a diverse array of needs.

3. *Competition.* As long as the new towns engage numerous organizations beside the developer, they must all be challenged if breakthroughs in thinking and technique are to occur. Design problems, technical problems and the sheer management task of launching a massive building program should be considerably eased if the industry and the professions are sufficiently motivated to apply their best expertise. So the practice of holding competitions has been adapted from its narrow architectural tradition and applied on a scale unprecedented in France. More than a score of competitions have been launched in building design, neighbourhood planning and construction technology. Innovative in their very conception, they have already shown the value of the new towns as realistic testing grounds for urban change.

Development organization

Launching new regional centres of the scale and scope envisaged in the policy was clearly going to require a major injection of talent and a strong local organization that could pay single-minded attention to the development process. Consistent with the basic sequence of planning and development operations, a two-phase organizational strategy was adopted.

Between 1966 and 1968, following on the initial studies of the regional planning agencies, Research and Planning Commissions were established for each new town. In his initial directive, the then Prime Minister, Georges Pompidou, defined three main tasks: (1) preparing the master plans for infrastructure and development; (2) initiating and co-ordinating land acquisition and development; and (3) working out the programming, budgets and timing of development. The heads of the Commissions were appointed by the Prime Minister and each was staffed by some 30 to 50 specialists in city planning, architecture, law, engineering, and public and business administration.

To encourage their identification with local problems and to promote day-to-day contact with local officials, they moved to the site of the new town from the beginning. Moreover, they reported directly to the region's chief executive (Prefect), who was given special responsibilities for the new town(s) in his area and empowered to co-ordinate joint action by the ministries directly concerned.

Thus firmly established, the planning teams could tackle the broad aims of the program with relatively open minds. The only specific requirement in Pompidou's message was that the Commissions should create 'attractive and modern town centres', and, as we shall see, considerable design innovations have resulted from this brief. Beyond that, the planners were largely free to experiment, bound only by two pragmatic rules: their plans should evoke general regional and local support and they should be capable of implementation with present technology and skills. Innovation was not to be compromised by Utopian daydreams but should produce practical solutions to current problems.

As the Commissions were designed solely for study and analysis, neither their powers nor their organizational styles were suited to the development task. A new structure was required to use government and regional finance and technical support, assume overall responsibility for the project and ensure co-ordinated local action, while avoiding the pressures of local politics as much as possible.

In 1968 a formula for public development corporations (EPA—Etablissement Public d'Aménagement) was finally devised that embodied some of the best features of the British new towns model but was more limited in its functions. Set up at the Government's instigation after consultation with local authorities, there is one EPA for each new town. Their Management Boards include seven elected representatives of existing local government bodies—commune, administrative department, region—and seven civil servants appointed by the Government to represent the ministries concerned (Housing and Infrastructure, Economic Affairs and Finance, Interior and Cultural Affairs). The Board Chairmen are elected from among the local representatives, while the chief executives are appointed by the Government. The Research and Planning Commissions become part of the EPA staff, and all land and development operations are transferred from other agencies.

Under its terms of reference, the EPA may develop the land and define the conditions under which land can be used by public or private builders—but it cannot itself build. It is empowered to construct essential public services—but only as an agent of the local authorities. It is compelled to initiate and maintain a dialogue with builders on the one hand, and local and state authorities on the other. It must persuade others to accept its views, since it cannot impose them. While EPA officials may complain of unimaginative or conventional solutions from private builders and developers who are accustomed to judge commercial and financial risks and plan accordingly, they must pay greater attention than their British counterparts to the wishes of prospective residents and users as reflected in the builders' product/market analyses. Perhaps in retrospect, the EPA's most important function will prove to be providing neutral ground for the various participants to thrash out new solutions with relative objectivity.

65

Local government organization

However effective, a development organization alone cannot cope with the vexing problems of fragmented local government structure and conflicting parochial interests. Since the boundaries of the new town overlap a number of largely rural authorities, and since each of these authorities has its own fiscal system, discrepancies inevitably arise in the burden borne by the existing residents of different areas, depending on the degree and type of development in each part of the town. Leading first to conflict between the new and the old, such a situation could easily result in entrenched opposition that could thwart the most imaginative plans. The regrouping of these numerous bodies was therefore decisive in establishing a workable structure for decentralized responsibility and action, though the ultimate framework had to be painfully built in several different stages over a six-year period.

The most obvious solution was to set up an entirely new local authority, coterminous with the new community. Its land would be detached from the existing communes and, after a build-up period, a municipal council would be established in the usual way. It was argued that this would protect the existing residents from the financial, and possibly political, intrusion of an imported population, while the newcomers could share promptly in the management of their affairs. A clear-cut, comprehensive administrative structure could also be more easily established. In 1967 the Government proposed to set up an 'urban corporation' (Ensemble Urbain), managed by a council whose members would at first be appointed by the Government but rapidly succeeded by elected representatives of the new inhabitants.

However, local government mayors throughout the country jibbed, both at the surgery to historical boundaries and at the precedent of appointed rather than elected councils. They countered with a 'community association for development' (Syndicat Communautaire d'Aménagement) to safeguard the commune's existence, while providing a single structure for financial decision-making in the new town. This completely original concept enables the local governments to take up direct management of the new town through a committee composed of representatives elected from each municipal council. The new town's area is treated as an additional commune whose taxes are made uniform by using a notional tax that is collected directly by the association. Community facilities are developed under a single budget agreed by the committee and funded by local taxes, by loans and by a 'capital endowment' from the Government to facilitate the start-up. Areas not included in the new town continue to be managed by the municipal councils and their officials, and the association has no powers within them.

Finally, a law on local government organization in new towns was voted by the French Parliament and passed on 10 July 1970. The 'urban corporation' concept survives, but its first council must be formed of existing mayors and not of members appointed by the Government. The municipal councils of Le Vaudreuil chose this formula. In all other cases they preferred the creation of a 'community association for development', which gives existing local officials more lasting control over the new town's evolution.

Interagency co-operation

An important innovation in ensuring consistency of effort at the local level is the institution within the French national budget of 'categorical' budgets for the new towns. This means simply that the amounts for each general budget element (roads, sewers, schools, etc.) are explicitly appropriated for the new towns. Much of the apprehension of local authorities that the new towns will compete with, or drain, their scarce resources has been allayed by this device. Since 1966, categories have been progressively added to cover land, recreation, health and welfare.

The task of co-ordination was no less essential at the central government level. In 1966, together with the creation of the first Research and Planning Commissions, the Prime Minister established an interministerial work group for the new towns in the Paris region under the regional chief executive. It included representatives of the three main ministries concerned and directors of the Planning Commissions. It played a fundamental role in devising and proposing to the Government the institutional framework (development and local government organization) and the necessary financial support to the new towns, and in helping to solve day-to-day problems as they arose.

The new towns outside the Paris region gave the program a nationwide dimension. Moreover, many other ministries (Education, Posts and Telecommunications, Sports, etc.) would eventually have to be kept constantly informed and to take action on a closely co-ordinated basis. The categorization of budget appropriations also called for a forum where the requirements of the new town could be defined and the issues they raised debated at the highest level.

The Prime Minister therefore established a central committee for new towns (GCVN—Groupe Central des Villes Nouvelles), which has a secretariat attached to the Ministry of Housing and Infrastructure Development. It has two main purposes. First, it advises the Government on the administrative measures, capital grants and operating subsidies needed for efficient and effective operation of the projects. Second, it ensures that budgets for the various programs in the new towns are consistent with national and regional development policy and long-term financial stability. In consequence, it also produces the new towns budget for the five-year National Plan, which includes their priority objectives in terms of housing and jobs and the action programs that will be undertaken to achieve them.

As the key link between government departments and the EPAs themselves, the GCVN also serves an essential 'catalytic' role. Where a particular town embarks on a pilot project or experiments with a new technique, it may intervene to encourage, advise or act as an information centre. It may provide general support for those initiatives that have value for others and help them to find the partners and resources they need. Its position, its role and its scope thus give it a degree of influence simply unknown to its British and American counterparts.

Financial support

The new, decentralized structures for development and interagency co-ordination have been combined with various financial instruments and resources. Chief among these are land price controls, start-up subsidies and budget co-ordination.

An ambitious policy of 'deferred development zones' (ZAD—Zone d'Aménagement Différé) enables the EPA and other public authorities to control prices by pre-empting any land transaction in the new town area even before the master plan is made public. The ZADs are limited to 14 years and are essentially aimed at deterring price speculation rather than securing a particular price level. But they provide a useful basis for a land development policy.

Specific budget appropriations have also been made for land banking—the acquisition of long-term 'reserves' in strategically important areas that are likely to gain considerably in value. As these are held by the state, it can allocate the capital gains to build essential infrastructure, particularly for future urban centres that are to be developed over a long period.

Assistance in the start-up stage has been decisive in ensuring that critical research and initial facilities are amassed and that area development can be guided from the start. The Government bears the costs of launching the new towns, of initial land acquisition, preliminary studies, initial operating costs of the EPA, road systems and sewage, exceptional aid to the local authorities, and grants to cover the early years until new business activities and the new population can pay enough local taxes to guarantee its functioning and growth.

The financing of public services and facilities is being co-ordinated through a systematic policy, monitored by the GCVN, of ensuring that the 'categorical' allocations in both the annual national budget and the five-year plan are consistent with the goals and master plans of the towns. The aim is to see that facilities will be in place at the moment they are needed, but, at the same time, to prevent the high opportunity cost—experienced in US and UK projects—of capital investment exceeding the overall development pace. The 'physico-financial' control system that has been devised for this purpose is discussed in chapter 13.

The finance available to the EPA varies with the expected funds use. Land for the main town centres and strategically important areas is directly bought through budget appropriations and later resold to the EPA at the initial price plus 3.5 per cent interest a year. Other land to be developed and development works are financed with loans from a bank specializing in the finance of local communities and public housing (Caisse des Dépôts et Consignations). The loans are for six years, at a state-subsidized rate of 3.5 per cent (7 per cent for 'industrial zones'), with repayment deferred until the fourth year. These are very favourable conditions. But the loans are too short and, in practice, new loans are partly used to repay previous ones.

Primary roads are financed by central and regional governments. Primary sewers are paid for by local government, which gets a 50 per cent grant and a 50 per cent, 25-year loan. Other infrastructure costs are backed by the EPA and paid for through the price differences between agricultural land and land that is preserviced and ready for building. Because of French tradition and the fact that the EPAs only may benefit from six-year loans, land is usually sold to private builders. However, in order to keep the future 'value added' of land, some zones are now leased for from 40 to 99 years.

Discussions are currently under way on improving financing methods for land purchase by enabling EPAs to have a single land account. Finance for land acquisition from all available sources would be combined, and the legal link between the source of finance and a given piece of land would disappear. This would lead to a more efficient use of funds since, at present, there is often a mismatch between the available finance and the funds required for different uses. Overall, the EPAs aim to have recovered their investment by the time a new town is completed, when its assets are handed over, free, to the local government.

Public facilities and amenities are paid for by local government with an average of 40 to 50 per cent central government grants, and 20- to 30-year loans for the rest. Some EPAs finance those parts of them that are of specific interest to the new town with income from their operations, and they often pre-finance them to ensure that they are on time.

Special provision of sufficient funds to cover its share of expenditure is made to the local government in whose area the new town is located. This means not only that specific central and regional government grants match the first four annuities of local government loans for new town public facilities and amenities, but also that if a 'community association for development' (or 'urban corporation') meets real difficulties in covering its expenses at a 'normal' level of local taxation, it may apply for an 'equilibrium grant' through the GCVN. A number of these subsidies were given for the first time in 1975—at the price of many political and technical difficulties.

Design and building

Innovation in development is easier to identify when it appears in the tangible form of imaginative design or improved buildings. But all too often, improvements to individual buildings have little impact on either the functions or architectural quality of the area they are in.

The task of the EPAs was made more difficult by the absence of a strong urban planning organization and of good private consultants, as well as by the mediocre state of French architecture in the sixties. On the other hand, this gave them great freedom of action. Strongly supported from the beginning by M. Paul Delouvrier* and the Paris regional planning agency, each research and planning commission had to look for its own solution, the GCVN acting later as a forum where each new town could discuss its ideas and experiences with the others and with outside specialists.

The underlying precept was to avoid laying down rigid planning or architectural guidelines. Instead, each commission was encouraged to be innovative and flexible in looking for and adopting the greatest possible number of links, bridges and feedback

* M. Delouvrier, presently chairman of the French National Electricity Board, was, in 1961, nominated the first regional chief executive for the Paris region and chairman of the newly created Paris regional planning agency. He played an essential part in initiating the French new towns policy.

processes, from initial planning right through to construction itself. Great stress was put on establishing and strengthening within a common dynamic process relationships both inside the EPA, among engineers, planners, financial and commercial staff, and between the EPA team and builders, executive architects and local people. It has been a period of trial and error but, on the whole, the process brought imagination and new vigour to French planning and architecture.

Taking their cue from Pompidou's directive, the new towns have concentrated their efforts on the creation of town centres to set the stage for and to influence community activities, while providing offices and business premises. The scale of this undertaking is unprecedented. Its main purpose is to bring together the most diverse elements: housing, cultural, shopping, office, sports, craft and civic facilities. The proximity of such facilities is common enough in the old towns of France, but it is difficult to recreate in a new context, since it imposes a number of constraints and is subject to the whim of thousands of unpredictable and uncoordinated decision-makers. The effort, though still rudimentary, has relied on two instruments. *Levers,* however subtle, may provide an impetus or theme for the centre: an 'agora' at Evry, a university at Lille-Est, the creation of parks and leisure facilities, regional shopping centres and new railway or Métro stations. *Original procedures* may improve implementation: the design competitions for regional shopping centres at Cergy, Evry, Marne-la-Vallée, Lille-Est, a novel housing–office–shopping–swimming–skating complex at Cergy, and several pilot construction research programs. Recently, the EPA for Evry in conjunction with independent architects prepared detailed plans for a 1.5 million square feet 'street complex' that would link the regional shopping centre and 'agora' to the new railway station, and include university colleges, offices, houses, shops, artists' studios, and a huge youth centre. Promoters were approached for most parts of this complex only after the preliminary studies were completed.

Beyond this, integration of functions and facilities in the new towns has occurred both in single structures for complementary programs, such as schools, libraries, youth centres, sports, and at the neighbourhood and townwide level, incorporating a mix of different housing types, workshops, retail stores and offices. The value of integration is not so much economic as psychological: a difference of attitude in both suppliers of services and users who are geared less to conventional groupings (as shoppers, students, etc.) than to diverse individuals encouraged to co-operate through a variety of avenues.

The search for urban atmosphere, architectural quality and improvements in the building process led to a score of important and original national or international competitions. Some, based on carefully studied 'programs', related to the design and execution of whole 'quarters', ranging from 1,000 to 7,000 dwellings and including all public facilities and amenities. Others were open to teams of architects, consultants, promoters and builders (in some cases, the first stage of the competition was open to architects only). The most important and significant competitions occurred in Evry, Le Vaudreuil and Marne-la-Vallée.

The 'Evry I' competition, which was held in 1971, concerned the design and construction of a very dense 'quarter' of 7,000 dwellings laid out along a boulevard reserved for pedestrians and public transport, with road traffic being entirely underground. Special importance was attached to the imaginative use of the ground floor of buildings, the integration of activities in the town, the integration of public utility services, the introduction of the arts, and the possibilities of future development. The first 1,000 dwellings were to be occupied in 1975.

In 1974 the 'Marne-la-Vallée–Val Maubnée' competition (two neighbouring 'quarters' of 1,500 dwellings, each medium density) was designed to attract young architects to find ways of integrating a variety of modern buildings into the traditional framework of streets and public places.

There were also many small competitions and experimental design programs. A number of specific studies have been made either by the new town teams themselves or in conjunction with outside architects. Competitions were organized for street furniture and school furniture. In most cases these efforts were sponsored by the GCVN and received active support from the Ministries of Construction and Cultural Affairs.

Improving community services has depended on exploiting possibilities afforded by the corporation's capacity to act as a master builder on behalf of local government or of any other willing participant (university, government agencies, railways, etc.). They may range from modest but essential installations, such as young people's centres (including nursery schools) and community centres, to the ambitious Cergy-Pontoise civic centre, which will bring together a town hall, theatre, library, college of music and youth centre. In the Evry 'agora', opened in March 1975, the corporation is also acting on behalf of *private* participants, thus making it possible to associate in the same building, near to the regional shopping centre, five cinemas, shops, restaurants and an ice rink, as well as three theatres, a library, a youth centre, a swimming-pool, a gymnasium, crèches, the national employment agency and community association offices.

Community processes and functions

A particularly interesting outcome of the French program so far has been the combination of social and technical processes and the establishment of their interrelationships. As these processes are the elements that transform the new town from a spatial structure and 'work of art' into a living community, it is worth considering the types of innovation that have so far emerged.

As mentioned above, 'animation' is the novel concept that has been implemented in earnest since the first houses were built to engender social interaction. The traditional planning focus on spatial design was modified to take account of the importance of creating the right conditions for social relationships, to facilitate integration with existing residents, and to promote a sense of belonging. A 'preanimation' phase, in the year before the new residents arrive, is now an accepted part of the social development program. Multi-professional teams are set up in the EPA, consisting of representatives of the ministries involved (Cultural Affairs, Youth, Sport, etc.) together with outside specialists. Attention is focused on the basic needs of newcomers, such as meeting with neighbours, obtaining information on

71

public services, establishing relations with builders. The approach is to motivate and equip people to develop their own relationships, rather than emphasize facilities or create relationships for them. Hence, the 'animateur' is a catalyst—a 'social entrepreneur' encouraging the formation of community groups and providing them with help or resources.

In Marne-la-Vallée, an 'animation' team, on contract to the EPA, was created in 1972, consisting of two co-ordinators, two audiovisual specialists, a graphic artist, and a youth and sports leader. Its role was to start up the community associations and to be responsible for the sociocultural life of the new town. With financial assistance from central government, the team engaged in a variety of activities, including assistance in the preplanning, siting, design and management arrangements for amenities in the new neighbourhoods, and the cultural and leisure complex at Noisy-le-Grand. Following close co-operation with existing communities, elected representatives and voluntary associations, the planning and construction of the facilities were completed in time for the new arrivals in 1973–74. The initial social activities program included theatrical productions, music appreciation courses, photographic exhibitions and the establishment of a graphic arts and cinema workshop.

At Cergy, a social planner examined the social mix of the new town and the provision of services and institutions. He then contacted the people responsible for each aspect of community life. Working parties were created in each neighbourhood to liaise with the EPA on matters concerning housing and environment, leisure activities, and information about the new town in general. The 'animation' team now comprises the head of each service responsible for the major sectors of social development—education and social services, for example. Community workshops are particular features of the program for encouraging personal, family and neighbourhood relations. Group activities are regarded as the most effective means of stimulating social mixing and of helping people to rebuild the social life that has been disrupted by the move to the new town.

As the potential scope and aims of 'animation' go well beyond these initial sociocultural programs, there is still considerable room for expanding and intensifying this effort. But it represents at least an initial step in the embryonic field of institutional change.

The technical innovations are occurring in four fields. Major experiments in public transport are on the verge of completion: in Evry, for instance, a complete network of tracks reserved exclusively for public transport and capable of being automatically operated at a later date is being built; and the first fully automated public transport line in Europe, which will link the new town of Lille-Est with Lille as the first part of Lille's future Métro network, is under construction. More modest experiments are being conducted in parallel (the use of electric buses in several new towns) and in-depth research is being carried out on 'bi-mode' transport, automatic for part of the way, but also capable of being used on ordinary roads.

In the field of pollution control, Le Vaudreuil has for several years been playing a pilot role as a 'nuisance-free town'. This operation, the subject of close Franco-American co-operation, is supervised by an interministerial committee under the chairmanship of the President of the Electricity Board and sponsored by the Minister for the Environment.

The new towns also constitute a testing ground for cable television, which is already widely used in America but is new to France. This opens up new prospects for community activities as well as for educational and political affairs. Cergy is acting as a pilot in liaison with the French national radio service, while the other towns have study groups under way. The possibility of computer use is being explored in l'Isle d'Abeau and is now the subject of a national joint research project by the GCVN and central information agency. Initially, this is being concentrated on the problems raised by underground networks and, in liaison with the Ministry for Economic Affairs and Finance, on land registration data. The first experiments in large-scale all-electric heating have been launched in Marne-la-Vallée (for 4,000 dwellings) and in l'Isle d'Abeau; and a seminar organized at the beginning of 1972 with the Ministry of Posts and Telecommunications opened up forward thinking on the structure of the postal network in the new towns.

Concluding note

Making things possible: the ambition of the new towns can be summed up in these words. What things? Not spectacular gestures like Versailles or Brasilia, but those that modern society is capable of generating every day and that, in the case of old towns, have so far come up against fragmented local structures and uncontrolled growth. In this respect, the innovation lies in the methods used, the structures set up and the means employed. Nothing would be possible without these, and everything that has been achieved flows directly from them.

Although this chapter has been devoted to the promises of innovation in the French new towns policy, it would be as well to recall its extraordinary *vulnerability*. The new towns, as we have emphasized, are barely out of the cradle. Built for residents who are not yet there and who therefore have no voice, and involving in every field modifications to the spontaneous tendencies of urban development, they impose constant strains on those responsible for them. The daily work makes tremendous demands and gives rise to manifold difficulties and temporary set-backs, in situations that never offer the rewards of immediate or rapid results. Furthermore, the provision of the jobs and infrastructure that condition the very existence of the new towns can be ensured in the early stages only at the cost of constant and clearly affirmed determination at the regional and national levels. The fact that it has been sustained without faltering for six years during the most difficult phase is the best encouragement for the future.

References

1. A brief history is recounted in Lacaze, J.-P., *The Role of the French Towns in Regional Development and Regional Life*, Report to the VI Congress of the International Council of Regional Economies, Warsaw, May 1972, pp. 1–2.
2. The only exception may be the USSR's program, but statistics are hard to come by and even when they are available they are frequently not comparable.

3. Sixth National Plan, Towns Commission Working Party for New Towns, quoted in Roullier, J.-E., 'Administrative and Financial Problems of Creating New Towns in the Paris Area', *Techniques et Architecture*, Number 5, November 1970.
4. Symposium on 'L'expérience française des villes nouvelles', 19 April 1969, sponsored by Fondation Nationale des Sciences Politiques, quoted in Roullier, op. cit.

Part II

Shaping a strategy for successful development

From assessing national achievements we turn to the processes and techniques of development. Some of the most crucial aspects of the developer's task are best thought through before a single spadeful of earth is turned. The first of four chapters on this subject steps back from the development project to look at the development enterprise itself. Three factors vital to its success are pinpointed: a coherent strategy to guide the enterprise through change and uncertainty; a planning style that recognizes the nature of the job to be done; and the management characteristics—urgency, sensitivity, flexibility—needed for the realization of its plans.

Adroit response to change is the main theme of chapter 5, 'Developing the project strategy'. Rather than attempting to forecast the future in copious detail, the developer should sketch a coherent project strategy but keep his detailed plans—and expensive commitments—as short-range and flexible as possible.

In chapter 6, 'Planning for community management', one aspect of strategy formulation is examined in detail. Community management is often over-looked in the planning process, perhaps because its importance becomes evident only toward the end of the development cycle. Yet well-planned community services, facilities and mechanisms for governance crucially affect the community's ability to attract and retain residents—and thus its ultimate success.

The financial theme dominates chapter 7, 'Mastering development economics'. Here, we are concerned with the special characteristics of leverage, the elements of profitability and the problems of financing community services.

Like community management, community design is an area in which the interests of residents and of the developer should coincide. In 'Design: An integral part of strategy', Mort Hoppenfeld argues that good design can enhance the development's marketability and commercial success. He argues for a continuing design control function in the mature community.

Chapter 9, 'Genesis of a new city', provides an account from the firing line, so to speak, of how strategic issues affecting a very new town were faced and dealt with at the regional and local level. 'Planning with its feet on the ground' is how Richard Phelps describes the way he and his team tackled the problems of change and uncertainty in planning Britain's largest new town, the Central Lancashire New Town.

Chapter 4. Guiding the development enterprise

MAHLON APGAR, IV

The success of any large-scale community development effort depends ultimately on two elements. The first is a workable strategy that links the products and the processes of development to the main areas of human need, establishes what kind of community is to be developed and specifies how this will be done. This part of the book is largely concerned with the problems of and approaches to formulating a strategic concept. The second element is effective implementation—the way the development organization, whether public or private, translates the concept into buildings and programs. This is the subject of Part III.

Both strategy and implementation are shaped by a variety of factors that activate, inform and direct the thousands of decisions and actions composing the development process. The most obvious of these factors is the quality and motivation of the human resources involved—the entrepreneurial spirit and drive to identify unmet needs and new opportunities and marshal the resources to meet them; the leadership talent to guide and motivate individuals to give their best to the task; and the technical competence to handle its complex and extensive requirements. Indeed, enterprise and entrepreneurship, as used here, refer explicitly to public as well as private sector organizations and management styles. In my view, entrepreneurship is equally relevant in both—particularly in the community development field where, as I argued in the Introduction, the goals and tasks are largely the same though the mix may differ. Unquestionably, the aims and means of the 'social entrepreneur' are different from those of his classical economic counterpart—but he can pursue them in either sector with increasingly marginal differences.

Less apparent, though no less important, are management concepts and tools. In the development enterprise, unlike most public or private undertakings, these must be consistently designed and implemented at two levels at once—for the development project as well as the development corporation.

The project organization has to be small, flexible and responsive to new demands and rapid changes during the development cycle, while the structure of the enterprise must be designed to accommodate the needs of specialization, long-range planning and massive commitments. Its basic objectives and policies determine the character of both the community and the organization, setting the scene for myriad decisions of every kind. The roles it plays must reconcile the community's need for a full range of activities and services with the developer's ability to provide them effectively and efficiently. The systems for planning, executing and controlling the development process must weave routine day-to-day activities into the longer-term, more fundamental strategic pattern.

Thus, the strategic concept and implementation processes for both the enterprise and project need to be closely and continuously interrelated. While this requirement may be obvious enough in principle, its practical implications are too often obscured by the traditional gap between project planning for the community and corporate planning for the enterprise (where this exists at all).

For one thing, the disciplines, techniques, perspectives and even personal values of those who undertake the two processes are very different. For another, developers have traditionally preferred an essentially intuitive, opportunistic response to a strategic approach based on formal analysis of needs and opportunities. But perhaps the most important difficulty is that community planning is as yet a fragmentary art. Markets can be analysed *ad nauseam*, elaborate buildings and financial structures planned and ambitious social programs laid down. But to draw together, at the right time and in the right way, the disparate economic, social and physical threads that make up the fabric of a living community remains an awesome challenge.

This chapter highlights a strategic approach to planning that can help community developers decide their corporate strategy and guide its implementation through a variety of activities and projects. The approach comprises a number of processes and techniques. Not only will many of these be familiar to the reader but in some he may have a practised hand. It is the framework within which these are linked that enables the developer to take a distinctively different viewpoint, and this has been used with marked effect in the past few years in enterprises and projects of all types. Chapter 5 then describes a process for developing a community concept and commitment plan as a basis for public and private investment decisions.

Three aspects of management will be considered here from the wider corporate perspective. First, the functions of corporate strategy in the development organization will be outlined, together with a framework within which key choices can be made. Next, I shall propose basic reforms in current planning practices to enable developers to meet the challenge of new economic and political conditions. Finally, it will be useful to examine some features of management style that can keep the enterprise dynamic, flexible and sensitive to the pressures that threaten to impede success.

Strategy—purpose and practice

Strategy is a term that is rarely defined or consciously used in most development enterprises. The public development authority will claim that because its goals and

78

activities are clearly prescribed in statute, it does not have a strategic choice to exercise. The private developer will blanch at the thought of framing a corporate strategy, since his success has been based on good contacts, financial acumen, entrepreneurship and a 'feel' for the market. While they may spend millions on community project planning, neither will readily admit that they are in need of a formal, systematic process to define and continuously re-examine their aims, policies and plans as a corporate entity.

Yet it is hard to conceive of any type of organization more in need of an explicit strategy. On the one hand, the vast array of human needs and opportunities it might seek to meet, the broad range of powers and capabilities it could bring to bear, the activities that its decision-makers wish to undertake, and those they believe they should pursue—all these call for a persistent concept of both corporate purpose and the means for achieving it that will preclude some possible activities and include others. On the other hand, the inherent risks of over-commitment, excessive front-end costs, political uncertainty and insufficient flexibility equally demand a strategic approach to identifying and planning for the critical contingencies that will make or break the enterprise in financial, political and operational terms. In short, the large scale, broad scope and sheer complexity of community development require thorough charting of a specific course to maximize the prospects of lasting success with minimum risk. Without it, the most sophisticated planning and management techniques are unlikely to bring the desired results.

The strategic function

Rare as it is in development organizations, I believe that conscious attention to corporate strategy is needed for three purposes: (1) to clarify corporate values and points of view; (2) to relate the multiple goals and interests of its varied constituents; and (3) to shape and direct the organization for maximum effectiveness in managing the process of change.

Clarifying the corporate philosophy. Every development enterprise has its unique philosophy, stated or unstated. This set of attitudes, habits and values can be decisive in the organization's ultimate success. As Thomas J. Watson, Jr, when chairman of IBM, put it:

> ... The basic philosophy, spirit and drive of an organization have far more to do with its relative achievements than do technological or economic resources, organizational structure, innovation and timing. All these things weigh heavily on success. But they are, I think, transcended by how strongly the people in the organization believe in its basic precepts and how faithfully they carry them out.[1]

Typically, the development entrepreneur and key policy-makers are imbued with a strong personal philosophy that enables them to endure the extraordinary pressures and conflicts of the development process. These personal values, however, do not meet the need for a clear set of corporate guidelines on which all the policies and actions of many colleagues and subordinates can be based. In an era when

79

management by consensus has largely succeeded management by fiat, basic corporate principles need to be defined more carefully than ever before.

One of the main aims of a corporate strategy, then, is to crystallize basic ground rules into a working guide for organizational effort and detailed corporate and project planning. For example, one successful developer adopted this corporate mission:

> To plan, build and operate large-scale mixed-use development projects in the Southwestern US designed to achieve product/market leadership; set high aesthetic standards; serve a wide and diverse range of housing, shopping and employment needs; raise the base of ratable values to support the local community; and make an overall 22 percent internal rate of return on total assets employed.

Depending on the particular style and principles of senior management, it may also be desirable to articulate the standards of integrity and conduct expected of the organization. Columbia's executives set such a standard early in its development when they decided that 'under-the-table' pay-offs would not be made for political favours or official approvals. Against the custom of the area and the 'pragmatism' of other developers, they held that the community goals they had set would be contradicted if the integrity of the process were not maintained. People would much rather be informed of such principles and understand the ground rules than be left to assume, and then run the risk of misinterpreting, vague or unstated beliefs.

Relating multiple goals and interests. Few organizations have as wide and diverse a range of goals to accommodate as the community development enterprise. Whether public or private, it is expected to be *efficient* as a developer and builder, yet *effective* in catering for multiple interests (economic, financial, social, environmental) and *equitable* in serving the needs of many constituents (residents, public authorities, employees and firms).

The classical single-minded focus on one objective (e.g., 'build 5,000 houses', 'make a 20 per cent profit') overlooks this multiplicity of aims, constraints and criteria for success. Narrow but easily applied measures of return on investment still absorb the attention of both public and private developers, diverting them from the full range of economic, social and physical objectives and measures. Because the developer is in effect a funds manager, with either public or private money at risk rather than his own, he should use a variety of yardsticks—ranging from 'return on effort' and asset use to jobs created and housing needs met—to assess performance in meeting his multiple goals. He must also consider whether present returns or achievements—however measured—should be forgone and reinvested as a basis for greater returns in the future. At the same time, he must confine his role to viable activities that can be readily financed, and seek commitments from other organizations to supplement the resources on which he can draw directly.

A second purpose of strategy, then, is to articulate the multiple goals of the development enterprise in a way that clearly establishes the relationships between them, the criteria for judging them, the types of action required to implement them, and the policy issues they raise. But in this era of rapid and fundamental change, workable goals cannot be defined in a purely theoretical structure. The sequential steps of classical corporate planning practice—formulating goals, defining and evaluating alternative strategies—are not well suited to the development enterprise. Its goals and strategic options can be understood and stated operationally only in the context of a specific situation. Thus, in practice, I have found it more effective to begin with a broad statement of corporate mission, such as that stated above, that summarizes the overall philosophy, defines the basic product types and field of operations, and establishes the target rate of investment return. As chapter 5 explains, it is then much easier to formulate explicit objectives for each new undertaking from an initial review of the opportunities and constraints directly applicable to the location.

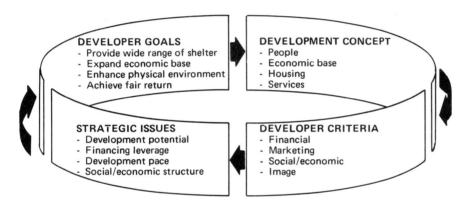

Figure 4.1 Analysis and clarification of developer goals is a continuing process

A continuing process of classification and analysis is therefore required to make trade-offs between potentially conflicting goals (Fig. 4.1), and define appropriate criteria for each of them (Fig. 4.2). The performance of both the enterprise and its projects—in character, quality, financial returns and prevailing ethos—are the direct result of the discipline that these multiple goals require and the innovation that ensues when, in pursuit of the goals, problems inevitably emerge.

The cyclical process will help to make clear the conflicts that are likely to arise not only between developer goals but among the many participants in community development activities. Much more than sensitivity to the public interest is required to resolve them. Tough and intensely political issues must be faced squarely. Who will gain from development? Who will lose? How will changes in tenure and housing mix affect the area? What roles should the developer play? Public and private enterprises alike are open to confrontation, embarrassment and possible failure if they cannot answer such questions.

In short, by anticipating participant concerns about profit, quality, innovation or risk (Fig. 4.3) the developer will be able to ensure a more consistent approach to reconciling the conflicts and strengthening further areas of agreement.

81

GOALS	CRITERIA
Achieve an acceptable level of profit	- Percentage ROI - Cash flow generated
Reduce to a minimum the financial and marketing risks	- Target groups as percentage of total available market - Peak debt
Provide opportunities for the widest possible range of groups	- Expected income structure - Expected occupation/employment structure - Expected age structure
Promote innovative approaches to community programs	- Specific opportunities for innovation
Create an environment that promotes inter-action among residents, shoppers	- Propensity of target groups to participate in community activities - Specific opportunities for meeting and establishing relationships
Reduce net expenditure on community programs where possible	- Ability of target groups to pay for community services - Opportunities for intensive use of existing facilities - Potential for non-developer funding
Ensure political acceptability	- Specific opportunities for links between new and old community

Figure 4.2   Goals and criteria for trade-off analysis

Shaping the corporate destiny. It is paradoxical that developers who devote massive resources and effort to planning projects spanning 10–20 years invest little time or thought in planning their own future corporate development; too many still rely on improvisation and 'gut feel'. The trouble is that community development projects are too large and complex, involve too many outside organizations, commitments and risks, and entail too many activities to change course instantaneously in response to

Figure 4.3   Anticipating conflict

new conditions. Indeed, most new directions are simply impossible without considerable time and preparation.

Moreover, innovation and the inspiration behind it—which are so critical in forging breakthroughs in institutions, procedures and programs—require prior determination of the needs to be met and extensive analysis of shortcomings in current approaches. Reliance on conventional wisdom, tried-and-true methods and external regulations leave the development enterprise unprepared for the wrenching changes it may face. Corporate planning may equip it to grow and to adapt to environmental change.

Many of the great planners, dreamers and developers have, of course, been characterized by a colourful, instinctive style. But the most successful projects have resulted, typically, from the patient and careful work of many associates and subordinates, whose efforts are inevitably less effective if they are continuously disrupted by the erratic, if brilliant, manœuvres of the swashbuckling entrepreneur or the grand designer. More than a few development groups I have witnessed in the past few years suffered greatly from the chaos occasioned by massive land purchases and costly financing arranged with a flash of insight on the basis of untested assumptions. The decision-maker's own vision, however inspired, is no substitute for a strategy that permits the rest of the organization to respond with their maximum contribution to common goals.

The roles of the developer, too, are changing with the new demands and constraints of development. Not only are the traditional distinctions between land developer, builder and property manager blurred, but new and different roles have emerged in initiating, planning, supplying and managing the panoply of community development programs and services required. Chapter 6 discusses these in detail; suffice it to say here that overall corporate performance is closely bound by the choice of roles, and that this choice in a given situation can be made more sensibly within the framework of an explicit strategy.

The final purpose of strategy, then, is to harness the will, the human energies and the material resources of the enterprise to manage its destiny rather than succumb to the ebb and flow of outside forces.

The strategic framework

In order to guide the development enterprise in the way described above, a strategic framework can most easily be constructed around three fundamental choices: *where* to develop, *what* to develop and *how* to do it. While devised in the first instance for private developers, whose field of choice is usually less restricted, the approach discussed below has also proved useful to development decision-makers in the public sector who face essentially the same choices, opportunities and constraints.[2]

The choice of location. The private development industry operates on a highly opportunistic, project-by-project basis, commanded largely by individual entrepreneurs who can move quickly without preconceived notions of strategy or product—but whose key skills are local knowledge, local contacts and local control. The public sector development process, though often begun by national or regional government, is similarly localized: the planning and zoning system is locally initiated, and largely directed and conditioned by local social and political forces.

The key to evaluating the impact of location is to recognize that significant differences exist between the regions and metropolitan areas of every country, and to assess closely the fundamental rather than surface trends affecting the market. For example, the rapid suburbanization of the postwar era led planners and politicians in many areas to try to capture growth in low-density subdivisions of single-family detached housing. However, rising prices in these projects diverted many potential buyers into town houses and condominiums or even rental units. Besides changing the dwelling mix of individual projects and reshaping the basic development concept, this has revealed unforeseen opportunities such as the second-home weekend retreat to complement the new higher-density life style and to succeed the former primary home as the principal housing investment. Superficial analyses of housing market factors have led many developers to overlook these implications and misread the local demographic, economic and environmental picture.

While the basic principles of location analysis, development plans, site layouts and marketing programs reflect universal requirements, the highly personal nature of the house purchase (or rental) and employment decisions make the differences between locations absolutely crucial. Tastes with respect to the site, room layout, colour and style vary considerably by income group and location, though planners all too often overlook the subtle distinctions. One recent project began with pseudo-colonial houses in a market that was built around suburban ranch styles. Another placed California Spanish in a Southern resort. Numerous local authorities have imported 'bastard Bauhaus' as their standard design. None of these aesthetic disasters is a commercial or social success.

Although a given development product can seldom be distributed nationally like toothpaste or colour television sets, this is not to say that national operations are ineffective. On the contrary, there is still considerable scope for economies of scale from industrial production techniques, bulk purchasing, product design and many other features of efficient operations management. But in applying such approaches, careful tailoring of the basic development product to the needs and tastes of specific client groups and markets in each location is essential.

Market research can, of course, aid the product decision by highlighting the local demand characteristics and trends. Models can be used to analyse growth, mobility and preference functions. But research and analysis of market forces alone will not provide the answers to questions of strategic choice or forestall costly mistakes like those cited above. Full evaluation of competitive strengths and weaknesses is needed. What value can the buyer obtain elsewhere? What distinctive features are being offered? Which of the competitor's sales techniques works best? For a regional or national development enterprise operating simultaneously in several locations, this competitive analysis must embrace all major development products and services.

Evaluation of the basic business conditions may not be so easy or obvious, as each area of development operations will have its own set of circumstances and local facts. For example, strong site management, effective political and public relations, contingency planning, detailed financial control and efficient sales force deployment are essential ingredients for superior performance anywhere. But the balance between them and the weight given to each will differ considerably from area to area. Thus, strategic analysis must be thorough enough to identify the environmental forces and competitive product/market conditions, and specific enough to plan and program investment and development to fit local conditions closely.

The choice of development products and services. Though he must consistently do his product/market analysis on a project-by-project basis, the developer may still obtain unusual leverage from a distinctive product/service mix and image. For example, a few builders have offered consistently sound value for money over a sustained period, gaining a national reputation that enables them to compete effectively in new locations. In the face of demands for quality standards as well as a better community environment, a careful approach can provide a strong competitive edge to developers whose products combine good design with well-conceived land use.

Market trends are already giving strong impetus to the community development concept that encompasses environmental objectives and community services as well as physical structures. As Fig. 4.4 shows, the traditional pattern of individual structures—apartment or office buildings, houses, churches and other pieces of the community fabric—is being supplanted by product groupings that aggregate several types of land use aimed at several market segments in single projects. Thus, the postwar shopping centre has become a regional centre with residential, commercial, office and civic uses. The traditional suburban subdivision has become a planned unit development with clustered housing, parks, recreation, community services—and

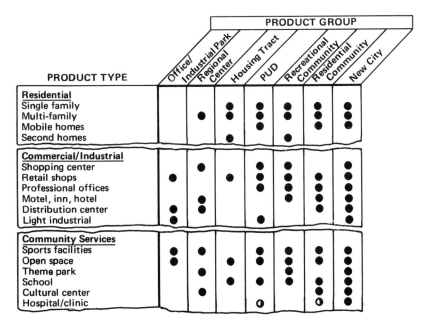

Figure 4.4 Illustrative product opportunities

even light industry. Resort hotels have metamorphosed into entire second-home or recreation communities. And the new community or city synthesizes nearly all these products in a single project.

The development enterprise planning its entry strategy or reconsidering its current role will be well advised, then, to take a broad look at both end-use product segments (e.g., single-family houses, offices, industrial parks) and development services or process segments (e.g., land-use planning, market research, engineering). Against such an assessment, project analysis can be done more quickly and comprehensively, and new products can be more closely related to the developer's other skills, resources and activities as a whole. This approach enables the organization, before launching into a major acquisition or large development project, to analyse possible linkages between individual needs, service activities and end-use products, thereby stimulating new product combinations.

Figure 4.5 illustrates a simple matrix to use in assessing the developer's potential 'fit' with the opportunities in both products and services. As can be seen, Developers

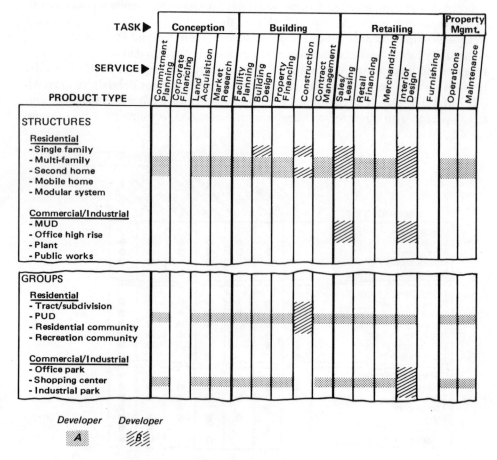

Figure 4.5   Assessing the developer's potential product/service 'fit'

A and B took entirely different approaches. Developer A chose a fully integrated strategy of planning, building and marketing a variety of product and project types in numerous locations. Developer B, on the other hand, was for many years a traditional builder of single-family houses in a narrow price range. But by thoroughly evaluating the possibilities of broadening his base, B was able to successfully enter other phases of the development process on a highly selective basis with existing management skills and little additional investment.

By contrasting alternative strategic patterns on this 'strategy map', the development enterprise can both examine the course of action it is now pursuing and assess the many new options it might follow. Since well-articulated markets exist for development services as well as for products, it may prove desirable to form an integrated operation with full service capability, both to support the developer's projects and to market separately. Rather than limit participation to individual segments, a developer might consider, for example, planning a multi-unit and multi-market mixed-use development; designing, engineering and building the individual structures; selling some to generate cash and retaining some for growth investment; and supplying the raw materials, talent and time on a fee basis to fit these parts together. Already successfully followed by both private and public enterprises in the US, such strategies are increasingly promising abroad as the prospect of community ownership and control of land forces a shift in roles between the sectors and a consequent change in the product/service mix of the developer.

While strategic definition is limited only by the developer's talent and time, the more successful have adopted one of three basic themes:

- *Product:* This strategy concentrates on a single end-product but embraces most or all of the service activities required to produce it. The large office developer and housebuilder, and the local government housing authority, are examples of developers pursuing this strategy. While it encourages specialization in skills, procedures and techniques, and permits the enterprise to focus its resources on a single development product, it also concentrates the risks of outside economic, governmental and environmental forces.
- *Service:* Just as the product strategy focuses on a single product line, this uses professional and customer service activities as a basis for either diversification into the product strategy described above or growth as a service enterprise. In shifting the risk from the building product to the development process, this approach requires more subtle and sophisticated management to succeed.
- *Product/service:* Here the developer expands to several different product lines, still entailing a wide range of services in the development process. This is essentially the pattern of most large private and public developers, and of course of the community developer, though the particular mix of products and services will differ for each organization. While it spreads the risk of vulnerability to outside forces and may benefit the development process through the synergy of different product/service combinations, this approach also requires especially strong management—and is most likely to fail for lack of it.

There are, of course, many possible variations on these strategic themes. For example, a developer with a large existing land bank would probably undertake a product/service approach to build on this key resource. The public authority with a vast building program, on the other hand, might move to acquire or build up its resource base of both land and building materials to ensure a sufficient inventory and even flow of work.

Having established a number of options, it is essential to take one final step in making the choice among products and services: evaluating which combination of opportunities best strengthens the enterprise and setting priorities on which of these to pursue. Here again, such basic decisions are too often made by the entrepreneur with more imagination or 'wishful thinking' than systematic thought. Conversely, where large corporate organizations are involved the analysis may be so exhaustive that demonstrable opportunities are pre-empted by market forces or so complicated that decision-makers become confused by it all and fall back on their intuitive judgement for want of anything clearer.

The problem is worsened because the attractiveness of a prospective project is tied to a specific locale with its own product/market characteristics, making direct comparisons between projects difficult and time-consuming. One aid that has proved helpful in screening the options is the 'portfolio matrix' often used in developing investment strategies. For instead of comparing opportunities by their market or operational characteristics, as market researchers typically do, the strategist arrays potential projects according to their importance in meeting corporate goals and criteria, and their expected contribution to the organization's overall ability to perform. Then, priorities for action are set according to the probabilities, risks and relative ease or difficulty of improving marginal performance through a given opportunity.

To illustrate this method, Fig. 4.6 shows a simplified matrix with several product/service possibilities that were considered by one developer. In this case, strategic importance and contribution to cash flow were the key parameters for decision. The particular MUD opportunity was rated 'high' on both and, in the lower right-hand corner, a resort community and a new contract market research service were rated 'low'. But in terms of short-term action, and the investment of fresh capital, time and effort, those opportunities in the hatched 'medium' and 'high–low' squares received a higher priority than the others. Why? Because their relative current positions could be improved with marginally greater returns on investment and effort and with lower risks than those activities at either extreme. Assessed against the developer's overriding interests, they would produce better results than either the 'high-flyers' or glamorous new ventures such as the MUD.

In short, the aim of these tools is to help narrow the range and variety of possible products and services, and to guide corporate decisions and activities in developing them. Figure 4.7 illustrates part of one developer's guidelines that were prepared as a result of these analytic disciplines. They enabled corporate executives better to control the specialists and project teams, thus avoiding costly, time-consuming mistakes and overcommitments, while at the same time allowing increased flexibility to local site managers to respond to day-to-day needs.

88

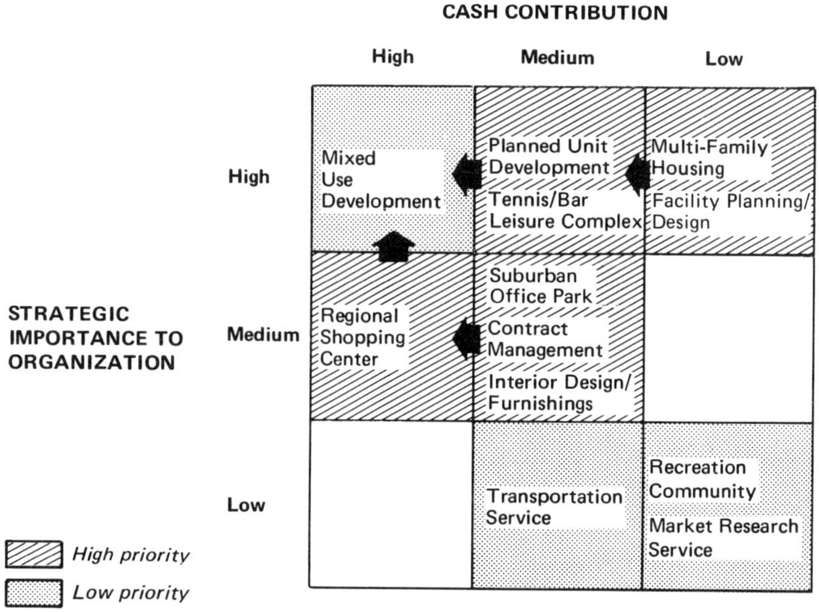

CASH CONTRIBUTION

Figure 4.6 Simplified portfolio matrix

The choice of development approach. When the choices of where and what to do have been assessed, the question 'how' can then be considered. Because the pros and cons of alternative approaches differ significantly, careful analysis and thoughtful decision are called for.

Many developers, however, opt out of this decision stage—particularly in public authorities where professional determinism easily overrides management direction. They turn to planners, builders and a host of other specialists whose studies of and proposals on individual projects and sites may easily bury the key operational problem of *how* they should undertake the chosen product/service strategy at the chosen location.

Three basic routes into community development have proved successful for both public authorities and private enterprise. Each has its own set of advantages and disadvantages, and its own unique requirements if the strategic aims are to be met.

1. *Acquire a development team.* During the past five years, the most common approach has been the acquisition, through either outright purchase or management contract, of an established development organization. This has not only enabled the immediate use of a team of project managers and key specialists and provided a ready capability to pursue development opportunities, but it has proved the best route to secure entrepreneurial talent and ensure their immediate contribution to the overall objectives of the enterprise.

89

CORPORATE CRITERIA

Financial

Net cash flow - 20-30% of revenues

Peak debt/revenue - 3X

Work in process - 3 months

Forced liquidation recovers 85% of investment at any point in project life

Marketing

No products under $18,000 income group

Housing guarantees used when local competitor offers them

Child care program in every first-home community

Etc.

Political/Environmental

Full cooperation with local authorities

80% protection of all sensitive areas; limit construction damage

Etc.

DATA FROM PREVIOUS PROJECTS

Leisure Center

Land needs - 30-50 acres

Location - intersection of main highways, near residential and office districts

Capital needs - $10 million (threshold size 2,000 members) + $1.5 million per 500 extra members

Preferred layout (see map)

Phasing
- Start-up - $2.0 million + land
- Phase 2 - $2.5 million

Programs - squash, tennis, paddle tennis, bridge club, three bars, two restaurants, etc.

CORPORATE ASSUMPTIONS

Money Cost

1975-76
- Development loans - 12%
- Construction loans - 14%
- Retail loans - 10%

1977-80
- Development loans - 10%
- Construction loans - 12%
- Retail loans - 9%

Land Value Appreciation

Basic - cost of living index + 2.5% for productivity

Personal Disposable Income

1974-76 - down 3% from 1973

1977-80 - up 12% from 1973

Housing % rises from 25% to 35% over next 7 years

Mortgage Forecast

1975-77
- Volume 20% below 1973
- Cost - 8.75%

1978-80
- Volume 25% above 1973
- Cost - 8.25%

Construction Costs

Earthmoving - 0.8%/month

Cement - 1.2%/month until 1977; then 0.3%

Wood - 0.7%/month until 1977; then 0.8%/month

Figure 4.7   Illustrative developer guidelines

However, several difficulties inevitably arise. First, it is usually difficult to fit a previously independent, highly autonomous development team into an established organization with its own—and often very different—styles and methods of work. Also, such an ambitious step is more difficult to undo if conditions change. Third, if continuing autonomy and a high level of activity is not assured, the management team may well part quickly. Fourth, the knowledge and expertise thus gained is likely to be highly localized. Assuming that the strategy is focused on the same locale in which the acquired team gained its experience, this may be a distinct advantage. But it should be recognized that this experience may well not be transferable within a national organization for the reasons discussed earlier in this chapter. Finally, their individual expectations for salary and benefits are likely to be higher than those of staff in comparable positions in the corporate hierarchy.

To succeed, therefore, this approach requires careful planning and close attention during the transition period. The management structure and relationships should provide for a high degree of autonomy with a separate management group to accommodate the unorthodox decision-making style in an entrepreneurial development team. They must be largely free of the numerous reviews, conferences, formal meetings and so on that characterize the large multi-departmental organization. A major shift will probably be required from short-term return on investment or payback criteria to careful monitoring of total investment performance over time with a close watch over short-term cash positions and detailed expense control. Radically different incentive programs will have to balance the current performance measures inherent in most corporate remuneration policies with the capital investment and growth objectives of the development entrepreneur.

2. *Undertake a joint venture.* If a private developer joins with a private investor/lender or a public development authority, for either a single project or a continuing partnership, thorough understanding by both partners of the particular characteristics of the project and the nature of the development risks and benefits that they both face is essential. As one observer put it:

> There are great rewards in joint ventures, but they go to the active, aggressive investor who either knows [about development] or is advised by those who do. He should, of course, be prepared for the worst [because] having an extra financial capacity is vital in exploiting those situations where success costs more than initial estimates.[3]

The joint venture has the main advantage of providing explicit parameters on both partners' involvement and exposure—i.e., maximum leverage with minimum risk. It also reduces or completely eliminates the need to build up an internal development organization, though monitoring roles will, of course, need to be defined. Moreover, it enables the public authority or private investor to learn the development process through participation in policy and program decision-making for the joint venture. It can also spread the risks of failure or delays by allowing continuing relationships to be maintained with several developers in different markets or types of project. And not least, for the investor and lender, the corporate balance sheet can be relieved of a large real estate debt burden—often a highly significant market advantage.

The greatest difficulties in joint ventures occur when the partner has negligible operational control, either by default through lack of experience and expertise, or by

91

design. Little knowledge or management skill is gained internally, so that if the project begins to overrun or to fail, there is neither the talent nor the depth of staff to turn it around. And if the overall objective for the private investor is diversification into a new business, the joint venture does not really establish a new, ongoing product/market strategy.

Unlike the acquisition approach, the enterprise or investment group must develop its knowledge of the 'different' economics and long project life cycle before structuring the joint venture, since the benefits to each partner are distinctive—e.g., capital gains, cash flow, tax savings—but they can only be optimized through careful prior positioning. It also requires a mutual appreciation of each partner's underlying motivation, whether it is building a monument, achieving social or ideological aims, or avoiding public exposure. Each can almost surely be accommodated, but not without thorough analysis of the roles each will play and the risks these entail.

3. *Build an internal development team.* This third route provides not only maximum control of growth and direction, but often better utilization of existing knowledge and resources within the organization. It may also ensure closer communication and greater rapport between the development group and other operating departments and staff. Found occasionally among the larger, multi-divisional private corporations, this also has been the most common strategy of most public development authorities. However, it is the slowest approach to moulding an effective team and carries a high risk of organizational atrophy as conventional bureaucratic attitudes and processes emerge without the leaven of an entrepreneurial management style.

Because of the length of time and the lack of momentum that this typically entails, it requires strong, in-house leadership by experienced and aggressive managers who have the wholehearted backing of the key decision-makers in the parent organization.

It is also appropriate at this stage to pin down the ways in which a contribution can be made to the developer's non-financial objectives. For example, the two key resources of land and skills may, if applied selectively, leverage the development's social contribution. Institutional uses that can be tied into the product/service mix will be worth far more to the community than their price premium would allow. Know-how can be shared by the developer with community organizations that are chronically short of technical and managerial skills yet whose contributions are indispensable to achieving the overall community purpose.

To sum up, the choice of location and product—based as they are on the overall objectives of the development enterprise—should determine the plans for land-use, financial and other resource commitments, and not, as commonly happens today, the other way round. The total development approach is thus based on the needs and demands of specific customer/client groups; the product and service characteristics that will meet their needs; the marketing programs that will best reach them—and finally, the most effective spatial structure to embrace this mix of people, products and programs.

The developer's last step in strategy-making should be to check the entry strategy and product/service plans against the profile of market demands and social needs.

Does the product/service mix match the current and prospective need/demand profile? Can the existing or available resource base—of land, finance, talent—support the strategic concept? Have any needs been overlooked that could be met with the available resources—even if they require a rethinking of the strategy? What is the impact of any special risks and critical contingencies on the expected results?

If any imbalance here reduces the viability of the proposed approach, the option of deferring the entry decision ought to be considered. Despite the momentum of planning and the inexorable commitments that harden as the decision nears, the costs of a wrong decision today are too great to skimp on this crucial evaluation.

The next chapter discusses a new approach to planning individual development projects within the strategic framework described above. It is appropriate here, however, to suggest how planning styles should adapt to the changed conditions within which today's development enterprise operates.

Planning and planners

Planning for an undertaking as complex as a new community entails rigorous analysis and conscientious re-examination of beliefs, hypotheses and working assumptions.

Until recently, decision-makers, planners and planning systems could rely on some basic assumptions with which everyone seemed to agree. For example, growth was regarded as a basic national objective as long as natural resources were plentiful, political, economic and social systems seemed reasonably stable—and, most important, the future could safely be assumed to be like the past.

But no longer. The past two years have shown marked changes in the basic economic, social and political climate of every developed country. Battered by raw material shortages, high and rapidly growing inflation, capital shortages and the 'environmental consciousness', the core assumptions of yesterday's planners and decision-makers are useless for tomorrow. Not only is growth now bad in the eyes of many, but real growth has been largely arrested. Financial systems have been seriously disrupted and the availability of external finance has become increasingly uncertain. High debt leverage not only entails huge carrying costs for working capital but is subject to rapid variations in interest levels. Trends are increasingly hard to predict, crises must now be expected and political stability may be threatened.

Preposterous materials prices and increased wage costs will vastly increase the pressure for effective cost control, value for money and overall performance. For private and public enterprises alike, earnings and asset growth will not be as critical as the generation of unfettered cash flow. Indeed, in the marketplace of resources, whether decided by politicians or businessmen, strength will be judged by survival—not by excessive growth—even for the largest and most financially secure development organizations.

For planning corporate strategy, there are two fundamental implications of this massive change in the rules of the game. First, the future can no longer be expected to resemble the past. Investment returns will tend to be reduced in real terms by the

93

combination of inflation and price controls as revenue growth fails to keep pace with rising costs. Profitability will decline as development and financing costs rise faster than revenues, while the margin between returns and costs declines. Cash flow will deteriorate as the funds generated from operations—i.e., profits before interest and tax plus depreciation—fail to match the growing financing requirements. Thus, liquidity—the prime need of large-scale development—is threatened at a time when the availability and cost of new finance is least certain.

Second, since neither individuals nor markets can any longer be relied on to behave in accordance with forecasts, planning can no longer be prescriptive. Instead, it should be indicative—providing guidelines for future decisions, without attempting to prescribe those decisions on the basis of today's forecasts. This means constant review, evaluation and short-term changes in direction to avoid pitfalls in the strategic path. This need for a flexible response to unforeseen changes must be reflected in the tools and methods adopted for strategic planning and operations management.

Assumptions, which in the past have been little more than extrapolations of past trends with a highly statistical bias but less regard for subjective forces, should be based on detailed, rigorous and continuous evaluation of the social, economic and political changes in basic needs and demands for development products and services. Challenge and review sessions, especially during new project planning, should be held at least bi-monthly, with issue-oriented reviews weekly.

Comparative analysis, rather than emphasizing relative performance and competitive positions to an extreme, should focus equally on cost control, financial position, and variances against agreed development plans to identify specific points of vulnerability. Reviews should include thorough consideration of alternative or substitute product/service mixes, both by project and by region. Management should accept replacement cost accounting as a basis for pricing decisions, tax assessments and performance review.

Plan documentation should no longer be focused on the production of comprehensive, formal plans that detail 10- or 20-year life-of-project projections. Instead the emphasis should be shifted to strategic scenarios and issue analyses, geared to a two- to three-year planning horizon, with semi-annual operating budgets highlighting costs against the product/service mix. Attention should be focused on identifying and planning for key contingencies and 'downside risks' (an approach to identifying risks in the community planning process is discussed in the next chapter).

Control mechanisms should concentrate not on monetary measures and the various indices of return on invested capital, but on funds flow, cash and productivity. Special emphasis should be placed on (1) contribution analysis, quantitative measures of output and real value-added in development; (2) detailed control over project planning and overhead expense—particularly design and other 'soft' costs that do not contribute directly to cash-generating sales and rentals; (3) installation of early-warning indicators for each critical stage in the process and each product and service activity; (4) careful monitoring of monthly utilization and productivity of professional staff by the chief executive; and (5) continuing review of strategic issues and contingency plans. Internal information and control systems simply can no longer neglect the impact of inflation as they often have been designed to do in the past.

In summary, planning tools must become more relevant and usable, fashioned for quick response to undreamed-of contingencies and new constraints. And for the same reasons, the planning staff of the development enterprise must be more closely integrated into the executive decision-making machinery.

In the public sector, particularly in Europe, a rigid distinction between line and staff is a legacy of traditional town planning, where the preoccupation with survey research, data and methodology, rather than strategic analysis, overwhelms the substantive policy issues that often are left to be decided 'politically'—that is, instinctively and without the informed consideration they deserve. In private firms, nearly the reverse may be true: the projects are so complex that enormous staff effort is consumed on detailed analysis, while strategic issues may go unrecognized.

Generally, planning is the province of a staff group who research and analyse information without direct and continuing policy guidance. Because their reports lack a strategic perspective, they are seldom highly regarded by the decision-makers.

In the British development authority, for example, planning is not only a separate staff function, but usually is represented by a separate policy-making committee. While the planners' work is often highly visible, few policy-makers really understand or appreciate what they do. And the planners, for their part, are content to pursue their traditional functions quite independently of other staff groups—finance, construction, social development—which may in fact have more direct influence on the decision-makers' actions through their operational analyses than through long-range plans.

Success in implementing plans and policies requires the careful development and effective installation of appropriate systems and procedures. For example, a land acquisition policy is impossible without considerable detailed knowledge of land availability and pricing. And this in turn requires a systematic method for gathering, analysing and disseminating relevant data in a timely and economical fashion.

Yet I have often seen soundly conceived strategies fail in execution because decision-makers treated policy formulation as fulfilment—rather than as simply the first step. Uninvolved in execution, they have overlooked the need to issue instructions translating the corporate philosophy and strategic concept into operating reality.

Management—ingredients for success

A sound grasp of the principles and practice of strategic and project planning is characteristic of those organizations producing communities that 'work' for all those concerned. However, there is another factor involved too, often discounted in importance but no less essential to success: sound management. I am not referring to organization charts, reporting relationships, budgeting systems or computerization. Getting these right is of course important, but they are implementing aids that can be readily detailed. I am interested rather in management style, the way things are done

95

that ensures the success of the enterprise. Three aspects seem to me particularly important as I have observed the work of a number of public and private development executives.

A compelling sense of urgency. When you embark on a 10- or 20-year development cycle, it is easy to be lulled into thinking that today's problems can always be tackled tomorrow. Yet community development is a singularly eventful process, with new problems constantly emerging from the interplay of multiple aims, interests and constraints. Without a keen sense of urgency in line and staff alike, even the most advanced management tools will not be effective.

Urgency is always thought to be a quality of private organizations, not of public enterprise. At the official level, where most of the day-to-day development work is done, bureaucratic procedures are not geared to the need for rapid progress. Agencies and projects alike are accustomed to slow, measured approaches. But pressure on resources and the taxpayers' intolerance of inefficiency are changing all this. In the past few years I have seen several examples of public development entrepreneurs who have infused a fresh spirit into their organizations. Consider two illustrations. When Peter Walker became Britain's Secretary of State for the newly established Department of the Environment in 1970, he inherited an agglomeration of the former housing, planning and public works ministries, 28 semi-autonomous new town corporations, and a variety of research and staff functions, which had to be moulded into a single unit of some 80,000 people spending directly nearly £4 billion a year, and influencing many times that amount of local authority spending throughout the country. The reorganization was by tradition left largely to the senior civil servants. Meanwhile, Walker and his junior ministers concentrated on instilling a sense of urgency about community problems and opportunities both in the country at large and within the Department. People at all levels began to contribute ideas, to search for innovation, and to criticize 'the system'. Fresh programs, such as the 'Inner Areas' studies, were launched to examine the interrelationships of community development problems, and others, like 'Operation Eyesore', to experiment with remedies. Interdepartmental task forces began to tackle common problems on a greater scale and with greater effect than before. Action ensued in a much shorter time than would customarily have been thought possible.

Walker appointed Dennis Stevenson (at the age of 26) to be Chairman of the Peterlee and Aycliffe Development Corporation, undertaking the expansion of two new towns in the North of England. Stevenson's task was to transform an agency mainly concerned with completing a building program in a long-established, tradition-bound mining area into an enterprise focused on enhancing, developing and revitalizing the community. He faced up to it with both the vigour of youth and a strong sense of urgency.

New ways of working were introduced, and the staff infused with a fresh sensitivity to community problems and desires, an open style of management and a lot of enthusiasm. Working relationships between the development corporation and local government improved measurably, resulting in better productivity, more aggressive—and effective—marketing and a variety of innovative community programs.

The sense of urgency is a way of thinking as much as a personal style. To paraphrase Marvin Bower, the dean of American management consultants, it comprises five qualities: the sense that time is precious, however much there may seem to be in a multi-decade project; a zest for undertaking the tasks at hand; decisiveness even under great uncertainty; seizing and exploiting opportunities to build on strengths rather than shore up weaknesses; and lastly, seeking out and facing up to problems.[4]

The achievement of flexibility. Flexibility is a prescription for success in every text I have seen, and most development decision-makers have learned to be flexible amid the strong currents of political and social change. The larger private developers are used to working in an industry so highly fragmented and localized that flexibility in both policy and procedure is a *sine qua non* for survival, let alone success. But the single-purpose public development corporation and its small-scale private counterpart have much greater difficulty adjusting to rapid change and multiple operating styles because of their limited exposure. Both, in short, need the capacity to manage under uncertainty, in situations where the most fundamental rules of the game have changed.

This means a constant, week-by-week scrutiny of the forces at work on the enterprise to ensure that the core assumptions underlying policies and plans are still valid. When an unforeseen marketing, financial, engineering or political problem arises, management must be able to evaluate its impact on the entire corporate and project plan and, if necessary, rearrange within days work scheduling, financing or even the entire development sequence itself.

In addition, a close and continuing dialogue must be mounted and maintained from boardroom to construction site, not only to communicate changes in assumptions and plans instantly, but to ensure that improvement opportunities identified on the ground can be immediately exploited at the top and throughout the organization. Finally, flexibility is needed in operating systems, not only to avoid the dulling effects of over-formalization and paperwork, but also to keep all the various activities responsive to immediate changes in the development environment.

Public sensitivity. From the moment development intentions become public knowledge until the project is a functioning community, the enterprise will be enmeshed in complex, often highly emotional issues and problems. Before planning permission is secured, long-time residents will be apprehensive about higher densities and declining land values. New residents, full of anxiety about the community being created around them, will increasingly seek to intervene in the development process, as will the relevant local and regional authorities.

The benefits of greater freedom of choice within a more responsive environment will at times set the developer completely at odds with the community over these issues. The organization needs far more than good public relations to handle these problems successfully. Senior executives themselves must be able to relate day-to-day issues to the overall community concept and long-range plans, and create mechanisms for integrating the new residents' perspective into the ongoing development process.

97

Since the designation and purchase of a site represent, for all practical purposes, a permanent commitment, the developer's viewpoint must be very long-range indeed. All those responsible for providing the funds and managing the process must likewise be convinced of its ability to sustain the desired level of development products, programs and services over its entire life.

Before making such a commitment, therefore, thorough analysis is required to assess the type and level of future benefits to be obtained from the project, and the expected costs that will be incurred. The next chapter describes an approach to this crucial but difficult task.

References

1. Watson, Thomas J., Jr, *A Business and Its Beliefs*, pp. 5–6, McGraw-Hill, New York, 1963.
2. The approach to corporate strategy for development organizations described in this section was originally developed in 1970 by John Forbis and the author to aid large private corporations in the real estate industry, and later extended by Peter Braun and others. For further discussion, see Apgar, 'Do Big Corporations Belong in Real Estate?' *Corporate Financing*, pp. 45 ff., May–June 1972; and Braun, 'Avoiding Pitfalls in Real Estate', *Harvard Business Review*, pp. 125–34, January–February, 1975.
3. Lootens, Donald M., 'Policing the Financial Marriage', *Business Horizons*, pp. 79–86, August 1974.
4. Bower, Marvin, *The Will to Manage*, pp. 38–9, McGraw-Hill, New York, 1966.

Chapter 5. Developing the project strategy

MAHLON APGAR, IV

> The dilemma of any statesman is that he can never be certain about the probable course of events. In reaching a decision, he must inevitably act on the basis of an intuition that is inherently unprovable. If he insists on certainty, he runs the danger of becoming a prisoner of events. His resolution must reside not in 'facts' as commonly conceived but in his vision of the future.—Henry Kissinger

In undertaking a community development project, the development enterprise faces precisely the challenge that Kissinger describes. Acting largely on the basis of intuition, its executives must constantly chart a course across an abyss of unforeseen events. Their vision, perhaps even more than that of Kissinger's statesman, must be tempered by immediate realities—delays, soaring costs, obstruction and opposition. In weighing alternative strategies for an individual project, they must therefore find ways to limit their risks without compromising their objectives.

This implies a shift in project planning from forecasting the future to preserving future flexibility. In today's uncertain climate, decisions entail financial, political and managerial commitments that must be rigorously structured and carefully phased to keep open as many options as possible for the longest possible time. This is particularly so during a project's early years, when the risks and the difficulties of achieving results are so great. The process of formulating corporate strategy discussed in chapter 4 should help in this task by making explicit the development mix that best meets overall corporate criteria. But this is too general a framework within which to tackle the needs and opportunities presented by a particular area or site.

The project strategy is thus a bridge between the guiding principles of corporate planning and the minutiae of implementation planning. Before detailing the steps in developing a project strategy and the distinctive features of 'commitment planning', however, it will be helpful to look more closely at the nature of community development commitments and risks, and the pitfalls in conventional planning, both of which underlie the need for a strategic approach.

The nature of development commitments and risks

The most significant risks in community development typically become evident only after initial commitments have been made. Purchase negotiations—and subsequent decisions to increase the investment—influence a project's entire direction and determine its prospective performance, since revenues are largely a function of specific site characteristics and the size and growth of the local market. Though the immediate *financial* commitment may appear small, this initial decision will entail substantial subsequent commitments (Fig. 5.1). The *market* commitment, made with

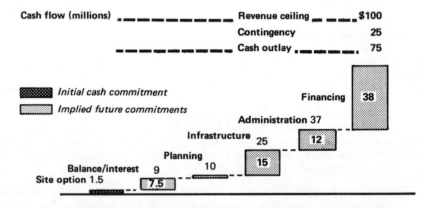

Figure 5.1 Impact of commitment decision

the choice of a site, is determined by local conditions that often are left largely unexplored. A *political* commitment is also involved, because to renege on intentions expressed at the time of purchase would destroy the developer's local credibility and reduce his ability to capitalize on other opportunities. Finally, a declaration of growth intentions, with its implied promise to staff that the project will be going ahead, amounts to a *managerial* commitment. But when a purchase or expansion decision seems urgent, as it inevitably will, the risks inherent in these commitments may go unrecognized until it is too late to turn back.

While simple in concept, the principle of limiting these commitments is rarely implemented, often because of the nature of the risks themselves. The time scale of community development, particularly in large projects, presents special problems. Early commitments based on optimistic assumptions about prices, sales rates, costs and development pace can later become a drain on the cash, time and energy of both the developer and financial institutions. What makes these decisions so demanding is not the task of projecting futures under a given set of assumptions, but the difficulty of arriving at the right assumptions to begin with and judging their probable impact. Because the development process requires hundreds—and even thousands—of critical assumptions, each with some degree of uncertainty, the combined uncertainties are frequently formidable. They are complicated by conflicting perspectives among the various participants in the project and the professional disciplines involved. Some 25 or more professions may be required, each with its own working assumptions and methods, and a number of other participants contribute to (or regulate) the process.

To accommodate the many uncertainties and competing interests, a community development project has to be conceived within an envelope of alternatives; a single strategic path will not produce the desired results. For most organizations, then, the risks inhere in: (1) their high vulnerability to political and economic forces, (2) the difficulty of changing the market mix or product characteristics during the development cycle, and (3) the long pull to reach the cash break-even point.

High vulnerability to outside forces. While operating under the keen eyes of politicians, environmentalists and other public interest groups, developers today must also rely on the co-operation or approval of a growing variety of outsiders. Substantial off-site support for basic infrastructure and services is vital—e.g. water supply, flood control, transportation and access, sewerage. Outside organizations will have to provide essential community facilities and services such as education, social services, main roads and common areas. The impact of development on the local ecology, economy, demography and resources will require lengthy and difficult negotiations with numerous bodies. Indeed, where large-scale development would once have been welcomed for its visible signs of 'progress', intense political opposition may now be aroused based on the popular assumption that higher local taxes and heavier burdens on local services will automatically follow. Even if these fears are laid to rest and the opposition eventually disarmed, months of costly delay in planning approvals or the provision of key site services may have resulted. Thus, the machinery to encourage an effective dialogue and to allow co-operative analytic work to take place has to be set up from the start.

The long time span of development also means that assumptions on demand for housing, jobs and services, and thus the mix of programs and facilities, may vary widely over the development cycle, and the demand for specific project features may change after the project is well under way. For example, in view of the present interest in telecommunications, failure to have planned a cable network on site could spell a major short-run competitive disadvantage and formidable long-run capital costs.

Constraints on changing direction. Once initial commitments have been made, the developer is hemmed in by numerous constraints in attempting to respond to changed conditions. Residents of an established community of single-family detached houses, for example, can be expected to resist any attempt to increase density—no matter how attractive the proposed development—or to change the land-use mix by extensive commercial building—even if the market is strong and local tax and other benefits can be clearly demonstrated. Existing political commitments, zoning and community facilities will further limit the alternatives, and the established economic base will impose constraints of its own. For example, a holiday development remote from centres of primary employment could hardly be successfully converted to a first-home project without massive further investment

101

—even assuming that a primary employment base existed or could readily be developed.

Although major cost increases may oblige the developer to curtail his activities sharply, commitments in infrastructure may keep him from easily winding down his project. Some developers have been unable to sell their more expensive products because mortgage credit simply has not been available. Yet political restraints, existing amenities and the expectations of present residents made downgrading of the product out of the question.

Deferred break-even. Because of the high-leverage financial structure of development projects, generating sufficient cash flow is the developer's primary task. Early cash outflows are massive while revenues lag; recovery of the original investment, therefore, will inevitably take a long time. Particularly in large-scale projects, the developer attempts to secure a sizeable site inventory through major options, outright purchase or compulsory purchase, in order to plan comprehensively, incorporate essential activities in close enough proximity, and prevent peripheral investors from siphoning off a major share of the value he creates. Large projects also require major front-end capital and overhead expenditures for infrastructure and initial facilities, extensive planning and design, and time-consuming zoning and environmental approvals before any significant cash can be generated.

This is not the problem of the private developer alone. Under pressure to reduce government spending, public developers find it increasingly difficult to get authorization for heavy development expenditures with no offsetting returns securely in sight.

Moreover, especially in residential developments, the prospective buyer or tenant may perceive greater risks and a less attractive investment in the early stages, until the project has attained its 'critical mass' and gained the local credibility essential for full market approval. Recent research shows that despite extensive promotion and early provision of amenities and services, major projects take at least 30–40 per cent of their total development cycle to reach their full market share. Attempts to bring forward the break-even point may only make matters worse. Opening up a site too early can harm the project's market image, create financing charges exceeding the revenues generated, and end by pushing the break-even point still further into the future.

Early analysis, therefore, has a critical role to play in aiding the developer to avoid these risks. From this brief summary, it might seem that the simple answer to over-exposure would be to reduce the scale of individual new projects. In Britain that has been the primary response of the larger housebuilders. In the US, even those who traditionally have undertaken 10,000–20,000-acre projects are now redirecting their efforts to PUDs on several hundred acres to spread these excessive risks. Major public authorities are now reshaping their strategies to undertake projects on smaller sites with less elaborate plans and lower investment. But increasing complexity and vulnerability still make development a high-risk activity requiring more subtle solutions. And in my experience, the place to begin searching for these is in the planning process, where the major decisions are made that determine ultimate success and shape the overall risks.

Pitfalls in conventional project planning

While methods for analysing sites abound, they are little help in assessing the impact of risks and selecting an optimal development approach. For one thing, key issues of project strategy—e.g., 'Should we achieve a complete balance of on-site employment and housing by Year 8?'—are likely to be obscured by the plethora of detail usually found in preliminary land-use, economic, financial and engineering studies. Without a clear conception of the essential elements in a project and the relative importance of the various issues they raise, much of the planning effort can be wasted on detailed research and analyses for project elements that are eventually dropped from the development plan.

Moreover, despite the volume and depth of detail found in the best of preliminary plans, the multitude of specialist techniques involved narrows the perspective of any single analysis and diverts attention from broader, more fundamental problems. Market research is all too often carried out with expensive surveys and complex gravity models but with only a cursory glance at the dynamics of market-share performance or competitive strengths and weaknesses. Financial structures supported by massive life-of-project cash flow projections often lack simple but vital break-even analyses and sensitivity tests.

Perhaps most critically in such an obviously uncertain activity, contingency planning is seldom undertaken or used as a basic management tool. The desire to create momentum in a new venture encourages an extensive commitment to facilities, programs and products, without full consideration of the resulting constraints on future flexibility. Preoccupied with the problems of site planning and construction, developers are prone to neglect even the most predictable contingencies. Economic, financial and physical plans are inevitably based on single-value assumptions of prices, sales rates, costs and space allocation, rather than on probable variations that could have a significant impact on project performance. The development plan is typically laid out for the whole site or structure, rather than staged to accommodate possible future changes. Land uses and infrastructure are determined for the total life of the project, even if it has a 10- to 15-year program—well beyond existing forecasting capabilities. Project image is defined and target markets are set by the amenities, product types, costs and prices chosen at that stage in planning.

To the well-versed manager, such practices may seem surprising. But they are not limited to small 'back-of-the-envelope' developers. The largest and best-staffed private firms and public authorities, teamed with the most sophisticated financial partners, exhibit the same limitations. Theirs is the legacy of traditional planning practice, which is still dominated by a spatial perspective—the built environment—rather than based on the economic and social processes that turn land, bricks and mortar into communities. Daniel Burnham's exhortation to architects, 'Make no little plans—they lack the magic to stir men's hearts and minds', largely governs the planning process, so that grand designs either precede, or even pre-empt, policy decisions on the type of community to be created in human terms or the scale and risks to be assumed. Even where so-called alternatives are considered, they may only embellish the building form with features of site access, layout or aesthetic effect; they are not subjected to sufficient strategic analysis.

The size of the resource commitments makes this single-faceted approach dangerous. One vignette from recent experience illustrates the point. The loan covenants for a $50 million multi-use project prescribed in minute detail the forecast sales, rentals and types of use—e.g., '5,615 two-bedroom cluster-type apartments'—all phased year by year to 1995. Not only were these assumptions impossibly detailed for planning purposes, but they had hardened into definite expectations and had even become legal obligations! Yet no contingencies whatever had been built into the agreement to accommodate unexpected product/market changes, nor had the key sensitivities of overall project economics been determined as a basis for financing arrangements. Moreover, while preliminary strategic analysis would have provided a basis for more prudent commitments, its potential value went unrecognized. Two major banks and an insurance company had insisted that all of the 20-year forecasts be recorded literally in the loan agreement. But though the developer knew from experience that such long-range forecasts were highly uncertain, he was unsure how to accomodate the uncertainties or restructure the project without jeopardizing his financing. Predictably, the development was in technical default almost from the day construction began, and radical restructuring was required.

Commitment planning: a strategic approach

Avoiding pitfalls such as these depends above all on distinguishing clearly between the five main stages in the overall development process: (1) *commitment planning*, in which the project concept is established and the major resource commitments are made; (2) *implementation planning*, in which detailed planning, programming and budgeting are completed for site and building development; (3) *site development*; (4) *building construction*; and (5) *community management* of the institutions, programs and services that the mature community comprises.

The remainder of this chapter discusses only the first stage, in which the most fundamental resource decisions are made. Whereas the ensuing stages are already well established, in most development enterprises the first stage is still undertaken haphazardly or not at all. The focus of project planning is commonly on how to implement a rather abstract concept in a specific location. Definition of the concept itself is too easily submerged, and the details of the land-use, financial and program plans may pre-empt it altogether. By deferring these detailed plans until the concept, commitments and contingencies are thoroughly evaluated, it is possible to limit the major risks and manage the subsequent stages more effectively.

While the aims and end-products of commitment planning and implementation planning are different, the distinction is chiefly one of emphasis. In commitment planning, goals for the project are established that meet the objectives of the enterprise and key participants. Feasibility for development is assessed from the opportunities and constraints of the economic, physical and social environment, and criteria for later planning and decision-making are established. A development concept is defined in terms of the kind of community to be created, and risks that could threaten its realization are anticipated.

But in implementation planning, the emphasis moves from the kind of community envisaged to how this concept will be brought into being: thus the project concept is translated into detailed plans as a framework for implementation. A full set of implementation plans will be likely to cover:

- *Land development,* including site layout and community design, schedule of infrastructure works and associated costs over time, and valuation estimates.
- *Housing,* including housing types and mix, price ranges, builder roles, year of construction, and the main marketing features.
- *Commercial and industrial development,* including location, design, values, costs, target customers and customer contact plans.
- *Production,* including the build-up schedule for infrastructure, housing, commercial and industrial construction, labour and other resource requirements, and construction methods.
- *Community programs,* including on-site facilities and services, community organization and financing.
- *Management structure and processes,* including project organization, planning networks, budgeting and control procedures.

Throughout both stages, the community concept is continually refined, gradually becoming more specific. The concept is, at the most general level, simply an outline of markets, products and timetables; at the most detailed level, it is a complete set of plans and programs.

The most difficult task the developer must face at the commitment planning stage is to distinguish the key strategic issues, whose resolution determines the shape and success of the project, from the welter of technical details that can easily overwhelm decision-making. Three features of the approach described below will help the developer highlight these issues: the comprehensive framework for development, the multiple perspective considered, and the careful staging of commitment decisions.

Development framework. From the 'gleam in the eye' of an initial concept to the completion of an end-product—new community, PUD, etc.—thousands of activities will be undertaken in a variety of tasks and programs. To establish the links and ensure consistency among them all calls for a framework embracing the essential aspects of development planning—financial, product/market, social, economic and spatial (Fig. 5.2). Besides helping the decision-maker to be better informed, a comprehensive grid will ensure that analytic methods, professional biases and working assumptions follow from the community concept for each task and program. In addition, important decisions about project strategy can be anticipated early enough to allow sufficient data collection and contingency planning.

Multiple perspectives. While this grid helps to tie the means to the ends, the issues and decisions themselves must reflect the different perspectives of the many participants in the project—e.g., central and local government, employers, private

105

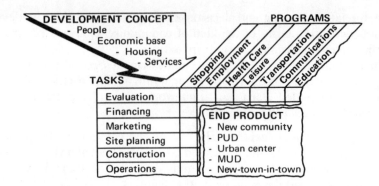

Figure 5.2   A framework for community development

builders, community residents, and the 25 or more professional disciplines involved—to ensure that maximum leverage is obtained where their objectives match or complement one another, while enabling conflicts in objectives to be identified and, where possible, resolved early in the process. As development is a highly political process, the prudent developer will capitalize on this opportunity. Political confrontations and risks can be limited by deciding who can best do what at the earliest stages of planning.

In theory, some ideal community 'meta-strategy' might attempt to combine the goals, interests and resources of all the public and private agencies that should be involved, and corporate planners in the public sector have long favoured this. But a corporate approach that attempts to co-ordinate all the agencies through a joint committee is rarely workable, because no one has the main responsibility. A more effective approach recognizes the role of a legitimate initiator to secure, through persuasion more than a legal charter, the co-operation and agreement of others. So the community strategy must in practice originate with the development enterprise—public or private—which is able to take the main entrepreneurial initiative, marshal sufficient powers and resources, and draw on the wide variety of other organizations that can help its implementation.

In so doing, the enterprise will be well advised to recognize in the strategy the alternative roles it can play in meeting project objectives, particularly where opportunities for social or environmental innovation exceed the interest or current capacity of public agencies or private entrepreneurs. Each type of community need will typically require a different developer role, and at any point in the development cycle the developer can adopt a number of complementary roles. Chapter 6 discusses these roles and the leverage—in political, financial, and staff terms—that can be obtained.

Staging decisions. As we have seen, the attempt to impose a single template on an uncertain future is doomed to fail. Multiple strategies are called for. In effect, the master plan of classical urban practice should be replaced with a strategic 'road map' by which development can proceed with changes in direction as unforeseen diversions are encountered. Decisions that will commit the developer to an irrevocable course of action or expenditure of resources should be carefully staged throughout the development cycle. Those that are most critical to project success should be highlighted, so as to avoid wasted effort and expense on unnecessary analysis and work, and to leverage staff skills, time and energy in the early stages when they are in shortest supply. The more rigorously this is done, the less will *ad hoc* reactions or current plans pre-empt urgent strategic decisions in the future.

Steps in commitment planning

Four steps are involved in commitment planning, each with distinctive end products:

- Evaluating potential sites or areas of opportunity quickly and economically before undertaking specific project planning.
- Defining a 'project concept' before the strategic decision to go ahead.
- Developing a commitment plan before any major investment in the project.
- Establishing guidelines for controlling implementation of the project concept before undertaking detailed planning or construction.

These steps are described below and illustrated with the type of working documents, necessarily simplified, that a project team using this approach might produce. The aim throughout is to inform decisions early enough in the development process to avoid overexposure and insufficient flexibility in a project, while providing a practical means of auditing numerous activities as the pressure on time and resources mounts.

While the approach was originally designed for large private developers in the UK and the US, it is equally applicable in the public sector. The balance of effort devoted to each of the steps can be adjusted to reflect the concerns of the development organization. A public authority, for example, might wish to spend more time on defining the social and economic aspects of the development concept, and less on the market-oriented steps of developing negotiating guidelines.

Evaluating development potential

Since all community development projects take place in an economic, political, physical and social context, the first step is to establish the objective factors that create the 'development environment'—e.g., site capacity, demand for and constraints on local growth, construction capacity in the area or region.

These conditions not only provide the context for development planning, but largely determine the manner in which the strategy, development concept and building activities are executed. Developing a new community in suburban Chicago obviously differs from undertaking the same type of project in an economically depressed rural area, in a fast-growing region, or in the inner city. Since the composition of people, houses, jobs and services in the project may vary substantially according to the assumptions employed in planning, the development environment demands continual assessment of the opportunities and limitations on action to determine whether goals are realistic and how they can best be achieved.

Rigorous selectivity is the key to assembling, quickly and economically, the information that decision-makers need to sharpen their intuitive judgements about a proposed site or opportunity area. There is no lack of data in today's development enterprise—but they are too often geared to the needs of the specialist rather than the decision-maker. Masses of irrelevant facts and figures that merely obscure the real issues can be accumulated by planners and research departments at great expense of time and money. Analyses of critical factors such as local needs, market shares and price premiums need to be updated and reviewed systematically with each change in plans or external events. Underlying assumptions must be made explicit. And all the key variables (Fig. 5.3) for each situation must be fully identified at the

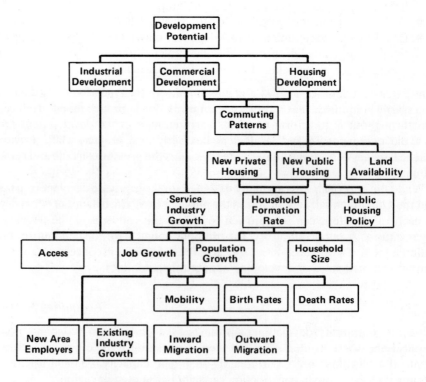

Figure 5.3 Evaluating development potential

start if a sound assessment is to be made. This does not require extensive new research on each variable where good judgement has been honed by experience. But it does mean a comprehensive, highly-disciplined review, recognizing the variables and the links between them.

In sum, information is needed that will help to: (1) judge the relative attractiveness of potential target areas; (2) identify the critical conditions and risks of a specific site within an attractive market area; and (3) establish criteria to guide site selection and project planning. For the purpose of strategic choice and major commitments, this information can almost always be gathered without inordinate effort or expense.

Area data provide a broad overview of the development forces and opportunities in the area and industry, and published sources usually suffice. Four types should provide the coverage required in most cases without excessive detail: (1) general economic conditions—e.g., household size and growth—to give an indication of the economic strengths and weaknesses of an area in relation to national trends and other areas; (2) market characteristics—e.g., population and employment—to provide an overall picture of demand levels and patterns: (3) product characteristics—e.g., house type and size, commercial features, amenities and community facilities—in recently developed projects throughout the area; and (4) political and environmental factors—e.g., building, zoning and pollution control regulations—that may impose development constraints.

For *site-specific information* on market, product and competitive conditions, prices, construction costs, and physical characteristics such as soil conditions, road availability, natural amenities, and drainage requirements, data can be gathered from local sources such as banks, civil engineers, newspapers, real estate agents—and, of course, observations from site visits. Whereas the more general background data on the area can mostly be obtained from published surveys, the planning team will have to dig a little to obtain the site-specific data and interpret their meaning for a prospective development. For example, knowledge of the local political climate, including the managerial competence of local government and its attitude towards planning and zoning applications, will require local interviews. It is often astonishing how much highly relevant information can be drawn from public records and local experts who know the area—yet how often these basic sources are overlooked because they are not so easily found or documented as are research reports and census returns.

Preliminary conclusions from the project feasibility analysis should be summarized for easy, more substantive review, as in the project summary illustrated in Fig. 5.4.

Planning guidelines are the final essential element of information needed to focus later efforts. In practice they are rarely defined in explicit terms, as planners are prone to forget that developer and investor aspirations, criteria and resources have as much impact on project feasibility as have the 'objective' opportunities and constraints identified in land use, market and project data. When these are not identified clearly at the start, disputes between the developer and technical staff (architects, market analysts, etc.), and haphazard control over the development process inevitably result.

Thus, criteria for evaluating project plans should be laid down at the outset, defining the limits within which the development team operates and giving a broad indication of both goals and aspirations. *Financial criteria* set the financial goals against which the returns on the project may be measured—e.g., 'Peak debt to be no

109

SMITHTOWN SITE – 300 ACRES

Economic Conditions

1. Growth: average - 325,000 residents over 30 years; 50% less than Phoenix, Tucson (Chart 1)

2. Mobility: below average at 50.7% (Chart 2)

3. Employment growth: high - about 12,500 jobs per year (Chart 3); low unemployment - 1.5-2.1% 1970-74; 8% 1975

Market and Competition

1. Residential income: second largest of target markets (Chart 12), 43% growth; 2% fewer affluent households, 3% more lower-middle income households (Chart 17)

2. Large-scale developments: none in 30 minutes' travel radius of site

3. Projects: prices typically above first-home community experience, but amenities are higher - especially technical innovations, electronic security, trash compactors, etc.; unit volumes total about 18,000 units per year, mostly in the $60,000-80,000 range

Product Characteristics

1. Developable land: 220 acres, limited by 100-year flood plain (Map 2), high slopes above river (Map 3)

2. Salable land: 175 acres, marsh lots on southeast of site near river (Map 2)

3. Natural amenities: tree cover, old stone millhouse, natural basin could be 25- to 30-acre lake (Map 4)

4. Ecologically sensitive areas: marshes, old Indian burial ground (Map 5)

5. Sewer: sufficient for 20 years' growth (Chart 21); development will require pumped sewerage for river frontage lots (about $375,000 required) (Overlay 2)

Political and Environmental Factors

1. Development situation by county: city center 95% complete; rebuilding of inner areas encouraged; rebirth of older district as young family area; Jones County imposed moratorium on multi-family development; 60% complete; dependent on city for water and sewer; Anderson County seeks large-scale development to enhance employment and revenue base; own water and sewer capability

2. Zoning background: agricultural, surrounding residential area 1.5/acre; PUDs refused zoning on tax grounds

3. Local government resources: strong chief executive who works closely with three of the five supervisors; staff limited in ecological, recreational planning and administration

Figure 5.4   Illustrative project summary

more than three times revenues.' *Marketing criteria* specify the standards to which the project will be held in relation to others and to the image it wishes to project—for example, 'No projects to be undertaken below the $10,000 market.' *Political and environmental criteria* are concerned with minimizing difficulties by maintaining the developer's government and community relationships. To this end the developer might decide that, for example, projects should make a significant contribution to the local employment base, or that the new project's burden should not exceed five per cent of the local property tax base. Finally, *physical criteria* are concerned with minimizing construction difficulties and creating the greatest possible value from the land available—e.g., 'Maximum separation of industrial and residential facilities.' Features such as layouts, facilities and equipment should be reviewed for possible adoption in the proposed project based on successful application elsewhere. These criteria will, of course, change as the developer's goals change. A decision to diversify into the economy housing market, for example, would mean modifying the marketing criteria.

In comparing the attractiveness of alternative development opportunities, the developer needs a consistent set of standards against which to evaluate them. Thus, besides defining explicit evaluation criteria, he should spell out his key working assumptions. Where variables are market-related or project-related, it is possible to eliminate much uncertainty by collecting and analysing data and projecting trends. But many variables will depend on unpredictable future conditions, and on these issues the developer must ensure that consistent assumptions are applied in project evaluation. These assumptions are primarily financial—including, for example, forecasts of inflation, interest rates and building costs for several years, availability of capital, levels of contribution to corporate overhead, and tax rates. Again, these assumptions will need to be reviewed annually and updated to take account of events in the preceding year—e.g., rising interest rates or a change in the amount of overhead to be allocated.

Defining a project concept

Equipped with concise and relevant information on the location and scale of the development opportunity, the developer can begin to link two elements: the *project concept*, which is a description of the eventual community to be created in terms of the target client groups and the products and services to meet their needs; and the *project scenario*, which specifies the phasing of construction, financing, services and participants' involvement. These help to ensure that all significant determinants of project results are defined and quantified as far as possible prior to commitment.

Much project planning is still done 'by the book', with attempts to state objectives before defining alternative strategies and operational plans. Because developers find it hard to think in abstract terms about their objectives, this process is often abortive. It is both easier and more effective to begin with a realistic course of action—or project concept—and force to the surface the specific objectives, criteria and policy issues it raises.

111

It is also common practice in conventional planning to allow the shape of a project to be determined by a fixed view of the needs and opportunities to be met. Partly by tradition and partly through oversight, the task of concept definition is typically left to the architect, site planner and engineer, who often lack the perspective to give proper weight to issues such as user acceptance even when these are well defined. Moreover, the full realization of social and economic costs and benefits depends entirely on the structure of the concept.

In reality, of course, there is usually a wide range of development options, but the extent to which these can be explored in detail depends on the time available and the analytic capacity of the development enterprise. Since it is important that at least several alternative concepts be considered, these should be concisely defined so as not to overwhelm the project team with unnecessary detail. For instance, alternative population profiles can be sketched using a few indicators, such as age, occupation and income groupings, family size and social characteristics. Changes to concepts can then be made easily and alternatives documented simply, without the time and expense needed to update masses of figures. As concepts are built up, descriptions should also be developed of the likely community structure arising from each. Such a description should indicate initial site layouts and distribution of housing and services, and ties with local, area and regional institutions, community groups and legislative bodies, to test the underlying assumptions about how these linkages will work in practice.

The concept ultimately selected for development must meet two essential requirements. First, it must be consistent with the fundamental goals of the major participants. While not fully articulated, nor matching one another precisely, there must be a broad measure of agreement to permit development to proceed. Second, it must be firmly based on the economic, social and physical environment of the project—i.e., the constraints and opportunities that it offers. The physical environment in which development will take place is obviously a key determinant of any project concept. However, the general economic and market conditions, and the opportunities for creating a desirable community structure and supporting institutions, are equally important and must be clearly identified, so that the wide-ranging, often lofty, goals for development can be grounded in specific actions.

Preparing the concept and scenario forces the development team to answer the questions, 'Why are we undertaking this project at this time?' and 'What will the resident, shopper, employee, other users and participants really value in this project?' This in turn will oblige them to re-examine the strengths, weaknesses and risks of the concept itself. Because the choice of a concept and scenario also determines the level of commitment required, as well as thousands of detailed activities in the development process, the steps in concept definition and selection are worth discussing in some detail.

Outlining a base case. The base case describes the project concept in broad terms, with preliminary definitions of the markets, products, phasing and roles of the developer. This brief but comprehensive definition of project characteristics and staging simplifies the planning process by acting as a focus for the detailed product/market analyses to come, identifying the most important opportunities and highlighting the issues that will make or break the project before any commitments have been made.

This planning task demands an open-minded approach, free of the bias of any one professional discipline or area of analysis—e.g., finance, marketing or land use—to make sure that all possible alternative uses for the site are identified. Brainstorming sessions with executives, members of the project team, and outsiders with relevant experience are a good way to identify promising development alternatives. The group may be able to suggest desirable modifications to existing products, and identify other opportunities by interpreting, in the light of their own experience, the data on needs, products and successful approaches developed in the first step (for example, segments of the market that are expanding rapidly, such as retired households, or products for which demand may be growing, such as town houses). Project data may suggest that certain facilities are particularly attractive in the area in question—e.g., a regional shopping centre, industrial research park or leisure complex. Corporate data will highlight successful previous approaches that the developer may wish to apply again.

In describing each alternative it is particularly important to make each element of the outline base case consistent with the others. For example, depending on the markets identified, there may be significant variations in the economic base; substantial on-site employment and a high proportion of upper-income housing are unlikely to be a viable combination. Similarly, appropriate community programs will vary; a community with a young family age profile will require up to twice as many schools as a community with an average age profile, and so on.

To ensure that project concepts will be realistic, it is important to establish the likely outer limits of feasibility for the key project variables. These variables will include: (1) *total project size*, determined by site capacity and developer resources; (2) *market absorption*, determined by the size and nature of residential, commercial and industrial markets; (3) *population profile*, determined by the above and relevant public policies governing mobility; (4) *development pace*, determined by regional construction resources and developer capabilities.

To establish the limits of feasibility in each case, historical precedents, current comparable projects, and the previous analysis of the opportunities and constraints of the project environment will all be used. Figure 5.5 illustrates how practical limits can be defined from relevant knowledge and experience in the case of two variables, population profile and development pace. The shaded areas indicate 'non-feasible' conditions, which should be avoided in the further definition of project concepts.

Choosing the base case from among these alternatives is a matter of applying (1) the development criteria—e.g., fit with local market opportunities and constraints, such as zoning or capitalizing on existing natural amenities; and (2) the corporate criteria, against which the attractiveness of the project to the developer can be measured—e.g., potential for creating development value, use of management strengths, consistency with desired image, compatibility with long-term corporate planning horizon.

Specifying markets. To compare the alternative concepts that will be built around the base case, it is important to make development markets consistent with

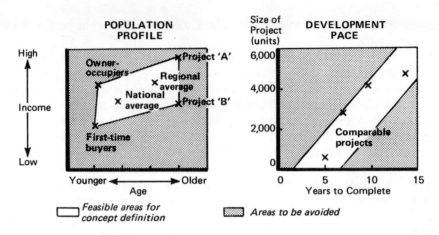

Figure 5.5 Establishing likely limits of feasibility

development products. For example, an issue of socioeconomic structure could not be determined without understanding the people, employment, housing and community service implications of alternative concepts; likewise, an issue of market potential for the project would need to incorporate all four elements in the analysis.

There is no single correct analytical sequence for defining project concepts, but it is usually easiest first to segment the two market elements—people and economic base—and then to define products—housing and community facilities. However, a private developer may find it easier to establish the housing mix first, based on his assumptions about the market, and then to determine the associated population and market characteristics implied by that product mix.

A productive way of determining *key market segments* is, again, through collective brainstorming backed by the knowledge gained from developing goals and analysing the environment. The precise approach will depend on who is initiating the project. The private developer is likely to model concepts on major market segments, with one primary group—such as commuters or first-time buyers—underlying each case. A public authority's approach is more likely to be governed by public policy statements or current planning theories of an 'ideal' social mix.

The target markets outlined in the base case should be defined in terms of their projected ultimate size, expected patterns of growth over the project life and expected key project needs. This definition will include the major demographic characteristics of the project—age, income, occupation, family size and the like—and an economic base that is consistent with the expected population, drawing on employment data to derive the most likely employment structure and patterns of shopping expenditure. The base-case assumptions on income growth and distribution, and on the trends in the size of target groups, should be compared with forecast regional and national trends over the project's life cycle.

114

To describe the economic base, the size of employment that would be required for the base-case population is estimated. Area and industry data will provide information on the typical area employment patterns and on trends as the project develops. The primary employment structure of industrial and commercial provision can be derived from the estimated share of projected employment growth in the area. From the total site population, the likely distribution of secondary employment in shopping and services can be derived.

Target groups summarize the characteristics of the alternative market segments, and therefore are the basis for deriving the products and services for each concept. The five target groups in Fig. 5.6 are a combination of age and income groupings for the head of each household. Concept 1 is a predominantly young, affluent, professional community. Concept 2 is also dominated by young families, but with a broader income and occupational spread. The Concept 3 community is more mixed in terms of age, income and occupation.

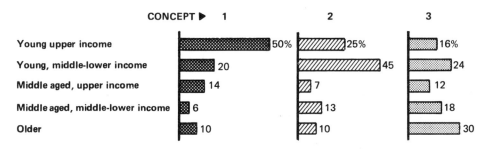

Figure 5.6 Formulating population 'target groups'

The basic analysis of alternative markets should be extended by identifying the important social and 'life style' characteristics of each. These will tie demographic characteristic to market segments. For example, in Fig. 5.7, Concept 2 contains a

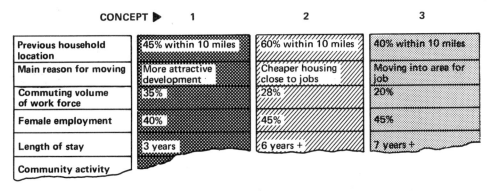

Figure 5.7 Identifying social 'life style' characteristics

high proportion of prospective residents not wishing to change jobs, while Concept 3 contains a high proportion of 'job seekers', hence a low proportion of households moving less than 10 miles.

Identifying required development products and services. The base-case population, with its consistent statement of the prospective economic base, represents needs and potential demands for housing (house types, sizes, etc.), community services (shopping, education, etc.), and industrial and commercial provision.

Defining housing products means first identifying family size and number of house units required for the projected population, and then estimating their ability to pay—i.e., income and mortgage capacity. For the rented sector, 'affordability' can be estimated from data on the percentage of income spent on rent in each income group; for owner occupiers, mortgage payments can be estimated as a percentage of income, and down payments as a percentage of price within each income group. In each case these figures should be projected over the life of the project.

A product range can then be drawn up to meet the projected need/price distribution, adjusted to reflect other important population characteristics such as age and stage in the family cycle. A check should be made here to ensure that the proposed product mix is roughly in line with that of similar developments elsewhere. Finally, these steps can be summarized in a housing product specification (Fig. 5.8).

| House Type | Total Units (000) | Distribution | | | Density (per acre) | Land Take (acres) |
| | | Price | | Phasing | | |
		%	($000)			
Owned						
- Single family (parcels)	1.0	45%	$10—15	80% in first 5 years	0.75	1,330 in first 5 years
		35	15—30			
		20	30—55			
- Cluster	0.5		45—65 evenly spread over price range	Evenly spread over 10-year project life	2.5	200, 20/year
- Patio	0.5	80	50—60	Evenly spread over 10-year project life	3.5	143, 14/year
		20	40—50			
- Villa	1.0	40	50—60	Evenly spread over 10-year project life	6.0	167, 17/year
		60	35—50			
- Modular	0.8		25—40 evenly spread over price range	80% in last 5 years, to match employment growth	4.5	167, 80% in last 5 years
- Other	—					
Rented	1.1	30	250+/month	Evenly spread over first 7 years of project life	10.0	120, 17/year over first 7 years
		60	175—250/ month			
		10	150—175/ month			

Figure 5.8 Housing product specification

Age and social characteristics have a significant effect on demand for community services and facilities as well as for housing. A young professional community, for example, will obviously make greater use of leisure facilities than an older, more socially mixed development. But the implications of these differences often go unrecognized until after commitments have been made. For example, of the concepts summarized in Figs. 5.6 and 5.7, Concept 1 would require 80 per cent more acreage and 15 per cent higher capital costs for leisure facilities than Concept 3. Conversely, Concept 1 would require 90 per cent less acreage and 60 per cent lower capital costs for education facilities than Concept 3. Estimates should be made at least of the need for the main capital-intensive community services (health, transportation, education and recreation) for the projected population. As some provision for each service will almost certainly be available locally, it is the gap between these facilities and the estimated demand that must be expressed in terms of initial land and capital requirements.

Finally, industrial and commercial requirements for the site should be determined by translating the projected employment structure into land-use requirements on the basis of local or regional norms—e.g., office floor-to-ground area ratios, manufacturing employees per acre. Shopping requirements can be similarly translated into sales-volume projections and hence into outline shopping space requirements.

The specification of target markets and required products completes the development concept. The project scenario consists of the implementation schedule and definition of developer roles.

Outlining the implementation schedule. If the base case is to be useful for evaluation (particularly for estimating cash flows), it must incorporate an implementation schedule that establishes the order and content of development. Such a schedule should be prepared in some detail for the first two to three years of the project, for which requirements can be foreseen with some precision, but need only be schematic thereafter since conditions governing staging and pace are highly uncertain until on-site works are actually under way.

Construction will need to be phased to achieve the maximum absorption rate—e.g., by creating a central core to the community, with a reasonable level of services and amenities, at an early stage of the project life cycle, so that prospective residents will not be too discouraged by a construction-camp atmosphere.

Several constraints must also be accommodated, however. The developer's financial objectives will determine the amount of construction that can be undertaken in any year, imposing limits on, for example, the amount of work in progress—e.g., unsold land or products— that can be borne at any one time. Physical development constraints—e.g., circulation patterns and the juxtaposition of land uses—will to a large extent determine the most logical schedule for construction, and the timing of development will also be constrained by the level and type of infrastructure and community programs that are in place at the beginning of the project.

The implementation schedule should therefore indicate the probable absorption rates for each product (based on estimates of growth of the market); the land required for development, in the form of a phased land absorption plan; the phasing of basic infrastructure—highways, sewerage, drainage, landscaping, etc.—required to meet these absorption rates; and the phasing of community facilities and services.

Defining contributions. The developer's ability to keep his project commitments to a minimum will depend significantly on the degree to which other agents can be induced to share the development burden. Thus, to round off the project scenario, the roles and contributions of each of the key participants in development should be determined.

Though often overlooked, there are many roles in any aspect of a project that the developer can play, and each entails a different level and type of contribution. As a *provider,* he is directly responsible for providing services or facilities, such as on-site roads. As a *social entrepreneur,* he may create a program for supplying a service, such as a community-run car-pooling system, without being involved in ongoing management. As an *advocate,* he persuades the usual providers of services to accommodate the project's needs on site—for example, putting to the local government the case for the timely provision of schools. Finally, as a *broker,* he acts as a middleman in collecting or distributing services—for example, selling building lots and putting purchasers in touch with a range of builders.

The choice of roles for each participant and for different aspects of the project will depend on the developer's interests, his financial and management resources, and the local capabilities of all the possible participants. For example, the local government would usually be the main provider of schools, and capable local builders would normally be relied on for the majority of housing.

| | | PARTICIPANTS | | | | |
PRODUCTS/PROGRAMS	TOTAL REQUIRED	Developer	Local Government	Builders	Community Association	Other Private Organizations
Housing	(units)					
Upper income	500	100		400		
Middle income	1,500	250		1,250		
Lower income	500		200	300		
Industrial/Commercial Space	(ф)					
Industry	1.5 million	350,000		1,150,000		
Warehousing	1.0 million	—		1 million		
Offices	400,000	200,000				
Shops	350,000	50,000				
Community Programs						
Leisure	27 holes golf 3 pools	18 holes 1 pool	1 pool		1 pool, 9 golf	
Education	300 daycare 400 primary 150 adult	100	450			200

Figure 5.9 Summary of contributions

Finally, a summary of contributions should be drawn up (Fig. 5.9), showing the developer's commitment in the provision of different products, and the contribution that other organizations are expected to make.

The project concept, now complete, consists of quantified working hypotheses that appear to offer the greatest development potential. But these are still largely independent assumptions that have not yet been shown to work well together. To finalize the concept, therefore, its elements must be tested against more stringent criteria. For example, marketing criteria can be related more specifically to the competitive situation in the area and to the facilities and programs that will be provided for the target market. Thus, the broad criterion 'Projects must preserve the developer's quality image' can be extended to 'Housing must be in all respects superior to local products in the same price range'. Product criteria, such as 'Recreation facilities must be within residents' income capability', can be refined in the light of the developer's knowledge of the target market's resources—e.g., 'Residents Community Association fee must be held below $25 per month'.

Evaluating the concept against such criteria will show up many issues that will need to be resolved if the project is to succeed. Perplexing problems will be found, since evaluation must involve estimates of the financial equivalent of as many of the concept assumptions as possible—e.g., deriving sales revenues from estimates of market share based on product competitiveness, and forecasting the cash flows that are likely to result. Although it is now common to use highly complex models requiring hundreds of inputs, a simpler cash flow planning tool with up to 30 input lines will probably be adequate for this purpose (Fig. 5.10), and may usually be

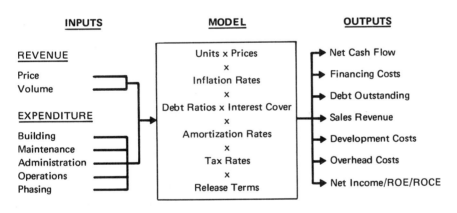

Figure 5.10 Simplified cash flow model

derived from existing models with only minor adaptation. In addition, the team should analyse those elements of the concept that have no direct financial equivalent, but that could threaten project feasibility—for example, environmental concerns that could seriously delay zoning approval. Evaluation of the most important of these issues will suggest further refinements, until the concept meets most of the criteria set for the project at the outset of the planning process.

Developing a commitment plan

At this point, the assumptions underpinning the project concept are still single-point estimates of costs, prices, timing and space allocation. Experience suggests, however, that original projections may prove to be far from the mark in four respects. Market shares may vary considerably from those expected because of the highly judgemental process of assessing competitive attractiveness, and developers' usual tendencies to over-optimism. The timing of key external events—e.g., delays in roads, sewage treatment or zoning approval—can radically alter the basic economics and phasing of the concept. Prices may be different from those anticipated, especially if they have to be reduced to counteract falling market shares. And the actual costs of financing and construction can affect expected performance, particularly because of the long lead times, difficulty of anticipating local variations, and random delays that may occur as a result of technical difficulties or labour problems. Such variations may call for significant changes in the project concept or even wreck its feasibility. So they must be carefully evaluated, since the commitments, once made, will be largely irrevocable.

To minimize these risks and preserve future flexibility, the commitment plan maps out all forms of commitment to the project—financial, physical, managerial, political—so that the maximum number of options is kept open for as long as possible during the development process. By dividing the project life cycle into phases, and specifying contingency plans for the key uncertainties of each phase, the management of the development enterprise is compelled to take the effects of uncertainty explicitly into account. Thus, the plan format itself, as well as the analyses behind it, are aids both to the decision-maker and to outside bodies in deciding on potential projects and evaluating existing ones.

The phasing of a development is, of itself, nothing new. But conventional project plans are usually phased either for the efficient programming of construction, approvals and operations, or for aesthetic and market acceptance, rather than with an eye to the project's risk profile. Similarly, although risk analysis has been refined to a considerable degree through industrial applications,[1] it is largely unknown as a practical working tool in development enterprises.

A commitment plan, on the other hand, highlights the contingencies that should be evaluated prior to making new or expanded commitments, and the options that may be pursued if expectations do not materialize. In place of single-value assumptions, the range of each possible variation is estimated. The impact of these variations on expected results is assessed so that terms can be arranged in full knowledge of both the upside potential and the downside risk. And the concept and implementation scenario can be revised to allow scope both for exploiting success if it occurs, and for surviving a crisis if it does not. There are two main phases in commitment planning: (1) pinpointing the key uncertainties that would most seriously affect project feasibility and investment performance; and (2) structuring the plan in light of the upside and downside potential to provide a framework for action.

Pinpointing key uncertainties. Possible variations in assumptions can, of course, affect both the basic feasibility of the project concept (site characteristics, street locations, sewer availability) and its relative investment performance (unit volumes, prices and costs). Feasibility assumptions may require some dramatic change in the project concept or the terms of the deal to ensure survival, and should be incorporated into the negotiation process. Performance assumptions are more likely to alter the details of implementation phasing and the amount and structure of early financing. Their impact can be drastic: if the residential sales in our illustrative project hit only 80 per cent of their target in Year 1, peak debt would exceed the planned limit by $6 million and wipe out the next three years' cash flow.

Experience and seasoned judgement will help to identify the most volatile revenue, cost and timing elements. But careful analysis is essential to determine which will have the greatest financial, marketing and political impact. The range of variation can be established in several ways—past experience, the extremes suggested by informed analysts, instinctive estimates. Estimates of the best and worst cases can be made—for example, assuming immediate funding and minimum design lead times versus a normal planning period with as much as a 100 per cent allowance for standard delays. Or the degree of optimism built into the concept can be estimated, for example, by setting the area norm of prices and volumes as the lower limit, and assessing the market premium that would be placed on the project as the upper limit.

The important task throughout is to concentrate on those few situations where a major change would seriously affect the project's feasibility or investment attractiveness. Figure 5.11 illustrates how key uncertainties can be pinpointed—in this case,

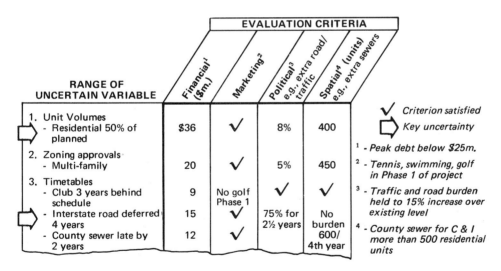

Figure 5.11 Pinpointing key uncertainties

they are most likely to affect cash flows (a high peak debt) and basic feasibility (inadequate access, heavy traffic burden).

Structuring the commitment plan. Having identified the few key uncertainties, the developer must decide how to minimize their impact on overall results. While the

121

122

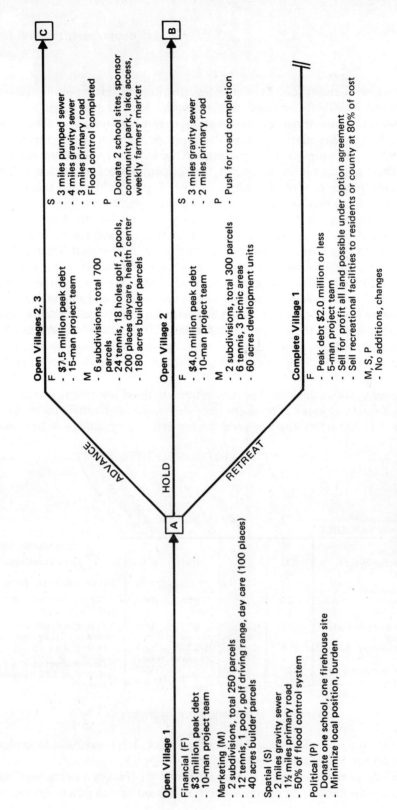

Figure 5.12 Illustrative entry strategy

Open Village 1

Financial (F)
- $3 million peak debt
- 10-man project team

Marketing (M)
- 2 subdivisions, total 250 parcels
- 12 tennis, 1 pool, golf driving range, day care (100 places)
- 40 acres builder parcels

Spatial (S)
- 2 miles gravity sewer
- 1½ miles primary road
- 50% of flood control system

Political (P)
- Donate one school, one firehouse site
- Minimize local position, burden

ADVANCE

HOLD

RETREAT

A

B

C

Open Villages 2, 3

F
- $7.5 million peak debt
- 15-man project team

M
- 6 subdivisions, total 700 parcels
- 24 tennis, 18 holes golf, 2 pools, 200 places daycare, health center
- 180 acres builder parcels

S
- 3 miles pumped sewer
- 4 miles gravity sewer
- 3 miles primary road
- Flood control completed

P
- Donate 2 school sites, sponsor community park, lake access, weekly farmers' market

Open Village 2

F
- $4.0 million peak debt
- 10-man project team

M
- 2 subdivisions, total 300 parcels
- 6 tennis, 3 picnic areas
- 60 acres development units

S
- 3 miles gravity sewer
- 2 miles primary road

P
- Push for road completion

Complete Village 1

F
- Peak debt $2.0 million or less
- 5-man project team
- Sell for profit all land possible under option agreement
- Sell recreational facilities to residents or county at 80% of cost

M, S, P
- No additions, changes

variety of possible approaches is unlimited, one practical step is to identify several main strategies for each opportunity—for example:

- *Advance*—the 'core' strategy that will achieve the results expected from the project concept if all goes according to plan.
- *Hold*—a 'wait and see' approach where neither advance nor retreat is possible, or sensible, in view of progress already achieved and commitments made but not yet implemented.
- *Retreat*—where no satisfactory holding strategy can be found to weather the storm, or the original prospects for success have simply withered away.

The developer will usually pursue an 'advance' strategy which represents a commitment great enough to ensure market acceptance but sparing enough not to sink the project under its financing and overhead costs should market expectations not be met, particularly in the project's early life. If unforeseen opportunities emerge, of course, the developer wants to be well positioned to exploit them. Hence, the advance strategy must be structured in specific building blocks, each planned to complement and strengthen the overall strategic position. The holding strategy allows a 'breathing spell' for careful scrutiny of both downside risks and upside potential before any further commitment is undertaken—under pressure, perhaps, from investment sources teetering on the brink of a decision to retreat.

Figure 5.12 illustrates how these strategies might be defined for the residential segment of a new community. Each is described on financial, market, spatial and political dimensions. Points A, B, and C are checkpoints at which current results are assessed against the conditions that have been defined for 'advancing', 'holding' or 'retreating'. These conditions for reviewing, and possibly changing, strategy will be dictated in most cases by the corporate criteria established in Step 1, which will indicate the levels at which results are unacceptable. During the early development period, the risk/return profile is low, and a single initial strategy is sufficient. But at point A, the options broaden and we can distinguish several clear routes forward, each representing a different level of commitment, risk and return. On route A–C, the developer exploits every opportunity with progressively larger commitments, high risk and return; on route A–B, he in effect buys time, and so on. In practice, of course, the profiles will be more complicated than this diagram since some plan elements are 'high-risk/low-return' and vice versa. Thus, it is wise to first consider each increment separately, and then overlay their risk/return profiles to draw out a composite picture.

Take a case where unit volumes have a major impact on peak debt. At unacceptable levels of debt, the project would be abandoned (retreat strategy). Where peak debt was 20–30 per cent above the desired level, attempts would be made to reduce investment by cutting amenities, overhead costs and work in process (hold strategy). Where it fell below the acceptable level, additional investment would be made to respond to the higher potential (advance strategy).

In addition to the conditions determining the strategy that should be followed, the elements of the next strategic phase should be sufficiently detailed to highlight new commitments that would be required and changes to the project concept that would

123

124

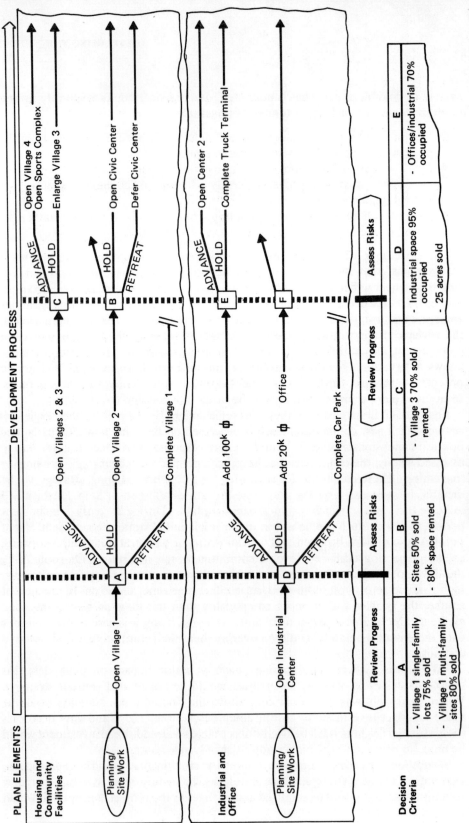

Figure 5.13 Commitment plan

need early attention. Returning to Fig. 5.12, it can be seen that these details are all framed in terms of specific actions and quantifiable project elements.

These strategic options represent the building blocks that form the basis for a commitment plan describing how the project will be developed over the critical early years. The essence of compiling the plan is to integrate the contingency strategies that have been built up on a piecemeal basis into a coherent structure around the phases of work that control and contain commitment, with checkpoints at the completion of each.

The format shown in Fig. 5.13 has proved a valuable aid in helping decision-makers to visualize these strategies. By displaying to development executives the alternative strategic directions open to them, it does for commitment planning what the land-use map has done for site planning, the architectural rendering for a proposed building structure, and the CPM network for construction scheduling.

But although the commitment plan may appear similar to techniques such as network analysis, PERT and CPM, there are two main differences of consequence to the manager. First, as a strategic planning tool, it is less cumbersome to use since it focuses on the few key performance indicators and 'make-or-break' activities of fundamental importance rather than the voluminous detail required for project scheduling and control. But even more basic, commitment planning is concerned with the performance results of community development and the risks entailed in pursuing them—not with analysis of physical actions and events. It highlights the sensitivity of each element in the plan that will change the risk, return and cash-flow profiles if events do not go according to plan. Thus, it provides a basis for setting overriding investment priorities, guiding as well as complementing other project management techniques.

Controlling implementation planning

While the commitment plan establishes a strategic 'road map' for development that minimizes the risk of overcommitment, it does not tell project staff how the concept should be implemented, nor afford the decision-maker a means of controlling the critical next steps. As mentioned above, the details of implementation are not our concern here because they are well known and in most cases expertly done. Rather, the key management task is keeping the complex, fast-moving process on track as detailed planning and site works begin. To this end, guidelines need to be established for negotiating the agreements that will enable the project to proceed, and for carrying out the detailed planning and design work. Negotiation guidelines force the decision maker and key project staff to prepare for that awful moment when the prospective lender refuses the proposed commitment or the planning authority mandates a change in concept. Implementation guidelines inform the numerous specialists involved of the specific criteria they must meet and the limits on their efforts.

To the manager who is familiar with the detailed preparations made by industrial enterprises in negotiating labour agreements or acquisitions, such steps will be obvious. But in development, *'adhockery'* is more the rule, and a structured, **125** well-documented approach the rare exception. Where these disciplines are imposed in the negotiation process, however, the developer is able to maintain a consistent position, take the initiative, enhance his credibility, and often, in the end, get better terms.

In implementation planning, the situation is similar. The intense activity undertaken by many specialists in a large project over a planning period of a year or more inevitably results in a good deal of wasted effort and cost: working drawings that have to be scrapped, unnecessary computer runs, even site works that lie fallow or have to be torn out. In scores of cases that I have seen, the basic flaw has been lack of clear guidance from the top and insufficient rigour in linking this detailed work to the basic project concept.

A comprehensive negotiation strategy should define the initial negotiating stance, fallback terms and ultimate limits on the key terms of the deal—e.g., site price ranges, inflation clauses, land take-down rates. A useful first step is to use the issues raised in defining the project concept to identify the constraints that could wreck negotiations. For example, analysis might show that a reduction in permitted zoning densities would sharply reduce the residual value of land and the rate at which it could be developed. Such constraints would then be converted to their equivalent in financial terms—i.e., maximum allowable values of prices and other requirements, and the contractual conditions that would be required to ensure protection. It is also important to document the evidence for these positions for later use as negotiations proceed.

Finally, it is well worth spending considerable time in rehearsing both the presentation and the debates that are likely to ensue when awkward questions are asked, so that complete consistency can be maintained. One highly effective developer I know spends a day in such 'challenge and review' rehearsals with his staff for every hour of planning negotiations—*after* all the homework is done.

Figure 5.14 illustrates a typical negotiation strategy defining the tactics used to reach the desired fallback position. Obviously, no amount of role-playing will identify all the possible paths that negotiations could take. But thorough preparation, coupled with selectivity in assembling the decision data, will permit a fast, flexible and confident response in the negotiations.

Once negotiations are complete, the details of the agreed project concept can be expressed as guidelines for implementation. Experience has shown that six types of guidelines will provide the means for effective control without excessive detail:

1. *A statement of the target markets,* including demographic description, numerical size and growth, main promotional appeals, and required product/service strategies.
2. *A product policy statement,* with details of residential products, features, prices and amenities; employment products—e.g., office, industrial and commercial sites or facilities—and their features, prices and amenities; and community programs, of both general and special appeal—e.g., health facilities, day care, club house, etc.

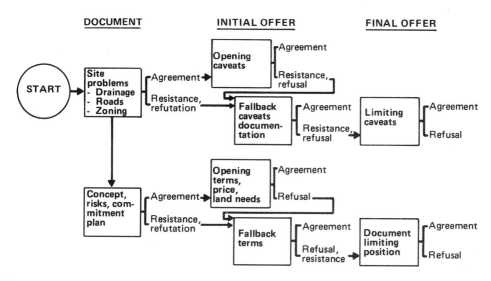

Figure 5.14 Illustrative negotiation process

3. *A layout plan,* including outline land-use, saleable land, circulation and infra-structure plans.
4. *A statement of participant contributions,* showing the role the developer will play in the provision of each product and program expected to be offered on site, and the level of participation of other agencies.
5. *The commitment plan,* in which money, manpower and land are committed to the project in stages, with contingency strategies defined to deal with the ranges of events that might be experienced. Each strategy should be described in terms of land take-up, infrastructure implementation, facilities, programs, developer role, financial demands, and conditions under which the strategy is to be used.
6. *A work program for implementation planning,* describing the tasks, end products, timing and responsibilities of all those involved—i.e., project and corporate personnel, outside consultants, and outside groups that must grant approvals or provide financing.

The preparation of implementation planning guidelines completes the strategic planning process. In contrast to the platoons of planners normally engaged on large development projects, only a small, high-level planning task force, supported by several experienced analysts, is needed to do the work. By using this approach, the development enterprise can avoid unmanageable and excessive purchase commitments, rapidly identify the most attractive development concept and scenario for a given site, structure purchase agreements to permit maximum future flexibility, and provide planners and project staff with a more useful data base and stronger direction as they embark on their complex, detailed and costly work.

127

Since strategic planning is focused on the basic commitment issues, it is naturally weighted toward the hard products of the built environment. As a result, early planning for the processes and services of community life is often neglected, at the expense of future residents and ultimate project success. Thus, we examine in chapter 6 the importance of and steps in planning for community management.

Reference

1. For the classic description of risk analysis techniques, see Hertz, D. B., 'Risk Analysis in Capital Investment', *Harvard Business Review*, January–February 1964.

Chapter 6.   Planning for community management

MAHLON APGAR, IV

Community management is the logical extension of community development. Because it begins last in time, and is not a 'step' but a continuing process, developers and planners commonly put off planning for it or, occasionally, assume it can be left to somebody else—that somehow the necessary mechanisms and processes will emerge.

Indeed, they most probably will. But if left to do so without benefit of planning, the resulting medley of programs and structures may submerge an array of major opportunities for innovation in meeting local needs—opportunities that neither the developer nor residents would wish to overlook. Yet a high proportion of projects signally fails to follow through on this final stage.

The impact and functions of community management

The economic and social viability of any project depends on an active community life, with residents taking full advantage of facilities and services. Every major aspect of planning and development is involved here. *Financial* viability is heavily influenced by the required front-end investment by the developer in community services and amenities. *Marketing* strategy depends significantly on services such as transportation and child care being staged at the right time and in the right way to support the overall community concept and attract the desired customer mix. In *spatial* terms, community services, including open-space amenities, represent as much as 50 per cent of total land use—and they must be carefully integrated with the core residential and economic activities. Finally, from a *political* standpoint, considerable leverage can be gained from a positive approach to services and amenities, while the penalty for neglecting them may be substantial.

Community services embrace a range of diverse activities that supplement a community's main function as a place for living and working. These include primary social services such as education and health care; technical services such as roads and sanitation; leisure programs for sport and entertainment; and services for groups with special needs, such as youth and the elderly. Since most people's largest single investment is their home, and its location a decision of paramount importance, it is essential that the community reflect the way its residents want to live. Whether it will do so depends to a great extent on the scope and quality of these community programs.

Moreover, as citizens as well as consumers, new community residents may acquire political experience that existing forms of local government have singularly failed to provide. The opportunity to share the challenge and responsibilities of deciding community matters that influence their daily lives is avidly sought, yet remains elusive, in the prevailing structure of government. For most people, local democracy is a vague concept rather than a working system in which they have a role. In England, only one-third of the electorate is actually represented; the majority don't even vote. And in America, a minuscule 0.1 per cent of the population serve as elected representatives. A complex community with heterogeneous, often conflicting, interests should present opportunities to broaden this narrow base. As the libertarian tradition is succeeded by a new communitarian ethic, self-fulfilment is occurring more through participation in group processes than through the exercise of pure individualism.[1] Community management, if properly planned, can help to make this happen.

In the wider public interest, the new community can serve as a laboratory where new ideas for improving community life and government processes can be tested more freely than in established cities and towns with their bureaucratic constraints. The way is open to experiment with different combinations of services and levels of administration, provision, policy-making and review. A comprehensive, central view, as distinguished from the partial view of special-purpose authorities, can be taken of community needs, opportunities and functions. To be sure, resident participation and open government have their risks. But if people are to gain the experience, mistakes will inevitably be made—and in a new community their adverse effects can be limited by a decentralized structure of decision-making and service delivery.

The interests of these 'stakeholders' in the development concept underlie the three functions of community management. The *civic* function of governance is the ultimate authority in managing conflict and directing local affairs. It is the only strictly public dimension, requiring a local government structure in the traditional sense, and the only one whose legitimacy is based solely on the consent of the governed. The *social* function is concerned both with the wide range of human needs to be served and with the interaction of people in meeting them. The processes and places through which they communicate and relate can be designed to relieve the ennui characteristic of much urban life while strengthening the community's social cohesion. The sense of identity and 'place' may even outweigh the value of social services on many an individual's satisfaction index. The *administrative* function exists to provide services and facilities, presumably based on the profile of civic and social needs.

It is the latter two functions that most facilitate community creation. They may be public or private, voluntary or commercial. Ideologies aside, there is no one 'right' institutional form for these functions, nor is there any reason to suppose that they should all be provided by a single institution. For the main concern of both developer and residents is whether the existing local authorities will deliver the services they need. Where they cannot, 'private' government can become an important force in new communities to supplement and stimulate public government. Precisely this has happened in America. In Britain and France, non-profit—but non-governmental—services have sprung up to meet a variety of needs. Even in the few cases where the existing local authorities could do the job, there will be numerous possibilities for improving public programs and monitoring their performance.

In formulating their strategies for community management, developers should recognize that efficiency is, in general, more important to residents than luxury. The developer cannot afford to waste money on gadgetry. Moreover, prospective residents are canny enough to know that both their original price or rental and future assessments will be inflated to cover the costs of any lush facilities they see. Most would vastly prefer adequate and attractive, but cost-effective, basic facilities, good after-sales service and a responsive system for problems and complaints.

The developer will be well advised, also, to maintain a low profile. The pervasive hand of the development enterprise is anathema in the new community setting. While the results of its efforts should be apparent, its influence should be as unobtrusive as possible—particularly in the delicate task of launching the community management structure in which its early dominance is inevitable and essential.

Finally, the prudent developer will keep his planning flexible. As in commitment planning (chapter 5), the community management structure should aim to keep tomorrow's options open. In a dynamic community, needs and institutions will evolve and change. Hence, the framework must be able to accommodate unforeseen problems requiring new programs, new leaders and different methods.

With all this in mind, let us examine four key steps in planning for community management: (1) establishing the likely demand for community services, (2) identifying opportunities for meeting this, (3) selecting initial programs for implementation, and (4) setting up the community management structure.

Estimating demand

If needs are to be met in an economical and politically feasible way, the developer must begin with an explicit *operative* definition. This means analysing the existing machinery for financing and delivering community services against a comprehensive profile of all community needs and services, however and by whomever provided, to identify weaknesses that call for correction. By assessing the problems with care, the developer can direct his effort and investment where it will do most good, while deferring action that does not meet the test of a rigorous cost-benefit trade-off.   **131**

As the main force behind the project, particularly in its early years, the developer must keep a firm grasp on community activities that affect the definition of the concept. Typically, the larger the project, the less homogeneous the social values and life styles of residents are likely to be—and, therefore, the wider ranging will be the requirement for community service support. The introduction of a substantial employment content into the project, for example, will have the effect of diversifying the on-site population base and creating a requirement for services, such as full-day pre-school child care, that may not be called for in the smaller or more specialized project. Moreover, service needs and demands vary substantially with the age, income and other social characteristics of the population. (Professional and managerial people, for example, spend twice as much time as blue-collar workers in active sports; the health-care needs of the very young and the very old substantially exceed those of the rest of the population.) Cumulative variations of this kind have a significant impact on costs, project commitments and management structures—and therefore on the viability of the project concept itself.

Beyond the inherent complexity of demand patterns, the nature of social change requires a tougher look at many key planning assumptions. Consider the types of evidence that have emerged in recent research:[2]

- Most residents care more about their own streets, and the areas immediately adjoining their homes, than about their 'neighbourhood' or 'community'—the usual planning areas. Their friends are scattered throughout the region, their contacts are mainly by telephone, and their shopping trips are increasingly to distant, larger centres. Beyond the street, most think of specific projects and facilities rather than areas.
- Most house buyers care less about services and amenities than about getting value for money and protecting their investment. What people think of most community facilities and services depends less on location than on quality, cost and the attitudes of suppliers; and their perceptions of the value of open space and recreational amenities vary sharply by income and race.
- Most people stubbornly persist in travelling by car, despite the planners.

While the implications of such basic demand patterns are clear, once identified, they do not emerge solely from historical census data.

The complexity of changing demands is matched by the variety of agencies involved in meeting them—not only the developer, but voluntary agencies, local *ad hoc* groups, private operators, local government, builders, community organizations and, of course, the residents themselves. Gaps in provision are therefore almost inevitable unless needs and demands are comprehensively identified. Special needs—e.g., for preventive mental health care or drug addiction clinics—can easily be shrugged off by conventional agencies as someone else's responsibility. Emerging trends, too, may be missed—e.g., short-term peaks in the school population generated by the intake characteristics of new residents. As initiator of the project, the development enterprise is better placed than any voluntary organization or public agency to identify these needs and make sure they are met by someone.

There are three main steps in estimating demand:

1. *Define programs.* The project concept described in chapter 5 will define the community profile, from which the structure of programs and services will naturally follow. Figure 6.1 illustrates a summary checklist that should be detailed to reflect both facility and service needs in each project. For example, leisure is subdivided first into types of recreation and entertainment, and then into various buildings, open spaces and activities. Pre-school education comprises several elements, including full-day care (nursery school, child-care centre), part-day care (child minding, special classes), and drop-in services (baby-sitting, play groups).

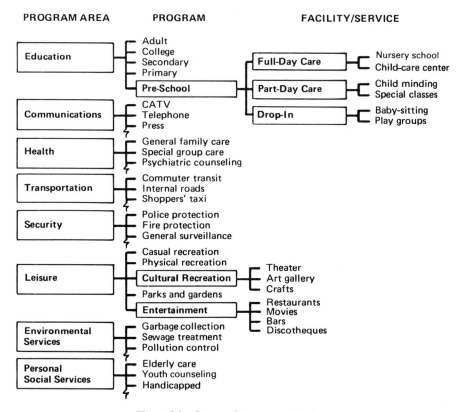

Figure 6.1 Community program structure

2. *Determine client/customer groups.* The structure and size of potential client groups for each program is determined next—e.g., for child care, the number of children in the $2\frac{1}{2}$–4 age group, and the number of working mothers involved.

3. *Adjust for local differences.* Conventional public program planning determines provision by applying prescribed or accepted standards or units of service—e.g., '6 acres of open space per 1,000 population' or '35 children per classroom'. This fails to take into account the requirements of the particular population. In reality, most

133

service demands vary directly with income, occupation, age and family size—e.g., adult education enrolments among clerical employees are three times those of professionals and managers.

As the pattern of needs changes over time, the demand for each service must be forecast over the life of the project: the mature new community will suffer a fall-off in primary school demand in its later years, while the secondary school population will greatly increase.

As we shall see in the next chapter, the implications in terms of capital costs for infrastructure, land and facilities, annual operating costs, and availability of the requisite specialists can be substantial. In project plans I have reviewed, the range of error has gone as high as $16 million in excessive costs and 100 wasted acres because the demand estimates were thus inflated. The political repercussions from such spendthrift planning can be awesome.

To adjust the demand function for differences in age, income, occupation, location and other characteristics, an 'activity budget' can be built up for each group in the future population, and demand for each activity estimated by multiplying the number of participants in each by the frequency of use. The capacity of facilities, measured in comparable units, can then be matched against demand. Daily, weekly and seasonal variations in activity, particularly activity peaks, also have to be allowed for. And differences in demand by men and women must be established.

The data required for the analysis can usually be drawn from various existing sources, including the census for basic demographic data, and studies by government and research institutions for data on major national and regional trends. Easily overlooked local sources—newspapers, banks, universities—can frequently provide invaluable insights on local variations. Although there are fairly extensive data in the fields of leisure, health care and general community provision, research in some areas is inadequate, and conventional standards may have to be substituted for individual service demand analyses. Demand estimates based on surveys also will reflect the experience of those interviewed, as well as the time and money they have available to take part in the activity. Moreover, demand can be influenced by quality of supply—e.g., by what people have been offered as well as by what they desire. These limitations will have to be allowed for when interpreting the usefulness of data.

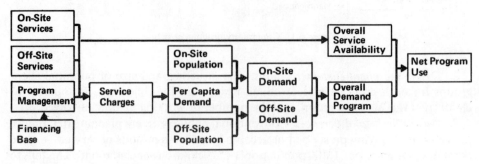

Figure 6.2 Variables affecting program demand

It will also be helpful to structure the demand variables to ensure that even the briefest evaluation is complete and consistent (Fig. 6.2) and to highlight any remaining uncertainties on levels of provision, delivery systems and means of local participation.

Identifying opportunities

Once needs and demands have been identified, specific approaches to meeting them can be developed. The emphasis here is on filling the major gaps in provision while stretching to the limit the resources available to the project, whatever their source. Not only will this tend to minimize the demands on developer and resident resources, but it is likely to result in better use of those facilities that are developed in the initial years when community program resources such as foundation funds are most stretched and to release additional new resources that would not normally become available without a positive initiative.

'Gap analysis' is helpful in setting priorities and targeting the actions of the community management effort. From the demand analysis described above, a level of provision is derived to meet each service need. The range and capacity of current and planned services—public, private and voluntary—should then be estimated to determine the met and the unmet demand (Fig. 6.3). This shows the program gap to be bridged, and usually fills the entire community program slate before any competitive or alternative programs are considered.

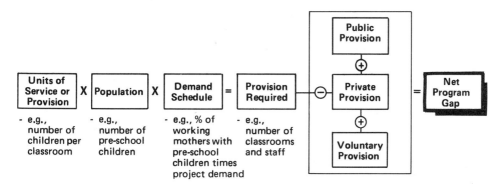

Figure 6.3 Analysis of program gap

The most important problems involved in estimating gaps in service provision arise from distortions in the demand/supply equation resulting from the dynamics of a population change. To meet the needs within likely cost constraints, innovative solutions are often required. Consider Fig. 6.4, which illustrates the likely education profile in a UK new community. The gap is the difference between projected family need and known education authority plans. Should it be entirely filled by new facilities, or by doubling up the old? Should the 'hump' between 1982 and 1992 be

135

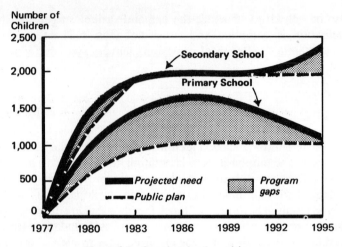

Figure 6.4 Gaps in school provision

met by permanent or temporary buildings? What impact will current teacher training cutbacks have on the supply of teachers during those high-demand years?

Beyond program provision itself, opportunities will abound for forging community commitment. Here the emphasis is not on facilities but on creating the institutions and programs that foster social interaction. When construction begins, the simple needs of newcomers are paramount: ensuring a positive welcome, launching and co-ordinating information sources on local services, providing introductions and guidance on shopping and transport and clubs. As development progresses, an ever-widening range of activities should come into play.

Social entrepreneurship

No single agency, and certainly not the development enterprise itself, should monopolize the task of community creation. Diverse populations and democratic politics require a highly pluralistic response. Rather than a monolithic, uniform structure of direct involvement in providing services, the developer can act as a social entrepreneur, identifying needs and opportunities, marshalling resources, encouraging other providers, and monitoring the results.

As *advocate*, he can ensure that community needs and demands are persuasively brought to the attention of the relevant public agencies, such as the School Board, and use various levers of influence with outside bodies who can encourage participation by their members in programs and services. As *broker*, he can act as intermediary in marshalling funds or skills from outside sources and providing staff assistance where appropriate. As *catalyst*, he can stimulate planning in collaboration with other agencies or local voluntary efforts—e.g., by setting up joint working groups—and take an even more active role, enlisting outside support and advice and providing 'seed' capital to launch new programs. In practice, of course, the developer

136

can confine himself merely to building, but whatever role the developer selects, attention to community needs is likely to suggest practical innovations in both services and working methods.

Where demand is not guaranteed, the developer can reduce his exposure to risk by subcontracting services to other agencies. On-site transportation, for example, can be chartered rather than large supplies of capital equipment purchased directly. The commitments can at least be staged to postpone the investment until absolutely necessary.

Figure 6.5 illustrates some of the many programs where social entrepreneurship can be effective. In the US, the main opportunities are basic services, such as health care and leisure, which are provided only sporadically by public authorities. Thus, several developers have negotiated arrangements with nearby hospitals to provide ambulatory and clinical care on site at no cost. And Columbia's famed community-wide health care program with the Johns Hopkins Medical Centre has been widely copied.

PROGRAM AREA	ROLE		
	Advocate	Catalyst	Broker
Education	Lobby county to improve quality of public schools	Initiate discussions with county for extension of dual use	Ensure coordination between child-care program and schools
Health	Liaise with health agency to position community in long-term hospital plans	Identify emerging health-care problems — e.g., drugs, alcoholism	Provide staff assistance to make grant application
Transportation	Monitor negotiations between city buses and county buses to ensure local service	Negotiate start-up service with bus lines Survey on-site transport-ation needs	Set up working group for planning with outside operator

Figure 6.5 Opportunities for social entrepreneurship

In both the US and the UK, discussions with local churches in this ecumenical age nearly always produce promising opportunities for sharing facilities and gearing religious and counselling services to the needs of various community groups. And even local education authorities are generally willing to make playing fields, gymnasiums, libraries, lecture rooms and the other expensive features of modern schools available for community use outside school hours.

The French *villes nouvelles* program has refined and broadened this concept to embrace many types of community affairs, from basic economic, political and cultural activities to voluntary groups to welcome newcomers and comfort the elderly. The principal aim has been to relieve the isolation and anonymity of urban life and to 'animate' the new community with programs and institutions that will help generate and develop social relations.[3]

Linkages

Fresh ideas for filling the gaps also emerge from analysis of linkages. When a new development is grafted on to an existing town—as in new-towns-in-town and many suburban satellite projects—numerous opportunities typically are presented for linking services for the new to the existing program structure of the old. For example, in one project to expand an existing small town of 10,000 by adding 20,000 new residents, analysis revealed that, in addition to the local authority, there were already some 120 local organizations providing 50-odd different services!

For most services, the developer will be well advised to spend some time and effort establishing a link rather than try to go it alone. Close integration between newcomers and existing residents is likelier to emerge from informal interplay among local organizations than from structured competition and formal negotiation of terms. This can also help to avert feelings of hostility between old and new residents, permitting a more constructive approach to community needs.

The forms these linkages could take may be suggested by surveying the local organization structure, program by program; identifying their coverage, strengths and limitations from informal local discussions; then evaluating the cost-benefit results to them and the new community of a partnership. Incentives (usually geared to their limitations) may be needed to encourage their participation. Figure 6.6

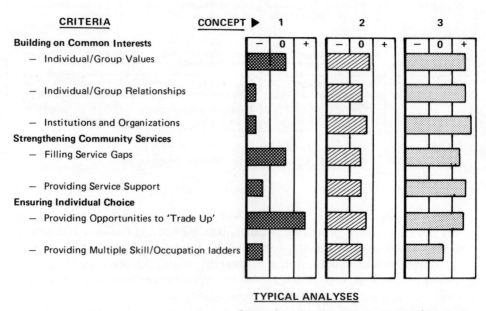

CRITERIA   CONCEPT ▶   1   2   3

Building on Common Interests
- Individual/Group Values
- Individual/Group Relationships
- Institutions and Organizations

Strengthening Community Services
- Filling Service Gaps
- Providing Service Support

Ensuring Individual Choice
- Providing Opportunities to 'Trade Up'
- Providing Multiple Skill/Occupation ladders

TYPICAL ANALYSES
- Occupation, class, income, age structure/distribution
- Length of Residence
- Structure of Official, Voluntary commercial service organizations
- Interlocking Memberships, Directorships

138   **Figure 6.6** Community linkage balance sheet

illustrates a community linkage balance sheet summarizing the opportunities for one project.

As well as organizational links between new and existing communities, possible links between users and facilities are worth looking at. Attention should be given at the earliest stages of program planning to exploiting opportunities for leveraging resources through multiple use of buildings and services. Schools, health clinics, clubs, churches and community centres are the most obvious places to begin, since each has a different single-minded client. To aid in the arduous process of negotiation and persuasion, the analysis must show not only the possibilities for multiple use, but the marginal costs of doing it and the potential means of financing and managing these extra requirements. For example, it is often possible to integrate commercial, profit-making activities with public non-profit ones serving the same general needs. A public library in one project was combined with a bookstore, record shop, discotheque and coffee shop around a central service core. Not only was the library considerably enlivened and its usage quadrupled, but the total complex was financed at a greatly reduced net cost to the local authority.

The design teams will also have to be brought in early to undertake additional technical work to link the programs. Chapter 14 discusses a practical approach to determining facility capacity for multiple uses and relating the design layout to program needs.

Programs focus on user needs within relatively narrow boundaries. It is equally important to look at the provision of all services from the user's viewpoint. For example, the mother with young children has a special set of shopping, educational, health-care and recreational requirements that might better be met at a single 'client-oriented' centre. Similarly, the basic information and service needs of older house-bound residents in a given area might be met by making use of the policeman, milkman, postman and community tradesmen who are their main outside contacts.

Consultation and testing

However imaginative the developer's staff, a variety of other sources can help to generate innovative approaches to meeting needs. Given some initial analysis and solid working hypotheses, brainstorming with experts is an easy way to identify the issues resulting from gap analyses and to identify program options suggested by experience elsewhere. Collaboration with the many public agencies will help the developer to understand the existing service structure and legislative framework, and to establish likely agency commitments, competing priorities and planning assumptions—all of which will affect what he can do. Enlightened officials may welcome the chance to bring together public and private resources, and co-operating with local decision-makers from the start will bring rich dividends in the long run.

Finally, a modest public participation effort before the development gets under way can produce results, if it is well prepared and the public is not led to expect too much. Treated as a form of market research, its object at this stage is solely to generate ideas—not to establish consensus or community approval for plans. Thus, individuals and relevant special interest groups can be invited, after appropriate briefing, to contribute their ideas. Open on-site meetings can also work if the developer is prepared to deal seriously with hostile responses. But the risks are high and the stage-management effort is only rarely worth it.

Selecting programs

Without selection of potential service areas, the sheer breadth of community needs and service possibilities can easily result in overspending budgets, overworking staff, and wrecking the developer's own credibility if he cannot keep his promises to residents. One useful set of screening criteria to establish these service priorities follows.

- *Community impact:* Will the service help to attract new residents, particularly during the critical early stages—e.g., golf or swimming? Is there likely to be significant resident need or demand during the first years of the project—e.g., pre-school child care? Can political or public relations leverage be obtained from giving the service early attention—e.g., health care?
- *Developer impact:* Is the developer likely to have to play an active role in providing the service, with a consequent need to anticipate well ahead of time what its contribution might be—e.g., transportation? Are extensive commitments involved that would require analysis in the context of overall project economics—e.g., security or cable telecommunications?
- *Service planning/delivery impact:* Are there significant benefits to be realized from imaginative, integrated program planning at this stage—for example, through multi-use facilities and cross-program synergy, such as health care/pre-school child care? Are there site-planning considerations that must be explored before the first phase land-use plan is finalized—e.g., physical recreation?

Once high-priority needs are identified, program strategies should be developed along the lines discussed in the previous chapter, ensuring rigorous analysis without excessive detail or premature decisions. A useful format for a community program strategy is illustrated in the appendix to this chapter. A range of possible programs to meet a need—in this case, for pre-school child care—is first defined, together with possible providers of the service. These options are evaluated against criteria similar to those above, but extended to include economic viability, risk, future flexibility and management burden. The chosen strategy is mapped out in detail for the initial development phase and schematically for the rest of the project cycle. Tasks to be completed before residents move in are highlighted.

Setting up the community management structure

140

Since the community management structure obviously must provide a wide choice of avenues for action to match the great diversity of residents' needs and interests,

	COMMUNITY ASSOCIATION	NEIGHBORHOOD ASSOCIATIONS	RESIDENTS' ADVISORY GROUPS	BUILDERS' GUILD	DEVELOPMENT ORGANIZATION
SCOPE	Community-wide	Neighborhood/subdivision	Housing cluster	Community-wide	Community-wide
ROLE	Provide/operate community service programs, facilities Stimulate provision by outside organizations Provide central maintenance to NAs Encourage formation of interest groups Carry out architectural review as developer agent Stimulate resident involvement in program planning and operation	Supplement CA services within neighborhood Decide maintenance policy Monitor CA maintenance contract Organize selected local activities - e.g., welcome teas	Advise CA on program priorities Consult NA on specific local issues Channel complaints to Builders' Guild Represent residents to developer - through residents' council Identify/advocate opportunities for resident participation	Coordinate builder activities to minimize community disruption Manage cooperative action where feasible - e.g., bulk purchase, storage Respond to resident complaints Review design/construction standards Coordinate/police sales programs to avoid complaints	Plan/organize start-up program - e.g., child care Organize community management structure Provide initial staff support to CA Operate selected services Plan/build start-up community facilities for CA Stimulate community "identity", action through marketing program
MEMBER-SHIP	Residential owners/tenants Commercial property owners/tenants Developer	Residential owners/tenants	Residential owners/tenants	Developer Builders Resident representative	
FINANCING	Annual property assessments Special assessments User charges Developer/external loans Foundation grants	Proportional block grant from CA User changes in selected activities	Grants Subscriptions	Developer assessment	
STAFFING	Community manager Professional program staff as required Developer staff support	CA staff support Paid resident volunteers	Volunteers CA staff support on ad hoc basis	Developer staff support	Project team

Figure 6.7 Community management structure

community organizations will do well to emulate the fine mesh of social institutions found in mature and well-established communities, rather than the monolithic structures that have characterized much new town planning.

The structure will need to be flexible to allow organic growth and response to new conditions. Since the ultimate range of services and facilities needed by residents cannot be anticipated at the outset, the developer should allow for the possibility of adding or removing programs, adjusting financial arrangements and changing organizations over the life of the project.

Other things being equal, services should be managed in the way that offers greatest value for money in delivery—e.g., through efficient use of scarce staff resources and facilities. However, the developer should retain the least control compatible with his own interests, and surrender control entirely to the community as early as possible; residents' interests in creating and maintaining value in the community will normally be identical with his own. He will thus escape the charge of paternalism, without risking political exposure or overcommitting his financial and managerial resources.

Although the structure of each community should be uniquely matched to its needs, five components typically will be required in some form. These are (1) a Community Association, to provide and operate services for community-wide benefit; (2) neighbourhood associations, to perform more restricted services (primarily maintenance and service delivery within groups of residential units) at a level closer to their users; (3) residents' advisory groups, to represent residents' views on community issues; (4) a builders' guild, to cope with residents' complaints and ensure better service during the massive construction process; and (5) the development enterprise itself. Figure 6.7 summarizes the roles of these bodies and the key relationships between them.

The Community Association

The Community Association (CA) is the centrepiece of community management. As the principal organization for supplementing conventional services provided by local government, it should manage and maintain common properties and services for the community, and sponsor and encourage a wide range of community activities.

Being close to the community and endowed with wide powers, the CA is better placed than any other agency to identify community needs and ensure that they are met. It should have scope to provide, either directly or indirectly, any services that the community may require in addition to those already provided by the local authority, commercial operators (including the developer) and voluntary agencies.

The CA's second purpose is to safeguard and enhance property values in the community by maintaining a high-quality environment. To this end it should maintain common properties deeded by the developer, and any other properties it acquires. Maintenance standards for each property will be specified by the developer as guidelines before the property is handed over. As an additional protection to ensure quality, the developer may reserve the right to delay conveying common

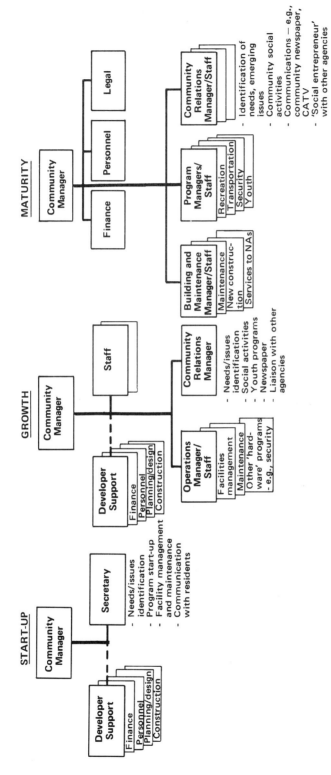

Figure 6.8 Evolution of the CA organization

START-UP

Community Manager

Secretary

Developer Support
- Finance
- Personnel
- Planning/design
- Construction

- Needs/issues identification
- Program start-up
- Facility management and maintenance
- Communication with residents

GROWTH

Community Manager

Staff

Developer Support
- Finance
- Personnel
- Planning/design
- Construction

Operations Manager/Staff
- Facilities management
- Maintenance
- Other 'hardware' programs – e.g., security

Community Relations Manager
- Needs/issues identification
- Social activities
- Youth programs
- Newspaper
- Liaison with other agencies

MATURITY

Community Manager

Finance | Personnel | Legal

Building and Maintenance Manager/Staff
- Maintenance
- New construction
- Services to NAs

Program Managers/Staff
- Recreation
- Transportation
- Security
- Youth

Community Relations Manager/Staff
- Identification of needs, emerging issues
- Community social activities
- Communications — e.g., community newspaper, CATV
- 'Social entrepreneur' with other agencies

143

property for up to, say, two years, even though the facility has been completed, if he is not yet satisfied that the CA can maintain the property to a high standard.

It is important for the CA to cover the whole area of the project. In Reston, the original structure was based on neighbourhood units, on the assumption that the only significant concern would be property maintenance; but emerging community-wide demands made the old structure inappropriate. As a result, a rather painful process of amalgamation had to be carried out in 1970.

A unified approach will be needed for managing services that will be used on a community-wide basis—e.g., community roads, bike paths, boating facilities. Besides ensuring economies of scale, such an approach will also reduce the risk of conflict between different parts of the community getting out of hand. At the same time, the developer will be better able to avoid the invidious role of arbitrator in intracommunity disputes.

The membership of the CA should reflect the main interest groups in the community: tenants, owners of dwelling units, owners of developed or undeveloped commercial land tracts, and, of course, the development enterprise itself.

The CA should be governed by a Board of Directors, small initially but expanding as development proceeds and control passes from the development enterprise to the Association. The Association's staff should also be small at first, to preserve flexibility and keep costs down. A Community Manager, an Operations Manager and a Community Relations Manager, with technical and accounting help from the developer, will be able to run the Association through its early years. As the community matures, however, it may well become a substantial organization resembling a small municipal authority. Figure 6.8 illustrates the evolution of a typical CA, from start-up through its growth phase to a full-fledged organization in the mature new community.

Neighbourhood associations

In addition to community-wide programs and services, further common services will be required for the use of residents living in their respective development tracts—particularly external and internal maintenance.

Because these services are best controlled at the point where they are actually used, they should be managed by an independent association for each neighbourhood, not by the CA. Neighbourhood associations would probably find it economic to use the CA's maintenance facilities on contract. However, they would be fully within their rights to change contractors in the case of inadequate performance. This should provide both owners and renters with far more control over important basic services than any other community association structure.

In addition to maintenance, the neighbourhood associations should manage any local programs utilizing common properties (such as swimming) and provide any local facilities or services for the use of their members that supplement facilities already being provided by the CA—e.g., children's play spaces.

They will also provide a valuable channel of communication between local residents and the CA on issues of local concern—e.g., the use of community recreation facilities adjacent to the tract, the quality of CA maintenance services.

Thus, two kinds of neighbourhood association are most likely to be needed: (1) to administer common properties (a legal requirement in the US wherever a condominium is established); (2) to provide local services and represent the mutual interests of the residents of any street or cluster of dwellings.

It is neither necessary nor desirable for the developer or the CA to prescribe covenants and operating mechanisms for neighbourhood associations. Particularly in large suburban subdivisions, experienced residential developers may have their own formula based on their previous experience. The developer should, however, provide guidelines to individual developers and to residents, particularly where neighbourhood associations impinge on the CA.

Residents' advisory groups

Both the CA and the neighbourhood associations will be established as management agencies, but there is a distinct and equally important need to be met in community organization—to provide opportunities for representation of residents' interests at the grass roots. Without an adequate 'safety valve' to direct the pressures that are inevitable in a new community, opposition is likely to be focused directly on the developer, and potentially constructive community contributions dissipated. Experience suggests that bodies conceived as service providers are unlikely to be effective vehicles for this additional safety valve function, particularly during the critical early years of development.

The developer should therefore anticipate the emergence of residents' groups to supplement the official service-providing agencies. These groups are likely to take two forms: (1) a community-wide residents' council; and (2) *ad hoc* advisory groups on specific community issues.

A residents' council deals on behalf of the new community with the developer on major development issues, with the local authority on identifying and meeting needs, and with the CA on services for which the CA is responsible. It also provides a vehicle for community participation in the planning process, and for citizen participation in government—e.g., by exploring the possibility of being given official advisory powers by the local authority.

The demand for a residents' council is not likely to be strongly voiced for the first two or three years, until a sense of community has grown up among the residents. When the demand does build up, the developer should leave the definition of roles and the precise form of the council to the residents themselves.[4] It would be desirable for the electoral basis of the council to be aligned with that of the local authority, if close working relationships are to be established.

The council also could well have a fixed life. Once the community has assumed control of the CA, it may well be found that the CA can serve as an adequate representative vehicle, in addition to its management functions.

The formation of *ad hoc* advisory residents' groups has often proved a valuable device for enlisting community help on specific issues and for resolving points of

145

conflict with residents. Many opportunities will arise for the formation of such groups—e.g., to decide the most appropriate uses for a lake, to plan additional tennis facilities, to expand the pre-school child-care program. Without attempting to impose a structure, the CA should encourage the formation of advisory groups to study issues of acknowledged community concern and to make recommendations to the Community Association Board. The CA should support their activities on a low-key basis with staff and material resources.

The creation of *ad hoc* advisory groups need not await the formation of the residents' council. On the contrary, they should be established as soon as residents express an interest and have a contribution to make.

The builders' guild

One of the most trying aspects of living through a community development process is the intensive building activity it entails. It is therefore not surprising that resident complaints are so prevalent, not only about the noise, dirt and confusion caused by large-scale construction, but also about the job done by building contractors. Indeed, in a recent survey of community leaders in Irvine, a new city in California, 60 per cent complained of poor quality, shoddy materials, insufficient landscaping and inadequate follow-through.[5]

Normally, complaints are directed either to the community developer, who does not have direct responsibility for building, or to the CA, which is unable to take remedial action. The purpose of a builders' guild is to provide an effective channel for coping with complaints, and to promote the co-ordination of builders' on-site programs, economies of scale in bulk purchasing, control of materials and overall resource management. Co-operatives, of course, already exist in many areas. But the key feature here is the organization of builder activities within the context of a single project. Moreover, the concept can be adapted to particular needs: at Flower Mound New Town in Texas, the builders' guild has the special purpose of co-ordinating the provision of prefabricated housing units.

To realize these benefits, the guild should discharge several tasks. To deal with residents' suggestions and complaints about housing deficiencies, resident and community opinion should be monitored and problems promptly tackled. Architectural standards should be reviewed, particularly in light of escalating housing costs, and recommendations should be made to the developer for possible incorporation as guidelines for subsequent development tracts. The benefits and possible scope of a builders' warranty program should be evaluated, and a program set up if the developer and builders agree on its merits. On-site activities should be integrated where economies of scale can be achieved—e.g., materials storage, materials purchase, site surveillance (individual builders would be charged by the guild for these services on a proportional basis). Marketing and sales programs should be co-ordinated—e.g., to avoid inconsistencies in sales approaches and prevent duplication of tasks between the developer and the builders. And on-site operational problems should be resolved through the guild—e.g., access obstructions, labour difficulties, co-ordination of delivery schedules.

146

The builders' guild should be a distinct entity with its own budget, but under the community developer's leadership and control and possibly with developer staff support. It should also include a residents' representative.

The community developer

The intention of the community management structure is to spread the basis of power and responsibility through the community. Nevertheless, the development enterprise—as initiator of the project—will remain one of the most important influences in community management. The most significant tasks for the developer are therefore to control the form of development through architectural review, to exercise specific controls over the CA, and possibly to direct the initial operations of community club facilities to ensure effective performance.

Architectural review. As we shall see in chapter 8, the developer is the key influence in shaping the physical form of the project. To ensure that the physical and aesthetic objectives of the community concept are implemented, he should initially elect to retain the powers of architectural review, rather than devolve these on any other agency. An Architectural Review Board can approve, amend or reject any development proposals. Additions and external alterations to structures will be within the Board's scope, as will landscaping proposals and changes. The Board should review proposals comprehensively—for location and general compatibility as well as for design, shape, height and use of materials. And its charter should cover *all* development proposals, whether from builders, the CA, outside agencies, such as churches, or the developer himself.

The Board should include appointed outside architects and at least one official voting member from the property owners. On significant or controversial proposals, the Board should consult the people and organizations involved—e.g., the CA, the residents' council (if established) and local *ad hoc* groups.

The CA charter may empower it to act as the developer's agent in architectural review at any future time. The delegation of the architectural review function (which should happen as soon as the CA develops the management capability—say, after three years of development) would shift effective day-to-day control to the CA, but still leave ultimate responsibility with the developer.

Controls over the CA. To protect its substantial interests in the project, to ensure the development of a professional management capability, and to represent the interests of future owners and residents, the developer should retain a series of specific controls over the CA. One typical formula illustrates how these controls might work.

First, CA Board membership should leave the developer with a majority until 50 per cent of zoned residential units are sold. The evidence of established new communities suggests that, while Board voting control is a useful reserve power, it is rarely necessary to exercise it. In Columbia, Board members tend to speak as individuals rather than as representatives of the developer or of the community 'interest'; as a result, differences of opinion on community issues between the two groups seldom become polarized. In Reston, the developer has publicly promised not to use his majority membership of the Board to veto any decision that clearly has community opinion behind it.

Second, the developer will be able to vote as a regular CA member, in accordance with the voting allocations for all members of undeveloped and developed property. For the first two or three years of development, this will give the developer absolute voting control.

Third, the developer will retain the right to add to the CA area at any time over the development cycle. The properties added should be consistent with the development covenants governing existing CA members. As property is added, the allocation of votes and the arrangements for electing directors could be adjusted either to maintain or to alter the control relationship described above.

Fourth, while committed to conveying specified common properties to the CA, the developer will reserve the right to delay conveyance if he feels that the CA is not yet able to provide high-quality maintenance. Moreover, at the time of conveyance, specific performance guidelines for property maintenance should be defined. However, once property has been handed over to the CA, control cannot revert to the developer.

Club operation. There is no reason why the start-up operations of community clubs should be any more difficult than those of other community services, such as restaurants or leisure facilities. Two practical considerations, however, call for careful definition of the relationship between the club and the rest of the community management structure.

First, since leisure activities will be prominent among the services provided by the CA, the question of who does what in developing new facilities and expanding existing ones can hardly be avoided. Second, with direct developer backing, clubs are likely to have substantially more leeway in charting their future than other private operators, so that the developer needs to be sensitive to the potential charge that he is 'taking the icing off the cake' and leaving the least profitable activities to the CA.

Without attempting to prescribe or pre-empt club policies, guidelines should be laid out to provide a general understanding of how the club will work vis-à-vis the CA. For example, club services should be allowed to adapt and evolve with demand for recreation, but not into activities that fall entirely within the scope of the CA. Conversely, the CA should not be prevented from developing facilities that it believes are needed and could be provided viably, even though similar facilities are already being operated by the club. Nor need the CA be excluded from managing specific services that happen to be located within club premises. A child-care facility, for example, could be developed as part of the club's physical structure to complement its services, and yet be operated by the CA (or by any other agency for that matter), with the space being rented out by the club for that purpose. Once the club is in operation, the CA should be consulted on any major proposals to expand or alter the scope of the club's services.

Successful community planning and management obviously require a sound financial base from the start. But in many projects, the community dimension is ignored or sacrificed through mistaken emphasis on narrow measures of economic performance. Chapter 7 discusses the issues in structuring community development economics.

References

1. Lodge, George C., 'Business and the Changing U.S. Society', *Harvard Business Review*, March–April 1974.
2. Kaplan, Marshall, *Social and Community Services Planning and Modelling*, unpublished paper, National Research Council, 1974.
3. Hughes, Derek W., 'Animation in French New Towns', *Town and Country Planning*, pp. 75–7, February 1975.
4. For one residents' council model, see *Toward New Towns Governance*, Reston, Virginia, January 1972.
5. *Irvine Community Associations*, Claremont Urban Research Center Report, p. 65, 1973. 1973.

Appendix: Initial program strategy: Pre-school child care

This appendix contains a program strategy statement for pre-school child care developed by John Griffith-Jones, illustrating the scope and level of analysis and program design appropriate to the decisions to be made in the strategic planning stage.

Introduction

The educational needs of children of five and over will be met through conventional public and private school provision. In the case of pre-school children, however, the public education authority carries no legal responsibility and the developer has a wide range of opportunities to secure provision through other channels. A well-designed pre-school child-care program will bring significant benefits both to the developer and to the community from the earliest days of the project.

First, it should increase the project's attractiveness. A substantial proportion of residential sales will be to families with one or more children under school age; an on-site program should appeal directly to this major market segment. By freeing mothers for work, it also will enable families to pool two incomes for house purchase (or rent) and thus broaden the market available. At Reston, for example, between 30 and 35 per cent of all homes purchased are now being financed with two incomes.

Second, it should provide an effective response to local demand for child care, both from the project and from the surrounding area. At the projected residential absorption rates, some 400 children between the ages of two-and-a-half and four are likely to be on site by 1983. Of these, it has been assumed that about 45 per cent will require some form of pre-school program. This assumption could be on the conservative side, compared with a participation level of about 50 per cent that has already been achieved in Reston. Regarding area demand, the nearest facility, 10 miles closer to the city centre on Route 1, is already at capacity. While no other facilities exist within a 15-minute drive of the project site, an estimated 360 three- and four-year-olds live within this radius. A capture rate of less than 25 per cent would be required to ensure immediate viability of a community facility. Thus, total demand is estimated to be about 100 children in 1975, rising to over 350 by 1983.

Finally, a child-care program should contribute to the image of the project as a progressive and socially active residential environment.

To achieve these benefits and capitalize on already existing demand, a child-care program should be in operation from the outset of the project. The first child-care centre should be ready to enrol children by September 1975. Initial viability should be ensured by tapping pent-up area demand. The centre should provide both full- and part-day care, and should also provide a focus for child-care activities in the community.

The program should be a self-financing, non-profit operation under the control of the CA. Initially, the developer should donate land and build the facility in Village 1. The facility will be planned to accommodate CA offices, along with the child-care program, and the CA will own the building. No commitments to further centres should be made at this point, in terms of timing, program content or management responsibility. However, the developer and the CA should encourage the opening of additional facilities as and when the demand arises.

The rest of this document explains (a) the possible child-care programs that should be considered and the reasons for focusing on a child-care centre as the core of the strategy, (b) detailed strategy recommendations, and (c) next steps in implementation.

Program evaluation

A wide range of possible programs exists for providing child care, each with distinctive features (Fig. 6.9): (1) full-day care, based on a nursery school or a child-care centre; (2) part-day care, including a nursery school/child-care centre, individual babysitting, play groups, and family home care; (3) drop-in services.

All of these programs will have their place in a total pattern of child care; the strategy should encourage all options as demand develops. The core of the strategy, however, should be the provision of a child-care centre, with both full- and part-day programs. From a marketing standpoint, this will provide the most visible demonstration of the developer's concern for child-care needs. Home-based programs—e.g., group babysitting—can be initiated without much action from the developer or the CA: the child-care centre, by contrast, needs careful planning to match the program with market conditions and site requirements. The quality emphasis being sought in the development can be achieved only through a purpose-built centre, with professionally qualified staff and specialized equipment and facilities. The centre will have the flexibility for subsequent expansion and development of programs—e.g., integration of nursery classes with home-based child minding. Moreover, the centre can (and should) be used as a community-wide focus for child-care activities, in addition to providing its own programs—e.g.,

PROGRAM	Program Emphasis	Quality Level	Child Density/ Room	Adult: Child Ratio	Management	Profit (P) or Non-Profit (NP)	User Fee Per Week	Revenues
Full-Day Care								
- Break-even, non-profit, high-quality program		High	20	1:8	PE	NP	$25 min.	Break-even
- Cash-generating, non-profit, high-quality program	Education, child development	High	20	1:8	PE	NP	$25 min.	Cash surplus for CA
- Cash-generating, non-profit, medium-quality program		Med.	25	1:10	Prof.	NP	$25	Cash surplus for CA
- Profit-making program		Med.	25–30	1:10	PE	P	$25–30	Generates profits
Part-Day Care								
- Part day at child-care center	Education and child development	Med.–high	15–20	1:6–1:15	D	NP	$5–20	Break-even
- Individual baby-sitting	Child minding				V			To baby-sitter
- Play groups (group baby-sitting)	Child minding, several children				V			To baby-sitter(s)
- Family home care	Child minding/education and child development		5–6/ home	1:5–6	V	P		Teachers' pay is net revenue
Drop-In Services								
- Child-care center	Child minding	Med.		1:10	PE	NP		To child-care center
- Commercial		Med.		1:10	D	P (poss.)		To commercial operator

PE = Professional educator   D = Developer   V = Voluntary

Figure 6.9   Child-care program options

providing information on the availability of babysitting and child-minding services, giving professional advice to parents, and holding discussion groups on child development problems.

With the centre identified as the main vehicle for child-care provision, the main issue becomes one of how it should be controlled and managed. Here the developer has three choices: (1) provide the program itself on a non-profit basis, under its own direct control; (2) allow a commercial operator to open a private for-profit centre, with no control by the developer or by the CA; or (3) sponsor a private non-profit operation through the CA.

There are strong reasons for recommending the third choice. Linked to the CA, the program can be structured to respond directly to community needs, and support

151

related programs such as recreation. Moreover, the idea of a community-based program should be an asset in marketing the project. Since the centre would be non-profitmaking, parents would not feel the resentment that can otherwise occur of 'someone making money off my children' (profitmaking day-care centres are often referred to by parents as producers of 'Kentucky-Fried Children'). Since the fees can be set to cover capital and operating expenses, the program also should not be a financial burden either on the CA or on the developer; present estimates of demand suggest that the centre can be fully viable financially and that the need for subsidy is unlikely. In addition, rental space could possibly generate income during off-hours. Direct control by the developer, however, would require extensive involvement in an area where it has no experience, where there is little or no return on investment and where other providers are available. Initiating the program will require some commitment of time and money, but no more so than for other community programs.

Although the program would be run as a self-contained operation, both the developer and the CA will have a significant role to play. The developer should take action to ensure successful initiation of the program by donating improved land, arranging for construction financing, and supervising centre construction. The CA will act as overseer once the program is under way, advising program staff on community needs and priorities, ensuring that the program is linked with related community activities—e.g., recreation for young children—and controlling the performance of the program, with the assistance of a small advisory committee of residents and parents.

Recommendations

This section contains detailed recommendations for the implementation of the child-care strategy.

Program design

Current educational thinking is that a child should be stimulated to think and do as much as possible on its own, within a framework of concepts to be learned. The child-care program should therefore be geared to child development, both alone and in groups, and in structured and unstructured form. Activities include drawing, painting, cutting and pasting, listening to stories, listening to music, and playing with toys and equipment.

The centre should be open from 7.00 a.m. to 6.00 p.m. Throughout the day children should be in groupings according to approximate age. A basic schedule should be devised and followed each day to establish a routine for the children. Education will be emphasized in the morning, the afternoon being less structured. A general pattern might be:

7.00 a.m.–8.00 a.m.	Arrival
8.00 a.m.–9.00 a.m.	Free play
9.00 a.m.–11.30 a.m.	Educational classes (with break)
11.30 a.m.–12.30 p.m.	Quiet period
12.30 p.m.–1.30 p.m.	Lunch
1.30 p.m.–2.30 p.m.	Quiet period
2.30 p.m.–4.30 p.m.	Supervised free play (with break)
4.30 p.m.–5.30 p.m.	Quiet play
5.30 p.m.–6.00 p.m.	Departure

In addition to full- and part-day care, a drop-in service should be available for pre-schoolers on an hourly basis. Classes could also be provided for children of five and above out of school hours, say between 3.00 p.m. and 6.00 p.m.

Staffing

Ideally, a child-care program should have an adult-to-child ratio of $1:5$ or $1:6$—i.e., one teaching staff member present for every five or six children. The costs, however, are prohibitive for any program relying solely on fees for revenues; state and charitable funds are normally only available for low-income programs. A more realistic teaching staff ratio would be $1:10$ (this also happens to be the minimum for many states).

The total staffing requirement, however, will be more than $1:10$, because of staggered hours, the grouping of children and the need for support staff. At its full complement of 100 children, the centre is likely to need a staff of 19 or 20—including a full-time director, an assistant director (optional, but very helpful), 4 head teachers, 4 assistant teachers and 8 aides, a cook and a maintenance person.

Salaries will depend on rates in the area for comparable jobs. In general, people working in pre-school programs are paid less than those working in the public school systems. The potential problem of high turnover might be countered by offering salaries slightly higher than the average. But it is more important to create an environment where teachers and aides realize that they are making a real contribution to the program and to the children.

Facilities

The following guidelines should be adopted in planning and designing the centre:

- The centre should be limited to a capacity of about 100 children. Unless very well designed and operated, a larger centre becomes noisy and too much like school, and it becomes difficult to work effectively with the children.
- The facility should be designed as a flexible open area rather than as separate classrooms. This is both more versatile, less institutional, and more economical in space required per child. A space standard of 36 square feet per child should be adopted.

153

● While class space should be maximized, space for other uses should be kept to a minimum. A small office will be required for the director. No hallways are needed. A central core should be established for storage, toilets and utilities. A kitchen for preparing meals and snacks should be provided, rather than reliance on heating pre-cooked food.
● A fenced outdoor play area of at least 5,000 square feet (50 square feet per child) should be established.
● 1,250 square feet of CA offices should be added to the child-care space, as an integral part of the structure.
● Parking spaces will be available for teachers and parents in the nearby parking lot.

Space standards for the centre should be:

Space Standards

(square feet per child)

Space	State Standard	Ideal	Acceptable	Minimum
Outdoor*	75	—	50	—
Indoor				
Facility with classrooms	—	100	75	50
Each classroom	35	—	—	20
Facility with open-class design	—	50–75	36	20
Open-class space	—	—	25	20

* Requirements for fenced-in outdoor play space vary with the amount of alternative open space available.

Location

The first centre should be located near the reception centre and the general store. The centre should be away from traffic, yet easily accessible for parents. Usually a location on a side street, half a block or so from a main road, is good. Since the centre should be visible to visitors and prospective house-buyers, a location near the reception centre is ideal. As additional pre-school facilities are needed, they should be located in village centres or (possibly) in residential areas.

Program economics

On the expectation that the demand estimates will be fulfilled, the program should be economically viable from the outset of the project.

1. *Costs.* Capital costs for building and equipping the centre are expected to be about $110,000, and operating expenses will be on the order of $110,000 per annum, broken down as follows:

Capital costs		$
3,600 square feet (36 sq. ft. per child)		90,000
Architects' fees		9,000
Equipment		
Kitchen	3,800	
Indoor equipment	5,780	
Outdoor equipment	400	
Miscellaneous	1,170	
		11,150
Total		$110,000

Operating costs*		$
Salaries		69,100
Food		17,540
Supplies		6,000
Utilities		3,080
Insurance		60
Replacement of equipment		1,000
		96,780
Amortization of building†		9,160
Amortization of equipment‡		2,220
Total		$108,160

* Assuming: Full capacity of 100 children. 75 per cent full day, 25 per cent part day.
† Assumes 9 per cent mortgage over 25 years, CA space excluded.
‡ Assumes 9 per cent loan over 7 years.

The centre will require a start-up loan to pay the director's salary for six months before opening and to pay initial operating expenses. This loan should be made by the developer, and repaid as quickly as possible from revenues.

2. *Revenues.* The program will not have access to government or charitable grants, since these are normally allocated exclusively to programs for low-income families or for children with special needs, such as the mentally handicapped. The program will therefore be dependent on fees for its revenue base.

Program revenues will depend on the fees charged, the number of children enrolled, and the mix of full- and part-day care. At the fee of $25 per week for full-day care and $20 for part-day care, the centre should break even at 78–92 children and yield a surplus of $10,000–$25,000 per annum at full enrolment (Fig. 6.10).

● The proposed initial fee of $25 for full-day care and $20 for part-day care is fully competitive with comparable schools in the area. The superior quality of

155

FEE LEVELS	FULL-DAY/ PART-DAY	ECONOMICS AT 100 ENROLMENT			BREAK-EVEN ENROLMENT
		Revenues	Costs	Surplus	
		$	$	$	
$25 p.w. full-day	50/50	112,500	87,530	24,970	78
$20 p.w. part-day	75/25	118,750	108,160	10,590	92
	100/0	125,000	112,220	12,780	90
$27.50 p.w. full-day	50/50	118,750	87,530	31,220	74
$20 p.w. part-day	75/25	128,120	108,160	19,960	84
	100/0	137,500	112,220	25,280	82

Figure 6.10   Child-care centre economics

the program may allow fees to be raised once the centre is under way. Raising the full-day fee by only $2.50 to $27.50 would increase the annual surplus to $20,000–$30,000, assuming full enrolment.

● The economics of the program are very sensitive to the balance between full- and part-day care. Financially, the optimum balance is about 50 : 50. In practice, however, community demand is likely to be nearer 75 per cent for full-day care and only 25 per cent for part-day care.

The surplus generated by the program could be applied to any of the following purposes: additional child-care equipment and services; lower fees for some or all parts of the child-care program, to ensure continued attractiveness to the widest range of income groups; or released for other community purposes determined by the CA.

Next steps

The program should be ready to open in September 1975. Pre-school educators state that September is the busiest month for enrolment, probably because it is traditionally the beginning of the school year. In order to meet this deadline, detailed planning and design steps must start now, involving the development team, the CA Manager, and the program director, when appointed. A child-care action plan identifying the required implementation steps, responsibilities and timing, must now be proposed.

Chapter 7. Mastering development economics

MAHLON APGAR, IV

Previous chapters have discussed more flexible approaches to strategic planning in today's climate of rapid change. But responsiveness alone will not ensure the success of a development project. It must be underpinned by sound financing. Though skilled planning and sensitive management can be decisive in improving results, they cannot shore up a weak foundation.

To state so basic an axiom may seem unnecessary. Yet even the most seasoned developers and lenders have often overlooked the unusual financing risks occasioned by community-scale operations. The heavy debt burden makes them especially vulnerable to sudden rises in interest rates. Traditional financing instruments are insufficient to meet the requirements for social investment. Inflation and eroding markets can wreak havoc without the protection of contingency funds or deferrable commitments. The sheer complexity of most ventures, coupled with the heady purpose that drives their developers and investors, can easily tempt the unwary to treat assumptions as facts and paper plans as cash-generating projects. Indeed, the basic problem community developers face today is that their unconventional planning and development processes have been financed with conventional instruments and measured by traditional performance criteria.

Rather than suggesting a new financing improvisation, which could be deceptive and quickly dated, this chapter therefore reviews the fundamentals of 'value economics' in large-scale, mixed-use development. This concept, analogous to profit economics in business, though different in several key respects, embodies the principle of creating value through the development and use of land and buildings to provide the financial base for realizing overall project objectives. Mastering this concept and associated techniques is in many ways the most important skill required of the community development enterprise.

After summarizing the role of land use in value economics, this chapter discusses five core economic elements: (1) the uses and limitations of leverage; (2) the sources and measures of investment return; (3) the effects of inflation on management; (4) the use of contingency planning to cope with rapid change; and (5) approaches to capturing the economic values of 'social' investment.

Land and building use provide the common ground for evaluating thousands of discrete activities in terms of their contribution to the project's aims and financial performance. The decision on how each site and structure can be used, and each use related to others, pervades many other key choices: development objectives, the size of sites required to meet those aims, the size and type of structures, the infrastructure to service them, the programs and services to operate them, the form of benefits that accrue from holding them, and myriad other decisions on buying, selling, improving, enlarging or demolishing them.

The value economics of community development are particularly complex because the relationships between uses may change radically during the project's life to accommodate new needs, shifts in taste and location preferences. The key to unlocking a project's economic potential is therefore to manage the *timing, phasing* and *mix* of uses that will best realize the development concept while responding to unforeseen changes in opportunities and constraints. The development cycle is simply too long, the multiplicity of objectives too complex and the operating environment too uncertain, to permit a single static financial plan. The private developer, for instance, may choose a mix that will initially contribute maximum cash flow and shift to an asset growth goal later on. The public developer, on the other hand, may pursue short-term asset growth at the start (to increase the taxable revenue base), but at the same time attempt to allocate a high proportion of space to non-earning public uses.

Thus, the uses prescribed in the project plan should be seen only as an initial definition that will need to be modified as new patterns of demand and shifts in the cost or availability of capital emerge. Regrettably, many financial staffs pay scant regard to the importance of this continuing process. Time and imagination are lavished on the initial financing structure, but once the plan is 'set', their attention turns to implementation, and to the budgets, status reports and cash management tools of prudent financial control. New conditions obviously arise, but the underlying assumptions are overlooked until it is too late to change course.

In short, creativity in structuring project economics is needed not only at the planning stage, but whenever significant changes in direction or additional investments are decided. Imaginative ideas, however, must be grounded on a solid understanding of both the possibilities and pitfalls in using leverage.

Leverage: uses and limitations

Leverage—the proportion of borrowed funds to equity capital used by a development enterprise—is the mainspring of development financing. A high ratio of debt to equity distinguishes the developer's capital structure from that of most manufacturing and service enterprises, and makes comparisons difficult.

Cash requirements are high, particularly in the early stages, since substantial front-end investment is required for land acquisition, preservicing and predevelopment expenses, such as architect's, legal and accounting fees. Consider the planning, land development and initial building costs in a typical 'satellite' project for 100,000 people:

	Costs	
	$ Million	%
Land acquisition	20.0	40.0
Planning and management	2.0	4.0
Infrastructure (sewers, utilities, water, grading, roads)	15.0	30.0
Phase 1 building construction	8.0	16.0
Total cost of land and initial improvements	45.0	90.0
Interest charges on net invested capital at 10 per cent	5.0	10.0
TOTAL	50.0	100.0

By the mid-point of the development cycle, this cash requirement may have increased five-fold.

The scale, lead time and comparatively low financial returns of new community projects make it impractical to use more than a tiny percentage of equity to cover these costs. Whether the developer is a company, an individual or a public authority, it will not normally have sufficient assets under direct control to finance the required investment. Yet a major corporate investor is unlikely to find this an optimum use of funds in the face of higher return opportunities. Most of the financing, therefore, will usually come from large institutions—in particular, insurance companies, pension funds and commercial banks—or a government development fund. These institutions normally underwrite 50 to 100 per cent of total investment requirements.

As building starts, refinancing can be used to increase the developer's effective overall leverage. Land values increase as a result of planning and infrastructure, enabling the developer to revalue the project and borrow substantial additional funds to finance income-producing sub-projects and further amenities.

In this way, the investor can exploit the earning capacity of the debt portion of total project capitalization to leverage a higher rate of return on the cash investment, or the equity portion of the financial structure. As a simple illustration, if a $50-million project earns $5 million (before taxes), the equity return is 10 per cent. But if the investor provides only $10 million in cash equity and borrows $40 million at 10 per cent interest for 25 years, his return is 19.8 per cent.

The danger in this otherwise attractive situation is that leverage can spell disaster in an ill-conceived project. Development financing is distinctive in that borrowings are made mainly against the potential value and earning capacity of the *project* rather than of the development enterprise. Thus, small organizations and individuals with minimal capital assets and net income can undertake large projects that will provide substantial long-term returns. The development costs of a single project may be 15 to 20 times the developer's total assets.

159

Capitalizing on this opportunity requires extraordinary competence in conceptual planning, problem solving and management control. If the developer cannot orchestrate the planning and building process effectively, the investment potential will never be realized. And if the product/market strategy and cost-to-value premiums are not intrinsically sound, using additional debt to increase investment returns will only further expose the equity base.

When costs soar and confidence sags (as in 1974), the developer may be unable to carry the heavy debt-servicing load: for example, the $50 million debt cited above at 10 per cent interest requires some $19,000 per day in financing charges; at 15 per cent—the debt cost in many projects during 1974—the daily cash drain is $29,000.

To guard against these risks, the developer must be able to arrange financing that permits deferral of principal and partial interest payments during the critical early years when revenues are not being generated. In return for this flexibility and cash infusion, the developer's financial partners may exact a substantial equity stake, require a share of any increase in cash flow, or both. The long-term institutional lender is usually unwilling to refinance large-scale projects in the face of clear market uncertainty, since development margins are too narrow to buffer major changes in the economic cycle.

The prudent developer will therefore seek to limit the potential risk of excessive leverage by careful planning, ensuring that the product and financial strategies are completely consistent, and that the resulting financial structure is shielded from major market uncertainties. If a 'buy-make-sell' strategy is pursued, return on investment results from both appreciation in land values and value-added in the development process, so the financial structure should be designed to allow for immediate refinancing if sales forecasts err substantially. On the other hand, if property is simply purchased and held, returns are realized solely from price increases, which must at least exceed the debt-servicing cost. In this case, the financial agreement would need to cover 5 to 10 years or more and would require the sales and rental income to be substantially in line with forecasts; otherwise excessive negative cash flows would result.

The project that achieves planned revenue and cost targets, and is seen as a secure investment opportunity, will have excellent prospects of sustaining the investor's interest and attracting fresh funds at moderate cost.

Sources and measures of investment return

Just as leverage must be employed with careful regard for its pitfalls, so must the types of return on investment be thoroughly evaluated in light of the project's financing requirements. For the relative attractiveness of large-scale development depends not only on the proper *use* of land and buildings to generate market volume, and on effective *leverage*, but also on an accurate understanding of the *sources* of profitability and risk.

Investment returns are derived from two interlocking sources: capital appreciation on land and buildings attributable to the value created by development; and cash flows generated by land sales, building development, refinancing and the operation of income-producing properties. Full capital appreciation on land is not normally realized until the entire project is completed, some 15 to 20 years after the land is acquired, but cash flows on individually marketed sub-projects can occur almost from the start.

The difficulty in assessing these returns is that most enterprises use as their main performance yardstick return on total capital employed—i.e., equity plus debt. By this measure, development produces only average returns. But by measuring return on equity, a much more enticing result is revealed due to the impact of leverage: a high debt to equity ratio combined with long-term financing and considerable tax shelters. Hence, cash flow net of debt services *is* the developer's return, and it is worth looking more closely at the way it is generated.

Capital appreciation

The primary financial objective in most projects is to increase property values as rapidly as possible through the development process and, accordingly, to derive the cash flows resulting from sales of developed land. This distinguishes the community developer from the property speculator who profits by holding real estate until external forces drive up the price, selling it only when a certain price multiple has been reached. His skill lies in purchasing sites in the right place and at the right time to achieve the highest multiplier; he does not add value through his own initiative or by major new investment. By contrast, the developer tries to minimize the inactive holding period and quickly add value by developing land and buildings for a higher economic use.

While this distinction is oversimplified, it highlights the importance of managing the capital appreciation cycle in community development. The earlier price increases can be obtained, the greater will be the developer's financing capacity for the project as a whole. Substantial revaluation over acquisition cost during the first few years will eliminate the lenders' initial exposure, provide a useful cushion against premature market slowdowns, and put the developer in a strong refinancing position. A 100 per cent annual value increase in the first three to five years has proved a reasonable target in metropolitan regions averaging five per cent growth in household formations.

The cycle is illustrated in Fig. 7.1. Undeveloped land values rise sharply, spawned by shifts in population, expansion of services and new road construction. When values mature, the rate of increase slows significantly and the carrying costs—generally, property taxes and any site-related debt—reach a level at which the land should be either disposed of or developed.

Both the scale and type of value created in any project depend on its financial structure (the mix of debt and equity and the term and interest rate of mortgages), on the timing of cash flows resulting from financial decisions (phasing of the initial equity investment, refinancing and the sale of sub-projects), as well as on its marketability. The level of appreciation depends not only on original price, location and development potential, but also on the specific number and mix of land uses and

161

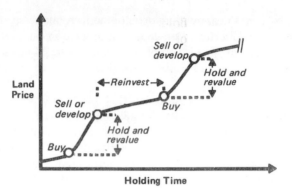

Figure 7.1 Value appreciation cycle

building types. Because they offer a concentrated mix of uses, new communities may enjoy higher land values after development than traditional single-use ventures. A combination of residential, industrial and commercial land in one area attracts users with different objectives but a common interest in the mix: retailers take advantage of the relatively dense market, while families are drawn by the proximity of stores, schools and employment. Each additional use of the land should be programmed to boost the value of the whole mix.

The developer must balance land investment and development costs against capital appreciation, and location is the fulcrum. If he locates far from existing residential development, his costs for raw, rural land will be low. But the farther the community is from existing job markets, the less will be its capacity to attract residents.

In economically developed areas, a new community's residential viability is generally the key to its success, because housing is the land use from which most other service and community uses spring. But easy access to available jobs is essential to sustain housing demand. Unless such opportunities are accessible outside the community in the critical early years, when internal industrial and commercial facilities are under construction, demand for houses is likely to be so low that the resulting price levels cannot sustain the project.

In developing regions, housing demand will be created by concurrent development of an extensive employment and population base—e.g., a regional growth centre or a large new program for industrialization—as in the massive development plan recently approved for Saudi Arabia.

Thus, effective management of the capital appreciation process requires considerable testing of alternative mixes of land uses and building types, both when working out the overall financial plan and throughout implementation. Economies of scale that would be impossible in a smaller project can accrue for each type of development and for the project as a whole. By trading-off uses and planning higher density clusters, the developer can provide community facilities and open space that would not otherwise be feasible. The result of the subsequent planned growth is a gradual but decisive shift from undeveloped to developed urban values.

162

As even the most prescient analyst cannot predict with precision the level of needs and the resulting values 10 to 15 years hence, rigid adherence to a financial plan is a sure way to failure. Rather, each major milestone of the commitment planning process described in chapter 5 should trigger a reassessment of underlying financial assumptions and detailed analysis of how well the total portfolio of land and building assets is being employed to generate sales, rentals and other forms of cash or earnings. For both the public and the private developer, this means keying development strategy to investment performance at each stage through the efficient and effective use of funds, land and other resources at his disposal to achieve the required results.

Cash flow measures

While capital appreciation is the ultimate source of value in a community development project, cash flow establishes the current value of its income stream or earning power on a continuing basis. It also determines the degree of financial leverage open to the investor and thus his potential profitability in terms of cash.

The developer's ability to generate cash for reinvestment is critical to his success because it will largely determine his capacity to multiply future cash flows, rapidly expand development and thus realize a higher ultimate return. As leverage increases, growth in cash flows will have greater impact in raising the overall rate of return.

Three cash flow measures are most commonly used. The simplest is *cash flow from operations* (CFO), the residual funds available in the project after taxes, debt servicing charges and operating expenses have been deducted from gross revenues. Though valuable as a measure of liquidity, it does not reveal the tax benefits of the investment nor the changes in revenues and costs over the project's life.

The second indicator, *net cash flow* (NCF), explicitly recognizes tax implications (in the US) by deducting depreciation from CFO. Although they usually appreciate in value, building projects are treated for tax purposes as depreciable assets. Since depreciation does not represent a cash outlay, however, these deductions for tax purposes reflect cash available for reinvestment.

While the depreciation life varies substantially for each type of property use, developers and investors typically choose the accelerated method, in which accounting deductions are greatest in the first year of project life and decline sharply thereafter. This means the developer can more quickly recover his early investment. Thus, cash flows related to amortization of loan principal and depreciation of the development assets are reciprocal—over time, amortization increases and depreciation decreases—resulting in low taxable operating income in the early years, which increases over the project's life. Where deductions are substantial and revenues negligible or non-existent in the early development phases, taxable income is negative and the resulting tax saving can be treated as a major cash inflow.

The most complex, and most useful, indicator—*investor's rate of return* (IRR)—is the discount rate at which the present value of all future cash inflows equals the present value of all future cash outflows. This includes the time value of money and in effect tells the investor what will be his 'true' rate of return on capital employed in the

163

project for any period he chooses. Properly used, IRR is the most important single tool for measuring the financial value of a project, because all the elements of return—sales, tax savings, capital appreciation—can be assessed in this one calculation. Expressed as an equation, IRR can be summarized:

$$\text{IRR} = I - \sum_1^n \frac{(\text{CFO})n}{(1+r)n} + \sum_1^n \frac{(\text{NCF})n}{(1+r)n} + \sum_1^n \frac{(\text{CFS})n}{(1+r)n}$$

Key: I (investment)
n (holding period)
r (investor's discount rate)
CFO (cash flow from operations)
NCF (net cash flow)
CFS (cash flow from project sale)

As the past year has shown, however, the problem in discounting life-of-project cash flows is the uncertainty of forecasting the future rate of inflation and its impact on the costs of financing and building. Consider the extraordinary changes that occurred between 1973 and 1975: inflation quadrupled, moving from 5 to 20 per cent, and interest rates doubled—from 6 to 12 per cent. The resulting differential between inflation and interest rates (+1 point in 1973 and −8 points in 1975) meant that debt could be secured at a lower cost than the rate of land price appreciation guaranteed by current inflation.

For this reason, many corporate analysts have reverted to evaluating returns in today's money, using a reasonable 'real' rate of return, net of inflation. Rather than try to predict the rise and fall of inflation and interest rates—a dubious effort at the best of times—the developer can plan on future differentials in real income terms. The next section expands on the impact of inflation on management.

Logically, an investor would not participate in projects with an IRR lower than his discount rate. But, in practice, too many investors include in their decision other criteria that have not been properly evaluated. Qualitative factors inevitably obtain in community development projects, but they should at least be weighed carefully against the objective IRR measure.

Although the evaluation of cash flow is simple in principle, it is complicated by the necessity to compute all cash flows over the duration of the entire project rather than year by year. In the planning and land-development phases, annual cash flow will understate the profit potential of a project, because actual land sales will be far below their anticipated future rate, and revenues from building development and operations will be limited. On the other hand, treating tax shelters and other forms of paper gains as investment returns may seriously overstate the actual cash position. It is therefore essential to assess the cash break-even (the point at which cash revenues equal expenses) on a regular and consistent basis and judge from this whether further investment can be sustained. Easy and familiar as a tool of corporate management, this analysis is often overlooked by developers, to their cost.

Consider the economics of a project that reports sales from the beginning although, for the reasons discussed above, it is operating below break-even for some

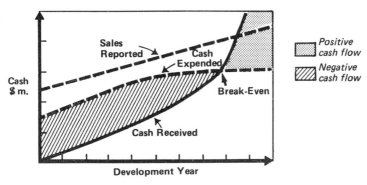

Figure 7.2 Break-even analysis

years into the development cycle. As Fig. 7.2 shows, actual out-of-pocket expenses for debt servicing, overhead and other current project costs exceed the actual cash revenues from sales, rentals and operations. As a result, the break-even point is deferred until these revenues catch up with expenses through value appreciation. The accounting impact of these characteristics can significantly affect the timing, location and investment level of each development component in the community.

Some of these issues are explored further in chapter 12. Suffice it to say here that a project's financial performance—whatever the measures used—depends largely on the accuracy of the assumptions in the economic model. Negative deviations, even if small in absolute terms, can seriously affect the arithmetic because interest and other holding costs will be compounded over the prolonged development cycle. As the usual source of trouble is over-optimistic assumptions about demand, a constant watch over the break-even indicator is an essential task in good project management.

Managing with inflation

Implicit in the foregoing discussion, and the strategic framework outlined in chapters 4 and 5, is the understanding that the recent conditions of high inflation have had a massive impact on the basic economic structure of the development enterprise. Only recently, however, has inflation been recognized for its effect on the way developers should manage. And even now, few organizations have actually changed their operating style or methods accordingly. While detailed prescriptions are beyond our scope in this chapter, and in any event must be worked out specifically for each enterprise, it is worth highlighting here the main effects of inflation on economic viability and performance measures, and the resulting priority tasks facing developer managements under inflation.[1]

Effects on viability and performance measures

We noted in chapter 5 that the combination of a dramatic increase in the rate of inflation, stagnating economic growth, eroding profitability and the high cost of finance had significantly increased the risks of development and reduced the overall return on investment. Moreover, even if the short-term countermeasures now being adopted were effective—and that is by no means certain—the inflation rate in 1976–80 will be nearly twice that of the 1960s, and real GNP growth will be significantly lower.

The implications of these simple but fundamental facts are startling. First of all, for the highly leveraged developer realizing high rates of return on equity with substantial amounts of borrowed capital, continued viability is seriously threatened. Operating cash flow tends to be reduced in real terms by the twin pressures of higher costs and stable or lower prices that result from declining buyer confidence. Similarly, CFO declines as a percentage of sales as revenue growth fails to keep pace with operating costs, while increased interest charges reduce the net realizable cash flow.

Because of inflated costs and limited revenues, the cash needs of each project, and of the enterprise as a whole, rise rapidly so that overall profitability, measured by the return on total capital employed, declines as NCF lags behind the rising capital requirements. As a result, the return on equity over time drops below the average cost of borrowed funds (Fig. 7.3 shows the actual pattern of one large developer) while even higher levels of debt must be sought to finance ongoing operations.

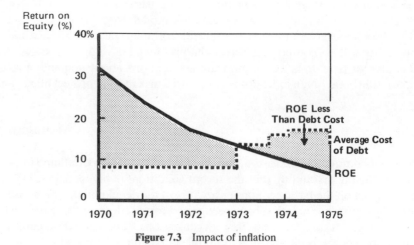

Figure 7.3 Impact of inflation

Finally, cash flow itself deteriorates and corporate liquidity is threatened as financing requirements exceed funds generated from operations (Fig. 7.4). Not a few developers, faced with a mounting cash drain in 1974, saw their borrowing requirements increase tenfold above the level of funds that would have been required with a pre-1970 inflation level. As their debt/equity ratio increases even further, borrowing capability weakens and the interest cover may drop as much as ten times.

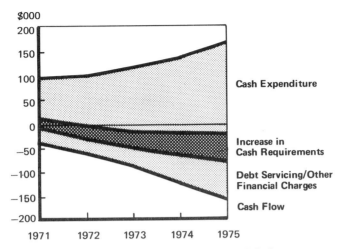

Figure 7.4 Cash flow deterioration under inflation

The second sobering result of inflation is that the traditional measures of financial performance become grossly distorted. The focus on sales revenues is particularly misleading for, as Fig. 7.5 shows, turnover may be rising rapidly but the financial position is in fact deteriorating. Conventional reported profits become seriously overstated because the costs used to determine them are based on lower, 'historic' costs rather than on (1) the higher current value of materials and (2) the higher costs of replacing the depreciable assets at current values. Conversely, the reported value of total capital employed in development is significantly understated at its historic cost before revaluation. Measures of return on net assets will further mislead as

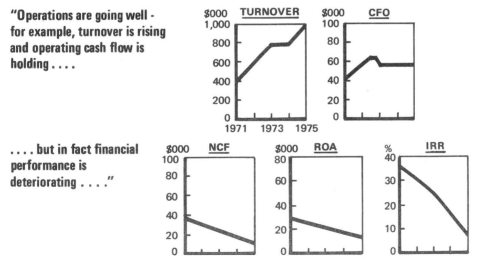

Figure 7.5 Conventional financial measures can be misleading

historic profits are overstated and historic capital employed is typically understated. For publicly held developers, reported earnings become increasingly divorced from cash flow even when existing levels of operation are maintained.

Thus, it is essential for decision-makers to recognize that conventional historic profits, and the profitability measures based on them, may well result in wrong decisions. They generally include funds required to maintain existing levels of operation and may therefore hide the fact that sales are insufficient to cover the current cost of development products sold or the productive assets used to build them. Tax payments and earnings distributions based on historic profits may exceed the gains from inflation, resulting in further borrowings merely to maintain current activities. And the conventional measures will disguise the inadequate levels of return on capital employed—particularly in relation to borrowed funds—until the lending institutions or the threat of bankruptcy expose them.

Priority tasks for management

Lest this prognosis seem too overwhelming, developers can take some comfort that in at least one respect—using cash flow as the key indicator of profitability—they are a step ahead of their manufacturing and retailing counterparts. However, ensuring survival as a viable going concern under conditions of high inflation requires more of management than simply measuring performance on a cash flow basis. Two immediate steps in particular must be taken in both private and public enterprises.

First, the financial management information available to and used by the decision-maker should be modified to reflect the impact of inflation at all levels of the enterprise. Cash flow forecasting and monitoring need to be strengthened and extended to cover *total* cash flows, not simply operating cash flow, and to highlight trends monthly rather than quarterly or less often as is typical. Internal management accounts should show the effect on net profitability of replacing both products sold and depreciable assets used on a current basis, while internal balance sheets should reflect the current value of fixed assets employed. The inflation impact on cash contribution and profitability of *each discrete project or operating unit* should be assessed, and designs, construction, marketing and financial plans revised accordingly. This means dividing the total organization into units that have common cash needs, cost structures, product/market characteristics and pricing constraints. These may reflect geographic areas, product/market groups, functional lines or distribution channels—but they are likely to differ significantly from the existing reporting or operating structure.

The second requirement is to move quickly to improve internal cash flow and 'current value' performance. As the action tree in Fig. 7.6 depicts, there are a number of steps that are likely to produce effective improvements—in particular: (1) increasing sales and rental revenues, mainly through price increases; (2) reducing current value capital employed in relation to turnover by reducing net current and fixed assets; (3) reducing operating costs; (4) improving design value for money through closer matching of design specifications with buyer/user priorities; and (5) reducing financial charges. Chapter 14 details a proven approach to steps 3 and 4,

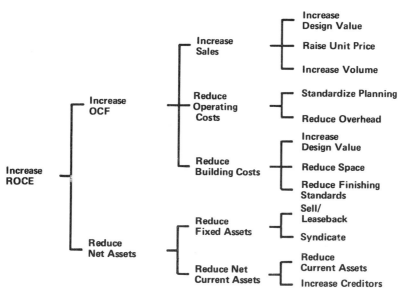

Figure 7.6 Improving performance under inflation

and chapter 13 describes an effective method for step 5. Once these are analysed, the impact on cash flow of alternative options can be assessed and possible scenarios arising from any option examined within the strategic framework presented in chapter 4.

Explicit recognition of inflation's effects also opens the way for a fundamental review of short-run strategies that many developers unwisely overlook—the process of contingency planning.

Contingency planning

Of late, market malaise, volatile interest rates and the other symptoms of uncertainty cited above have awakened many developers to the need for contingency planning, but they have been ill-equipped to respond. While conventional methods of financial analysis and planning are suited to the drive for growth, they are not designed for the radical surgery—or even preventive care—required to prune unnecessary or high-cost debt when inflation begins to take its toll.

Outlined below is a five-step approach that has helped developers to sharpen the definition of financial risks, problems and opportunities. While proven in practice, it is not presented as a definitive formula, but as a means of segmenting exceptionally complex financial structures into a manageable set of building blocks, each of which can be evaluated and repositioned as appropriate. Figure 7.7 expands on these steps, illustrating an actual analytic plan for resolving contingency issues and organizing the analyses.

169

ISSUES/PROBLEMS/TIMING	HYPOTHESES/REASONS	ANALYSES REQUIRED	DATA SOURCES
1. Do current plans solve known problems? - Refinancing project debt - Refinancing operating properties - Overhead cost reductions (1–2 weeks)	Debt structure modified; earnings problems may not be solved - Major refinancings reduce debt to 4:1 - Projects with largest positive cash flows spun off - Low cash return projects retained - But, interest cost may be reduced	Cash/earnings forecasts with proposed changes and impact - Assume current market forecasts unless recent data vary from plan - Include pro forma impact of current deals on cash, P & L, debt availability, DCF (?) Comparison of plans against longer-term target performance ratios	Current short-term plans, sales and profit data Proposed deal structures Economic models Earnings data and forecasts Cash Project data (if needed)
2. How much would financing gap increase if probable uncertainties occurred? - Refinancings deferred to FY76 or 77 - Operating properties not refinanced - Overhead reductions not achieved - Market performance below plan (1–2 weeks)	Gap could be an additional $7 million or more - $2 million/year interest savings - $1–2 million cash release - Target savings of $1.4 million could be only $1.0 million - Sales are 1/3 of last year; sales doldrums because of lack of clear product image; project behind plan on sales, ahead on cash needs	Relative performance versus plan and national market; reasons for 3–4 key projects Latest timetables/probabilities for implementing major refinancings; assessments of deal from potential partners' viewpoint; brokers' views on progress, reactions Latest results on achieved cost savings, timetables for further reductions	Marketing department Project manager interviews Market research Negotiators Loan documents Investment banker interviews Survey of monthly operating statements

| further overhead reductions and value improvements and what benefits would be achieved? E.g.
– Skeleton staffs in construction and amenity monitoring, design, administration
– Centralized financial reporting and control
– Limited architectural review, land planning, ecological planning and control
(3–4 weeks) | reductions are the most certain and rapidly implemented solutions and would have major impact (e.g., $____ million per year in cash and $____ million in earnings) because of
– Extensive operating overhead in past
– Tendency to overstaff specialist departments, overcontrol quality, image | tudes of expenditure, sorted into activity areas, with space, related overheads approximately allocated, fixed variables identified

Forecasts of levels of activity – by project – for design, construction, amenity and infrastructure operations, ecological and land planning burden, etc.

Estimates of process and data overlaps, duplications; outline of simpler, more centralized system; cost estimates of design and implementation | detailed budgets, job descriptions

Sales and construction plans, key projects

Reporting systems structure and review of operations

Systems design personnel

Public companies' data

Appraisers for G & A rates

Outside vendors' experience of projects

To be identified after initial analysis of opportunities |

Figure 7.7(a) Financial contingency planning: an illustrative analytic plan

ISSUES/PROBLEMS/TIMING	HYPOTHESES/REASONS	ANALYSES REQUIRED	DATA SOURCES
3. (Continued)		Comparative data from other large-scale developers for key activity areas	
		Survey of cost and availability of outside supply (seasonal or peak needs)	
		Comprehensive survey of key managers' ideas, opportunities, relative priorities of each activity area to short-term sales/earnings achievements	Key managers' analyses of development process by project
4. What potential exists for short-term sales increases, and what benefits might be achieved? (3-4 weeks)	Sale of lots to non-developer syndicate that might tap a new money source; 'for fee' development at appropriate time in project cycle	Cash and earnings contribution analysis by product type and customer/sale type – by project, if structure varies	Analysis of existing prior syndications / Existing project data
	Increased presentation of low-capture SMSAs by highly targeted mail shots, junket-	Definition of deal and comparison of tax, cost benefits to potential syndicate	Deal terms, present costs, etc.

...crease closing rate – e.g., holiday discount on purchase of lot, selective price reductions, cash discount for DU tract purchases, free year's club membership

But legal and registration problems, risks and costs may limit short-term actions – e.g., New York state injunction, Illinois moratorium

...high and low capture regions to identify saturation level, reasons for variations in results

Estimates of capture by region

Costs, benefits for each proposed change – e.g., estimates of initial costs, B/E volume increases required to justify changes, price/volume relationships from historical data or estimates

Figure 7.7(b) Financial contingency planning: an illustrative analytic plan (cont.)

173

ISSUES/PROBLEMS/TIMING	HYPOTHESES/REASONS	ANALYSES REQUIRED	DATA SOURCES
5. Are there any other solutions possible through a changed corporate/ project relationship, allocations of activity or reporting arrangements? (1–2 weeks)	Additional resources could be transferred from corporate to project	Model of financial flows between corporate and project for one specific case	Project finance staff for one project
	Short-term marketing efforts should, in particular, be focused on the most 'cash generating' products	Review of current budget allocation between corporate and project for all projects	Corporate financial staff
	Increase selectively accounts payable (e.g., renegotiate terms of purchase with key vendors)	Impact on financial structure and financial availability of past and possible additional future shifts in resources between corporate and project and staff terminations	
		Evaluation of roles with financial staff	

Figure 7.7(c) Financial contingency planning: an illustrative analytic plan (cont.)

1. *Review current plans.* Contingency planning begins with a quick assessment of the developer's near-term plans, the assumptions underlying them, and the impact of current or proposed action programs on foreseeable problems. The entire financial portfolio should be included, whether the development enterprise has several projects under way, or only one large-scale project with many separately financed sub-projects.

All possible actions and events should be considered, even if they seem highly improbable at the time. If a full commitment planning process has been completed (as described in chapter 5), then the critical contingencies will already have been identified. But it is only prudent quickly to review the internal and external factors that could precipitate a financial crisis, since these may change fundamentally in a time of uncertainty. A contingency matrix (Fig. 7.8) is useful in assessing the interactions between events and their impact on the financial health of the enterprise.

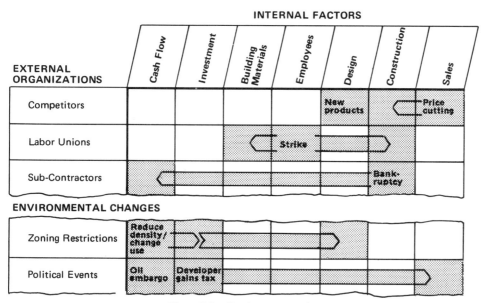

Figure 7.8 Contingency matrix

The major end product of this crucial first step is an updated financial plan and project concept (chapter 5), with revised cash and earnings forecasts to reflect likely short-term changes, and comparisons of these with longer-term performance targets reflecting overall financial prospects.

2. *Identify probable financing gaps.* Since contingency planning is a means of averting financial jeopardy, potential cash-flow gaps need to be evaluated in terms of both their range and their downside impact on cash and earnings. Here considerable use is made of 'what if' analyses of the key assumptions highlighted in step 1. Starting from the assumption that no countermeasures would be taken beyond those already proposed helps to pinpoint the most significant contingencies, and prevents the issue

175

being clouded by too many bright but unworkable ideas that may emerge to solve the problem. While sequential analysis and simulation runs are essential, the extensive models typically used for strategic planning are too cumbersome. Hard thinking with a pocket calculator, and a large supply of midnight oil, are less costly and more useful.

As indicated in Fig. 7.7, the cash-flow gap may not be covered by the projected refinancings being negotiated under pressure. In the evaluation, one thorny problem is to determine what cash contribution will be made from existing sources and the degree of downside risk in each. Since a major project typically involves a number of separate sub-project deals, each with its own source, terms and risks, the practical difficulties of preparing a composite picture cannot be dismissed lightly. Cash contingencies that depend directly on sales are more easily tracked, but those that are a function of other aspects of the development process are particularly difficult to analyse. Figure 7.9 shows a practical format for analysing these independent cash contingencies.

3. *Evaluate potential value improvements and cost reductions.* While it may not always be practical to cut costs significantly without cutting corners and ultimately damaging a project's viability, it is nearly always possible to increase the customer or user value in the project and directly improve the financial results. At a minimum, this strengthens its competitive advantage and further contains any market risks, but it may also create price premiums and release considerable resources for more effective redeployment elsewhere.

When considering cost reductions, overhead is the natural expense item to pin-point for detailed review. Because of their mammoth projects and entrepreneurial styles, developers have difficulty keeping their overhead down at the best of times, and in a crisis this may be as productive an opportunity for saving as the financing structure itself.

Overhead reduction must, of course, be approached with a delicate hand, because it raises sensitive issues of corporate and project staffing. It is usually best to begin with an analysis of the basic development tasks and an estimate of the minimum staff that would be required if one were starting afresh. To start from the other end, dissecting the existing structure and the personalities within it, is to risk overlooking high-potential opportunities, as well as embroiling executives and analysts in highly charged debates before it is clear where the major problems and opportunities lie.

Detailed approaches to value improvement and overhead analysis are discussed in chapter 14.

4. *Assess short-term market potential.* Because of quirks in the market, the short-term potential for achieving sales or rentals may differ from the original estimates. It is therefore worthwhile to re-examine opportunities that were discarded in earlier analyses and to identify those raised through unforeseen events. For example, individuals who convert securities into cash for safety may also be inclined to capitalize on the discounted prices they can obtain by investing in high-quality land and housing. Such opportunities are unique to particular locations and buyer segments, but a number of developers have been able greatly to improve their short-term performance—and long-term viability—by quick and effective action to exploit erratic markets.

Project/Cash Contribution to Year 1976	Contribution Source	Assumptions	Downside Risk
Smithville/ $1.6 million	Bank loan supports overhead to $200,000 a month cash deficit ($2.4 million/year) besides funding project

Funding to end FY75 is not directly contingent on performance | Loan has exceeded original $5 million limit and reached new $20 million limit; loan ceiling will be extended to $30 or $35 million; bank will continue funding overhead | Bank will probably renew loan, because alternative is to manage project directly

20% probability of reduction in funding; bank may fund hard costs only |
| Oldfields/ $2.7 million | Project supports developer overhead to maximum of $175,000/ month

Funding originates from $30 million loan; $15 million limit on outstandings | Loan and interest reserve ceilings will not be reached before March 1976 | Added drain of $600,000/ month could start April 1976 or sooner depending on sales level

Performance criteria have to be met by FY77 or interest and overhead funding will be discontinued |
| Lake Retreat/ 0 | Bank has halted contract | 20% chance developer may get $500,000 but imprudent to include in FY76 cash flow | $15,000 moving costs |

Figure 7.9 Illustrative analysis of cash contingencies

The key to this, however, is to assess the opportunity costs of immediate action against the benefits to be obtained. Even substantial untapped demand would not justify a major marketing effort if the actual cash impact was likely to be minimal or deferred for several years. Similarly, an action program targeted on immediate cash-generating sales would have to be carefully vetted to ensure that it did not pre-empt the longer-term strategy or create an impression of over-aggressive promotion.

5. *Develop and execute an action program.* Ideally, contingency planning should be undertaken before a financial siege begins, but it is seldom initiated until repeated warnings have come from institutional investors and lenders, who will be reassured only if the revised plans are clearly realizable. Moreover, in a time of unusual stress,

	MAJOR SOURCE OF FINANCE			IMPACT		
Proposed Transaction	Purpose	Structure	Probability	Cash	Earnings	Balance Sheet
1. Development loan	Reduce developer leverage and financial exposure; secure incremental funding for development; reduce working capital lines and other debt	1/3 debt guarantee for 1/2 cash flow	Low, FY75 High, early 1976	$11 m.	50% reduction	$70 m. debt reduction; contingent liability; D/E drops from 11.8 to 7.6
2. Joint venture	Fund further expansion; reduce working capital lines and other debt	Give up 35% cash flow Gain $3–5 m. equity	Medium, FY75 High, FY76	$3–5 m. available cash	35% reduction	$40 m. debt reduction
3. Sale (and leaseback)						
(a) Income-producing properties	Secure financing of new offices; generate some short-term cash	11–13% lease rate for $____	Medium to low, FY75	$13.8 m. from initial proceeds $2 m. for working capital	Ultimate expected increase in earnings	Switch debt to lease (no significant impact)
(b) Purchase land on joint venture	Reduce debt burden and carrying cost	75% cash to bank, 25% to developer	Medium, FY75	Repay $13 m. debt $1.5 m. available for working	75% reduction	$13 m. debt reduction

						November 1975		None
	manent corporate debt; 'take out' bank; secure all additional $1.8 m. contingency financing up to December 1975 if possible	pledged for − $3 m. commitment increase from banks − $1.2 m. repayment leaving net $1.8 m.					None	
5. Retail site refinancing	Refinance existing retail debt to take it off existing lenders; gain contingency financing from existing lenders; secure future retail financing	Secure $15 m. in refinancing debt Reduce outstandings of current lenders from $17 m. to $7 m. while keeping current $21 m. commitment Switch from prime +2.25% balance to prime +4	Medium, FY76	Increase loans from $21 m. to $31 m.				

Figure 7.10 Financial contingency planning: illustrative analysis of possible transactions

179

normal management responsibilities, relationships and processes may be overtaken by events unless a complete and detailed action program is designed. Such a plan should designate not only who is to do what, but who should pursue each contingency strategy with the lenders concerned. It should also specify who must be kept informed of issues that arise and progress in structuring the refinancing. Contingency reporting is likely to differ substantially from the normal hierarchy. The 'need to know' principle is therefore a wise one to adopt, not only to secure confidentiality and so maintain staff and investor confidence, but also to avoid information overload among already stretched project executives and analysts.

Finally, the action program should specify the analysis of possible transactions that will meet contingency needs. Figure 7.10 shows the type of synthesis that will help decision-makers to keep abreast of the refinancing and inform their judgements on a specific course of action.

This completes the contingency planning process. Events of the past 18 months have given convincing proof of its value in a period of crisis. Not a few developers have benefited accordingly, but many more need to follow their example.

Capturing the economic values of social investment

Social investment—i.e., in infrastructure, schools, clinics, community centres and the like—benefits the community in tangible, though non-financial, ways and can result in real, albeit unrealized, savings for local government in the long term. Indeed, a set of community accounts would show a net positive impact from planned development, and all of the community impact studies done over the past 10 years show these benefits conclusively. In total, cash expenditures are substantially lower. Funds for parks and open space may be higher, but expenditure on roads, water and sewerage is generally lower, because more rational land-use relationships and higher planning densities permit a more compact infrastructure and the provision of basic services at lower *per capita* investment. Moreover, good planning can generate substantial savings in public programs—savings that should be possible in existing communities but that often go unrecognized. In Columbia, for example, the simple fact that most children can walk to school is expected to save the state $1 million annually by 1980 in transport and running costs that would have been unavoidable within most traditional patterns of development.

In providing community services, however, the developer is not simply a benefactor. Social investment, properly managed, helps to create value. In both privately financed projects and public projects where a return is expected from borrowed funds, the overriding issue is whether the values created by investment in amenities and other community assets will provide sufficient collateral either for long-term development without the need for a guarantee or subsidy, or for giving the lender a substantial equity stake in the development to secure his risk.

Managing the required social investment presents the developer with two main challenges: how to finance it and how much to invest. And each element of the total

180

mix of uses must be carefully evaluated to ensure the right balance. To leverage his limited funds, the developer needs to draw on a wide variety of outside sources of funds, matching them, as far as possible, with the ultimate beneficiaries of a given investment.

A range of methods, each with its own sources and users of funds, has proved workable in community development:

Method	Source	User
1. Land price discount	Developer	Local Government (LG)
2. Land price premium	Buyer	Developer
3. Fixed annual fee	Buyer	Community Association (CA)
4. *Ad valorem* tax	Buyer	CA
5. Loan	Developer	CA/LG
6. Grant/subsidy	Developer	LG
	Government	CA
	Foundation	Developer
7. Service charge	Individual user of service	CA

Each method is briefly discussed below.[2]

1. *Land price discount.* The developer assumes that he will sell a substantial number of acres for community programs at a minimum price. Cash flow is not affected provided these programs do not infringe on saleable acres. He may, however, use his cash flow to fund programs that do not require substantial cash.

The developer may also subsidize programs through reduced land prices. Free space, services and cash subsidies are often given to religious, medical and cultural groups that will bring additional resources to the community. To stimulate minimum cost housing, price concessions may be offered to builders, since house prices are directly influenced by lot prices. Generally, a finished lot price represents 20–25 per cent of the builder's selling price for a house. So, if a developer can sell all the lots that he can produce at $8,000 per lot, houses will range above $40,000; to provide houses in the $20,000–$30,000 range, lot prices will have to drop to $5,000–$6,000. A similar relationship exists in multi-family dwellings between unit prices and rental levels.

However, the market often eliminates lower cost housing units on first resale, giving substantial windfalls to the seller. In Columbia, several hundred town houses sold in the opening year for $14,500–$17,500. The builder had built the units because of a substantial land subsidy and working capital assistance from the developer. Within 18 months the price had risen to over $22,000, even though similar units were being offered by the same builder in a new area for less than $20,000. So the developer's initial objective of providing lower cost housing was quickly lost, and the difference between the market price for land and the subsidized price was also forgone.

181

2. *Land price premium.* This method establishes the definitive level of amenities that a developer can afford to provide within the project budget. Funds are sourced mainly through current residential sales, so no continuing charge is made to residents. Price-sensitive commercial and industrial land purchasers show little interest in increased amenities. If all other factors—especially price—are equal, the commercial and industrial user will select the site with the highest level of amenities, but he usually will not pay a premium for them.

While recreational facilities, like golf courses and swimming pools, are easily added to the price of middle- and upper-income residential units, problems occur in supporting lower-income housing. A community developer can provide some lower- to middle-income housing through land subsidies. But as we have seen, land that could be sold at market prices for higher-income units *must* be sold at a discount if lower-income units are to be provided, and few if any amenities can be funded from these subsidized prices. This method of recovering amenity costs therefore runs counter to the objective of providing lower-income units in the new community.

3. *Fixed annual fee.* This will normally provide more funds over time than the above methods. It also gives the resident a prepurchase understanding of his commitments. However, it usually does not apply to industrial and commercial buyers. Moreover, with high inflation the fixed fee is insufficient, so the level of services must fall or the charge must be increased by agreement of a substantial majority of the residents—a difficult and often unrewarding process. Again, a fixed charge puts a greater proportionate burden on the lower-income unit than on the higher-income unit. If rates are raised, the lower-income resident might be forced to leave the community.

4. *Ad valorem tax.* This is a more equitable way of raising funds, since it is applied annually to the full established assessable value of land and buildings, and can easily be applied to all properties in the community. The commercial and industrial buyer will accept an annual tax-deductible charge much more readily than a higher land price that cannot be expensed.

Compare an *ad valorem* tax with an increased land price as a means of generating funds. A one-time 25 per cent increase in land price from, say, $40,000 to $50,000 would yield $10,000. The same parcel, developed for investment, would yield $2,025 annually in perpetuity, or $25,300 capitalized at 8 per cent.[3]

It is also more equitable for low-income residents, who receive the same level of services for a substantially lower charge by paying only in proportion to the value of their property. Furthermore, the method is inflation-proof as long as assessed values are revised regularly to reflect increased costs.

Perhaps the most important benefit, however, is that the developer is able to preservice the community with amenities because he has a means of recovering the front-end financing. Because a developer would normally be reluctant to advance funds to a community association without some assurance of repayment, this method best ensures the CA's risk.

Ad valorem charges should be supported by a lien on property values. If this is superior to the basic development financing, the CA should be able to establish its own funding at an early date, enabling the developer to be repaid. Without the prior lien position, ultimate finacing by the CA of its capital facilities program is sure to be deferred, and the developer is less inclined to advance significant funds to the CA.

Since the annual charge is small in proportion to the total value of the property and mortgages, there is little increased risk to the lender in having the smaller charge in front of the mortgage if default occurs. On the other hand, the value of the lien as a source to a financier of community needs is substantially reduced if the mortgage holds a priority. By allowing the lien to precede the mortgage, little risk is assumed but benefits accrue to the community, thereby increasing values and affording additional protection to the developer.

5. *Loan.* Loans are extended to acquire for community use properties other than those deeded by the developer, to construct and improve community facilities or to supplement local public services. Provided by the developer, public agencies or institutions, the terms and conditions for borrowing will depend largely on local requirements. Without a first lien as collateral, the CA would find it difficult to raise external funds on acceptable terms. But with the first lien, the CA will be in as strong a position as a public authority with its own capacity to issue securities. For example, rather than properties automatically being transferred by the developer free of debt, the CA could carry a high proportion of the debt burden for community facilities. This could have the double advantage of reducing developer exposure and using the favourable terms of interest rate available to CAs.

The local government will normally accept responsibility for services that they already provide to the existing community, but they may not have sufficient sources of funding. Indeed, if accelerated growth results from the new community, 'reverse' funding may occur, where the developer loans funds to the municipality to accelerate school, sewer and water programs. When the community has an adequate assessable base, bonds can be floated to amortize the local government's obligation to the developer.

6. *Grants and subsidies.* Local government is less apt to be politically courageous in providing facilities or services to the new community if they are not already provided to the existing community, so the developer may have to accept that responsibility until the new constituency can 'negotiate' them. The growth potential of the assessable base, local tradition and the developer's sensitivity to local needs are the major factors in a developer's relationship with the local government. But if he is too effective in finding alternative sources of funding, the local authority may not assume responsibilities that it would otherwise have accepted eventually.

New communities do not have sufficient cash flows to fund programs that have traditionally required national government support. Mass transport, for example, is beyond the developer's financing capacity, just as it is beyond that of many existing cities. Assistance in providing for sewer, water and open space development is usually needed because local authorities cannot provide adequate funding and the developer's cash flow is limited.

The US Title VII program provides for grants to support basic services without which development cannot proceed (e.g., sewer, water), and for other services that are important to fulfilling new community objectives but are not essential to the physical structure (e.g., transport, day care). Basic services must be accounted for in

183

cash flow projections through some funding source, but community services may be included without firm commitments. The developer's cash flow will benefit in one of two ways. If the grant replaces funds that the developer had assumed would ultimately derive from cash flow, the total cash flow is increased and the peak debt requirement is reduced. Some developer agreements require 80 per cent of these funds to be applied to meet social objectives. On the other hand, if the grant replaces funds that the developer had assumed he would supply but would recover from some other source (e.g., sewer rebates), his ultimate cash flow is unaffected but his peak debt requirement is reduced. The developer might benefit from reduced carrying costs but would have no cash savings to apply elsewhere. However, the community receives a service that might not otherwise have been provided, assuming that grants and other aids are based on the lack of alternative sources.

Existing institutions and foundations may be eager to participate in a new community, particularly if they might derive some competitive advantage from it. In Columbia, for example, the Columbia Bank and Trust is the only local bank to date with a president living in the community. The developer recognized this fortuitous circumstance and requested that, in view of its identification with the community and assured market growth, the bank allocate 10 per cent of its earnings to the Columbia Foundation. The bank now contributes $10,000 annually but by 1980 the amount is expected to be $100,000 or more. The Foundation uses these funds to provide 'seed' money to new community institutions, supporting a wide variety of community services.

7. *Service charges.* Used to supplement the regular assessment base, service charges provide a fair means of paying for community services that are not demanded or used by the whole population, and for which a particular clientele can be identified—i.e., swimming pools and tennis courts, but not common open spaces and access roads. Furthermore, they can be designed to give flexibility of access to users other than residents—e.g., on-site employees, visitors, people living adjacent to the project—thus reducing the charges of isolation that may be levelled at the project and, at the same time, increasing CA revenues.

Having assessed ways to finance social investment, the developer still has to determine the level of non-financial benefits that may support the financing request. As the appendix highlights, the evaluation of social, economic and financial value is an issue that plagues every community development program. Drawing up a 'true' balance sheet would clearly be an enormous task, but is probably more feasible than is generally acknowledged.[4] A format could be devised for reporting the sources and uses of investment in the community; the various types of return, using social and economic as well as financial indicators; the achievements and gaps in services and product performance; the kinds of problems that have emerged, and the ways they have been tackled or left unresolved. By comparing each area and community project with others, some approximation of overall social as well as financial return should be apparent.

Though no purely quantitative method yet exists for integrating these costs and benefits, decisions must still be taken to invest funds that may not realize financial returns, and some assessment is needed of the value of that investment. Despite the difficulties, both public and private developers have alternative uses for funds, and thus need to know whether the community development has been, or will be, a good investment. Policy-makers too need to know whether they have made a sensible investment—that is, 'what went in, what came out, and was it a good buy?'

An initial attempt at evaluating the full costs and benefits has been made in the course of planning for community facilities and services. As shown in Fig. 7.11, the

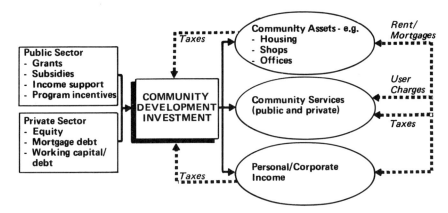

Figure 7.11 Funds flows in community development

first step is to analyse the basic fund flows and investment entailed in the development process. For example, the flow diagram in Fig. 7.12 shows how capital costs and operating cash flow can be estimated for each of the planned community services discussed in chapter 6. At this stage it will not be possible to be precise about capital costs, since costs will be determined as the project matures. To take account of this element of uncertainty, the decision-maker's judgement should include an

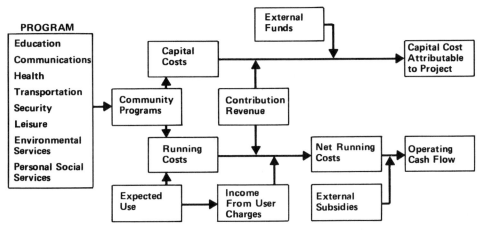

Figure 7.12 Flow diagram of capital costs and cash flow for community services

185

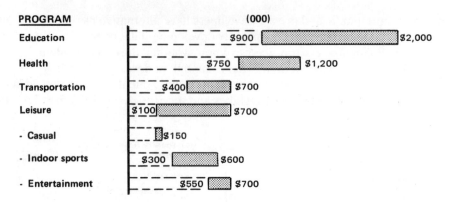

Figure 7.13 Range of capital costs for community facilities

indication of the possible range of capital costs that might be incurred in providing some of the community facilities (Fig. 7.13). Then the expected costs that would be required if historical development patterns ensued are established as a basis for testing whether the planned front-end investment of public and private funds in the community development model would result in greater ultimate savings and thus release resources for community use. These relationships are illustrated in Fig. 7.14.

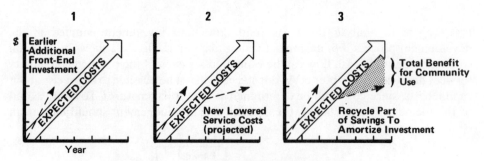

Figure 7.14 Financing community services investment

The special economics of large-scale development, and the difficulties of accurately communicating them through conventional accounting and management information, underscore the need to evaluate each project thoroughly, on its own merits, in light of the factors discussed above. Project characteristics differ so greatly that any effort to design or apply a single investment yardstick is likely to be futile. Too often, hasty analyses fail to take account of the unusual economics and the special risks of community building and ignore the significant benefits that underlie its long-run success.

It is particularly essential that the financing concept for a project clearly distinguishes development uses that have commercial real estate market potential from those designed to meet community objectives. In contrast to the European programs, perhaps the main shortcoming of much US community development financing to date has been confusion between commercial and social objectives, which has placed such an intolerable burden on the underlying financing structures of the programs, on the institutions that have supported them and, ultimately, on the community residents.

While new instruments for community financing will require specific design and analysis beyond the scope of this chapter, they should meet these four basic principles: (1) *simplicity* to ensure ease of administration and review, avoiding the need for a large bureaucracy; (2) *long maturity* with deferral of interest until the nominal break-even is reached; (3) *policy-oriented control*, based on measures of local need and results, as well as on traditional financial and building measures; and (4) *paired investment* between the financing and value-creating potential of growth areas and the reinvestment needs of outworn inner city areas. In applying these principles, the crucial challenges for community development economics still lie ahead.

References

1. Derek Finlay and Richard Norton of McKinsey & Company recently completed an extensive series of analyses on the impact of inflation on corporate management, and they made a number of helpful suggestions that have been incorporated in this section.
2. I am indebted to Richard L. Anderson for his contribution in developing this description of alternative methods.
3. 15,000 square feet at $30 generates $450,000 of value, assessed at 60 per cent with an assessment rate of $0.75 per $100 ($270,000 × 0.75 ÷ 100 = $2,025).
4. See Apgar, 'Using Social Indicators: Guidelines for Urban Decision-Makers', *Papers and Proceedings of the 1974 World Congress*, International Federation of Housing and Planning, pp. 173–94.

Chapter 8. Design: An integral part of strategy

MORT HOPPENFELD

The words 'design' and 'community' together conjure up visions of beautifully rendered plans, perspective pictures and elegant three-dimensional models, all depicting an ideal of a completed 'new community'. Architectural journals and books reinforce this association. But designing for publication and designing for the realities of a community in the processes of development are vastly different. The Utopian image is acceptable in one case. In the other, only sensitive, analytically sound and demonstrably feasible work will carry the day.

Community building is a live activity and by definition subject to continual change. It is a process that thrives on the involvement of many people with many skills. Principal among these committed participants must be the community designers. In this chapter I shall first discuss what we mean by 'good design', and why it is important both to the resident and to the developer. Then I shall describe the design process itself, the designer's working relationships and some of the dilemmas he must resolve. Finally, I outline a framework for an architectural review that could help reconcile public and private interests in the continuing growth of the community.

Quality in design

Designing is the deliberate process of giving visible shape to a community by creating its physical environment: ultimately, in every last detail, and in response to *all aspects* of a program. Designing the environment is not something that is done after many development decisions have been made.

Levels of design input are often required in the earliest stages of concept development, program definition and general planning in order to assure project feasibility. As Fig. 8.1 illustrates, the designer's initial conceptual diagram helps to visualize the relationship between program elements before the specifics of building size and shape are known. These activities should be thought of not as sequential but

188

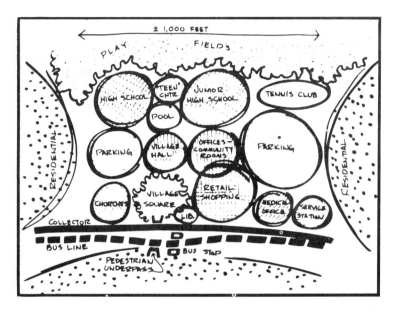

Figure 8.1 Designer's conceptual diagram

as interactive and continuing throughout the development stages of a community. Only the *role* of design changes according to the progress of the project. Even in the earliest phase, such as site selection, designers should participate by engaging in a careful analysis of the land in question, to establish the desirability of a given site in light of the objectives for the new community. There is hardly a step in the community development process that does not require participation by knowledgeable planners/designers if the project is to be both economically sound and functionally and aesthetically satisfying.

In essence, designing is a way of solving problems. In community development, the design problems lie in resolving the sets of complex requirements placed on the physical environment in order that all of the physical and social pieces that make up a community can best function. To design is to analyse the problem, to identify its respective components and their interrelationships and to synthesize the components into a harmonious, working whole.

What is good design?

The medium of community design is the physical envelope for community life—the important buildings and places, the circulation systems between them, the paraphernalia of the landscape (trees, signs, lights, benches, etc.), the natural setting, and sets of housing and other repeated building types. The fundamental test of 'goodness' is how well the resultant places meet the requirements of the program—i.e., how well they solve the problem. A good design process, therefore, should require that the designer first state in words what is meant to be accomplished by the configuration of

189

land, buildings and circulation systems. If you cannot articulate your purpose verbally, there is little likelihood of knowing when you have satisfied it with a completed building, place or community.

There are innumerable forces at play or criteria to meet simultaneously throughout the life of any project. Good design must strike the delicate balance among these forces. Three broad categories can describe them. First, *economic*: the basic construction budgets, the time frame, cash-flow requirements, maintenance costs, the techniques of financing, etc. All of these have significant effect on design decisions. Second, *social purpose*: the ability of the physical environment to ennoble and to enhance or, by poor design, to inhibit the behaviour of people and influence their lives. The designer must share in the values of the community's stated social purpose. Within this category must come issues of design process, how and with whom work is done and whatever is appropriate to achieve political approvals. The third category of *aesthetic or sensual delight* is important in its own right. The goodness of a place should in part be judged by its ability to make people smile and feel good, to linger, to be awed or excited—that is, to satisfy the senses in ways appropriate to the basic purpose of the place. Unfortunately, it is here, in the realm of the senses, that designers often pursue their own values—leaving behind the client or user community. The mystique of 'beauty' and the sometimes prestigious name and domineering personality of a designer can often lead to design that is poor when judged against *all* criteria.

These three categories set goals for design, expressed sometimes in detailed programs such as the precise areas and dollar construction costs to be allocated to each unit, sometimes in vague, inarticulate terms such as 'it should be beautiful but inexpensive'. At various stages any one force can dominate the other two. All three are needed, kept in a continual balance. When a design does meet all three of the general criteria, without the serious negation of any one, only then should it be considered to be good design.

The designer must have no hidden agenda, no private aesthetic or other goals that he intends to pursue. This is not to say that he should not have his own values and opinions, some held so strongly that he may not wish to participate in a design process that violates his own sense of right and wrong.

Once there is agreement in concept (words and diagrams) between the designer and the client, which establishes the fundamental purposes to be served and the basic attitude toward aesthetics together with the allocation of resources, then the designer must begin to make this agreement operational. He needs to articulate a design program. As the design process continues, new information and choices will emerge, and it is to be expected that the program itself will evolve.

Typically, design programs are couched only in quantifiable terms—e.g., so many square feet for such and such a use to be constructed at a given cost. Sometimes added to this is a description of relationships between buildings or spaces. These are all necessary. But equally important and seldom included in a design program is a description of how the completed environment is intended to affect the people using it. For example, if we are designing a grouping of houses, I would want to know what role privacy will play in the well-being of the families. For which activities do they need visual privacy? How important is audio privacy in their personal lives? How can the environment facilitate neighbouring and friendship patterns? How can the activities of children and adults be encouraged without encroaching on each other? How is the relationship between a mother and her children affected by the environment? How might the cultural heritage of the residents influence aesthetic decisions?

I hold the fundamental belief that the designer alone cannot significantly alter the interpersonal or intergroup relationships of a large or small community. These are most affected by socioeconomic conditions. But over time the man-made environment can aggravate difficult human relationships or can reinforce and facilitate happy ones. We should know in advance what feelings we mean to engender and what activities are meant to be encouraged. The consummate skill of a designer is in the ability to predict human response to an environment or object (not discounting the felicitous accident).

Determining quality in design requires study and time. Beware the immediate impact of dramatic spaces and unique forms. Good places have the special quality of *congruence*, where a social and physical environment is mutually reinforcing and supportive of defined human interests and activities. I like to use words such as 'appropriateness' and 'fit' in judging elements of a design. A well-designed place is seldom startling. If it is appropriate, it may seem 'natural' (as it should be), and evade immediate awareness.

The design should aim to create an environment that is responsive to the needs and aspirations of people 'where they are now' (culturally), to offer the comfort of recognition and familiarity. It should simultaneously evoke higher aspirations for environments that are beyond people's experience—i.e., it should transcend the present. What a difficult task for a designer to achieve: to sense a possible and desirable future, design for it and still satisfy the felt needs of today.

Large and complex communities are seldom built 'at once'. Yet it is often necessary to have most, if not all, of the pieces together before a place can be sensed as whole and inclusive enough to serve the community well. Most people are aware of this problem and hesitate to move into an incomplete environment. At each stage of growth, there should be a stated design objective to have that fragment evoke a sense of completeness, even though it is only a part of a yet unfinished whole. This is a very difficult task, but it must be met lest the community look always unfinished until it is, in fact, completed—often years in the future. The reason for articulating this as a design criterion is the effect that such concerns have on the designer's approach to creating community places. Identifiable geometric patterns with a side left incomplete for lack of the town hall or the next wing of the shopping centre can be terribly obvious, and therefore wanting in providing the sense of wholeness for those who are there now. The Piazza San Pietro in Rome (Fig. 8.2) is a perfect example of a single-purpose, monumental place. It would be difficult to imagine it being incomplete or subject to change.

Having talked about congruence and wholeness as conditions of quality, I must now add what will seem to be a contradictory requirement—that is, the ability to adapt to change.

191

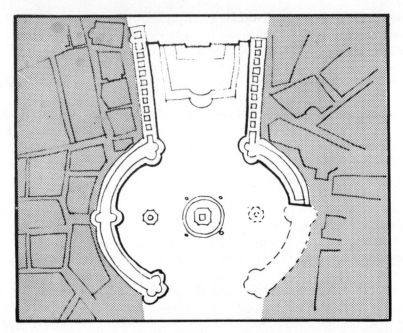

Figure 8.2   Piazza San Pietro

Since it can be assumed that change in need and circumstances will occur during the course of building a community, it is desirable that these changes be manifest in new programs and new design. Recognizing change and the unknown requires that places can be added to or altered in unanticipated ways. This leads to the concept of 'open-endedness' in the forms that places take. The designer's skill is taxed when trying to accomplish the sense of completeness and the reality of open-endedness at the same time.

In this connection I tend to prefer complexity in the built environment rather than simplicity or formalism. Carried to extremes one will lead to possible chaos and the other to boredom. But my underlying assumption here is that people are more likely to find satisfaction over time in an appropriately complex setting because, over time, our moods and demands on the environment will vary greatly and the ideal environment will be rich enough to be responsive to this variety of needs. Figure 8.3 illustrates a site plan where complexity is inherent in the 'completed' urban place. Complex shapes and places tend almost by definition to have 'openings' that can become 'joints' to future building. It is a move away from the monumental, which tends to evolve from concepts of single purpose, toward the informal, or softer setting, which can accommodate many uses over time with little adjustment. In Fig. 8.4 the designers sought to create the main urban complex of the new city next to a lake, allowing the earliest buildings to appear 'complete' in their park-like setting. Growth can thus occur in alternate directions with each new unit enhancing the

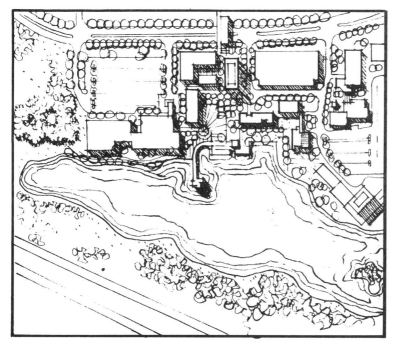

Figure 8.3   Complexity in a completed site

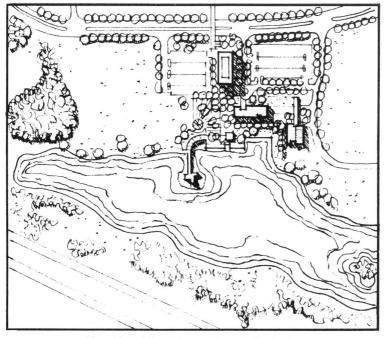

Figure 8.4   'Completeness' from the beginning

194

Figure 8.5 Unfinished yet 'complete'

Figure 8.6 Informal activities in an urban setting

existing place while creating new urban scenes. Figure 8.5 shows the actual unfinished—though visually 'complete'—place as seen from the water's edge. At the same time, these informal urban settings can encourage a variety of impromptu activities that enrich and enliven individual and communal life (Fig. 8.6).

In summary, a philosophy that leads to good design has *no preconceptions* as to what should be built or the form that it can take, but does demand (1) that what we build serves a soundly expressed social purpose; (2) that what we build should evoke a generally positive, highly satisfying aesthetic and emotional response; and (3) that (1) and (2) are accomplished through the expenditure of reasonable and previously agreed-upon commitments of time, money and manpower.

My philosophy would have the designer struggle to optimize these three conditions, knowing full well that the ultimate satisfaction of one is likely to be attained only at the cost of another.

The nature of the balance cannot and should not be solely decided by the designer. In fact, it should come forth as a proposal by him to be affirmed or adjusted by the client—ideally, the user of the thing intended to be built. *This requires that the designer conceive of himself in the role of facilitating others to make the decisions that will directly influence their own lives or business success.*

Why is good design important?

The essential importance of good design is that it creates the environment for a sought-after quality of life. Good design will therefore benefit a community in every respect.

An environment that works well for its people will inevitably evoke love and loyalty. Feeling good about a place can add dimensions to a person's life, away from anomie and toward belonging. A good environment can encourage social interaction and the workings of a communal life. The simple comfort of a wooden bench in the shade will encourage two to sit and talk while a concrete slab in the sun or wind will limit the visit.

A well-designed community should evoke the kind of response that ultimately makes people decide to stay, to buy, to invest, because it is a better alternative to other, less well-designed places. A well-designed community should create value far beyond its cost. This is one of the essential objectives of real estate investment. A place with the qualities of beauty and sound functioning should generate immediate consumer response. Good design is, in essence, a way of increasing sales. It is a marketable product. It is often its own advertisement. But the developer must recognize that the imaginative and appealing rendering (Fig. 8.7) may be taken as a kind of contract by which the buyers and future residents will soon expect him to deliver.

In the most measurable terms, good design can conserve land and minimize and/or optimize infrastructure and costs in general. While it can affect first costs, good design decisions can also help keep project life costs down by proper detailing and use of materials. Good design is without question a means toward increased profits.

196

Figure 8.7 Design: a contract for the future?

Good design skills are also necessary to establish a project's feasibility in economic terms and in the sociopolitical arena of consumer response and public agency approvals.

Conversely, poor design can make life's activities difficult, expensive, and unpleasant. A community shopping centre that is unprepossessing and difficult to get to, or which makes the shopping trip chaotic and unpleasant, will fail to attract shoppers. In any reasonably competitive setting, people will choose to go elsewhere. The economic costs to the developer can be disastrous. The social costs of additional trips to other places, the loss of a sense of place within a community and the consequent disintegration of likely social contacts are harder to put dollar value to. But any aspect of a whole community that evokes user dissatisfaction rubs off on all other aspects.

In more measurable terms, poor design might lead to early estimates that proved to be unfeasible later; to projects that were rejected by public approval agencies; or ultimately to the lack of sales, and to consumer dissatisfaction. There is no way to separate social and economic costs—it is simply a bit more difficult to quantify some than others.

How often places are deemed well designed when what is meant, in fact, is that they are beautiful. That quality alone is not sufficient. Too often beauty is purchased at a high cost—in budget or functional terms. If these construction costs are caught before building, then redesigning means losing time. But if the costs are hidden—or if bad process is combined with bad (beauty only) design—then money is wasted. Projects can be broken and community developers destroyed, and the user community loses in the end as well.

This high value placed on the aesthetics of design is most typical of architects and other designers. It is reinforced by their professional journals and trade magazines. Most awards and peer group recognition are generated not from the qualities of the completed community or project tested in use, but from the promises of elegant plans, perspective drawings and photogenic models, or at best from photos of the freshly completed 'design for publication'. In other words, it is the bold form and shape of things that typically turn the designer on, while the client and user has a much broader concern. This broader concern must be equally shared by the design professionals involved. This is not to suggest that symbolism and aesthetic satisfaction are not important. Occasionally they are critical— but seldom are they sufficient.

The design process

Well-designed places are most likely to result from a good design process. It could be said that designing a community is too important to be left only to designers. It is too complicated as well, and beyond the competence of any single area of specialized skills and knowledge. Good design process, therefore, is necessarily interdisciplinary, interactive, participatory and iterative.

Good process can not only create good places but also affect social institutions and ways of delivering social services. The designer can become a conscious agent of change because the questions raised in programming, when asked of the right people, provide the opportunity to 'do it better'. The rigours of time and budget accepted in designing and building can assist change-resistant institutions in making difficult decisions simply in order to keep up with the building schedule. In most cases, such change is beneficial to all.

The designer and his client

The environmental problems that design must solve are typically identified by many parties, whose interests may diverge. But the ultimate recognition and statement of 'what is to be done' must come from those who will be responsible for building and/or using the community. They are the ones who will bear the financial, sociopolitical risk of decision-making and they are the rightful 'client' for the designer. In this sense, the designer's responsibility is limited. The community designer is only one of many skilled people to whom the client-developer will look for help. It is important in the community design process that this distinction between roles be kept clear. The designer must have the proper frame of mind, viewing himself as a servant to and participant with client groups, *being responsive to their needs and interests.* It is not uncommon for the designer to cloud this relationship with personal biases, and to state his own problems and set his own priorities, becoming, in effect, his own client and being ultimately irresponsible in his designs. This is easy to do, since the real client is often inarticulate in the language and media of design. The misconception of the designer as his own client has been fostered, historically, by the idea of the designer as artist—'the cutting edge of society', who leads the masses to a better environment. This has seldom been the result in fact. Not that the design role is passive—far from it. The process is interactive; it often requires leadership; but, above all, it should be responsive to community needs. This involves a degree of participation in the design process by non-designers.

The word participation is a relatively new one for designers. Many jokes revolve around the concept of designing by committees. The fact is that designers are at best insufficient for the multitude of tasks involved in community design. Moreover, practising in a democratic society today requires real participation in environmental development procedures—people will no longer tolerate the 'elitist-expert' approach of having it done for them. The parties who have the ability to implement or to delay and deny development should be involved at all stages of the planning/design process if the concept of success is to include actual construction, user satisfaction and a real sense of ownership by the using community. This kind of participation can often furnish insight, feedback and creative energy to willing designers.

While project success may require non-designers to influence design decision, it is equally true to assert that the designer should be in a position to influence others. The design skill must be well represented on the management team (be it public or private) and have the same respect from top management as that given to the typically key interests of economics or construction engineering. The design skills (preferably an in-house staff) should be involved through the life of a project.

199

In addition to ensuring a quality product, a basic mission of a planning and design department (it could be one person) should be *continually to improve the knowledge and techniques for planning and design within the development corporation as a whole.* This improvement should not be limited to the designers, but should include project managers, sales and construction staff, social service officers and many others. A staff designer should also be a 'teacher' of design, just as he is a 'learner' of all other aspects of community development. An integral relationship to all other operating departments in an organization is essential to this end.

Designers working as part of a project team should become aware of the critical relationships of all aspects in the life of a project, from economic feasibility studies through maintenance. In this corporate environment, design principles, attitudes and standards are continually distilled and incorporated into written and graphic programs and into the operational behaviour of the entire group. The use of design consultants without such in-house staff minimizes the value gained from each experience. Such value leaves with the consultant. The value of consulting design talent and the quality of work done is directly related to the skill of the design managers as programmers, critics, and members of the client team.

Community planning and design requires many design and design-related disciplines. All must make their appropriate contribution to each project, in the right way and at the right time, through the project schedule. Project design co-ordination is an essential function and best carried out by one skilled in a design field. The project design co-ordinator does not have the overriding right to make design decisions, but should know the parameters for decisions, and how to go about getting them made.

What follows is an effort to delineate, in some detail, the kinds of work designers undertake to feed into the overall development process at different stages. At each stage, material is usually prepared for public or interest group meetings, and the designer is often most skilled in such presentations.

The sequence of steps in the design process

Stage One: Establishing project feasibility. At this point, a project area is delineated—land is either purchased or optioned, though boundaries are not necessarily finalized; a concept program is articulated; and a development team is assembled. The overall feasibility of meeting the space needs of the specified program on the given piece of land needs to be evaluated. Simultaneous analyses and evaluations are likely to be under way by lawyers concerned with zoning and all other conditions relevant to the use of the land; by engineers for critical on- and off-site conditions (sewer, water, roads, power, etc.); by marketing and sales for the potential for various 'products', pace, etc.; by economists for financing and the disciplines for economic modelling.

The cumulative evaluation of all relevant factors establishes the basis for decisions needed to move on to the next stages in the development process.

Steps in Stage One

1. *Collect existing information.* Search to identify all relevant base data and to establish their validity—i.e., topo maps, land-use maps, road maps, etc.

2. *Prepare usable base materials.* Prepare base maps to appropriate scale, with control topo, known and questionable conditions marked; identify all ownership and right-of-way easements and other legal constraints.
3. *Carry out intensive site visit.* Make photographic reconnaissance, take specific and panoramic views with emphasis on eye-level observations, aerial obliques where appropriate and possible.
4. *Analyse and map existing surface conditions.* Record vegetative cover by appropriate categories—i.e., trees, brush, etc.; also record roads, and relevant structures.
5. *Analyse and map surrounding existing land uses and public agency plans.* Include infrastructure elements, roads, sewer, water, power, schools, etc.
6. *Make land quality analyses and inventory.* Map slopes by degree relevant to likely building types (0–10 per cent; 10–20 per cent, etc.); catalogue soil analyses by potential effect on site use and development costs.
7. *Analyse land structure.* Map elevations by appropriate intervals (1 ft., 2 ft., 5 ft., 10 ft., etc.); show ridge and valley designations.
8. *Carry out hydrology analyses.* Map established drainage patterns, existing and potential optimized sewer patterns, water courses, flood plains, marsh and areas of other potential hydrological import.
9. *Carry out visual analyses.* Identify special opportunities or problems that affect aesthetic and use potentials.
10. *Carry out ecological analyses.* Identify, evaluate and map *pertinent* ecological concerns—i.e., animal life, special plant material concerns, climatological factors and pollution implications.
11. *Make preliminary land capacity analyses.* Assuming density, building type, and land utilization from concept program, establish preliminary capacity of land to hold the program requirements based on all above constraints.
12. *Make initial on-site cost estimate.* Provide engineers with necessary schematics to establish basic cost items—i.e., road sections, alignments, basic cut/fill requirements, landscape, lighting, utility, and other factors.
13. *Prepare summary maps for presentation of above critical items.*

Stage Two: Program development. The task here is to assess carefully the capacity of the site to satisfy the social and economic objectives of the program, or to discover in the process those areas where physical constraints or unforeseen opportunities would warrant *changing the program.* This design-program feedback loop often requires many iterations. In essence, this is a first cut (schematic) at a detailed illustrative site plan, the results of which will serve as a basis for further commitments, such as zoning applications, commitments regarding financing, and other deal-making. The level of detail is conditioned by the amount of land involved, the complexity of the programmed uses and the time and money allocated for this step.

It is common at this stage, if not in the previous one, for the development team and manager to ponder the dilemma of wishing to have the 'best data', which would come only from intensive design investigation. The level of accuracy in cost estimates and land utilization can drastically influence later project economics. Yet these **201** studies are time-consuming and costly. The question is whether to invest in such detail before all necessary deal components are in place.

Steps in Stage Two

1. *Revisit site* and internalize summary analyses.
2. *Set up map and subzones* as basis for design work quantification, parcelization, etc., using 'buildable land bays' as points of departure.
3. *Re-evaluate concept plan* regarding distribution of land uses and circulation from Stage One.
4. *Develop schematic site plan* using realistic building types, qualities, parking ratios, etc.
5. *Establish numbers—i.e., plan vs. program.* Develop parcel-by-parcel basis for quality take-offs regarding units, floor space, coverage, etc., as relevant.
6. *Ancillary facilities.* Identify and quantify space requirements for all ancillary programmatic requirements—i.e., schools, play space, public and semi-public facilities.
7. *Refine in-tract and off-site cost estimates* based on above.
8. *Prepare appropriate graphics.* These should include an illustrative site plan, sketches, etc. to be used for information and 'turn-on' purposes.
9. *Prepare all special appropriate documentation* for zoning and other political and legal presentations and requirements.

Stage Three: Detailed design development. At this point decisions will be made as to the nature of the development approach—i.e., bulk sale, subdivision and small parcel sale, or in-house developments. Pending a decision among these, the plans are brought to further stages of refinement sufficient to accomplish the sales objective with appropriate controls through development.

Steps in Stage Three

1. *Establish key land design criteria.* On a project-wide and parcel-by-parcel basis, establish critical road alignments and elevation grading requirements, areas to be preserved or specifically treated, etc.
2. *Identify critical building settings* regarding setback height and key configurations, develop means to describe these graphically for further design development.
3. *Establish landscape concept* and basic planting requirements, plans and sections.
4. *Establish lighting and graphics concept* and specify requirements.
5. *Document design requirements* appropriate to purpose—i.e., for in-house use or as development criteria to serve as review guide between buyer and seller.

Stage Four: Prepare construction documents. Assuming that the project moves into actual development, the design team will now work with appropriate architects and engineers as contract drawings are prepared for construction.

Stage Five: Carry out design review and on-site supervision. This description of the design steps at each development stage is idealized. It does not take account of the problems that are likely to occur, which will change conditions and warrant recycling. The time and manpower costs of plan changes can be painful. How can we decide when they are warranted? The process is full of uncertainty and costly alternatives.

The following section discusses this dilemma and suggests a way of thinking to allow living with it.

The designer's dilemma

It is difficult to imagine a situation in which a developer could proceed without some kind of comprehensive general development plan as prerequisite.

The developer would himself want such a plan to help him test out the economic feasibility of the project. The plan would be the basis for cost estimates and sales proceeds. Any approving agency at a county or municipal level would similarly need such a plan to anticipate the cost-income-benefit situation before giving political approval. Certainly any user groups or prospective buyers would want a plan to understand how their piece fits the whole and to appreciate the general context for development. The plan would have to indicate its socioeconomic concepts with clarity and credibility; a good plan must have integrity—that is, the basic pieces must clearly be part of a whole and not subject to arbitrary change. Last, any lending or investing parties would require such a plan to help insure their financial stake.

The dilemma arises because although the continuing need exists for a general development plan that is complete and rationally whole, the lengthy development process requires open-endedness in plan and design sufficient to respond to changing social, economic and market conditions. Premature design parameters may turn out to be inconsistent with the very activities you want to encourage.

I used to believe that once you had a design solution, you should come to a conclusion, act on it, get it formalized and tied up so that you could relax and move on to something else. This was one of my most prized skills—getting a job done. But there is another way of playing the design and development game. It requires keeping many options open simultaneously, and it is a much more effective way. If you can postpone making a decision, don't make it today, make it tomorrow. Experience convinces me that in the intervening time something is likely to happen; you may get more information that will make a better, more inclusive decision possible. One could describe this balancing act as 'the subtle art of non-decision'.

In most cases, the 'open design' attitude and procedures will be relevant at the level of detailed site planning for specific parcels identified for specific projects. Achieving flexibility to enhance sales potential is difficult and sometimes costly to manage. If public approvals are time-consuming, it may be necessary to make firmer design decisions before having buyers in hand, thereby limiting the sales options considerably. But a good general plan can withstand much internal movement before it too must be altered. In general, 'this design is subject to change' must become a comfortable working philosophy in designing for development. If you are not tuned-in to non-decision-making, you will find it hard to cope with the inevitable uncertainties, and this will destroy design effectiveness in the development process.

This 'closed–open' planning dilemma can only be resolved if the process is right. There has to be a common understanding among all parties involved that this situation is necessary, if not desirable. The planner-designers must be skilled enough to deal with such conditions. Most essential to success is the trust that all parties will be acting in good faith.

203

So far, this chapter has dealt with ideas about 'community design' as opposed to building design. Even the best community design must be complemented with good buildings and the detail spaces between.

This is not easily achieved because the typical commercial builder is not accustomed to have to fit his product into a larger community, nor are individual builders typically required to answer to any design interest beyond their own. In order to merge the design interests of all parties, a special process is needed.

Architectural review

Most of the US (is it very different elsewhere?) is built by individual property owners or speculative builders adding their bits and pieces to an existing or emerging urban area. Working within the legal development criteria, established by typical zoning and building codes, they are left to 'do their own thing', and do it usually with little regard for neighbouring buildings or other environmental conditions. In other words, the aesthetic and social interests of the existing or future surrounding community are subject to the relatively unpredictable effects of individual decisions to build, with no opportunity for the community to have its group interests set forth and considered in the overall design process. The results of this typically American city-building process are visibly lamentable. One would be hard put to defend this *laissez-faire* approach on aesthetic, functional or social grounds. While our cities do get built, the results are generally agreed to be aesthetically grim and functionally chaotic.

While the predominant concern here is one of 'aesthetics', this value-laden concept must in all cases take its appropriate position in the larger set of community values. These include moral and legal private–public rights as established and continually affirmed by a given community; the need for other functional qualities of a project to be affirmed, such as safety and convenience; the need for developing and maintaining a sense of community involvement through a sound process by which the community can identify with and support the efforts; and last, but by no means of least concern, the need for continued economic viability, which enables a project to be developed in the first place and maintained over time, and allows the community at large to continue to build well.

I have absolute confidence in the potential of a design review process to make a valuable contribution to community building. Even when I worked in the public sector, I tried to establish such procedures in both Philadelphia and Washington, DC, knowing that in some European cities there is typically a chief architect (a most respected man among his peers), who is deemed responsible not only for the quality of public buildings and places but for the general aesthetic quality of the city.

The word 'responsible' is the key to the whole process and its success. If one can accept the premise that total freedom (within health and safety codes) in the improvement of real property is neither an absolute right nor an absolute social value, then it should go unchallenged that there is the need for someone (or group) continually to make the often difficult decisions between the private interests of an

204

individual builder and the public interests of the larger community. The only issues remaining are who this person or group should be, to whom it should be ultimately responsible, and what should be the nature of the restrictions placed on its freedom.

Responsibility for review

In a managed community development, it is the developer's responsibility through his design staff to set forth design and other criteria for each project and for the whole community. It is then their responsibility to see that these criteria are made public and lived up to. In fact, the criteria may be subject to change over time to reflect public input.

In every aspect of quality control, there will be many judgements to make, rather than clear objective facts to review. The role of sitting in judgement is at best a difficult one, particularly when the issues involve aesthetic satisfaction—which can often be in conflict with other community values, such as functional efficiency, economic viability, or the most strongly felt rights of private property and the freedom of personal taste. The point of all this is that the developer must establish the criteria for making those judgements, for *ad hoc* decisions will not suffice. It is then *his* responsibility to live up to those criteria or, failing that, to bear the cost. That cost can be felt in consumer dissatisfaction (with the product or with the lack of control exercised by the developer), community uprising, erosion of competitive position, and ultimate economic loss.

Throughout the community development process, the developer cannot hand over to any individual or group those responsibilities that he agreed to fulfil at the outset—i.e., agreements with himself (made public), his customers, his lenders, and the community at large—until he has in fact fulfilled them or is absolved from doing so by mutual agreement. The process of architectural review must remain close to the seat of project management and must be responsive to all project goals and management-determined priorities.

To accomplish this, the person or group undertaking the architectural review must have the confidence of top management and the ability to represent it. This role requires an unusual kind of professional, one with keen design ability and a balanced aesthetic judgement. He must be able to work with countless project architects and their respective clients, since a large community is never the product of one design team. He must command their respect as a professional and must be able to draw the best from them without imposing a strong personal aesthetic throughout. The manager of this process must also be a good communicator and a kind of teacher for those lay persons involved who wish to understand what could be 'the mumbo jumbo of design talk'. This requires a long-term commitment and kind of loyalty to the overall community development, and to the development process itself, wherein the whole is valued over the individual parts.

This is not a very rewarding job for a designer, and I have found very few architects prepared to undertake that kind of mission over a period of time. Architects, as a rule, have no trouble in expressing concern for aesthetics, often with great force and conviction, but always assuming that the ultimate decision for wholeness will not

205

have to be theirs and that they are in essence only lobbies for 'good taste'. (Fine arts commissions often function in this manner with dubious results.) This rules out one alternative to keeping design review as a staff function—namely, that the continuing role of architectural review in a community development process could be played by independent 'uncommitted' consulting architects. Lacking long-term responsibility and a commitment to the overall success of the project, these part-time 'critics' would only create situations of unwarranted stress between a project architect, concerned resident groups and the one with the ultimate responsibility for the overall quality of the community, including its aesthetics—i.e., the development manager. Management authority could not long survive the imposition of third ('independent') parties for project-by-project design review. With all their objectivity, they could well be killing a project for lack of procedural or balanced judgement. Over time the community as a whole might be seriously damaged, if builders concluded that 'this place is too hard and too costly to build in'. New communities have the opportunity to be distinguished by their design—they should provide great variety, harmony and a pervasive sense of beauty—but they must remain economically competitive with surrounding developments, generally ugly but free of aesthetic control.

Although the developer's responsibility in design review is paramount at the start of the development, the resident community has an important role to play once it begins to be established. A formal process of community participation is essential at the outset. During the development stage (i.e., the first round of construction) the community can make representations in an advisory way, but it is essential that it later take over a decision-making role as the developer properly relinquishes his responsibility for maintaining the community's aesthetic value systems and procedures.

A Residents' Architectural Committee should ultimately take on the review responsibility, recognizing the personal and intimate level of concern that will emerge as homeowners begin to seek alteration and improvement to their property. At that stage, the decision regarding the design or functional quality of such improvements should not be made by a third party (the developer). In recognition of the difficulties of making sound design judgements and the need for known rules and criteria, developers should prepare guidebooks—for landscaping, the construction of fences, etc. They should set forth principles rather than firm requirements, which should serve as a common base for a dialogue on the subject. These would then be modified by the resident community.

In essence, the Residents' Architectural Committee should view itself as presiding over a delicate process in which the community developer was only the starting agent. The continuing healthy balance between the individual, his aesthetic and functional objectives, and those of the community is at stake. Moreover, so is the opportunity and necessity to use these review occasions continually to invigorate and reinforce the 'human community' that the environment is meant to facilitate (too often people attribute some absolute values to the built environment instead of viewing it in relation to its human purpose).

The Residents' Architectural Committee should view itself in relation to the community of people as well as to their buildings, seeking always to bring occasionally divergent personal and community interests together by one means or another. It should use its wisdom and skill to enable individuals to achieve their objectives, while not destroying community objectives. This attitude would place the Residents' Architectural Committee in the role of helper to individuals, and not their watchdog or policeman. It would regard the review sessions and the dialogues that should characterize them as an opportunity to create a better solution (everybody wins) rather than to deny the expressed interests of a neighbour wishing in some way to modify his or her surroundings.

Guidelines for decision

The Architectural Review Process is meant to deal with matters of functional and aesthetic concern that arise when aspects of an individual's property might impinge on neighbouring property and the community at large. In other words, the community should have no interest in those improvements or alterations that are essentially internal to a site or of such modest scale as to have virtually no wider impact. For example, the size and placement of house numbers, door colours, or the construction details of a railing or balcony should not be of concern to the larger community and, therefore, not subject to the review of the Committee.

While the courts have maintained the right of a community to act with regard to aesthetic considerations, it behoves the community to act with consistency and reason in its decisions; the courts will not uphold capricious actions, nor for that matter can a community long survive them. Most architectural committees will seldom have the benefit of trained and skilled designers to add their wisdom in the decision-making process. Where the issue at hand seems moot, as in a matter of a subtle difference in colour choice, such an obvious area of 'taste' should typically be resolved in favour of the homeowner. Where proposals for change are dramatic and jarring to the eye, the question must be asked of the homeowner, 'Why this degree of change?' The answer might indeed be sound and convincing, if the proposal is a good design solution for the functional purpose to be served and in relationship to the immediate environment of the new building. The larger question must then be asked as to whether that internally valid design solution is equally valid in the context of the larger community. It is in the realm of relationships between objects and their environment that design skill must be applied. One must assume that there is an acceptable design solution to almost every felt need of the homeowner—the task is to find it.

The Architectural Review Process is obviously not a simple activity. It is fraught with the potential for conflict and emotion. Homeowners naturally invest a great deal of themselves in their desire to improve property and express their personal choice and style. It is essential that the community work to maintain a larger harmony. Only goodwill and a continuing dialogue on this subject will suffice. 'Good design' and 'good taste' are not to be achieved at the cost of a friendly community—a sense of humour must persevere whenever the absurd is allowed somehow to be built. How else could a visitor know that mere humans reside there?

Chapter 9. Genesis of a new city

RICHARD W. PHELPS

The Central Lancashire New Town, the most recently designated area under the British New Towns Act, is now three years old. My observations in this chapter therefore concern problems encountered in the early and critical phase of a new community's development in these rapidly changing, highly uncertain times. I shall concentrate in particular on describing the 'real life' aspect of some of the themes that occur elsewhere in this book.

The historical background

As a brief account of its history will make clear, many of the problems now besetting the project stem from various pressures, local and national, political and economic, that developed during the long planning period before the Development Corporation was established.

Central Lancashire is distinguished from most other new town projects by its sheer size, with respect to both the designated area—35,000 acres, or 55 square miles—and its planned population growth, already nearly a quarter of a million and planned to increase by another 180,000 by the end of the century—or just under three per cent annually. This is a very different proposition from the typical new town project of the late forties and early fifties, which aimed to create a town with an ultimate population of 50,000 or so, on a virtually 'greenfield' site in quick time. In Central Lancashire we have a much larger task, centring on building around existing communities and integrating new and existing development into a new city-region, rather than on creating a self-contained town.

The economy of the Central Lancashire area has weathered many changes over the years. The area felt the full benefits (and paid many of the costs) of the Industrial Revolution in the eighteenth and nineteenth centuries. More recently, as it became a significant centre for truck, aircraft and armament manufacture, in effect a second industrial revolution took place. The collapse of the domestic cotton industry in the fifties demanded the urgent redeployment of large local labour forces, which was most successfully achieved.

These changes were in general unplanned. Because responsibility for the area was fragmented among a great many local authorities with limited powers and resources, the public sector investment in new facilities was minimal. The pattern of local government organization in the area remained substantially unchanged from the late nineteenth century until 1974. By then, of course, most of the functional boundaries had long since been rendered largely meaningless by economic growth and change. By 1965 rural district councils were already administering large areas of suburban development, while urban authorities had to grapple with all the problems of urban renewal without being able to avail themselves of the social or financial resources of thousands of affluent commuters who came daily to work in the city centre.

Against this background, the New Towns Act seemed the obvious vehicle for bringing additional public investment and government direction to bear on local problems. Unfortunately, however, events moved only slowly. The two conurbations of Manchester and Liverpool, instead of welcoming planned developments within reasonable distance to help relieve their worst rehousing problems, were unwilling, for various reasons, to support the concept of a new town in Central Lancashire. In 1965 the then Minister of Housing and Local Government, Richard Crossman, announced his intention to commission a planning study with a view to establishing a new town. The proposals of the consultants (Robert Matthew, Johnson-Marshall and Partners), published in 1967 in a report entitled *Study for a City*, aroused further suspicions that the new town would be a large and unwelcome cuckoo in the regional nest.

The Government reacted by commissioning another study to investigate whether on the whole the new town project would benefit the neighbouring towns of North-East Lancashire that were suffering from the collapse of the traditional cotton industry. Although not suffering from high unemployment, these towns feared that the new town development might cause stagnation in their areas. This 'Impact Study' concluded that the new town would be likely, on balance, to produce a net benefit to surrounding areas.

Armed with this report the Government pressed on, and in 1969 a Public Inquiry was held. The Government eventually confirmed the development but, by a sorry stroke of timing, a General Election intervened and various major government projects were put on ice while the need for them was reviewed. Normally, immediately after the Designation Order is confirmed by the Secretary of State, a new town development corporation is established and detailed planning and development begins. In the case of Central Lancashire, however, almost a year elapsed before the next Secretary of State for the Environment announced that the project would go ahead. The appointment of the Chairman of the Development Corporation was announced a month later, but it was nine months before I took up my appointment as General Manager, and over a year before the Corporation had a staff 20 strong.

I have described the historical record at some length to emphasize the time scale. The democratic processes of planning—participation and consultation—are time-consuming. Add to these problems the natural tendency to consider projects in bigger and bigger terms and the ever-growing appreciation of the interactions of planning decisions, and you risk creating a planning process so complex, expensive and time-consuming as to be quite counterproductive. The freeze that planning studies put on the solution of immediate problems may simply create more problems than the plan can solve.

What happened during this long planning period, which lasted in effect from 1965 to 1973? For one thing, development pressures within the area were banked down, only to erupt outside it in the very villages and areas of high-value agricultural land that the concentration of new urban development in the new town was intended to help conserve. The consultants and local planning authorities naturally felt unwilling to allow substantial projects to go ahead within the new town area until they felt there was an adequate framework to support them. But the consultants did not have the same influence on the local planning authority's decisions in the surrounding areas. Even more seriously, because a new town project was in the offing, the designated area received far less investment in new highway construction than it would otherwise have obtained.

Another critical factor was that during the planning period national population forecasts were in flux. Falling birth rates and progress in the reduction of 'overspill' housing needed for the Manchester and Liverpool conurbations changed the character of housing needs in the region. The planning studies, and the consultants' original development strategy, had assumed that redevelopment within the conurbations would provide a flow of immigrants into the area who could be channelled into certain well-defined growth points. When this hypothesis was vitiated by external events, a much more flexible development strategy had to be worked out after the Development Corporation had been established. The consultants' studies towards an outline plan provided much useful background information, but the pressures of external events in fact demanded the production of much simpler studies.

Even after the establishment of the Corporation, we had to work against a background of rapid economic change—in particular, the energy crisis, and new government legislation affecting the taxation of capital gains on land, rent control over business premises and levels of subsidy for public housing. Despite these difficulties, the Corporation embarked on a very large program of land acquisition. Badly needed sewerage schemes were developed; and, though not without difficulty and delay, housing schemes were started.

But what was the true cost of all this delay? As I write, there are nearly 6,000 families on the housing waiting lists of the local authorities in the area, but it will be two or three years before we see any substantial increase in housing completions. An enormously complicated and expensive planning procedure seems quite unable to meet the most simple human needs either in reasonable time or at reasonable cost.

The basic problem in the planning of the Central Lancashire New Town was that the 'best' was the enemy of the good. Because the project was so large, the planning studies for the project became bogged down in their regional implications. If some way could have been found to allow more limited, incremental planned development while the overall studies were continuing, the project would have got off the ground much more quickly, and human needs would have been more immediately served.

I now turn to some more specific problems we encountered in the first three years. Three in particular merit discussion here: the way in which we adapted the traditional development corporation organization structure to meet the particular needs of Central Lancashire New Town; our approach to planning in the face of uncertainty about the future; and our experience in consulting the public.

Adapting the organization

In Central Lancashire we made radical departures from the traditional development corporation structure because, as I have emphasized already, the size of the area designated and the very substantial existing population make ours a very different task from that of the earlier corporations. We felt it essential from the outset to set up an organization that would be able to cope both with the effective control of dispersed construction operations over a large area, and with the political (in the broadest sense) problems inevitably arising in an area with such a large existing population and so many established institutions.

The solution we have devised is, in effect, to establish two self-contained groups within the Development Corporation, each able to operate as independently as possible. The first—the Policy and Planning Group—deals with all aspects of general policy, including negotiations with other authorities, and general physical and social planning. The Executive Services Group takes over from the planning side the fairly detailed briefs for each project and executes them, where the works concerned are to be carried out by the Corporation. An organization chart appears as Fig. 9.1.

A few words of comment about the work of the two groups may be useful. First, the Planning and Policy Group is responsible for carrying out all land-use planning down to 1/500 scale and identifying the boundaries of parcels of development. This group defines the planning principles with which individual schemes must comply, and also prepares all briefs for developers. It monitors the town development program and it is responsible for all research. In its relationship to the general policy group, the executive group differs little from outside consultants who may be employed by the Corporation in cases where we lack the resources to carry out the work involved.

Some such allocation of functions seems to me inevitable in large-scale projects. Planning is so complex and large-scale construction projects so expensive that both activities need independent professional management. This type of organization also gives greater independence of action to a wider range of professionals in reporting to co-ordinating and directing managers.

Its underlying principles may appear more controversial in this country than in, say, France or the US. Traditionally, development corporations in Britain have tended to carry out the bulk of the design process on an 'in-house' basis, particularly in the case of public sector housing—that is, housing for rent. It is usually cheaper to do so. But if—for whatever reason—the pressing need is for the development organization to produce quick results, a key problem is to organize for major

211

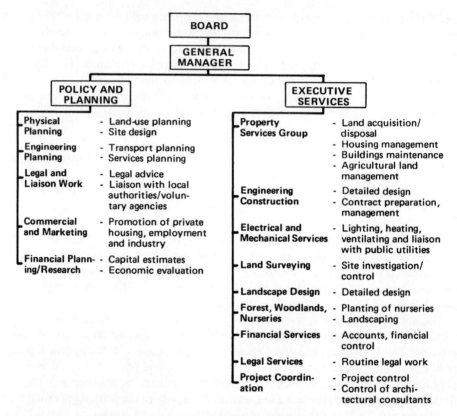

Figure 9.1 Central Lancashire Development Corporation

development as quickly as possible. The necessary flexibility in the employment of consultants can be achieved only if the development agency possesses a really effective planning and project control organization; otherwise the consultants will always be operating in a vacuum.

The introduction of the new organization form met general acceptance because, having decided on it before recruitment began, we could discuss our proposals with potential Chief and Principal Officers at the interview stage. In this way they all took up their appointments with clear information about their duties and the way in which their functions would differ from those of similar positions in other development corporations. The opportunity of establishing a new organization is rare; but if it is to be fully exploited, the principles must be established at the outset.

Planning for an uncertain future

The early new town projects in Britain were, as already noted, relatively limited in their scale, and housing problems at the time were so serious that 'end state' planning was appropriate. That is to say, problems during the growth period could be regarded as transitional, as the new town would probably be realized relatively quickly. In circumstances of burgeoning growth, over-provision of facilities during the development period does not matter too much, since growth itself will soon ensure their full utilization. If money costs only four per cent per annum and the population using a road is going to double over five years and double again over the next seven years, it makes sense to put in immediately the road you will ultimately require.

But we operate today in an entirely different climate. The undeveloped parts of the Central Lancashire New Town area are not so much sites on which urban development is to be designed and building immediately constructed, but rather a regional reservoir of developable land to cope with growth in a rational and economic way. This situation requires a very different style of planning. We do not consider that, because the new town has been designated, we should produce a detailed physical plan for the whole area at once. Instead, our outline plan suggests a set of fairly firm proposals for about half the development while leaving the detailed planning of the balance until we have a firmer base of experience. Thus, we distinguish between those parts of the new town likely to be required for development in the medium term and those that are better regarded as forming a land bank for future urban development, the timing and need for which is inevitably uncertain.

I would like to discuss briefly three studies we have undertaken that attempted to define the limits of uncertainty and to ensure that planning would be robust enough to stand up to events within those limits. The first exercise was a study of the best long-range forecasts we could lay our hands on to identify the ways in which our planning might be affected if the future developed within the parameters suggested by these long-range forecasters. The second related to the planning of new highways within the designated area. The third was a study of the extent to which the future population of any given hundred acres of housing land could vary, depending on such factors as variations in tenure, likely ranges of housing density and family size.

The first exercise resulted in the publication of a small booklet entitled *Towards 2001*. This summarized the relevant long-term studies of social change carried out recently in Britain and the US, covering population mobility, education, health, economic activity, leisure, transport and communication. *Towards 2001* provides us with a solid body of relevant forecasting data against which we shall be able to check real situations as they materialize. The limitations of such studies need to be recognized, however. The energy crisis and recent changes in birth rates are only the most obvious examples of unpredictable events that can vitiate any forecast.

We did no original research for this pamphlet. One of the battles that I suspect most newly established development corporations have to fight is with those who feel that it is necessary to engage in basic research. Basic research is best done in the universities, by specially trained academics. If special agencies like development corporations require fundamental research, then they should commission it. The role of a development corporation is to apply the results of research to particular local situations. While it would rarely be cost effective for a development corporation alone to commission such academic research, there is a growing need for applied policy and program research and analysis.

213

Our approach to planning for an uncertain future can also be illustrated in relation to new highways. For various reasons, highway planning has become a highly emotive and political subject in Britain, as elsewhere. In the mid-sixties, when the initial planning studies for the new town were commissioned, there was a broad measure of public agreement and support for the need to plan in order to be able to cope with very greatly increased levels of car ownership. Later in the sixties, however, the environmental and social consequences of adapting to higher levels of car ownership, at least in the larger cities, became a major concern. These fears were reinforced both by the new awareness of the long-term need to save energy and minimize the use of irreplaceable natural resources, and by the immediate impact of sharp increases in oil prices.

In Britain two further factors complicated the debate. On the one hand there was increasing concern that, unless positive measures were taken to discourage the use of private cars, the level of subsidy necessary to maintain public transport services, whether rail or bus, would become insupportable. On the other hand, the prospect of national self-sufficiency in oil supplies by the early 1980s led many to think that it would be possible to supply sufficient energy at reasonable cost to allow the growth of car ownership to proceed without any artificial fiscal or other restraints.

All this is well known. But for the Corporation the issues were not academic: our policies had to be defended at a public inquiry. We decided, as a matter of principle, not to plan for any particular level of highway facilities to open up the new areas. Instead we suggested that certain corridors of land should be reserved, and we sought to demonstrate only that some level of facility (initially, a single lane highway) would be necessary inside these corridors in whichever direction national transport policies developed. We assumed that public transport would receive no special external assistance in the new town area, and that policies would have to reflect generally accepted national practices. Any further development of the highway network must depend on, and reflect, national policies as they develop over the years to come. Development agencies cannot presume that they will be able either to pre-empt public resources in the future, or to direct the development of national social policies in their own area.

The third study relates to 'area' or 'sector' planning, covering areas of between about 800 hectares to 1,200 hectares (or 2,000 acres to 3,000 acres) and a time scale of 15 years. Fundamental to the success of these sector area plans in land-use terms is the accuracy of the population forecasts for them. These depend more than anything else on the number of houses in each area. We take the view that housing density is not something we can impose on an incoming population, for several reasons. First, the project must compete in an open market: we cannot compel people to come and live in the area. Second, housing for sale will be financed by private developers, and while we can influence the style and quality of their development, they have the ultimate responsibility for determining the market in our area.

Another complicating factor is that we cannot predict the ratio of public sector rented housing to housing for sale—demand in these two sectors in recent years has been extremely volatile because of Government decisions and economic circumstances over which we have no control. This ratio has an important effect on population because different levels of family size are normally associated with demand for new dwellings in these sectors. In fact, public rented housing is likely to be provided at densities within relatively narrow ranges, because the design and cost criteria we have to meet for financing effectively dictate density ceilings.

In the face of these uncertainties, we asked ourselves what the highest and lowest populations could be on any hundred acres of housing land. We arrived at a range of 2,500 to 4,500 people, based on variations in the following factors: (1) dwellings per acre—from 9.6 to 13.44; (2) persons per dwelling—from 2.58 to 3.375; and (3) population density (persons per acre)—from 24.77 to 45.36. From this we can work out how precise the area plan needs to be in allocating land for facilities such as shops, schools and roads and where it can be left flexible.

As I write, we are still examining our hypotheses, and some narrowing of the range of uncertainty may result. Nevertheless, this exercise does demonstrate how flexible the planning of social facilities must be in any area plan that has to be produced before a stable pattern of population intake has established itself in a new area. If the degree of uncertainty inherent in the early stages of the planning process were more explicitly appreciated, very great financial savings as well as a better fit between social needs and facilities could be achieved.

It is relevant to discuss here too our efforts in the field of social planning. From the outset we made a conscious effort to use the results of relevant social planning studies. We set up a small Research and Intelligence Unit, which has carried out a number of useful studies, practical and problem-oriented. Particularly relevant have been those relating to mobility and housing preferences.

We have also tried our hand at monitoring the views and preferences of the local population as part of a program of long-term social surveys. These have, as yet, had little effect on our decision-making, though this is to some extent to be expected since the benefits can really accrue only in the longer term.

However, our experience so far in the field of social planning has suggested that some disciplines can make a more immediate and relevant contribution to positive planning than others. In our case economists have proved more valuable than have other social scientists. This may be a reflection of personal qualities or the failure of recruitment selection to sieve out those academics who find difficulty in identifying with a highly pragmatic research process. Our main problems with research have perhaps been typical: a leaning towards over-emphasis of concepts such as objectivity and accuracy; unwillingness to accept the real constraints of available resources of time and money; and a reluctance to admit that simpler studies, whatever their drawbacks, could be of great and immediate practical use.

Finally, of course, most of the principal social problems in a new community do not require fundamental research for their solution: they need money. And a good fund raiser—one who can winkle out the limited resources, whether from the local authorities, private trusts or individuals—might be the hero and driving force of social planning activity.

Consultation with the public

No account of my experience during this initial period would be complete without reference to our prolonged public participation and consultation process. At the end of it all, I am left with a sense of unfinished business and the appreciation of many issues that those who advise on the organization of the process, and the participants too, often either do not face up to, or choose to ignore. The best I can do is to list a few here. On some of them we formed firm views, but others remain unresolved in our minds.

First, with a settled population the problem is twofold: how to get more than a tiny proportion of the population to take an interest so that you can test general opinion; and, paradoxically, how to sift the overwhelming volume of opinion from vocal minorities so that you can differentiate between public opinion and vested interest. With a plan for a new community, there is a more fundamental difficulty, because those being planned for are unidentifiable. It is bad enough when the majority is present but silent; much worse when it is by definition unknown.

Second, when and at what level do you try to communicate? If you present plans in such detail that they can be interpreted in relation to particular properties, you certainly provoke a response—violent and local. If you produce more general plans, the cry is 'don't come to us with half-baked schemes', 'you're evading the real issues', 'you don't know the problems of ordinary people', and so on. If you consult the public at every stage, you won't lay a brick before the planned completion date of the whole development.

Third, how can you keep discussion about a long-term project within reasonable bounds? Of course, we had thrown at us the problems that have baffled scientists, philosophers and politicians through the ages. More difficult still was how to explain that you indeed have plans—for better health services, for example—but that it is for another authority to set standards and determine the timing of implementation. 'Ducking the issue as usual' comes the cry from the back of the hall. Express agreement with the shortcomings of the local service—whatever it is—and the next day the local newspaper headlines read 'New Town Chief Slams Health Provision—Condemned as Inadequate'. And if that happens you can write off co-operation from that quarter for a decade at the least!

Fourth, those who set the 'rules of the game'—and in large measure these were laid down in central government reports, etc.—ought to be more realistic about the inbuilt limitations in political and practical terms of the consultation process (can you ever hope to achieve a reasonable consensus of opinion from a quarter of a million people of widely differing political ideologies?). Our consultation was designed to lead up to a public inquiry by an Inspector, appointed by the Secretary of State. It was *not* supposed to be a referendum; it was *not* supposed to be a decision-making process; it was *not* supposed to be concerned with all aspects of people's lives; it was *not* supposed to be a propaganda process, although it was one in which we were from the outset committed to a set of policies. It was *not* supposed to be a Perry Mason court-room drama. It was supposed to be an informative and educative process, culminating in consultation searching for genuine informed public opinion.

Fifth, at the end of the day, it was human contact that mattered. Films are useful aids but expensive to produce. The written word, exhibitions and so on all have their place. But in my view the public meeting, more than anything else, serves to debunk the conceit of the expert, the arrogance of the bureaucrat, or the obtuseness of the local bore, and also to elevate to their proper scale the simply and sincerely expressed views of very ordinary people. One important point—we always allowed time not only for general discussion before and after meetings, but also for individual communication. Planning problems can be just as personal as health problems, and public participation should include the right to private consultation.

The whole process was exhausting: 27 evening meetings in addition to normal work in 35 days when we were going at full steam. All the participants from the Corporation were influenced—perhaps permanently—by the process. But I think to some extent we were the scapegoats for the idealistic objectives of others. We were not fooled: but on us may rest the blame for failing not merely to achieve objectives but to reach the unattainable!

Summary

In this contribution I have not attempted to describe our experience in any synoptic way. Instead, I began by questioning the relevance of many of the planning studies carried out because I felt they were unnecessarily complex and created a totally false sense of certainty and inevitability about the development process that certainly does not exist now, even if it ever did. Second, I emphasized the crucial importance of thinking hard about organization and structural problems, if possible even before the top-level appointments are made.

In the latter part of my chapter I tried to illustrate by reference to three studies our approach towards planning against an uncertain future rate of growth. I have tried to show how we have endeavoured to take account of external factors that we cannot hope, or expect, to control, so that our plan provides a robust starting point and framework within which our development can take place. This sort of planning is not pretentious, but I would suggest that it is realistic: it has its feet on the ground and acknowledges the limitations imposed by the amount of social data available to us.

Part III

Managing the development process

'The appointment book of a general manager' sets the scene for a shift in focus from strategy to implementation. Micheal D. Spear's worries in one week in Columbia, Maryland, ranged from a major land deal to neighbourhood swimming pools, from racial problems to a tree-planting program. Dedication to the task in all its complexity, he concludes, is essential for the sake both of the project and of those administering it.

Chapter 11, 'Managing for results', addresses this complexity by describing the management tools needed to ensure that 'all things happen on time and according to plan'. Charles E. Wallace first discusses the way in which project organization may need to be adapted as the project matures. Emphasizing that good organization is only half the story, he discusses the management processes that will facilitate good communications, co-ordination and control among the many activities of which the project is composed.

Communications is also the theme of chapter 12, 'Key issues in the accounts'—in particular, communicating a true picture of the financial health of the project to those with an interest in it. Richard L. Anderson singles out the allocation of costs, recognition of income, and inflation as the main problems confronting the developer, his accountant and the investor in the field of financial reporting.

In 'Establishing the tools for control: the French solution', Pierre Blanchard shows us how the French new towns program has overcome the shortcomings of traditional mechanisms in designing a new planning and control system. The allocation of overheads among different elements of the new town, and the method adopted for comparing physical progress against budgeted costs, are among the innovations he describes.

219

Finally, in 'Beating the value squeeze', R. Donnell McArthur takes up a subject that is bound to become increasingly important to the developer and indeed to any form of corporate undertaking. His aim is to cure 'tunnel vision' in facilities design—that is, failure to consider cost-benefit trade-offs. McArthur suggests two remedies: value improvement, which involves every user of the end-product in its design from the earliest stage, and overhead value analysis, a method of identifying the relative contribution at each stage of the project life cycle for overhead functions.

Chapter 10. The appointment book of a general manager

MICHAEL D. SPEAR

For some time now I have begun each week in the same way— with a detailed review of the week's calendar. I began the practice soon after I became General Manager of the new city of Columbia, Maryland. Two aspects of my appointment book are still hard to get used to. First, the week's time is almost filled even before the week begins; if a couple of hours a day are still available at the start of a week, I feel blessed. Second, there is little to signal the end of one week and the start of another. In many other executive positions you can start most weeks with a number of tasks—problems—to be resolved and by Friday look back at tasks completed, problems solved. It is now 12 years since Jim Rouse began to acquire the first of 15,000 acres for the new city, and it will be another 15 years—almost 800 weeks—before the last remaining acres are developed and sold. In one week, therefore, little can be viewed as completing a task or solving a problem that affects the whole undertaking—building a city for over 100,000 people. The sewer or water problem that is resolved this week will be back in some form a year, five years, or maybe even 10 years hence. All this takes some getting used to.

My calendar for the week of 4 March 1975, while judiciously fictionalized, is representative of the issues, problems and activities found in a typical week of managing a new town project—the aspects that make managing a new community exhilarating and exhausting, rewarding and frustrating, challenging and humbling. Six aspects will be apparent.

An enormous *amount* has to be accomplished on a day-to-day and week-by-week basis. Very little scheduled for the week of 4 March could have been postponed and not much could or should have been delegated.

The weekly schedule reflects the *demanding role* of the new town developer. While the creation of new towns in the US has been undertaken to date by private developers, many of their activities are public in nature. By this I do not mean tasks that affect the public (for this is the case in almost all business undertakings) but rather activities that would normally be undertaken by and, in fact, are most often the financial responsibility of, local or even state government: constructing major roads, water and sewer facilities; developing, maintaining and operating community centres and recreation facilities; or even establishing and taking initial responsibility for systems of governance, as in the case of the Columbia Association, and setting up systems for village representation. These responsibilities, however, are an integral part of the new town development model if the developer is to obtain local approvals.

Third, in a typical week decisions taken by management vary dramatically in *scale*. At one extreme, it may be involved in budget decisions involving 100-dollar line items for current administration, and at the other it may be dealing in strategy decisions involving hundreds of millions of dollars over 15 or 20 years. This change in scale can occur from one hour to the next. It cannot be avoided or delegated, however, since the development business, even at the new town scale, is a business where each and every dollar counts. In Columbia, for example, savings of millions of dollars can result from a cut in development costs of $200 per single family detached lot applied to 15,000 lots, or from a reduction of a dollar per linear foot for pathway construction applied over 50 miles of pathway. The adage: 'Look after the pence and the pounds will look after themselves' is particularly true in the new town development business, notwithstanding its scale.

Fourth, the *range* of decisions faced in a typical week is imposing. There are few decisions that do not in some way or another touch on aspects of design, law, market research, finance, construction, politics, administration and organizational relationships. This is, of course, characteristic in most businesses but is made particularly acute because of the private–public role of the new town developer.

Fifth, almost every decision has very real social, political, market and economic implications which very often *conflict*. The right decision ('right' from a budgetary standpoint) concerning the operating hours for a swimming pool, for example, can have serious implications for community relations, in turn affecting the developer's ability to gain support for, say, a zoning request before the county. Taking a tough position on a sewer or water problem with local government for the sake of direct savings to the project can, on the other hand, mean delays that, in the long run, may be more costly than having accepted the immediate costs of solving the sewer and water problem. Or, in the case of lot prices, meeting the economic model requirements may be inconsistent with meeting the project's social objectives for housing low- and middle-income families.

Finally, general management of a new town involves unusually *complex* relationships, each with its own degree of accountability. Like most new towns, Columbia is managed by a development company within the context of a separate development corporation. Management, therefore, is typically accountable not only to the parent developing company but to a subsidiary corporation, which, in most instances, includes representatives of the major lending or financial partners. In Columbia, the General Manager has overall management responsibility for the new town project; he is also a Senior Vice-President and Director of the New Communities Division in The Rouse Company. In addition, however, general management is also accountable to the community in a very real sense. The new town development process is dependent upon success in the political arena, and there are numerous ways in which the developer's relationship with the community and local government can affect the outcome of the project. Since commitments are made to local government for years ahead, trust and confidence are essential.

Possibly the greatest challenge is to keep process subordinate to results. Because the new town development process is so complex, it can easily become an end in itself, supplanting the goals it is meant to serve. Success must be measured by *what* is being achieved rather than by whether or not the project is simply proceeding—and the calendar must reflect this constant discipline.

Calendar for week of 4 March

Monday Morning

6.30–8.00 a.m.   —Correspondence

—Review of calendar for week

—Draft response to newspaper article on housing for low- and middle-income families in Columbia (deliver by noon)

Note: Must focus on four major items this week: (1) materials for next week's Directors' meeting must be in the mail by 5.00 on Tuesday; (2) Columbia Association* (CA) budgets for community facilities and services must be approved by the end of the week; (3) must solve the sewer problem that became acute last Friday; (4) need to find a way to get to the major but unknown land sale prospect (referred to by Sales as the Mystery Man)—could be a $2 million plus deal.

8.00–9.00 a.m.   —Monday breakfast meeting with Glassberg, McGregor, Godine and Barker

Note: The reorganization has made a real difference. At one point, 13 people reported directly to me. Now there are only four major functions reporting to the General Manager: Business and Finance (Glassberg), Land Development (McGregor), Sales and Marketing (Godine), and Legal Services (Barker). Must remember to discuss the final draft of the Board Meeting agenda with them. Godine has asked to leave time to discuss the process for lease approvals, which has been giving him problems. Importance of defining the parameters of an acceptable deal before the leasing men begin.

9.00–10.00 a.m.   —Phone calls (call to Connecticut General† to discuss final draft of agenda for Board meeting)

Note: I'm learning to rely more heavily on Nancy's ability to handle things for me. She can save me many hours a week by arranging to get answers to dozens of questions that emerge in reviewing each day's mail. She and Genevieve handle or refer to others more than half of the almost 50 phone calls a day that come into the office.

10.00–12.00 noon   —Sales Progress Meeting

Note: In light of current economic conditions, it was the right decision to set aside two

---

* The Columbia Association is a self-financing, non-governmental, non-profit organization, providing a wide range of facilities and services to Columbia residents beyond those of public agencies. See chapters 6 and 7 for a further discussion of community associations.

† Connecticut General Life Insurance Company is the principal source of development financing for the Columbia project.

hours at the start of each week to review in detail the status of sales, leasing and marketing activity. The half-hour presentations by the Directors of residential, commercial, industrial and office land sales have gotten sharper and more helpful. Jim Rouse's attendance has added a sense of importance and urgency to the meetings. Need to confirm with Godine that a special presentation on the Spring advertising program will be made. Also a good time to discuss the overall strategy concerning the Mystery Man deal. Things are not going well. We need to find out who this Mystery Man is and to get in touch directly with the senior management of the company.

Monday Afternoon

    12.00–2.00 p.m.   —Lunch. Weekly Agenda Meeting with Jim Rouse

Note: First half hour with JWR alone. Three major items to discuss—original representations with regard to neighbourhood swimming pools; which one of us ought to see the group regarding teen centres in Columbia; and, follow up on Rouse's question concerning the appearance of the Village Centres.

Half hour of JWR meeting with Doug Godine to decide on strategy for approaching the Mystery Man prospect. Final hour to review Board Meeting agenda with Rouse, De Vito (Rouse Company President) and Keidel (Rouse Company Senior Vice-President—Finance).

    2.00–2.30 p.m.   —Meeting with Personnel re salary range adjustments

    2.30–3.30 p.m.   —Lot repricing meeting with Godine, McGregor and salesmen

Note: Will reducing the price of certain lots help stimulate land sales? Have some leeway within Board-approved price levels, but if a major price decrease is deemed desirable—below approved levels—include as Other Business on Board agenda. Also, consider equity with regard to other builders. New lots sold at a discount could put builders holding lots at previous prices at a competitive disadvantage. Ask Godine to prepare memo on builder inventory by product and location, indicating original purchase price plus carrying costs to date.

    3.30–4.00 p.m.   —Reporter from the *Baltimore Sun*: introduction to his replacement

    4.00–4.45 p.m.   —Review of Hecht Company warehouse deal

Note: Should we make the deal at a price significantly below our established price levels? Do we need to preserve or establish our position in the market-place in the new industrial park? Arguments must be compelling to make the deal on the terms requested. The competitive park in question is in the position we were in several years ago when we needed to make deals below the market in order to get started.

    5.00–6.30 p.m.   —Tennis

    7.00–8.00 p.m.   —Home for dinner

Monday Evening

    8.00–10.00 p.m.   —Final review of materials for Board of Directors meeting

Note: Need to determine at Sales Progress Meeting whether to revise Budgets document to include additional advertising money. Look at Cash Flow Projections closely. In earlier draft, while end-of-year position on target, additional cash needed in second quarter. Economic Model generally looks in line. Revise the Board agenda to leave time under Other Business to discuss lot pricing issues. Will need Glassberg with me to review material. Nancy, would also like to see land development projects summary—this is list of projects totalling ±$87 million.

5 March, Tuesday Morning

6.30–8.00 a.m.	—Correspondence
	—Prepare Columbia section for The Rouse Company Board Report
8.00–8.30 a.m.	—Meeting with Mickey Dunham, Community Relations Representative

Note: Mention to Mickey significant improvement in our relations with the new village as a result of her working closely with the newly elected representatives. Discuss agenda for monthly Communications Meeting with the Village representatives. Items for discussion: tree-planting status, role of the community in architectural review, status of Columbia's public transit, storage area for trailers, our view of new subdivision regulations.

8.30–9.00 a.m.　—Meeting with McGregor to discuss personnel matters

Note: Need to reassess objectives for key personnel in light of decision to slow land development in the new village.

9.00–10.00 a.m.　—Meeting with financial analyst

Note: Be candid about difficulties given current economic conditions, but emphasize seven-year land sales record and our favourable position once housing starts begin to increase again. Emphasize 10,000 acres still owned in and around the city—today 36,000 people, 500 businesses and 101 industries. Make key point—land prices have increased steadily since the start of Columbia—annual rate of 17 per cent per year. Last year with low land sales, prices increased by 14 per cent. Be ready to deal with the Economic Model and price assumptions.

10.00–10.30 a.m.　—Meeting with Glassberg re third quarter financials

Note: Remember to increase reserve to cover two new tenants now behind in rent. Nancy, extend meeting to 11.30 so I can discuss this situation separately with Glassberg.

10.30–11.30 a.m.　—Review of tenant problems with Glassberg

Note: Minority tenants involved here. Have Leasing prepare a report on minority tenants in shopping facilities and their current status. Check with the bank if possible to determine their position with regard to loans that may be in trouble. If a minority tenant problem, prepare for questions which may emerge at Thursday press conference.

11.30–12.00 noon　—Free for phone calls

Note: Nancy, set conference call with the Nederlanders for this afternoon re summer entertainment program at the Merriweather Post Pavilion under new lease of the facility.

Tuesday Afternoon

12.00–2.00 p.m.　—Lunch session on sewer problem with McGregor and construction people

225

Note: Set meeting with the County Executive for some time next week to discuss sewer situation and a number of other issues. Ask McGregor to prepare information relating sewer delay to land sales and the impact on assessable base over the next several years. Show, if possible, how loss in income to the county, associated with loss of business and industrial growth, more than pays for the sewer improvements necessary. Also, need list of projects previously approved for sewer service. Can projects on list be traded for projects that are not on the list for sewer service? Discuss this possibility specifically with County Executive.

      2.00–2.30 p.m.   —Meeting to discuss Merriweather Post Pavilion program

      2.30–3.00 p.m.   —Conference call with Nederlanders

Note: Need to talk with Mathews, Howard County Police Chief, regarding rock concerts at the Pavilion this summer. Also call June Cameron and Mary Alice Walker re the community's feeling about the program for the summer. Elections this summer—can't afford to have problems at the Pavilion (riot of last summer!).

      3.00–5.00 p.m.   —Hold for CA budget review

      5.00 p.m.   —Confirm Board materials sent out

Note: Nancy, have all CA budget materials for my review. To discuss at 5.00 p.m. weekly agenda meeting with President of the Columbia Association.

      5.00–6.15 p.m.   —Meeting with CA President, re budgets

      6.30–7.30 p.m.   —Home for dinner

Tuesday Evening

      7.30–10.00 p.m.   —CA budget hearing—open to public

Note: Early childhood education, transportation and the rate structure for CA swimming pools are likely to be the 'hot' issues. Prepare comments concerning original concept for the CA re assessment income used to service the debt on capital expenditures and meet corporate overhead and land maintenance while user fees used to meet all other operating costs.

6 March, Wednesday Morning

      6.00–7.30 a.m.   —Correspondence

                                —Catch up on reading

                                  —Review final draft of The Rouse Company Board report materials

                                  —Prepare notes for talk before American University Professional Real Estate Society

Note: Have Marketing Department update Quarterly Report figures on Columbia. Will want to use for American University speech. Major focus of talk to be present status of Columbia and other new towns in light of current economic conditions.

      7.30–9.00 a.m.   —Breakfast meeting at Columbia Inn with Howard County Farm Bureau President

Note: Discuss with Farm Bureau representatives current zoning request for the Middle Patuxent Valley area. Proposed cluster planning and development concepts are in accord with the Farm Bureau aim to preserve farm lands in the western portion of the county.

      9.00–11.00 a.m.   —Rouse Company Operations Committee

Note: Review with Glassberg latest internal budget report. Personnel issues to be discussed at Operations Committee— the bonus system and the company's affirmative action plan in conjunction with recent Equal Employment Opportunities Commission program.

    11.00–11.30 a.m. —Meeting with Concerned Fathers of Columbia

Note: Group lobbying hard for CA budget funds for the teen centre. Discuss with them recent racial problems at the teen centre.

    11.30–12.00 noon —Free for phone calls

Wednesday Afternoon

    12.00–1.30 p.m. —Lunch with industrial prospect

Note: Who else will be attending the lunch? Do I make any comments? What are major points that Industrial Sales want me to emphasize? Also, get for me from Godine a report on the status of negotiations. If JWR not to be at lunch, see if it is possible to stop by his office for several minutes at 1.15 with sales prospect.

    1.30–3.30 p.m. —Site inspection with McGregor

Note: Nancy, indicate to Doug that it has been about a month since I have had an extensive tour of new land development activity. I am particularly anxious to see the Clemens Crossing area. Would also like to visit the models that are about to open. Ask if we can stop by the Miller residence that will be coming before the Architectural Review Committee for appeal next week.

    3.30–4.30 p.m. —Reserve for additional discussion of sewer and water problem

Note: Check to see if meeting set with the County Executive.

    4.30–5.00 p.m. —Meeting with Townwide Open Space Committee

Note: Compliment the group's Chairman on outstanding report prepared by the Committee. Very difficult situation. Proposal for the naturalization of major open space areas makes a lot of sense in long run, but requires short-term funding, which isn't likely to pass the CA budget process this year. Need to find out whether state or Federal funds are available for work proposed by the Open Space Committee. Ask McGregor and Barker to sit in on meeting.

    5.00–7.00 p.m. —Meeting with Barker and Nippard (outside legal counsel) re county matters

Note: Nancy, see if McGregor can also attend meeting. Let Barker know that I would like to discuss in some depth the following items:

—New subdivision regulations. Do we join the builders in their appeal?

—Our appeal of the zoning decision

—Strategy for pursuing the Little Patuxent Valley proposal

—Do we want to take a position on the proposed Board of Education budget?

—Legal recourse if we are unable to work out the current sewer or water problem at the county administrative level

What are additional items to be discussed?

    7.00–7.30 p.m. —Dinner

    7.30–9.30 p.m. —Reserve for final hearing on CA budget

Note: Prepare closing comments on the budget process, particularly the role of the   **227**

community in that process and the willingness on the part of the resident elected representatives to 'bite the bullet' on tough budget matters. Stress importance of this to ability of CA to sell its bonds and to overall lender confidence in Columbia.

7 March, Thursday Morning
> 7.00–8.30 a.m.   —Correspondence
>   —Reading
>   —Prepare guest column for newspaper

Note: Need American University notes. Use same theme for my guest column.
> 8.30–9.00 a.m.   —Free
> 9.00–10.00 a.m.   —Meeting with Columbia builder

Note: Ask McGregor and Glassberg to sit in on meeting. Fletcher will want an extension of his financing. Ask McGregor to prepare a status report on builder, number of lots he has in inventory, etc. Ask Godine to sit in on meeting, also. Who will builder bring with him? What can we do? This is a difficult time, will want to do everything we can to keep good builders intact in Columbia.
> 10.00–10.30 a.m.   —Free
> 10.30–11.00 a.m.   —Meeting with Director of the Baltimore Symphony

Note: Remember in phone conversation with Nederlanders to bring them up to date on conversations with the Baltimore Symphony. Good chance that the Baltimore Symphony will make the Merriweather Post Pavilion their summer home. Would go a long way toward relieving the Pavilion of its image as a 'rock palace'.
> 11.00–11.15 a.m.   —Review charts to be used at next week's Directors' meeting
> 11.15–11.45 a.m.   —Free
> 11.45–12.00 noon   —Preparation for press conference

Thursday Afternoon
> 12.00–2.00 p.m.   —Bimonthly Press Conference (over lunch)

Note: Make point of introducing new representative from the *Sun*. Major issues likely to be touched on:
> —Subdivision regulations
> —Effect of economy on land sales
> —Summer program for the Pavilion
> —Status of zoning appeal
> —Potential impact of current sewer and water problems.

Check with Baltimore Symphony (depending on outcome of meeting) whether we can announce their being at the Pavilion this summer.
> 2.00–3.00 p.m.   —Ryland design review

Note: Nancy, ask McGregor for Ryland drawings in advance of meeting. Would like to review. Design to prepare comments for my review. Also ask for a site plan showing the new village and indicating lots proposed for Ryland product.
> 3.00–3.30 p.m.   —Prepare remarks for opening of Long Reach Village Centre
> 3.30–4.30 p.m.   —Opening ceremonies for Long Reach Village Centre
> 4.30–5.30 p.m.   —Free (check to see if Mystery Man prospect identified/called)

Note: Need to meet with Mickey Dunham to discuss several items relating to this evening's Communications Meeting.

    5.00–6.00 p.m.   —Free
    6.00–7.00 p.m.   —Dinner

Thursday Evening

    7.30–10.30 p.m.   —Resident Communications Meeting

Note: First meeting since the election of the new village representatives. Review purpose of Communications Meeting and overall concept with regard to citizen participation. Three points:

    —Residents' right to know what is going on
    —Knowledge that we gain from resident experience in 'living' Columbia
    —Pragmatic considerations re avoiding conflict in public approval processes

Reiterate meeting is 'off the record', not to reach specific decisions, rather to share views in an open, candid manner. Invite each village to appoint a representative to work with our planning team for the next village.

8 March, Friday Morning

    6.00–7.00 a.m.   —Correspondence
                        —Review draft of guest column for newspaper
    7.00 a.m.   —Leave for airport. 7.45 flight to New York

Note: Arrange to have car picked up at Friendship (International Airport), brought back to Columbia if I have to take shuttle flight into National in Washington. Also have following items available Thursday evening (can use the travel time to read and make comments):

    —Memo concerning water and sewer from McGregor
    —Internal budget report for February from Glassberg
    —Revised cash flow projections for CA
    —Copy of proposed county budget, particularly capital improvements section

Also include for briefcase material relating to University of North Carolina speech on future of new communities. Need to prepare over the weekend.

    10.00 a.m–1.30 p.m.   —Meeting with account representative at First National
                                    City Bank

Note: Confirm with Glassberg this meeting in New York. Ask Glassberg to bring a copy of Board meeting materials (cash flow projections, budgets and economic model) for Citibank plus copies for other lenders. Also need source and application of funds summary. Also ask Glassberg to prepare breakdown of $75 million investment in commercial properties by lender. Remember also to discuss CA working capital needs. Nancy, call Teachers (Insurance Company), Chase (Bank), Manufacturers (Bank) and Morgan Guaranty (Trust Company) re Glassberg and I to come by some time between 1.00 p.m. and 3.00 p.m. Friday to drop off new budget, cash flow and model materials.

    3.00 p.m.   —Catch 5.00 shuttle to National
      or
    3.00–4.00 p.m.   —Shopping—Lisa's and Judy's birthday
    5.00 p.m.   —Catch 6.00 shuttle to National

Note: Arrange to be picked up at office at 7.30. Will leave from office for dinner in Baltimore.

9 March, Saturday Morning
    7.00–11.00 a.m. —Correspondence
                      —Professional reading
                      —Preparation of notes for North Carolina speech
Note: Please pull speeches/notes files. Also have available CA final budgets for weekend review.

10 March, Sunday Evening
    4.00–6.00 p.m. —Cocktail party for new Village Board members

What can we learn from this week's calendar about the requirements for management of a project like Columbia? First, the nature of the requirements changes dramatically over time: one week's activities, issues and problems in the tenth year of a new town's development are very different from those that would be encountered in the first year of a project. This means that over time the capabilities, expertise and experience required for management must change too: over the first six years of Columbia's planning and development, there were three general managers, and at one point the project was managed by committee. Certain other aspects seem to emerge for this one week.

A fundamental question in managing a new town development project is the delegation of responsibility (within the overall development process). Because of the especially critical interrelationship between all elements of the project's development, a new town General Manager cannot delegate as much responsibility as a business executive in many other areas. It is not enough for him to be familiar with the general status of the legal, financial, marketing, political and development aspects of the project. He must be sufficiently well briefed and involved in them all to ensure that activity in one area will not have an undesired adverse effect on any of the others.

There are several other major requirements for the management of a new town development project. First, competent general management requires specific and deliberate training of key personnel to meet the multi-faceted and interrelated activities and issues involved. Seminars in finance, for example, increase the designer's understanding of the relationship of pace, density, staging, etc., to the project's financing needs. Second, there must be a special degree of organizational flexibility: as the focus changes, for example, from zoning to development, different skills must be brought to the organization by the General Manager or possibly the project's directors. The organizational relationships within the management structure must change too. For example, in the zoning phase of the project it is desirable for land planning and engineering to report directly to the General Manager. Once the project is under development these functions could report to a director of land development. Third, because control is essential, new town development requires extensive, intensive and rigorous reporting systems and comprehensive documentation. It is important, for example, to have a precise idea of the situation with regard to

230

land resources, which means that the history of land utilization as well as projections of probable future land utilization must be readily available, up to date, and accurate. A relatively small error or misjudgement on a per unit basis will be magnified into millions of dollars, because of the scale and duration of the development process. Fourth, control for the overall management of the new town project must be concentrated. Decisions must be made quickly and based on detailed as well as general understanding of all aspects of the project. Any kind of management by committee or major decentralization of functions, with only loose overall control from the top, will inevitably lead to major problems throughout the life of the development process.

In the final analysis, however, the most important ingredient in managing the community development process is dedication to the task. Development of such complex ventures puts demands on almost everyone involved in a key position far beyond what would normally be considered tolerable limits. A review of the management succession of most such projects would reveal a high rate of turnover in key personnel, resulting from these unusually intensive and extensive demands. Commitment of management, dedication to the task and a focus on results are therefore essential to the survival both of the project and of the individuals involved in administering it.

Chapter 11. Managing for results

CHARLES E. WALLACE

Earlier sections of this book have described how to develop a project strategy. During this process, an overriding determinant of success is the existence of a high degree of entrepreneurship—characterized by creativity, thoughtful analysis, and imagination. Typically only a handful of people are involved, and flexibility and the free flow of ideas are critical.

Once the strategy has been developed, however, and the entrepreneurs set out to implement the project, an important new key factor for success emerges —that of management. While it is true that in the strategic planning stage overly formal attention to management may be a hindrance, in the implementation stage the reverse is certainly the case. More people become involved, activities must be closely co-ordinated, time becomes money, and, in general, all things must happen on time and according to a plan. 'Management' is the tool that can effect this co-ordination and bring the needed discipline and vigour to the implementation stage.

Implementation of any idea requires consideration of how the venture will be managed. Community development, however, poses several special needs for effective management. First, the development process is simply too complex to be managed informally. Characterized all too often by the 'one man show', the industry's scale of activity precludes such a style of operation from being successful. And, where top talent is scarce, there is a substantial premium to be gained from using good people most efficiently.

Thus the purpose of this chapter is to describe how the developer can manage the resources available to him to achieve the results he seeks as outlined in his strategy. From the developer's vantage point, the primary benefits of establishing a good management system are that it will:

- Encourage broad delegation of responsibility—thus freeing him and his top people from the morass of day-to-day details and enabling him to focus on the viability of his strategy;

- Pinpoint accountability for results—thus enabling him to get the performance he expects out of his staff, and at the same time eliminate confusion about who is responsible for what;
- Facilitate co-ordination among a complex web of interrelated and interdependent activities—thus enabling him to meet tight schedules; and
- Monitor progress—thereby enabling him to look ahead and take corrective action in time to avoid costly problems and delays.

The term management is used here to describe the process by which the developer plans, schedules, controls and monitors the implementation of a project. A management system has two important aspects: organization and management processes.

Organizing for project implementation

During the early stages of strategic planning, a formal organization structure is virtually non-existent. So few people are typically involved that an organization chart is not needed. Because the emphasis is on the easy exchange of ideas and frequent brainstorming sessions, the kind of 'free form' relationship shown in Fig. 11.1 is usually adequate.

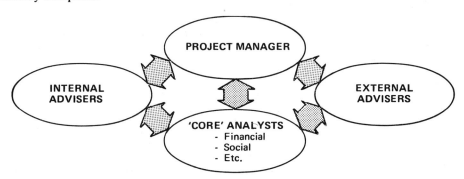

Figure 11.1 Relationships at the early stages

Once the project moves into the detailed planning, design, and implementation stages, however, more people become involved and relationships among activities become more complex. At this stage, a more precise assignment of responsibility becomes a necessity. To appreciate the dimensions of the personnel problem to be dealt with here, consider the impact of the changes that typically occur over the life of a project organization.

First, more and more people will be employed as the project moves from basic feasibility studies towards full implementation. This challenge of staff expansion is compounded by the continually changing mix of staff required, from a preponderance of planners and analysts at first to the professional disciplines of engineering and architecture at later stages. Finally, the need for careful organization planning is further highlighted by changes in the 'source' of staff—that is, (1) staff hired specifically for the project; (2) staff 'borrowed' from the parent; and (3) outside consultants. Figure 11.2 shows how these groups might be used over the life of a project.

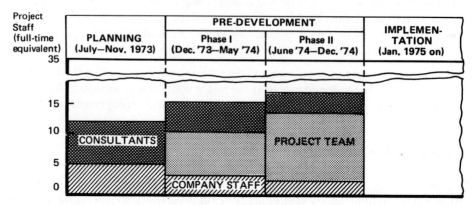

Figure 11.2   Sources of staff

Successfully coping with these changes clearly requires a well-thought-out organization plan. The first step is to define the types of skills needed and the number of people. A project network, which shows all of the major events to occur during the project, provides the basis for identifying the kinds of jobs to be done. The network

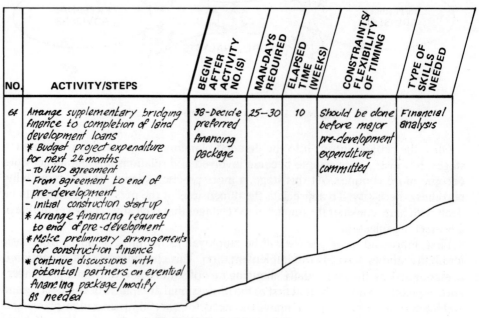

Figure 11.3   Activity worksheet

enables an estimate to be made both of the type of skills and of the amount of effort required to complete each major task or set of activities. A worksheet similar to the one shown in Fig. 11.3 can be used for this purpose.

Next, the activity worksheets can be summarized on a staffing requirement 'balance sheet'. The balance sheet need not be overly precise, but without such forecasting, at least in gross terms, management may find that it does not have sufficient lead time to acquire the people it needs.

Once management has estimated the kinds of people needed and the numbers, it can begin to consider the options for obtaining them. Figure 11.4 outlines the advantages and disadvantages of the three types of staff described earlier and suggests additional factors that management may want to consider in deciding among the options.

SOURCES	ADVANTAGES	DISADVANTAGES	OTHER CONSIDERATIONS
Hired Staff	- Least expensive - Easy to control - Choice of best people	- Hard to turn on and off; generally limits flexibility	- Extent of need for special skills
Borrowed Staff	- Less expensive than consultant - Easy to turn off (may not be so easy to get)	- May be subject to unanticipated recall - Loyalty to project may be suspect - May not get best people - May be difficult to control	- Nature of relationship to parent
Consultants	- Easy to turn on and off - Offer specialized expertise	- Per unit cost high - May be difficult to control	- Duration of need

Figure 11.4   Assessing staff options

Finally, management should define patterns of responsibility assignment—i.e., develop the organization structure. Just as the numbers and kinds of staff required change over time, so will the way in which responsibilities are assigned.

Project organization alternatives

Organization experience in the development industry can be boiled down to two basic alternatives—project organization or functional organization.

In the *project* form of organization, shown in Fig. 11.5, the full range of development responsibilities is assigned to separate project-oriented units of organization. Hence a project manager for a village centre would have full responsibility for the planning, design, financing, marketing and construction of his project. In theory, the manager would have a full complement of staff under his direct control to carry out these functions. In practice, as we will see later, the project manager may 'buy' staff from a core corporate staff.

235

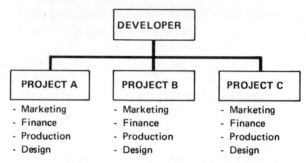

Figure 11.5 Organization by project

In direct contrast to the project organization, the *functional* organization groups together all staff performing similar functions. As shown in Fig. 11.6, staff within each functional unit are assigned responsibility for each project.

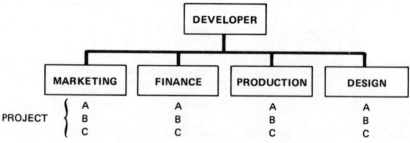

Figure 11.6 Organization by function

However, development is a dynamic business. A typical development organization will have a portfolio of projects, each in different stages of development. With new communities, as shown in Fig. 11.7, this portfolio may be continually shifting over a period of 20 to 25 years.

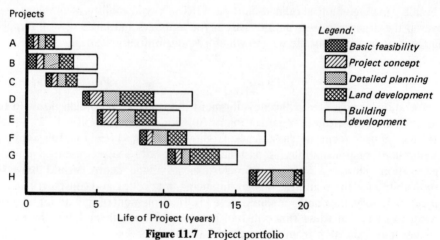

Figure 11.7 Project portfolio

For this reason, a development enterprise seldom finds that either a project or a functional organization fully meets its need. Rather, the project will typically be organized around a core team from the beginning of four or five highly professional executives skilled in several functional areas (e.g., construction, marketing, finance, design) who work well together. From this core, staff will be added or subtracted over time to meet the needs of the organization. The exact nature of the combination form of organization that emerges will depend on several factors, including the number and the size of projects in the portfolio, their timing and relationship, their product/market characteristics, and their geographic location.

Depending on the project mix, some tasks may be better administered on a functional basis, and others on a project basis. The decision to adopt a combination organization—such as the one shown in Fig. 11.8—involves determining how the organization can be most effective, and at the same time achieve maximum efficiency and economies of scale.

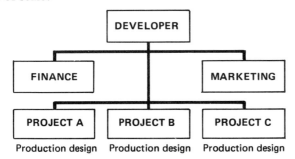

Figure 11.8 A combination of project and function*

*A classic form of the combination organization is the 'matrix' organization, characterized by having project managers who draw virtually all of their staff, as needed, from common pools of specialists.

In designing a combination organization, management usually starts by analysing the advantages and disadvantages of a more functional organization and a pure project organization. For example, functional co-ordination will be extremely important in situations such as financial analysis and control; in other cases, it may be possible to identify potential economies by grouping functions differently. Each alternative should be analysed in terms of likely effectiveness of both internal and external reporting relationships. Of course, some unique characteristic of the company may override other considerations. For example, if uniformity of architectural design is critical to the company, it may decide that such control can be achieved only through a functional organization.

Typically, this process goes on throughout the life of the organization. Let me describe how one organization adapted its structure to respond to the dynamics of the business.

A chronology of organization change

Certain-To-Succeed-Development, Inc., was founded in January 1972 to develop a 5,000-acre tract on the fringes of a medium-sized Midwest city. The tract was originally owned by a railroad, and options to acquire 70 per cent of it had been arranged by a large retailing firm, which ultimately planned to develop a regional distribution centre. The retailing firm created CTSD, Inc., to develop the tract with the intent of spurring growth in the area, which it hoped would ultimately benefit its retailing business. At the same time, CTSD, Inc., was charged with preparing a number of alternative development plans and projections of financial return; for the directors of the retailing firm made it clear that if a more profitable use for the land could be established that did not necessarily support the retailing business, they would seriously consider such a use.

As originally constituted in January 1972, CTSD, Inc., comprised only four full-time staff (Fig. 11.9). Several part-timers were used to round out the balance of required skills. For most of the next eighteen months, while alternative development plans were prepared, analysed, and reviewed time and again with the Executive Committee, this basic organization was retained, and the increases in work load were absorbed by the outsiders.

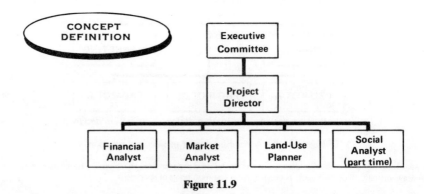

Figure 11.9

Early in the summer of 1973, CTSD's Executive Committee approved a development concept calling for a mixed-use pattern of development. A distribution centre would be included, but the bulk of the tract would be directed towards capitalizing on the recent growth of a nearby suburban area; included would be a wide range of commercial, distribution/service, and residential development.

To help it take on the increased complexity of planning for the new project, CTSD expanded its staff slightly. A full-time network analyst was added to help program the multitude of development tasks to be arranged. Subsequently, a part-time development estimator was also brought aboard.

After about six months of development planning, CTSD was prepared to begin moving ahead with its project. Since the first stage of the project was to involve the development of the distribution centre complex, it was essential that CTSD's project director get some back-up in the physical development area. Accordingly, as shown in Fig. 11.10, a production manager was hired to begin overseeing the site improvement activities. Similarly, with the project moving away from planning into the development stages, it was also necessary to begin actually controlling project

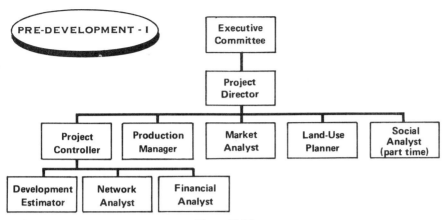

Figure 11.10

activities as opposed to simply planning them; thus, the next change in the organization, also shown in Fig. 11.10, was to combine the estimating network analysis and financial analysis functions under a single project controller, whose job was to keep the project directors fully abreast of project status so that they could take prompt corrective action should activities begin to slip behind schedule.

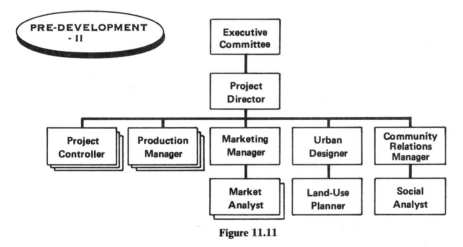

Figure 11.11

As the pre-development activities for the distribution centre progressed, it became time to work out many of the front-end tasks for the balance of the project. As shown in Fig. 11.11, three main changes to the organization were needed:

1. Because of the increased scope of physical production activity, the production manager gradually acquired a staff.
2. To consider in detail the way in which the balance of the project would be structured, skills were added in three key areas—marketing, urban design and community relations.

239

3. The project controller also required additional staff to keep pace with the expanding scope of activity.

By the time CTSD was about two years old, implementation was well under way on the distribution centre and the organization had expanded appropriately to handle the work load. For the most part, the basic project structure evolved over the past two years met CTSD's decision-making needs, and as the scope of activity expanded, so did the size of the organization. But the structure remained intact.

However, once implementation began on the residential and commercial aspects of CTSD's development project, it became increasingly clear that the current organization would be inadequate. Production schedules began to slip because of difficulties in setting priorities among the different elements of the project—distribution centre, commercial, residential. Marketing development work, on the other hand, was not taking full advantage of the range of development offered by the project. Moreover, financial investment decisions continued to be made primarily in terms of their impact on the distribution centre, and did not reflect CTSD's broader financial goals.

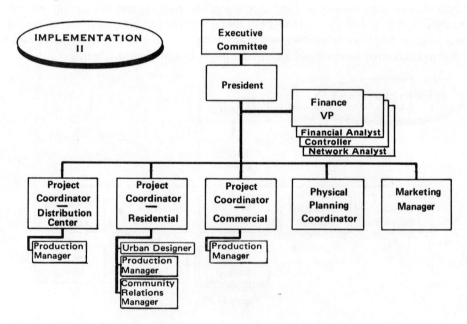

Figure 11.12

As a result, CTSD decided to alter its organization and adapt to a combination of project and function, as shown in Fig. 11.12. A CEO was hired to replace the project director (who, in turn, became the project co-ordinator for the distribution centre). His job was to ensure a proper balance among the three main elements of the project, each represented by a project co-ordinator. To alleviate the production scheduling problems, each project co-ordinator had a production manager reporting to him.

A corporate physical planning co-ordinator helped to smooth out inter-project problems. Marketing was centralized under a marketing manager to encourage development of a balanced marketing program. Similarly, a corporate financial vice-president was created to balance CTSD's financial program.

The above organization is currently in place at CTSD, and appears to be serving the company well. Undoubtedly, however, as the project matures and goes into a more operational mode, further restructuring will be necessary.

Developing management processes

A well-designed organization structure is important to a successful venture. It clarifies responsibilities and sets the stage for exercising them well. But good organization represents only half of a good management system. The other half is the management processes used by the organization—the way work is assigned and the way in which top management ensures that everything that needs to happen does happen. Most important, good management processes also enable top management to monitor the progress of development and take corrective action on the basis of early warning signals before serious problems emerge.

Controlling and evaluating performance in a complex development project is just as challenging as developing a strategy. First of all, relationships among activities become increasingly important. As demonstrated in earlier chapters, it is difficult enough sorting out the relationships among the various streams of activities when developing a plan; however, in the implementation stage, the interrelationships

| | | PERSPECTIVES | | | |
MEASURES		Local Government	Central Government	Developer	New Community Residents
MARKETING					
What is the percentage of low to moderate income housing?		2	1	1	3
Does the commercial space absorption match resident needs?		2	2	1	2
Does on-site industrial employment provide an adequate job base for residents?		1	3	2	4
How many square feet of office space have been leased?		4	3	3	4
FINANCE					
Is there a strong positive cash flow?		4	1	1	4
Is the fiscal impact adverse?		1	2	3	2
Has the Escrow draw-down been consistent with HUD guidelines?		4	1	1	4

Degree of Importance

1 High

4 Low

Figure 11.13 Project perspectives

become real, and great care is needed in managing activities to take these interrelationships into account. Moreover, the need for tight control is critical in the implementation phase because each of the main participant organizations in the community development process obviously has a different perspective on the relative importance of its activities and the impact that its actions may have on the overall project (see Fig. 11.13). From the viewpoint of controlling project progress, these different perspectives are important because they are often accompanied by priorities that may conflict with those in the project plan. A good project control system is thus essential if the actions of all participants are to be kept on track.

The schematic diagram in Fig. 11.14 shows in conceptual form how the control system fulfils its two main purposes. First, it tracks activities and results against plan to determine whether performance is adequate. Second, it evaluates results to determine whether the plan is still adequate. This aspect of control is particularly important for community development because of the many unknowns that exist when the original plan is drawn up, and because of the long time it takes to complete the project. Hence, the system must be an iterative one that continually uses the most current experience and information to update the plan.

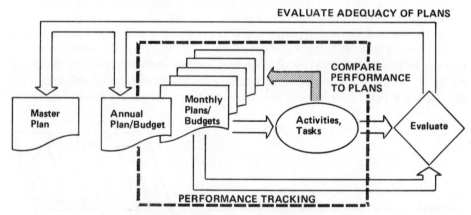

Figure 11.14 Project control cycle

The sections below describe how three aspects of a management control system—the annual planning and budgeting cycle, activity control mechanisms, and management information—can be developed to serve the above purposes.

The annual planning and budgeting cycle

The heart of the management control system is the annual planning and budgeting cycle. Based on the master plan for the project, the annual planning and budgeting cycle defines in detail the work plans and budgets for the project for the coming year. A typical cycle has three phases.

In *Phase* 1, which usually precedes the start of the firm's fiscal year by about six months, emphasis is directed towards reviewing and evaluating the progress and performance of each component of the overall project. The main purpose of this phase is to determine whether the project master plan still makes sense and to what extent projections must be changed. Hence, each project component is evaluated to determine the project's overall status in terms of financial projections, physical status and social planning projections. The analyses performed at this stage are similar to those described in earlier chapters on developing a strategy. For example, just as value analysis was applied earlier in developing the physical plans for the project, so can it be applied again at this stage to cut out excess fat that may have accumulated during the detailed design.

In *Phase* 2, the results of the reviews and evaluations in Phase 1 are consolidated into an annual operating plan and budget for the coming year. At the same time, revisions to the project master plan and its multi-year projections are assembled. Typically, a combined package will be presented to top management for review and approval.

Phase 3 is the execution phase and runs throughout the operating year. In this phase, progress is monitored and course corrections are made as needed. Control is typically exercised both through quarterly performance reviews and by exception reporting.

How the planning and control cycle is carried out in a particular company will, of course, depend in part on the personalities of the people involved. As a rule of thumb, the most successful plans in my experience are those that are prepared with the full participation of line managers. This is not to say that there is not a proper role for staff in gathering planning data and challenging assumptions; but the plan is more likely to be realistic if the person who must implement it also has a guiding hand in preparing it.

The way in which the planning and budgeting cycle is carried out will also depend on the development stage of the projects in the portfolio; a portfolio with a majority of projects still in the detailed design stage will need an emphasis different from that of one where most projects are in the construction stage.

The annual planning and budgeting cycle provides the basis for the coming year's activities. Using the approved operating plan and budget, line managers prepare detailed plans and schedules for all of the program activities to be carried out during the coming year.

Activity control mechanisms

A community development project consists of a myriad of different actions that must be carried out in a timely and co-ordinated fashion if it is to be a success. The project master plan is the basis for identifying the activities to be carried out, and it is ultimately converted into a project network.

From the analysis conducted during Phases 1 and 2 of the annual planning and control cycle above, an annual 'slice' of the network is agreed for action during the coming year. This slice of the network then provides the basis for developing a series of work schedules for individual organization units and managers, as shown in Fig. 11.15.

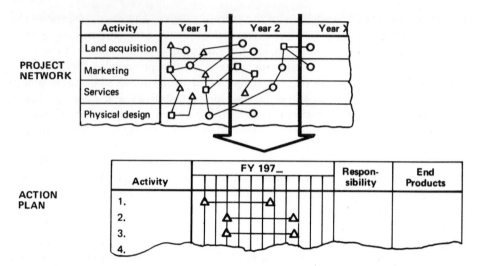

Figure 11.15 Overview of annual work planning process

To help management ensure that the various actions in these plans are carried out on time, it is useful to prepare more detailed activity plans. In our experience, during the peak of project activity, it is advisable for each manager to prepare a bi-weekly activity plan, in which he lists the specific steps that must be accomplished during the coming two-week period. Each activity is analysed in detail to identify long lead-time steps. Managers then regularly review their progress, scanning the bi-weekly plan to determine possible schedule slippage.

To help maintain overall project control, the project manager will typically assign to one of his staff responsibility for monitoring overall schedule progress. This can be done very easily, using the bi-weekly activity plan format. The scheduling co-ordinator maintains a master list of all activity milestones and their planned completion dates. Managers then regularly send a marked-up copy of their latest bi-weekly activity plan to the scheduling co-ordinator. The marked-up copy shows any anticipated problems in achieving a milestone on time. Using this information, the scheduling co-ordinator can then prepare an exception report for top management on scheduling status.

Activity control as described above is an important part of project management. It helps ensure that planned tasks get done on time. But project managers must be concerned with more than just task accomplishment. They must be satisfied that the right things are being done and that what is being done is producing the impact that was anticipated. For this they need good management information.

Management information

Few businesses run themselves, and community development is no exception. If a project is to be completed successfully, management will undoubtedly have to make

244

numerous decisions day to day. A good management information system can help improve the quality of those decisions and ensure improved project performance.

The first step in developing such an information system is to define the kinds of information management needs to make decisions. Figure 11.16 shows a summary of how information might be structured for presentation to the manager. Once reports are designed, the next step is to determine how they should be used. This requires laying out the overall flow of information throughout the organization. Decisions about who receives which reports will be based on the design of the organization structure. That is, the reports flow should be consistent with and should support the patterns of delegation of decision-making authority throughout the organization. Taking the reports and the prescribed information flow, the 'technicians' can then design an efficient information system.

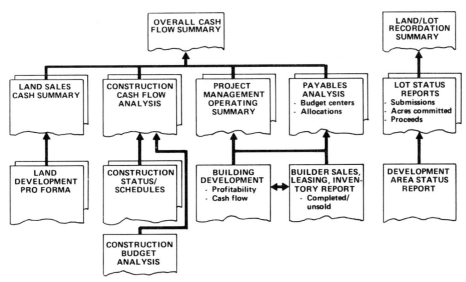

Figure 11.16 Overview of information reporting structure

Development of the types of management systems described will not automatically ensure a successful project. They will, however, give management a way of controlling implementation progress, and—if coupled with a soundly conceived project strategy—an increased chance for success.

Chapter 12. Key issues in the accounts

RICHARD L. ANDERSON

Accounting practices as we know them today are of little value in preparing meaningful financial statements for the dynamic and evolving community development enterprise. Developers acquire large parcels of land, spend considerable time in planning, obtaining zoning permission and financing, and then begin construction of the major infrastructure systems essential to develop the new community site. Before the first parcel of land is sold, therefore, the developer will have created substantial values that are not recognized in either the balance sheet or the profit and loss statement. Essentially, the community developer is in the business of converting those values into cash, either by the sale of land to others, or by the development for its own account of properties within the community that generate cash flow through revenues from rents that exceed operating costs and debt service. It is his success in this process that should be the yardstick by which his financial viability is judged.

While there are many economic issues relating to community development, discussed in chapter 7, the challenge is to communicate them to those with a financial interest in the project—in particular, the peak cash investment required for the project, the length of time until positive cash flow is generated, the length of time until debt retirement can be initiated and ultimately completed, and the expected excess cash over investment available for distribution to the investor. The investor measures return based on cash he actually receives, not on some illusion of values created but not realized. Lenders want to be certain that debt will be serviced and that loans can be retired on a timely basis. Investors, lenders and government regulatory agencies alike are therefore pressing for a way of presenting the financial status and results of development activities that will give a more accurate and realistic picture than is now available.

This chapter discusses three important issues that arise in accounting practice in community development—the allocation of costs, the recognition of income, and the effects of inflation—and shows how these can best be treated to give the most accurate picture of the developer's financial health at any one time. To illustrate the various financial reporting issues, a highly simplified community development model

Acres		7,000
Residential:	4,000	
Detached 2,000		
Multi-Family 2,000		
Industrial	800	
Commercial	500	
Public and Open Space	1,700	
Units		24,000
Detached: 2,000 acres at 2 to the acre	4,000	
Multi-Family: 2,000 acres at 10 to the acre	20,000	
Land Cost		$10,000,000
Total Development Costs: Including sewer, water, roads, planning		$20,000,000
Annual Costs: Including real estate taxes, marketing	Years 1-10: Years 11-20:	$ 1,000,000 (annually) $500,000 (annually)
Total Financing Required*		$25,000,000
Annual Interest		10%
Amortization ($000)	Year 8 9 10 11 12 13	$ 5,000 2,500 2,500 2,500 5,000 7,500
Development Period		20 years

* – While the cash flow model reflects a peak 'year end' cash requirement of $20,750,000, experience would cause the developer to have a commitment for at least $25,000,000. Any excess funds could be invested by the developer in short-term secure paper.

Figure 12.1 Community development model: basic assumptions

is shown in Figs. 12.1 to 12.5. All illustrations are based on the assumptions used in this cash flow projection of revenues and expenditures.

Allocation of costs

The cost of major facilities (sewer and water lines, major roads, townwide amenities) relates to the development of the total community. It is reasonable to conclude,

247

	Years				
	1-5	6-10	11-15	16-20	Total
Residential (units)					
Detached	500	1,000	1,000	1,500	4,000
Multi-Family	4,000	6,000	6,000	4,000	20,000
Total Residential Units	4,500	7,000	7,000	5,500	24,000
Residential (acres)					
Detached	250	500	500	750	2,000
Multi-Family	400	600	600	400	2,000
Total Residential Acres	650	1,100	1,100	1,150	4,000
Industrial	150	200	200	250	800
Commercial	100	100	150	150	500
TOTAL ACRES	900	1,400	1,450	1,550	5,300

Figure 12.2 Land disposition schedule

	Years			
	1-5	6-10	11-15	16-20
Residential (per unit)				
Detached	4.0	6.0	8.0	12.0
Multi-Family	1.5	2.0	2.5	4.0
Industrial (per acre)	15.0	20.0	30.0	40.0
Commercial (per acre)	50.0	75.0	100.0	150.0

* - Average prices, reflecting value increases without inflation.

        Figure 12.3 Land prices ($000)*

	Years				
	1-5	6-10	11-15	16-20	Total
Residential					
Detached	2,000	6,000	8,000	18,000	34,000
Multi-Family	6,000	12,000	15,000	16,000	49,000
Total Residential	8,000	18,000	23,000	34,000	83,000
Industrial	2,250	4,000	6,000	10,000	22,250
Commercial	5,000	7,500	15,000	22,500	50,000
TOTAL PROCEEDS	15,250	29,500	44,000	66,500	155,250

These proceeds are spread within the 5-year period on a basis that assumes pace and prices are accelerating, with the third year of the period representing an average. For example, years 1-5:

1	$ 1,000
2	2,000
3	3,250
4	4,000
5	5,000
	$15,250

Figure 12.4 Land sales proceeds ($000)

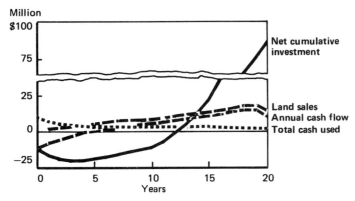

Figure 12.5 Annual cash flow from development

therefore, that the cost of these facilities should be allocated to both revenue- and non-revenue-producing acreage. The case can be made that such facilities benefit open space (in the case of roads, for example) and therefore that the non-revenue-producing land should bear a portion of the cost. On the other hand, the primary business activity of the community developer is to create values and generate cash from revenue-producing land; the non-revenue-producing acreage simply comple- ments the value-creation process. Therefore, a better case can be made for allocating all major facilities costs to the revenue-producing acres. There are several methods of allocating costs to particular parcels.

Method 1

The simplest method is to take the total costs to be allocated and divide them among the revenue-producing acres equally (Fig. 12.6(a) Method 1). The drawback here is that community development is a continually evolving process in which estimates of

Land	$ 10,000,000
Townwide development, planning, roads, utilities	20,000,000
	$ 30,000,000
Method 1	
Saleable acres	5,300
Per acre	$ 5,760
Each time an acre is sold, $5,760 of 'townwide' costs are charged off.	
Method 2	
Total projected proceeds from land sales	$155,250,000
Townwide costs	30,000,000
As a percentage of projected sales (rounded)	20%

Figure 12.6(a) Allocation of costs

total costs to be allocated and even the number of revenue-producing acres may fluctuate. For example, the community developer may add to his inventory by purchasing new sites, or may alter the number of acres to be used for residential or open space uses, based on his development experience. He may not change his total density but may, through good planning, be able to preserve more open space while providing a higher density of units on the remaining acres. In terms of residential use, therefore, a dwelling unit appears to be more appropriate than an acre for purposes of allocating costs:

Allocation of costs on an acreage vs. a unit basis
(see Fig. 12.1)

Residential acres	4,000
Residential units	24,000
Costs to be allocated:	
Per acre ($5,760)	$23,040,000
Per dwelling unit (rounded)	$1,000

Obviously, the per dwelling unit figure, if used equally for all densities, would produce significant differences:

	Detached Single-family	Multi-family
Units	4,000	20,000
Acres	2,000	2,000
Units per acre	2	10
Cost allocated per acre using the 'unit' method	$2,000	$10,000
	Years 1–5	
Acres (Fig.12.2)	250	400
Units (Fig.12.2)	500	4,000
Price per unit (Fig. 12.3)	$4,000	$1,500
Proceeds (Fig. 12.4)	$2,000,000	$6,000,000
Allocating cost per acre	$1,440,000	$2,304,000
Gross contribution to profit	$560,000	$3,696,000
Allocating cost per unit	$500,000	$4,000,000
Gross contribution to profit	$1,500,000	$2,000,000

Why consider the per unit method then? For two reasons.

1. *To accommodate changes in planning, development and marketing strategies.* Zoning will generally limit the total number of dwelling units to be built, and there is every reason to believe that the developer will build to that limit in order to maximize proceeds. Let us assume, then, that the 4,000 detached and 20,000 multi-family units

251

are fixed. It would not be uncommon for the developer to have the flexibility to reduce the number of residential acres, without changing the number of units, provided that the residual acreage went into open space or some other public use.

The developer may wish to reduce the number of residual acres for any of several reasons—for example, local market conditions, or development efficiency. If the developer reduces his saleable residential acres by 15 per cent (4,000 × 15 per cent = 600), as in our illustration, his remaining residential acreage will be 3,400 acres. If this change evolves over time and is not recognized until the end of year 10, and if the acreage method is used, the following situation will arise:

Acres sold years 1–10		1,750
Cost allocated per acre		$5,760
Total cost allocated years 1–10		$10,080,000
Original acreage	5,300	
Acreage reduced	(600)	
Revised acreage		4,700
Revised cost per acre		$6,383
Costs that should have been written off		
(1,750 × $6,383)		$11,170,250
Year 10 adjustment		$1,090,250

If the per unit method had been used, no change would have been required, assuming that the number of units did not change.

2. *To establish a better relationship of costs and revenues.* During years 1–5, revenues from multi-family units are $6 million. By allocating on a per unit basis, $4 million of costs are allocated, versus $2,304,000 on the acreage basis. I believe that land and townwide development costs should be related to land use. More productive use of land requires greater development costs, produces higher revenues, and therefore should absorb a greater proportion of these costs.

There is a drawback to this method, however. To stimulate the production of low-income housing (as required under the US Title VII Program), a developer must often offer land at a per unit cost substantially below market. Our $1,500 per unit average during years 1–5 reflects, in effect, an average of all units sold, ranging from $1,000 to $2,000 per unit. If each unit bears the same per unit cost, gross contributions to profit may quickly be turned into gross losses. I believe, therefore, that Method 2 below, which allocates costs on the basis of gross revenues, is more appropriate.

Method 2

This method (Fig. 12.6(b), Method 2) relates the total costs to be allocated to the ultimate value to be created on each revenue-producing acre. This requires a projection of the ultimate development costs and the ultimate sales price of each revenue-producing acre, expressed in current cash. A ratio of major costs to total revenues is established and updated annually, based on current projections and experience to date.

	Years				
	1-5	6-10	11-15	16-20	Total
METHOD 1					
Land Sales Proceeds	15,250	29,500	44,000	66,500	155,250
Allocated Costs	5,184	10,064	10,352	4,400	30,000
Net Contribution to Profit	10,066	19,436	33,648	62,100	125,250
METHOD 2					
Land Sales Proceeds	15,250	29,500	44,000	66,500	155,250
Allocated Costs (20%)	3,050	5,900	8,800	12,250	30,000
Net Contribution to Profit	12,200	23,600	35,200	53,250	125,250
Period Difference	2,134	4,164	1,552	(8,850)	-0-

Figure 12.6(b)   Comparison of effect of Methods 1 and 2 ($000)

This method better matches the cost of major facilities with the cost of high value sales, which typically have generated more of the requirement for the major facilities. For example, road systems will be sized to carry greater loads of traffic for office-building sites than for single-family detached dwelling units. In turn, the office-building site will generate a significantly larger sales price per acre than the detached unit site, and therefore it seems appropriate to allocate a greater cost to the office-building sale.

In the community development business, the majority of costs are often incurred at the beginning of the project, or in the first three to five years of a 15-year project, for example, while the majority of values are realized in later years. The number of acres sold per year might be greater in the early years than in the later years because of the preponderance of residential sales in the early years and the relatively small number of commercial and industrial acres being sold for higher unit values in the later years of development.

The first method of allocation would create greater operating deficits than Method 2 during the early years, with greater profits at the end of the development period. If all other conditions were equal, the reader of the financial statement under Method 1 would be led to believe that for at least half of the development period the developer was losing money or making a relatively small amount of money, while in the later years he would see tremendous profits being realized. The second method, on the other hand, would provide for a constant gross profit percentage and more appropriately allocate front-end costs to revenues generated in the later years. The risk in Method 2, from the accounting point of view, is that the method is based on projections that go 10–15 years into the future and that may or may not be fulfilled. There is an understandable concern about current financial statements reflecting cost write-offs based on future projections. However, the burden for producing reasonable projections and keeping them updated currently falls upon the community developer, and I suggest that such a system is both feasible to produce and essential to the very success of his business. This system is in use in certain large community development projects in America today and is used in preparing official audit statements.

Under either method of allocating costs, there may be transactions that appear to distort completely the cost-to-value ratio established. For example, if the developer

	(Millions)	
ACTUAL	Previous Amount	Adjusted Amount
Total Projected Proceeds from Development	$155	$159
Townwide Costs	30	35
As a Percentage of Projected Sales	20%	22%
REPORTED	Specific Identification	Revised%
Sale Amount	$3.75	$3.75
Allocated Cost: Cost of Site	5	.83
Contribution to Gross Profit (Loss)	$(1.25)	$2.93

In year 5 the developer decides for sound business or marketing reasons to acquire an additional 500 acres of land at $10,000 per acre for immediate resale to a large industry (or community use), for $7,500 per acre. Is this out-of-pocket loss a loss to be reflected in the current year? If we are correct in our comments regarding specific identification, then this acquisition, had it occurred as part of the original acquisition program, would not have had land cost and revenues matched.

Obviously the developer is motivated to make the sale because the development of his total community is enhanced. Shouldn't this parcel be treated in the same way as the others?

There is a $4,175,000 difference in the reporting alternatives, but both have been used in reporting extraordinary sales.

Figure 12.7   Extraordinary revisions to townwide costs

acquires a large tract of land three to four years into the development process for a relatively high cost and immediately sells that piece of land for a modest profit or no profit, while sustaining major improvement costs, the ratio can be substantially changed. It is doubtful whether the developer would deliberately enter into such a transaction simply to change the established ratios. It is entirely possible, however, that a transaction of this nature could eventually reflect a gross profit on the operating statement of the community developer, when in fact he had an out-of-pocket loss (see Fig. 12.7). In these special—but material—cases, it would seem appropriate to disclose the effect that the transaction has had on the current operating statement.

Method 3

It is possible to allocate land acquisition costs on a parcel-by-parcel basis as sales are made ('specific identification'). This method is used by some developers, but has several drawbacks. First, land is normally acquired before any real planning is done, and the cost of a particular parcel bears no relationship to its ultimate use. The lowest cost parcel may end up being used for the highest value commercial use, and the most expensive land for open space. The developer does not determine the use of a particular parcel solely as a function of the parcel cost. Then, it is a much more cumbersome method to use and to monitor. And the arbitrary assignment of the cost of non-saleable acres to saleable acres adds further complications, becomes very subjective, and may also be subject to the developer's manipulation.

Let us now turn to the second of our major issues—the recognition of income.

Recognition of income

The community developer disposes of land in a variety of ways: sells land to a second party for cash with no residual rights; leases the property on a long-term or a short-term basis to a second party; develops the property through a wholly owned subsidiary; and develops the property as a joint venture—with a homebuilder or an office developer, for example.

Accounting principles require the community developer to carry all the land he owns at acquisition cost. Improvement costs can be capitalized, but the creation of values on the balance sheet or in the income statement are recognized only when land is conveyed to a second party in an arm's length transaction for consideration. Accountants still spend a considerable amount of time trying to agree on when a transaction is properly completed and, therefore, recognized as a sale with the recording of an appropriate profit or loss.

Sales for cash

If a parcel of land is sold by the community developer to a homebuilder for cash, the sale is recognized when title passes to the purchaser. The income is recorded, the

255

related expenses allocated, and the profit or loss recognized. The homebuilding industry traditionally has been composed of numerous small builders who are reluctant to make large commitments for land acquisition programs. Whenever possible, they try to negotiate for options on lots, or at least attempt to make small down payments for annual development programs, so they can take down lots on a basis corresponding with their sales to the final customer. True options, of course, enable the holder of the option to back out of the deal, and therefore it would be inappropriate for the community developer to record the option as a sale. Creative marketing and financial management on the part of the community developers have created a circumstance more difficult to evaluate in accounting terms. The community developer may sell a number of lots to the homebuilder, transferring title to him on an unsubordinated basis, and taking back a note and a deed of trust for 80–95 per cent of the purchase price, with the developer and the homebuilder sharing equally in the settlement costs.

The main issue involved in the recording of these transactions is how to depict accurately those settlements that are legitimate sales and therefore reflect the activities of the community developer during a particular period of time, causing the profit or loss on the sale to be recognized. The community developer has the ability to influence his operating results by negotiating for a down payment that will require the sale to be recognized or not, as the developer chooses. If a developer, for example, wants to delay sales either for the purpose of delaying losses or for the purpose of pushing profits out into a future period, he will obtain a down payment from the homebuilder that is less than needed to recognize the sale, while giving up full rights to the particular lots in question to the homebuilder.

This issue becomes far more important in high-value commercial sales. For example, it is entirely possible that an industrial firm with triple-A credit could purchase a 50-acre site for $30,000 per acre, equalling $1.5 million, make a five per cent down payment of $75,000, and give a six-month mortgage while construction, financing and development plans are finalized. Clearly, the community developer would be willing to agree in order to entice the company to his community. But equally, the company has no intention of returning the site to the community developer and, in fact, if the $30,000 figure is a market price and the company decides not to proceed with its development plans at the end of six months, it is apt to complete the payments on the mortgage in order to sell the property at a higher market price in a relatively short period of time.

Under current accounting guidelines for recognizing sales, this transaction would not be considered as a sale unless the company made a 10 per cent down payment. If the developer wanted the sale to be recognized, he would obtain 10 per cent down; but if he did not want the sale to be recognized, he would obtain a five to nine per cent down payment, deferring recognition of the sale and therefore the income or loss on the sale to a future period. Rather than permit this manipulation of sales, and therefore earnings or losses, on financial statements, the guidelines should require that the activities reflected in the financial statements should reflect the spirit of the transactions consummated during the period.

Leasing property

Short-term leases of, say, 5–10 years are particularly attractive to the community developer, who can obtain cash for non-productive land and reap the benefits of urbanization at the end of the lease, either by releasing or by selling the property for higher values. The income from short-term leases is recorded as lease income, and the investment by the developer in the land continues to be carried on as an asset, since the property rights revert to the developer at the end of the lease.

On longer-term leases of, say, 25 years or more, the developer has the opportunity to 'bank' the lease and, if the lessee's credit is substantial, he may be able to borrow up to 100 per cent of the capitalized value of the lease. The community developer, therefore, generates the same amount of cash or even more than he might have generated had he sold the piece of property, because the lessee may pay an amount of money that, when capitalized and financed, provides the developer with more cash; the lessee is willing to pay this amount because in effect it provides long-term financing. The developer therefore achieves his objective of creating values and converting those values into cash, perhaps even more cash than he might have achieved through a sale, while retaining the residual values of the property.

Leased income is reflected annually in the profit and loss statement, as lease payments are received. If the lease is 'banked', the cash received is reflected on the balance sheet along with the corresponding debt. There is, however, no recognition in the profit and loss statement or in the equity section of the balance sheet of the actual values created. The reader of the financial statement is therefore severely handicapped in trying to determine the success of the business activities of the corporation. The developer may well be accumulating excess cash that he cannot distribute as dividends because his right to distribute cash may be limited to earnings. Most community developers would reinvest the cash in the development process or simply reduce high-cost debt and therefore carrying costs.

Intercompany sales

The community developer will often preservice his community with commercial, office and multi-family facilities in order to gain momentum, establish certain market places, and provide essential services to his community. In the early years of a project, he may not be able to sell commercial parcels to second parties for adequate consideration. He may, therefore, elect to develop an office building or a retail centre through a wholly owned development subsidiary.

He transfers title to the land to the development subsidiary and develops a program for completing the facility. He then obtains financing—which in some cases may be for 100 per cent of the cost of the project, including land at full market value—based on the capitalization of the rent roll he projects. There may be 'holdbacks' by the lender until established rent rolls are achieved. Financing in excess of 100 per cent cost would seem to confirm 'value', which to the reader of the financial statement is more important than cost.

At the completion of construction and financing, the cash is recorded on the balance sheet and the related mortgage liability is reflected. This transaction, **257** however, has no effect on earnings and the creation of value in the land is not recognized, since it is an intercompany transaction, and intercompany sales are not considered to be at arm's length. If the community developer sold the same parcel of land for the same cash to a second party, the sale would be recognized, and the resulting profit or loss would be recorded. It is possible for the community developer to develop up to 30–50 per cent of the land within his community for his own account, and particularly those acres that have the highest values. If this happens, the financial statements will not reflect the values created or the successful fulfilment of the developer's objectives of creating values and converting them to cash.

The present accounting treatment of these transactions meets the accountants' requirements and no one else's. Cumbersome footnotes are not adequate for helping the reader to understand what is really going on in financial terms. The investor and the lender require and deserve better financial information.

Joint ventures

The community developer may joint-venture projects for several reasons. First, he may not have the expertise or capacity to handle all of the development opportunities within his community. Second, he may want to influence a homebuilder to develop a style of housing that fits a certain economic situation. In a dynamic market, homebuilders generally will be pushing house prices up in order to maximize profits. The community developer may wish to provide units in lower price ranges to widen housing choices for those who work within the community. So the developer will stimulate the builder's interest in the lower income housing market by providing land at less than market prices. There is a correlation between lot price and the final price of a home, as there is between land sold for multi-family development on a per unit basis and the resulting rental level that the apartment developer establishes.

In a largely residential community, the ratio of land cost to building price increases. The developer, in selling land at below market price, recognizes that the homebuilder may have a windfall in profits resulting from strong market demand, which reduces the length of the building period, promotion costs and related overheads. Therefore, the community developer may structure a joint venture relationship with a homebuilder, selling the land at a reduced price, but sharing in the ultimate profits derived from the sale or rental of the dwelling units. The developer may be forced, in the early stages of development, to follow this route in order to stimulate the homebuilder's interest in the lower-income project. The land can be sold to the joint venture on the same basis as it would be sold to an independent homebuilder.

In a joint venture situation where there is a 50–50 relationship, the land sale to the joint venture company is not recognized in the developer's earnings statement until the joint venture company ultimately disposes of the housing units. In the case of multi-family rental units, this means that the profits are reflected only as rentals are achieved. The value of the land is eliminated in consolidation, and so the value of properties held for long-term rentals is not reflected.

258

Where land is sold to the joint venture company, it would seem appropriate to recognize the sale and the related profit or loss at the time the land is transferred, provided that the other criteria established for recognizing sales have been met—i.e., that the joint venture company has the demonstrated capacity to complete the program to schedule and that an option situation does not exist. The developer can cash in the joint venture notes as he would if the sale were to a second party. Assuming that the price per unit is not significantly above market price, in most circumstances the transaction will reflect a smaller profit than would normally be achieved, or a loss. The profit or loss that the community developer achieves in the building of the home should be recognized when the joint venture transfers title to the property to the ultimate purchaser.

Effects of inflation

In recent years the effects of inflation have become of increasing concern to investors and lenders. Experience has demonstrated that inflation affects both expenditures and revenues, although the impact on revenues may lag the effect on costs by as much as a year.

The long-term effect on project cash flow will be positive, since a larger proportion of development costs is incurred early and is fixed. For example, land acquisition, long-term financing rates, planning and predevelopment, and major facility costs are usually incurred within the first two to four years. Inflation will have an impact on annual operating costs, but at a cost far less than the impact on revenues, which are much higher in the middle and later years and therefore benefit from inflation in greater proportion. Lenders almost always want to see the effect of a range of assumed rates of inflation (5–15 per cent), but since the impact is always positive they revert to the non-inflation model.

One note of caution. If there is a lengthy predevelopment phase (up to five years), inflation could cause the fifth-year net cash requirement to be borrowed to escalate rapidly, since there would be no cash flow from development. One should always be certain to provide for adequate borrowings to cover this short-term adverse impact of inflation.

The case for a financial model

To measure the financial impact of planning, marketing and development strategies, the developer must have a working tool that expresses these strategies in financial terms. The financial model, often called an economic model, reduces strategies to an annual cash flow projection reflecting peak debt requirements and ultimate cash flow available for distribution.

The allocation of townwide costs, the determination of the exact time when a sale is a sale and the resulting profit or loss recognized, the creation of values, the recognition of those values and the generation of cash are the major issues in

259

preparing financial statements that can convey to the reader the financial status of a business at a given point in time or the financial results of business activities for a given period.

The financial model, on the other hand, is rapidly becoming recognized as the only consistent and accurate method by which the community developer can portray the potential financial results of his business activities. The financial model is expressed in terms of cash flow (Fig. 12.5) and reflects the projected revenues and costs on the basis of when cash revenues will be received or expenditure incurred by the developer. The financing of intercompany sales, which create greater values and therefore more cash, can be properly recognized. The issue of allocating costs to particular sales is eliminated because costs are projected for the entire development period and relate to the total development of the project. It is meaningless in many ways to try to relate development costs to particular transactions. The important issue is to determine the total revenues less the total cost, reflecting the net investment that the community developer has in a project at any point in time, and the positive cash flow that he can expect to achieve over a period of time. The question of whether Road A relates to Parcel X or Y is irrelevant to the reader of the financial statement.

I believe that investors and lenders interested in the community development business will require quarterly financial models to be prepared by management, perhaps with a review by some independent party of the validity of the assumptions on which the financial model is based. The financial model will need to be updated regularly to reflect experience to date and adjustments in market conditions and development strategies. It is just possible that a whole new profession will be required, as will new reporting methods, to respond to the information and evaluation needs created by the evolving community development industry.

Chapter 13. Establishing the tools for control: The French solution

PIERRE BLANCHARD

By 1973, work on all nine new towns in the French new towns program had begun, eight Etablissements Publics d'Aménagement (EPA) had been created, and project planning and development were under way. That year the national new towns administration (Groupe Central des Villes Nouvelles—GCVN) launched a major effort to design and implement a set of management tools to help the EPA to cope with the heavy financial responsibilities entailed in running their new operations.

At the end of 1975, the total expenditure of the EPA will be about 700 million francs. In 1980, their borrowings will amount to more than Fr. 1 billion and, in 1985, the nine EPA will have invested Fr. 6 billion and spent about Fr. 1 billion in operating expenses. State and local authorities together will have then spent about Fr. 20 billion on the new towns program. With such enormous sums in the pipeline, appropriate financial planning and control tools were needed urgently. A simple system was designed to allow the EPA to deal immediately with their most important problems, keeping for later the design of more sophisticated systems, both at the EPA level (cost accounting, and service planning and control) and at the GCVN level (centralized financial analyses of EPA performance).

My purpose in this chapter is to describe (1) the basic needs of the EPA as they appeared in 1974 when the effort to improve EPA financial management was launched, (2) the main characteristics of the financial plan, which was designed to cope with long-term strategic issues in the financial management of the EPA, and (3) the financial control system now being implemented to deal with operational financial problems. Although these systems are tailored to the French environment, some of the same issues may arise elsewhere, and some of the solutions might be adapted to other situations.

261

The needs of the EPA

The overall financial management needs of the EPA were established by determining the factors governing their financial stability and the key requirements that a financial control system should meet.

The first basic factor governing the financial situation of the EPA is the 'project concept'—that is, the overall size, type and location of the project, and the relationships of its various component parts. Creating a new town is a major undertaking, and one that goes far beyond traditional incremental development. Its ambitions for an enhanced quality of life, its size, and the interplay of all its basic elements add up to a project of considerable complexity, and the high level of political, economic, social and technical uncertainty under which the EPA must operate complicates still further the problems that must be mastered.

The second factor is the timing of the various project components. Many of the major determinants of the new town are outside EPA control—for example, the development of major infrastructure, such as roads or railway lines; fluctuations in market demand for housing or office space; and political reactions to the project. And the financial effects of other important elements cannot be entirely controlled by the EPA, such as land assembly, construction pace of on-site infrastructure, sales rate and so on. The timing of these can be modified by local authority decisions, the work pace of other public undertakings, market trends, and other outside influences. Clearly, financial management tools need to be sensitive to possible changes in external factors and to reflect these changes with speed and flexibility.

In France, as elsewhere, heavy front-end expenditures are required before any appreciable income accrues to the project. Even when this revenue lag is accepted, the EPA have to raise the money to balance their books in the short term. In the longer term, they have an important role to play in providing a high quality physical environment and services; their ability to finance these facilities depends on their success in generating a surplus from their other operations. The third important factor is therefore the balance between the cash flows involved in both the short and the long term.

To keep control over these factors, the financial planning and control system must enable management to answer several key questions. At the planning stage, it will need to know projected action on land purchase, infrastructure, housing, employment, and services—and when and where. It must show what income and expenditure is implied for each action, and when. The costs of EPA, State or local authority investment, and the operating expenses of the EPA must be estimated and set against income from sales or services. To balance financial flows, management will need to know the temporary deficit for individual elements, the total cash deficit, and possible financing sources. The final question is how the final equilibrium will be reached. To answer this, the balance of surplus and deficit on various EPA activities, and the ability to repay loans and to finance high quality facilities, must be estimated. The answer will also depend on how the financial burden is shared among project participants (EPA, local authorities, and the State).

During implementation, the emphasis shifts to controlling and correcting action. In other words, are all the project elements proceeding according to plan? Are costs under control, both against budget and against physical progress? Are revenues and the planned surplus for high quality investment being maximized? Is cash management satisfactory, in the short and long term? Should the plan be revised?

A management system that answered these questions would get new town operations off to a good start. However, analysis of the situation in early 1974 showed that traditional financial tools were not able to deal with these problems satisfactorily. The budget, prepared annually for the 'autorités de tutelle' (control authorities), depicts the financial flows for all EPA activities during the year. But the one-year horizon is not sufficient for managing and controlling more than thirty operations, each lasting at least three years (six years on average for a normal Zone d'Aménagement Concerté, more than 10 years for urban centres), and with a minimum 10-month time lag between expenditures and income. Zones d'Aménagement Concerté (ZAC) are the basis of all urban development in France. These zones have a legal existence: to be allowed to build on a tract of land, the EPA must create a ZAC in which this area is included, and for each zone financial statements have to be presented to the administration responsible before its creation is agreed. The existence of the zones has to be reflected in the structure of the financial plan.

Furthermore, results are compared with forecasts in financial terms only. The lack of any link between the financial elements and their physical counterparts leaves unanswered some fundamental questions. Have we paid what we planned for the actual construction thus far? Did we stick to the budget by building less than intended? If so how does this endanger the long-term financial equilibrium of the operation? This is not to say that the traditional budget does not have its uses for cash management purposes; but it does not answer the questions of primary concern to the EPA.

The conventional financial plan (Bilan de ZAC) is a compulsory document that every developer of a ZAC must prepare when submitting his project to local or national authorities. However, it does not reflect the financial management concerns of the EPA because it is prepared only once before development begins and is not updated later. Furthermore, it covers only the financial flows directly related to the operation, and is usually perfectly, and therefore artificially, balanced to comply with official requirements.

The standard income statement prepared by some EPA is intended to compare the sales of an organization with the costs of goods sold, to determine whether or not a given year has been profitable. As the financial objective of an EPA is not to make a profit in a given year but to reach a long-term balance, the preparation of an annual income statement may be an interesting analysis, but it cannot answer EPA problems, which go beyond yearly results and profit planning.

The standard balance sheet suffers from the same drawback. As the EPA are new creations, their balance sheets today cannot be an accurate basis for evaluating their chances of reaching a sound financial position in 10 or 15 years' time. Short-term

263

decisions might have led to an apparently sound financial situation today, while compromising all chances of realizing the long-term goals of the new town.

The shortcomings of the traditional financial planning and management mechanisms highlighted the need for a new approach, tailored to the precise needs of the EPA, and offering a basis for the adaptation of current administrative requirements. The system that resulted is described below—the financial plan for long-term planning, and the financial control system for forecasting and controlling activities in the short term. These systems are already being implemented, and new refinements, such as computerization, are now under way.

The financial plan

It may be useful to outline at this stage one important aspect of EPA financial strategy, which should be reflected in the financial plan. The EPA plans the overall new town project to meet its objectives under one fundamental financial constraint—final equilibrium. The operation should produce an excess of direct revenue (sales and subsidies) over direct costs (land acquisition, research, building). This surplus is used to finance the costs of facilities and services that go beyond what ordinary development would require. These added costs fall under two heads—operating the EPA, and financing facilities to provide a high quality of living for the community—and they reflect the ambitions inherent in a new towns program.

The overall financial strategy will therefore aim at realizing the objectives of the EPA through the creation of a *gross surplus* (difference between direct revenue and direct costs) and the allocation over time of this gross surplus to enhance the quality of the new town. This allocation is not only a choice among physical investment alternatives: it might be better to hire five additional specialists in 'quality of life' problems to contribute to the conception of the town, or to finance a good theatre company to promote cultural activities, than to finance and maintain a grandiose stadium or an exotic garden. As the gross surplus is limited, however, the issue must be seen as one of resource allocation.

Of course, the problem is complex, and there is unlikely to be an optimum solution that is obvious and unquestionable. In particular, some choices are subjective or political: to what degree should we economize in the first stages to enable provision of better facilities in future ones? Can we avoid this dilemma through incremental commitment planning? How can we choose between quality of service and quantity of physical facilities? How much financial aid should be diverted from existing local communities towards the new town? Resolving these issues fully requires the development of more explicit measures of environmental quality than we have as yet.

The role of the financial plan in this strategy is to describe the most suitable way to achieve the final balance of all the operations involved in building the community, and to present up-to-the-minute information on the overall activities of the EPA.

The financial plan is also a way of drawing together the management, planning and control activities of the EPA. It is linked with the general accounting systems, with 'commitment accounting',* and with the control of expenses and income, so that physical and financial information can be readily compared, and a data summary describing the overall operation can be quickly drawn up.

As an internal tool, the financial plan also helps the other participants to play their role in the development of the new town, strengthening and illuminating the relationships between the Administration and its various agencies, the local authorities and the financial institutions from which the EPA borrow to meet their capital needs. While the financial plan presents a synthesis of all the activities of the EPA, and therefore of all expenses and income, loans and financial transactions with its various partners, it excludes the financing of operations carried out by the EPA for others under contract. These imply a technical but not a financial responsibility and therefore appear in the financial statements or forecasts of the financing partner (in general, local authorities).

Timing

To give a total picture of the evolution of the overall financial situation of the EPA, the financial plan covers both past and future years. Historical results are given in the general accounting statements. After an examination of the time span of EPA operations, it was decided that a forward time horizon of less than five years would not give a picture of any value—a period consistent with France's national five-year planning system. The plan should cover at least the current five-year plan, the previous one and the next one. For instance, in 1974, the plan had to cover the 1970–74 and 1975–80 periods. In 1976, it will cover the 1970–74, the 1975–80 and the 1981–85 periods.

That the plan does not extend to the completion of the new towns (none will be completed before 1990) has been accepted for practical reasons. The ideal solution would have been to cover all the building years of the new town, when the plan would have been complete and the final balance sheet of the operation drawn up. Except in one case, it has not been possible to be so ambitious. The choice of the two five-year periods as a minimum was dictated by the difficulty of planning any further ahead for an activity where crucial decisions would have still to be made, and for which the next five-year plan has yet to determine some basic options.

Allocating income and expense

The financial plan summarizes the financial flows recorded or forecast for the entire EPA. To simplify this process, the total project is subdivided into Units. To some extent, it is already subdivided by the zoning process. However, in several cases, we observed that this subdivision did not provide a sufficient basis for the preparation of the plans.

---

* Commitment accounting—fundamental to French administration—consists of registering an expense or receipt when the decision to incur it is made—i.e., at the commitment stage, rather than on billing or payment. An excellent way of forecasting future flows, it does not replace real cash flow accounting, which measures what actually happens.

The financial plan is therefore subdivided into elementary Units, which must be compatible with the ZAC zoning, but could be smaller. In most cases, the subdivision is land based, so the Units are geographic plots; but in particular instances they might have a narrower definition—for example, construction planned on a given parcel during a specified period (ZAC No. 1 between 1971 and 1977 defined as Unit 1; ZAC No. 1 between 1978 and 1982 defined as Unit No. 2). They can even represent an element of infrastructure (heating, for instance) that deserves special treatment, despite the fact that it is used by several ZAC. The Units may be adjusted as implementation proceeds or to reflect changes in strategy. An intermediate level of aggregation can be created to accommodate sets of territorial Units that form a coherent area within the project as a residential neighbourhood or a town centre.

Each EPA determines its own subdivision plan within this framework, and the possibilities described above allow for many variations. The decisive criterion is that the zoning must facilitate the management of EPA operations. In particular, the subdivision chosen must simplify the allocation of expenses and receipts. The Units are the common basis of both the financial plan and the financial control system.

However, some financial flows cannot be directly allocated to single Units, and this poses problems. To simplify the allocation process, each expense or receipt is first recorded at the level of aggregation at which it is most directly relevant. In case of doubt at one level, it is allocated at the level above. For instance, land purchases in a Unit are directly allocated to that Unit, but advertising expenses for a group of industrial development zones are taken into account only at the EPA level.

In most cases, only two levels of aggregation have been chosen—Unit or EPA. All financial flows related to the EPA level are 'indirect'; but when an intermediate level has been determined, such as a group of Units, the expenses and income may be direct at Unit level, direct at intermediate level (while indirect at Unit level), or indirect (EPA level).

Indirect expenses and income should cover only financial flows resulting from the overall activity of the EPA. Indirect expenses are mainly EPA operating expenses (personnel, advertising), and contributions to major facilities (parks, etc.) that are not managed as a Unit. Indirect receipts are mainly the grants and subsidies of the Ministry of Equipment, and payment for services. This distinction between direct and indirect expenses is a simple and practical basis for the financial analysis of new town operations.

Preparing the plan

The plan consists of four 'building blocks' prepared in sequence. These are discussed below.

1. *Definition of the physical scenario.* The purpose here is to describe the timing and scale of the major construction elements on site. The EPA have already prepared general physical descriptions of the new towns, which have been presented to local and national authorities, modified and accepted. Based on this overall description, the EPA then divide their sites into geographic Units, as described

above, and allocate housing, office space, industrial acreage, commercial space, community facilities and services among these Units. Once the subdivisions are defined, objectives by geographic Unit are set (housing, service, employment, etc.) and phased over time.

2. *Translation of the physical scenario into financial terms.* From the physical scenario for each Unit, the expenses and income directly allocated to each Unit for each year (direct financial flows) can then be estimated. Expenses and income at EPA level (indirect financial flows) are also estimated on the basis of this physical scenario and of other economic and technical factors: yearly operating expenses depend on the tasks ahead, the capacity required and the number of specialists needed; advertising expenses depend on the expected market and on the ability of the EPA to reach it or to control it; and so on. These evaluations lead to the preparation of the first part of the financial statements for each Unit and for the EPA as a whole.

3. *Total financial flows after loans and interest.* Once all direct and indirect income and expenses have been sequenced over time for the period covered by the plan, the gap between cumulative income and expenses can be determined and the resulting borrowing needs and the schedule of loan and interest payments gauged. After the necessary adjustments have been made, the amalgamation of all flows ('definitive' flows resulting from expenses, sales and other revenues, and interest payments, and 'temporary' flows resulting from loans and repayments) is then presented in the overall financial plan (the Value-Added Tax financial flows are treated separately, as all income and expenses have been computed without VAT).

4. *Financial statement by Unit after allocation of indirect and temporary financial flows.* Because of administrative requirements (the ZAC or other geographic Units of a new town have to prove their individual viability) and for management purposes (comparisons among Units), the overall financial statement has to be split into Unit financial statements. Indirect income and expenses, as well as loans and interest payments, have therefore to be allocated among Units, although this allocation is largely arbitrary.

These various elements of the plan are presented in a single document with the structure indicated in Fig. 13.1. A complementary set of documents is added,

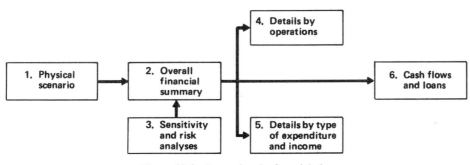

Figure 13.1 Presenting the financial plan

267

illustrating through sensitivity analysis and future asset value calculations the sensitivity of the results presented for the last year of the plan, and the balance of the assets and equities forecast for the last year at market value.

Adjustment and uses of the plan

The first draft of the plan is prepared according to the sequence described above, but this is only the beginning. All the documents have to be adjusted or revised in order to improve the performance of the EPA in meeting their objectives. The financial plan was conceived originally as the basic financial tool for strategic planning and policy making in each new town. Now it has become an official document, used by national authorities to evaluate the financial situation and needs of each EPA. Its preparation is therefore more than an exercise, and it must be continually revised until an acceptable version has been obtained.

There are many criteria for deciding the plan's acceptability. The ability of the EPA to achieve final financial equilibrium is perhaps the main criterion, but the ability to achieve quantitative objectives in terms of housing, employment, social balance, infrastructure, services, etc., is also important. Qualitative objectives must also be expressed, in terms of urban design, services, and community life. All financial, technical, and social requirements must be taken into consideration, as must the EPA ability to develop new towns in a balanced way. Finally, the realism of the hypotheses on costs, income, and timing will be appraised.

These criteria are demanding, and often conflict. The preparation of the financial plan therefore requires many analyses, comparisons, and trade-offs between conflicting elements. All the decision-makers concerned, both inside and outside the EPA, must be involved in preparing a scenario that represents the best synthesis of all points of view: financial, technical, urban, social, and political. The active management of this internal and external negotiation process is essential to ensure a feasible and credible plan, representing a real consensus among those concerned.

Once the plan has been prepared, it becomes the basic control tool of EPA strategy, as at this point it is the only clear summary of the strategy.

At the time of writing we have insufficient experience to detail all possible uses of the plan, but in those EPA where it has now been installed for more than a year (three out of nine), it appears that it was mainly used for four practical purposes, beyond the opportunity it offered to formalize EPA strategy in detailed form for the first time.

First, it acts as a data base, showing results quickly, and forecasting action and results expected, especially through the physical scenario. Second, it can be used to evaluate the choices and alternatives within a given Unit to improve the quality of the service at minimum cost, finance new equipment or react to market changes. Third, it can be used to reorient the overall strategy and to recalculate Unit-by-Unit revenues and costs and indirect financial flows, in face of new needs or unexpected market changes. Finally, it communicates financial needs in an articulate and convincing way to the national and local authorities, to justify EPA requests.

On the other hand, the potential uses of the plan in discussing with the GCVN and other authorities the preparation of more sophisticated financial controls for the EPA have not yet been realized. The second year may well fill this gap.

The financial control system

The plan for a new town is a coherent expression of its physical, social, economic and financial aspects, and the financial plan and the budgets enable results in each area to be compared against objectives and forecasts, so that slippages can be identified early enough for corrective action to be taken.

But an important part of new town objectives is expressed in physical terms. A prime requirement for financial control is therefore that it should show whether the EPA are able to realize physical objectives within planned financial guidelines. The other main requirement is to assist cash management.

Financial control requirements

The financial evolution of a development project over time can be represented as in Fig. 13.2, which shows a Fr. 500,000 overrun on a planned road network. The initial plan (forecast line) indicated that the construction of the road network of Unit X

ROAD NETWORK OF UNIT X

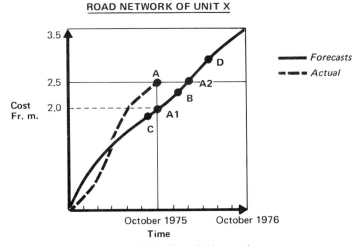

Figure 13.2   Financial forecasting

would be completed in October 1976 at a total cost of Fr. 3.5 million. By October 1975, Fr. 2.5 million had been spent, exceeding the Fr. 2 million forecast in the initial plan (Point A). Five interpretations of the overrun might be made:

1. After a slow start, the operation is now ahead of plan. Costs are exactly on target and the results for October 1975 correspond to the forecasts for January 1976 (Point A2).

269

2. What was planned for October 1975 has now been done, but at a higher cost (Point A1).
3. Physically, implementation is ahead of plan, but so are costs (Point B).
4. Implementation is behind plan, but costs are much higher (Point C).
5. Implementation is ahead of plan, and costs are much lower than planned (Point D).

For the EPA, these five situations are obviously different, even though the financial results are the same. Mere consideration of the financial slippage is therefore not sufficient. Diagnosis of the situation requires a comparison of the physical and the financial results to know whether the situation might lead to an overrun (A1, B, C), to the planned cost (A2), or to a lower cost (D). (It should be noted that although A2 and D are better from the overall financial point of view, they might entail cash management problems.) The evaluation of the physico-financial situation is thus essential to a sound understanding of the operation. Many risks of slippage are, of course, entailed in what remains to be done. It is possible to identify these risks; and this information is essential for updating forecasts and may even lead to a revision of overall policy and strategy.

The need for sound cash management, the other main task of the financial control system, can be easily illustrated. If the EPA had to increase its cash needs by Fr. 10 million, the interest payable would represent the cost of more than 10 people (EPA employ 100 people on average), or more than 50 per cent of the average total promotion budget.

A basic requirement of any control system is to record the information as soon as it becomes available. In the case of EPA cash management, the volume of financial flows is determined as soon as the contract is signed and the expense or receipt committed. This commitment is an unavoidable financial transaction for the EPA and must be translated immediately into cash flow forecasts. Although the volume of the flows is known at this point, the timing of course remains uncertain. However, with experience this can be fairly well anticipated.

Implementation principles

While the basic requirements of the financial control system are the same for all EPA, experience has shown that its implementation can be tailored to the needs of individual organizations, to reflect specific characteristics, i.e., type of project, present or planned organization, personality of the management team members, current and planned management tools and methods. It is therefore not possible to describe the implementation 'solution'. However, some general implementation principles appear to be common to all, and I shall briefly review some of these here.

The first principle concerns terminology. In identifying the multiple financial flows that affect EPA, a common terminology is necessary to ensure a proper understanding of all information, requested or received, and to enable information to be transferred from one document to another. To a large extent, the language used in the financial control system is determined by existing documents and procedures,

270

and also by French administrative tradition. However, the opportunity and the need arose in the implementation of the financial controls for some innovation and standardization of terminology, especially in the definition of expenses and income.

At the moment, the terminology used to define expenses and income in the financial plan is the same for all EPA, but this homogeneity does not extend to nomenclature of construction details—e.g., land purchases, building. These represent 75 per cent of total direct expenses, and the uncertainty attached to forecasting them is important. A special index has been developed to cope with this situation. Currently, each EPA team uses a different categorization of these expenses in its control report. The criteria for deciding the categories, however, have been the same in each case—namely, the ability to encompass all types of direct expense in this field; the homogeneity of each category; and the need to limit the number of categories to avoid 'shopping lists'. At present, the lists contain between 10 and 14 expense categories.

Some aspects of control techniques and documents are also common to all EPA— including physico-financial control, operations control and cash flow control. Experience to date has resulted in satisfactory solutions to some of the problems arising in these areas.

The basic technique for physico-financial control is the comparison of sales construction progress with the percentage of money spent or received, in light of initial or updated forecasts. All categories of income and expense can be controlled in this way, with varying degrees of analysis. However, experience has shown that it is more efficient to deal with the main expense and income categories first.

To do this, committed funds must be compared with corresponding physical targets. Once a commitment has been signed, whether for a sale or for a purchase (land, construction), the objective is to evaluate whether this commitment represents an under- or over-spending compared with initial forecasts. To this end, the value of the commitment is expressed as a percentage of the budget for this expense category (e.g., the value of the contract signed for two road sections of a Unit as a percentage of the total road construction budget for this Unit) and compared with the physical target of the work contracted as a percentage of the total physical target involved for this Unit according to the current plan. Thus, if the commitment represents 80 per cent of the current budget in financial terms and 60 per cent in physical terms, then it has been more expensive than was budgeted for and there is an overrun risk.

For example, in Fig. 13.3 the road commitments represent 90 per cent of budget and 100 per cent of planned construction. Unplanned road works costing Fr. 150,000 remain to be done, and the total forecast cost is Fr. 4.65 million, compared with Fr. 5 million that was budgeted. The commitment situation measured in physico-financial terms indicates a possible saving. (The form shown in Fig. 13.3 is currently used in some EPA.)

Expressing a commitment in physical terms is not as difficult as it may seem at first, and experience has shown that it can be further simplified by adequate preparation of the forecasts. For instance, Fig. 13.4 shows the secondary road network of a Unit. When the plan is drawn up, the approximate percentage that each section of road represents in physical terms can be calculated. As the contracts are usually signed for

271

CONSTRUCTION EXPENSES

| Nature of Expenses | Actual (Fr. 000) | | | | Forecast (Fr. 000) | | |
	Budgeted	Already Committed	Physico-Financial Comparison (%) ▨ Physical ▢ Financial		Estimated Remaining Commitment	Probable Total	Budget Variance
			0	100%			
Grading	1,300	1,200	94	97	100	1,400	+100
Drainage	2,500	2,300	89	92	400	2,700	+200
Roads	5,000	4,500	100	90	150	4,650	−350
Services	970	300	75	37	200	500	−470
Street Lighting	600	450	60	75	200	650	+50
Pedestrian Areas/ Equipment	1,000	800	80	80	200	1,000	0

Figure 13.3 Physico-financial control

a coherent set of sections, this computation is easy to prepare. In several EPA, physico-financial control has been used in this way for 90 per cent of construction expenses and 95 per cent of direct income (i.e., for office space: percentage of square metres sold compared with percentage of total income expected).

Once the physical and financial aspects of the recorded commitments have been evaluated, the project manager can estimate what is still to be done or sold, and for

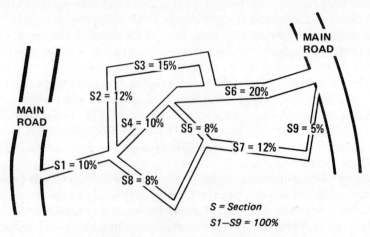

Figure 13.4 Secondary roads network

how much. This evaluation of remaining commitments is of primary importance in forecasting positive or negative slippages and eventually in taking corrective or defensive action. In this way forecasts can be updated at any time. However, this is not an argument for continuous revision, which would negate any attempt at objective planning.

Let us now turn to operational control. This is based on two control mechanisms: operation status reports and the commitment authorization document.

When the control system was implemented in the EPA, three types of operations reports were used (Fig. 13.5): the *physico-financial* reports, covering income and expenses (e.g., that shown in Fig. 13.4); the *commitment forecast* reports, detailing the total commitments forecast in previous reports, and the timing of corresponding payments; the *gross result* control report, providing for each operation a complete picture of its status to date, future developments and their financial implications.

Figure 13.5   Operation status reports by unit

The commitment authorization report is needed because of the importance of the commitment decision, which should be recorded and introduced into the control system as soon as possible. As a result, for each commitment, a report is filed and submitted for approval to the proper decision level, detailing the nature, the purpose and the impact of the commitment. In this way senior management can control financial developments and estimate risks incurred.

Through a synthesis of the operation status reports, it is possible to follow the gross result of all operations at EPA level (Fig. 13.6). Commitments affecting indirect income and expenses, and corresponding cash flows, can be traced through reports similar to those shown for direct expenses. The EPA are thus able to forecast and

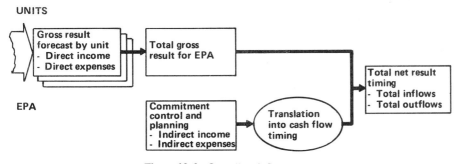

Figure 13.6   Overall cash flow control

273

control all their cash inflows and outflows, and in this way have the basis of a simple but efficient cash management system, linked to the reports needed by decision-makers.

To sound a final cautionary note, let me describe some traps to avoid. EPA experience has shown that, if ignored, these can be very expensive and frustrating.

The first is excessive ambition. The desire to design and implement a complete system covering all flows with the same frequency and accuracy, or the attempt to implement several new systems simultaneously, such as a good control system and the computerization of all data processing, will be doomed to failure. One must always be realistic about the quantity of paper a responsible manager can read, analyse or prepare without losing touch with his normal daily tasks.

The second trap is excessive prudence, such as keeping both the old system and the new going, to avoid cultural problems with traditionalists; or oversimplifying the system, to avoid an excessive work load.

Deviating from the original purpose of the system can also lead to problems—for example, using the tools as censorship devices without real feedback from the control cell members; or multiplying requests for supporting evidence or explanation, as the new control system allows for more and better questions. It may become too easy for one person or one section to control all the information and to acquire a privileged position at the expense of co-ordination within the organization. Or elimination of informal working contacts might lead to a purely formal set of relationships instead of the rich, even if disorderly, relationships existing before the system was introduced.

This list is neither complete nor original, but real life experience has confirmed that problems do not need to be new to ruin ill-prepared plans.

Chapter 14. Beating the value squeeze

R. DONNELL McARTHUR

Community developers in both the public and the private sector are caught in a value squeeze. House buyers are increasingly price conscious and selective, so developers must continually inject extra value into their communities in the form of additional or superior facilities or better value for money to make them competitive with established communities. But rising costs have so eroded margins and reduced flexibility to cope with market fluctuations that most developers are finding it difficult to stay afloat, let alone to enhance value by adding new and costly features. Therefore, they need to reduce their costs while making sure that every incurred cost creates something of value.

Current facility planning and design processes rarely achieve this. The central problem is a kind of shortsightedness. Architects, designers, builders and other participants concentrate on perfecting their own contribution, regardless of cost and too often without considering the needs of the ultimate user. Pride in translating an innovative concept into an exciting building can easily overtake the purpose the building is designed to serve. In the same way, specialists who provide services within the organization are concerned to give the best service possible, and often fail to balance the cost of refining their systems and procedures against the expected increase in value they provide.

This chapter describes two techniques designed to overcome this tunnel vision:

- *Value improvement* helps to reduce the construction and operating costs of facilities by involving users in the early stages of facility specification and design. 'Users' include *all* participants in the development—i.e., buyers, operators, maintainers, builders and the owner, as well as the architect and developer. Incorporating their knowledge of what is practical and feasible at this early stage ensures that detailed design effort is not wasted and protects project viability by providing facilities that are compatible with users' needs and priorities.
- *Overhead value analysis* is a way of minimizing costs by involving those who use and provide information and services within the development organization in

275

systematically challenging the need for them and redesigning the ways in which they are provided. By identifying the direct contribution each activity makes to ultimate sales and rentals, and assessing the impact of eliminating those that make only an indirect contribution, the process can be used to reduce the fixed costs of a project while protecting its marketability.

Value improvement

The most important cost reduction opportunity open to the public or private developer is to reduce the cost of providing facilities, as these normally constitute about half of total project costs. Large-scale developers have particularly high facility costs because they have to shoulder larger burdens than do smaller-scale 'infill' developers. To compete successfully with established communities, they have to make a heavy initial investment in basic physical infrastructure and frequently have to finance project access roads, and extensions of sewers, water mains and processing facilities, as well as on-site facilities. They are also involved in a substantial outlay in creating social programs and amenities—i.e., health facilities, commuter transport, nursery schools, and adult recreation and community meeting space.

Few of these investments can be considered optional extras because without them the project's life style would be bleak. In fact, private developers have generally found it necessary to provide above-average recreational facilities and on-site convenience shopping to create a competitive advantage. The critical need is to achieve the maximum value from the additional costs incurred in providing more and better facilities by ensuring that the facilities actually do meet users' needs and priorities, and that they are provided at the lowest possible cost.

The best time to take action on facility costs is at the initial design and implementation planning stage, since decisions made then determine most of the costs incurred later—not only the building costs incurred by the developer but also the ultimate cost of running the facility. If designers are more aware of user needs and priorities at this stage they are better able to achieve the maximum value from the costs incurred. Value improvement, a four-step process, helps to achieve this by focusing development effort on programs rather than facilities, defining these programs to meet user needs and involving them at all key stages of the design process.

1. Derive facility needs from program requirements

The first step in the value improvement process is to define the programs that will be required in the total community or project—e.g., shopping, education, community meeting space, medical services, employment—and then, and only then, to determine the facilities required to house these programs.

At present, design and development teams concentrate mainly on physical structures rather than on the programs they are designed to shelter. Economic realities require that the developer thinks of selling or letting buildings rather than programs, and mortgage financing typically centres on a building as collateral. Moreover, most government controls tend to focus on physical facilities. The HUD registration requirements in the US are concerned with the infrastructure and amenities to be provided, and the Parker Morris standards in the UK specify architectural and design criteria, preferred site layouts and basic requirements for safety and privacy, but set no standards for recreation, education or community facilities.

The developer's justifiable desire for a sense of personal achievement reinforces the overemphasis on the physical facility. In the early stages of a project, the developer's only tangible evidence of progress is the 'vertical development'—the buildings and the community and recreation facilities. Almost inevitably, therefore, he devotes himself to perfecting the physical object. This bias is reflected in the architect, who realizes his primary non-financial gain through professional recognition of the degree of innovation and adaptation of his design to the constraints and natural features of the site in question.

To counteract this overemphasis on the physical facility, and to ensure that the programs and services provided actually do meet users' needs and priorities, the first and in many ways most important step of the value improvement process is to define program or facility requirements in conceptual terms, before thinking of physical structures.

Program requirements worksheet

Program requirements are established in detail by completing a program requirements worksheet (Fig. 14.1) that assembles in one document the space, infrastructure and staffing needs of each program or facility under consideration, and the expected pattern of demand on the facilities and the growth requirements over the first few years of the project. Each column of the worksheet records information that will help the developer to identify the minimum provision required to launch each program.

Facility needs are the major categories of space normally found in a development. In general use space, a variety of activities could be performed with only minor adjustments in layout—for example, a community meeting hall could also be used as a waiting room for an adjacent clinic and a temporary theatre for an amateur dramatic society. While toilet, kitchen and storage needs are self-explanatory, some special features may be required—for example, a kitchen for preparing group meals might need special facilities for reheating frozen food. 'Special facilities' highlights uses that could not readily be varied—for example, a handicraft laboratory for an adult recreation program or a woodwork shop for a do-it-yourself club.

Layout constraints are those special needs that might restrict facility sharing. In a clinic, for example, the need for privacy in consulting rooms and related toilet space

277

TARGET PROGRAM	FACILITY NEEDS							PEAK-USE HOURS (Weekly)							GROWTH NEEDS Year			
	General Use Space	Infrastructure				STAFFING												
		Toilets	Kitchen/Storage Features (sq.ft.)	Special Facilities	Layout Constraints	Specialist	Utility	S	M	T	W	T	F	S	1	2	3	4
1. Health Care	3,750	Child 5 M 5 F Adult 1 M 1 F	200 sq. ft.; Large freezer Plastic crockery Milk dispenser	Sandbox; Pool Space for art-work displays Child fittings	Kitchen adjacent to classrooms Fenced outdoor play area adjacent to classrooms	4 qualified teachers 3 assistants 1 kitchen helper	1 maintenance 1 cook					8.30 a.m. to 1.00			Places 75	125	230	400
2. Pre-school (day care, kindergarten)				Outdoor play equipment														
3. Community Center																		

Figure 14.1 Program requirements worksheet

would dictate that they be kept separate. Similarly, a kitchen that would be used for a 'cordon bleu' cooking club would require extra space for spectators.

The *staffing* for each program is broken down to show both the professional or specialist staff required and the utility or general staff who could possibly support other programs using the same facility (e.g., cleaners and maintenance staff). Completing this column helps the developer to estimate at a later stage the potential staffing economies involved in any sharing opportunity.

The *peak-use hours* column records the expected pattern of demand—for example, the peak demand of a pre-school program would be from 8.30 a.m. to 1.00 p.m. each weekday. These estimates will form the basis for identifying opportunities for sharing facilities.

The final column is used to show the *growth needs* of the program over the project's life. Value improvement concentrates on the *initial* needs of each program—i.e., the minimum possible investment needed to launch the new community. But if the developer is to retain the flexibility to expand or contract, he needs some estimate of expected changes in demand to guide decisions on building a separate custom-built facility for any given program or accommodating increased demand by designing flexible facilities that can later be expanded.

The information for this worksheet is obtained from field interviews with the normal suppliers of the programs to be provided—for example, existing operators of public or private daycare programs who might be interested in taking up this role in the new community or who would be prepared to help with advice. In many instances, detailed design assistance can be obtained without charge, as long as the developer makes a reasonable commitment to consider that source as a supplier when the project is launched.

Consulting users

At this early stage in design, potential users can help to ensure that the programs and services provided actually do meet their needs and priorities. Too often, the urge to innovate has meant that proven formulae that are well suited to users' needs have been discarded in favour of newer and more exciting concepts—leading to extra costs in public and private developments alike.

In one recent project, a series of neighbourhood shopping centres, combined with a small swimming pool and recreation centre, were built. The range of shopping and social contacts that could be achieved in these neighbourhood centres was not enough for the residents, who preferred the larger facilities in the town centre. Further, since the shopping centres were purpose built, they were not suitable for conversion for alternative uses and ultimately fell into disrepair, so that a substantial investment was utterly wasted.

Expensive mistakes have also resulted from ignoring the costs that residents are prepared to bear for facility use. In another project, an elaborate equestrian centre was built for about $2 million. But the break-even fee level for the horses at that level of investment was about $40 per hour, which severely limited the appeal of the equestrian centre to local residents. And only after massive operating losses, the developer found that a variety of other uses would have better served their interests anyway.

Consulting users at the earliest stage of the project helps developers to avoid these expensive mistakes and allows them to identify those features that would meet effective local demand, so that programs and facilities really do add significant value to the development. One US developer found that most of his competitors offered no on-site doctor's offices or clinics, so that residents had to travel five to seven miles to consult a doctor. By encouraging a doctor from a local group practice to attend an on-site clinic three days a week, he substantially improved the project's appeal to growing families, and was also able to fill one of his office premises about 18 months sooner than planned. Another developer enhanced the value of the 'green belt' between groups of houses by providing a recreation area with swings, a sand pit and a basketball/climbing frame structure that was as demanding for adults as for teenagers. The recreation area became the focus of social contacts among residents and played a large part in pulling the community together. In both cases, by concentrating on meeting user needs, the project's appeal was increased without extra costs or facilities.

2. Define minimum facility needs and layout

Having determined the basic program requirements, the project team can develop a design that will meet users' needs with the most efficient use of space and resources. The usual development process makes little provision for this type of analysis, so that unnecessarily heavy commitments to facilities are often made prematurely. Developers will typically erect a purpose-built facility for every program, and tend to think in terms of the ultimate rather than initial requirements for programs and facilities. They become adjusted to thinking in terms of several daycare facilities, two or three schools, three shopping centres and the like, losing sight of the fact that they need provide only for the *initial* residents to create a project that meets development aims.

This can be expensive initially because of the carrying costs of under-utilized space in the early stages of the project's life, and similar expenses may continue later in the project if the expected demand does not materialize. For example, a purpose-built, six-room child-care facility in one project had only two rooms used because there were fewer children and fewer working mothers in the community than had been forecast. Had it been built only to meet demand in the first year of the project, the shortfall would have provided early warning that further building for child care would not be required. And if the program had been housed in a multi-use facility, the under-utilized space could have been converted for more needed services.

Some of this overcommitment is, of course, unavoidable, because the developer understandably wants to create a strong sense of momentum and permanence in the early stages to attract new residents and serve their needs. The tendency is reinforced by planning regulations in all countries that require early and tangible evidence (let contracts, for example) of the provision of key community facilities. Some may even argue that heavy commitments to physical facilities in the initial stages can be justified by economies of scale and timing. Building costs, for example, typically escalate rapidly, so that the addition of an extra 20–50 per cent of space to a facility seems a small incremental cost in relation to the possible cost in three to five years. In some cases this may be true, but the financial planning process seldom provides the developer with the sort of data he needs to balance potential economies against the carrying costs and financial penalty of owning and operating additional facilities. The value improvement process provides the developer with just this sort of data. It lets him know which features will have a genuine impact in the early stages of a project, and gives him an indication of how demand is likely to grow over the project's life, so that each facility commitment can be more carefully evaluated in terms of the incremental value added to the project.

Evaluating opportunities for sharing

Having established which programs he intends to provide in the early stages, the developer needs to identify the extent to which these programs can share facilities. Figure 14.2 shows a sharing opportunities worksheet used in evaluating such opportunities. Typically, these arise when different programs have similar uses for space and when their needs for these facilities occur at different times. In a community centre, for example, kitchen space, meeting halls, offices, committee rooms and toilets serve similar needs for all users, and few differences in design will be required. When programs use these facilities at different times of the day, it would be wasteful to provide separate space for each—yet that is typically what happens.

The first column of the worksheet is used to determine when different uses will occur—in this instance, the expected loading on kitchen space in a community centre over a normal weekly cycle is set out. Almost all uses are separate, but the overlap between the Women's League and the pre-school daycare program indicates operational problems that may require some rescheduling.

Then, the extent to which facilities can be shared is shown. Here, almost all kitchen facilities can be shared, so the four programs can share the general maintenance and cleaning costs.

While the worksheet establishes that sharing is an attractive possibility, there will usually be potential operational and technical difficulties arising from the special requirements of each group of users. One of the strengths of the value improvement process is that these practical difficulties are anticipated before construction so that solutions can be built into the original design. Such problems are recorded in the third column of the worksheet to show the extent of the difficulties that the designer will need to try to resolve.

The final column is used to record possible solutions for these problems. Though some problems (e.g., a poor standard of cleaning up between uses) are not conducive to design solutions, the majority can be resolved. Frequently, problems can be avoided by dedicating a portion of the space—particularly storage space—for the sole use of one program. Food and special utensils for each program, for example, could be housed in separate lockable cupboards, or sliding partitions can be used to

281

Hour				Program Peak-Use Day				Sharing Potential	Problems Arising From Sharing	Possible Solutions
	S	M	T	W	T	F	S			
6								Washing, cooking facilities; counter space, serving areas	'Pirating' of food	Lockable storage for each program
7									Damage to special dishware	
8										
9										
10										
11										
12										
1								Costs of general maintenance, cleaning	Overlaps in cleaning preparation	Clearly separated service areas
2										
3										Fast-cycle dishwasher
4										
5										
6										
7									Poor standard of cleaning up between uses	Cash penalty for poor cleaning up
8										
9										
10										
11										

COMMUNITY ASSOCIATION PROGRAMS   PRE-SCHOOL PROGRAM

Women's League

Teen and Pre-Teen

Adult Education

Figure 14.2 Sharing opportunities worksheet: kitchen space

BEATING THE VALUE SQUEEZE

PROGRAM	PROGRAM NEEDS				SHARING OPPORTUNITIES				POSSIBLE MINIMUM FACILITY				NET SAVINGS (over purpose-built facility)			
	Offices	Toilets	Kitchen	Common Space	Offices	Toilets	Kitchen	Common Space	Offices	Toilets	Kitchen	Common Space	Offices	Toilets	Kitchen	Common Space
1. Health clinic	3	4	–	250	2	2	–	250	3	4	–	250	–	–	–	–
2. Pre-school programs	1	10 2A 8C	200	1,500	1	2 A	–	1,400	3	4A 8C	200	1,500	1	2	–	250
3. Community associations	2	2	100	600	2	2	100	600	3	4A 8C	200	1,500	3	4	100	850

A = Adult   C = Children

Figure 14.3 Net facility requirements

close off space for privacy or to protect special equipment. The arts and crafts space for a pre-school daycare program, for example, could be sealed off in this way so that the teachers would not need to clear up after each session.

Having identified the special program needs and decided whether potential sharing opportunities can be turned into practical working arrangements, the designer will be able to determine the minimum facility requirements. Figure 14.3 summarizes the total facility needs of three programs to be housed in a community centre, showing how sharing can reduce space and equipment. In this instance, building one facility to house all three programs allows the developer to save three offices, four toilets, 100 square feet of kitchen space and 850 square feet of office space, representing a considerable saving in capital investment and significantly lower running costs for the program operators.

Developing the optimum layout

Once the total requirement for each category of space is established, this must be converted into a layout that will, as far as possible, accommodate the constraints identified in the program requirements worksheet. First, the optimum layout for each separate program is drawn up and then combined for all programs by balancing the requirements of each until a workable compromise is reached.

Information on the most effective layout for each program in isolation can be obtained from existing operators or from field research. Figure 14.4 shows optimal layouts for a health clinic, a pre-school daycare facility and community association space, showing the space required for toilets, offices, kitchens and general use. Each is designed to meet the special needs of the program—i.e., security, privacy, controlled access and convenient circulation. The layout of the health clinic, for example, clearly separates the waiting and reception area from the toilet and doctors' consulting spaces. The daycare facility design gives ready access from the kitchen to the classrooms, allows all children to get to the play space during recreation periods, and keeps the sand and pool play areas separate from the classrooms.

The community association space is also organized to minimize operating problems. The kitchen space and toilet areas are adjacent to the general use space, and the offices overlook this common area so that all activities can be supervised. The general use space is designed with partitions so that it can be used either as a common meeting area for the entire community or as committee rooms with a separate games area.

Having established the optimal layout for each program and defined the most important constraints, the designer can sketch out the combined facility. It must be recognized from the outset that some compromises in operating efficiency for all of the programs will be involved. The objective is to try to find the *least inconvenient* arrangement for the majority of the programs, and this may sometimes involve dispersing secondary space users like utilities to ease layout problems. In doing this, it may be necessary to increase the cost of, for example, the plumbing of the building, but typically these extra costs will be more than offset by the savings achieved in reducing the total space and maximizing utilization for the total project.

284

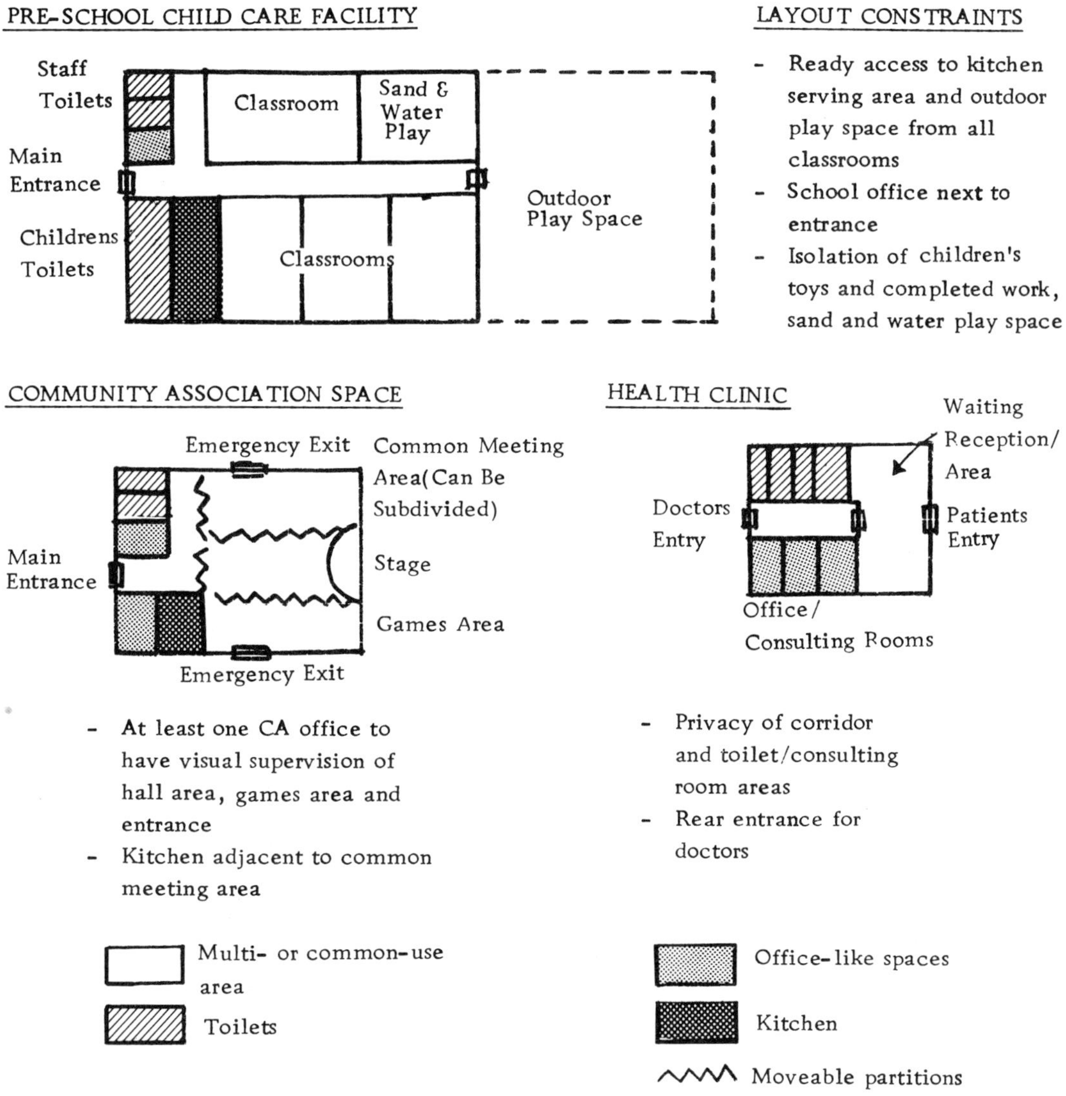
PRE-SCHOOL CHILD CARE FACILITY
Staff Toilets
Main Entrance
Childrens Toilets
Classroom
Sand & Water Play
Outdoor Play Space
Classrooms
LAYOUT CONSTRAINTS
- Ready access to kitchen serving area and outdoor play space from all classrooms
- School office next to entrance
- Isolation of children's toys and completed work, sand and water play space
COMMUNITY ASSOCIATION SPACE
Emergency Exit
Common Meeting Area(Can Be Subdivided)
Main Entrance
Stage
Games Area
Emergency Exit
- At least one CA office to have visual supervision of hall area, games area and entrance
- Kitchen adjacent to common meeting area
HEALTH CLINIC
Waiting Reception/ Area
Doctors Entry
Patients Entry
Office/ Consulting Rooms
- Privacy of corridor and toilet/consulting room areas
- Rear entrance for doctors
Multi- or common-use area
Toilets
Office-like spaces
Kitchen
Moveable partitions

Figure 14.4 Optimum layouts for each program

The optimal layout will not be achieved through a perfectly rational and formal process; some element of trial and error is inevitable, but certain practical tricks can help to simplify the task. The first is to reorient the original layout so that similar kinds of spaces are in the same 'compass quadrant' of the combined layout. This will show similar patterns of use and expose possible overlaps and clear conflicts that exist. For instance, in Fig. 14.4, the general use space is divided into classrooms by solid walls for the pre-school program, but the community association prefers

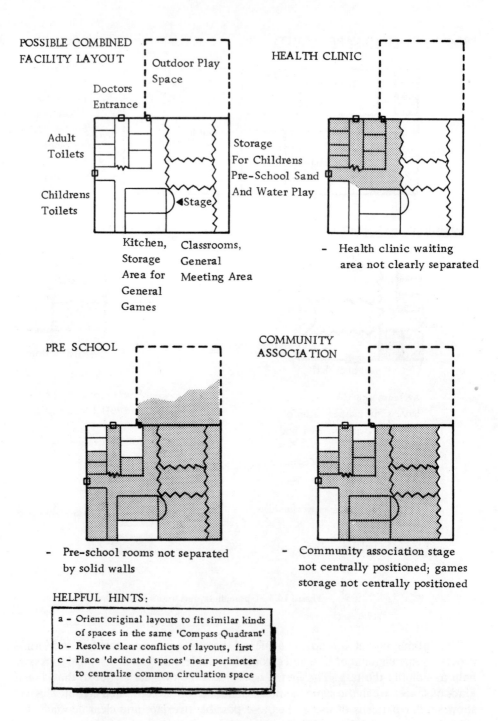

POSSIBLE COMBINED
FACILITY LAYOUT

Outdoor Play
Space

Doctors
Entrance

Adult
Toilets

Storage
For Childrens
Pre-School Sand
And Water Play

Childrens
Toilets

◄Stage

Kitchen,
Storage
Area for
General
Games

Classrooms,
General
Meeting Area

HEALTH CLINIC

- Health clinic waiting
  area not clearly separated

PRE SCHOOL

- Pre-school rooms not separated
  by solid walls

COMMUNITY
ASSOCIATION

- Community association stage
  not centrally positioned; games
  storage not centrally positioned

HELPFUL HINTS:

a - Orient original layouts to fit similar kinds
    of spaces in the same 'Compass Quadrant'
b - Resolve clear conflicts of layouts, first
c - Place 'dedicated spaces' near perimeter
    to centralize common circulation space

Figure 14.5 Combined program layout

movable partitions. Resolving such conflicts is an essential step in the process if the final layout is to be workable for all the programs concerned.

Once major conflicts of this type have been resolved, dedicated spaces should be marked out to ensure that the final layout meets the needs of all programs. The pre-school program, for instance, needs special storage for children's artwork and sealed-off sand and water play areas, and the community association needs equipment storage. The most effective layout can usually be achieved by siting these dedicated spaces near the perimeter of the building, centralizing the general use space so that it is easily accessible for all program users.

The principal conflicts can usually be resolved by juggling layouts and requirements. The combined layouts will often be radically different from the traditional optimal layouts for each program but should meet the major needs of each. Figure 14.5 shows a possible combined layout for the three programs I have been discussing. Clearly this involves some compromises—the health clinic waiting area is not clearly separated and the pre-school rooms do not have solid walls—but it is the layout that best meets the needs of all programs taken together. However, it should not be considered as the final layout but as a specific starting point for working with program operators to adjust the design to meet what they see as their priority needs.

Clearly, the more facilities can be shared, the lower will be the developer's building costs and the ultimate users' operating costs. One UK developer, for example, was able to provide an adult recreation centre at a quarter of the cost of a purpose-built facility, by working with a local school and adjusting the design of its planned assembly hall. By incorporating separate toilet facilities, dedicated storage space, a higher ceiling suitable for volley ball, etc., and an outside entrance for adults quite separate from the interior school access doors, he was able to minimize operating costs both for the school and for the adult recreation group, and cut his own building costs to £5,000 instead of the £20,000 that would have been required for a purpose-built facility.

3. Consult users on key design details

The pace of the early planning cycle of a project often encourages designers to gloss over critical design details. By this stage of the project, the developer has made major financial commitments leading to significant cash outflows that must be financed through debt. He can stem this outflow only by speeding up the design and construction of physical facilities, so designers usually are encouraged to 'second guess' user requirements in their designs. The third step in the value improvement process is therefore systematically to consult the full range of users and participants—the customer, the operator, the maintainer, the builder and the owner—to identify these key design details.

Small details may appear so insignificant to the designer as to be safely ignored, but this is dangerous, since the entire economic viability of facilities can be put at risk by a failure to comply with user requirements in these 'trivial' features. In one city parking lot, the architect did not check the dimensions of the coin-operated exit gate. The

287

concrete platform that he designed was some 12 inches too high to be reached from a normal vehicle, so that most drivers had to leave their cars to insert the token in the machine. This inevitably caused queues at the exit, and the inconvenience discouraged motorists from repeat visits. In effect, the car park's usefulness was destroyed by a detail that seemed trivial at the design stage.

In some cases, this type of second guessing simply results in inconvenience. In a recent US project the layout was such that the only access to the community centre kitchen was down a winding path and up two flights of steps. This meant that all deliveries had to be hand-carried to the kitchen, involving a needless expenditure of effort and considerable inconvenience—a situation that could easily have been avoided if the designer had anticipated the problem and installed ramps instead of steps.

Other projects have been more seriously affected by lack of thought at the design stage. In the design of one US golf course, a great premium was placed on creativity in layout and little attention was paid to the practical details of its maintenance. As a result, most of the sandtraps have to be maintained by hand because the shapes and widths are such that mechanized maintenance is impossible. And because the drainage of the course was not sufficiently thought out, the course is unplayable during the summer rainy season when an inch of rain can fall in less than an hour. This has a serious effect on the total project, because the golf course is a major recreational amenity for residents and others.

Small design details can also have a significant impact on staffing costs. In a recent project, for example, the clubhouse design required three support staff to put every golfer in play. Apart from someone to man the pro-shop, the club needed a starter because the pro-shop operator could not see the first and tenth tees, and a special attendant in the cart barn, because this was some distance from the pro-shop. A layout that brought these activities physically closer together would have permitted the golf shop pro to handle all three responsibilities during the mid-week quiet periods.

Few developers have the financial resources to maintain on their team experts in all the disciplines relevant to community development, so this type of second guessing seems almost inevitable. And because new communities take several years to complete, there are only limited opportunities for using the lessons learned in one project to avoid similar mistakes in another. In this situation, the developer needs a way of gaining access to the real experts—the operators and users of the various facilities. Field interviews in the first value improvement stage will have shown the developer which programs and facilities potential residents will appreciate. Given the relentless pressures they are under, however, developers need to be sure that these facilities actually do meet users' needs and that the essential but little known details of design that can reduce capital operating and maintenance costs are included.

This information can most easily be obtained from prospective users and participants.

In designing a golf course, for example, the customer, typically an enthusiastic golfer, would be able to give some idea of the features of a course that make it

288

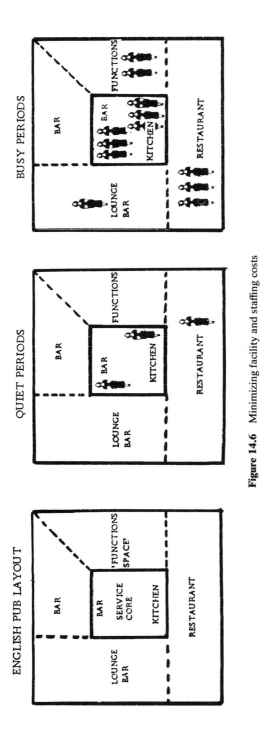

Figure 14.6 Minimizing facility and staffing costs

interesting, demanding and satisfying; an experienced operator would know what would make the place easy to run—e.g., automatic watering and a layout that minimized staff requirements; a maintainer would contribute his knowledge of the best type of grass for fairways and greens and the minimum sandtrap size that would accommodate automatic machines; a builder would know what materials could be obtained locally and what design features would be difficult to accommodate; and the investor or financing source would be able to set a limit on the total outlay he would be prepared to bear. Once identified, the key features can be built into the detailed specification that the designer will use in preparing construction plans and equipment schedules.

Including this step in the design process ensures that expensive mistakes are avoided for both the developer and the ultimate user. The developer saves effort, since these details are identified before detailed plans are drawn up and can therefore be incorporated in the original plans, avoiding the need for redrawing at a later stage. Users avoid making the heavy capital outlays that would be involved in adjusting facilities to meet their requirements after they have been built, but more important, they are assured that the ultimate facility will have the lowest possible operating and maintenance costs. Figure 14.6 shows how creative design, taking account of user needs, was able to minimize facility and staffing costs in a typical English pub. It has a public bar, a formal lounge, a restaurant and space for functions such as weddings and group meetings. Normally, separate facilities for each purpose would be housed under the same roof, but in this case by placing the service area at the centre, and arranging the 'dedicated spaces' around the perimeter, the design minimized both building and staffing costs. Because peak and valley staffing needs were taken into account, the resulting layout allows three staff members to run the entire pub at quiet periods, but it can also accommodate the additional staff required in peak periods.

4. Verify project plans with users

The final step in the value improvement process is to review project plans and design with representatives of all participants to ensure that the approach is valid.

Ideally, the plans will first be reviewed in outline, and the detailed design brief drawn up in the light of users' comments. Clearly users will be interested to review the proposed layout, but it is also useful at this stage to be able to demonstrate to each participant how his own program will be incorporated in the final layout. A summary of the relevant details should include sketch plans, facility details, the special arrangements that have been devised to resolve possible operational problems, and an indication of the target costs and implementation timetables. This can be used to agree the approach, costs and timetable with key participants, and invite their opinions and suggestions on refining the plans and provisions that have been made for sharing facilities and reducing operating costs. Any modifications can then be incorporated into the total facility specification for the project, and from this a detailed design brief against which architects and other specialist designers produce their detailed plans can be prepared.

Once the detailed plans are drawn up, participants can also be given an opportunity to validate the design approach and confirm that all essential details have been properly included. This two-stage consultation helps to conserve design resources, since detailed design is not entered upon until the concept has been approved in outline.

The approach in this final step would be similar to the canvassing process used earlier, and again participants are likely to be eager to co-operate, recognizing that it is in their best interests to support a process that will reduce their costs and ease their operating and maintenance burdens.

The benefits of the value improvement approach speak for themselves. It is far more cost effective than the traditional method of designing custom-built facilities, and the resultant design greatly increases the value of the project to the ultimate users. The design process is cheaper, since detailed designs are not drawn up until the ultimate users have confirmed outline plans. Users are provided with facilities that closely match their needs and cost parameters and are more convenient and cheaper to operate and maintain. And developers, having involved key participants at all critical stages, can protect the market appeal of their project by providing only those facilities that are compatible with user needs and priorities.

Overhead value analysis

Overhead costs represent a significant burden on the development process, particularly in the early stages when no revenues are earned from property sales. In a typical large-scale project, they may account for 25 per cent of the land development value over the life of a project, and in a development enterprise with several projects, up to 35 per cent of total fixed costs, or about equal to the debt service required.

The major element of overhead costs is staffing, which can amount to 75 per cent of overheads. In relation to the total development investment, however, the investment in staff in the crucial stages of a project seems relatively insignificant, so that even the most cost-conscious developer may feel justified in ignoring the potential for pruning. Personnel costs of perhaps $1–2 million a year in a $100 million project seem small in relation to the asset values to be created, but they are a major element of overall project costs and returns. Each extra staff member, paid $25,000 per year with normal rises and fringe benefits, and financed on the development loan for a period of 10 years, reduces project pre-tax returns by about $750,000—i.e., as much as five per cent of the pre-tax returns of a typical large-scale project.

How to do staffing costs get out of control? Clearly developers need to contain these costs, but a number of forces militate against careful control. First, the complexity of the planning stage implies the need for a wide range of highly skilled staff, and because of the heavy time pressures involved in meeting planning deadlines, developers tend to prefer 'captive' teams to temporary staff from outside organizations.

291

In the early stages of a project, a high level of staffing is almost inevitable. The number of specialist areas that must be planned in detail in itself warrants a large project team. In the 6- to 12-month start-up period, culminating in the final planning permission or zoning approval, many different planning streams have to be controlled and co-ordinated. Different aspects of the development need to be presented for approval and master construction plans have to be drawn up, with detailed plans for the first phase. Amenity and social program plans have to be outlined, and the developer's staff have to evaluate the project's economic and environmental impact. At the same time, staff are preparing marketing materials, financing proposals and carrying out the myriad other pre-development tasks.

The nature of development is such that many people have only a short-term involvement, depending on the need for their specialist skills. In general terms, there are four critical project deadlines that create peaks in the demands on project planning staff: (1) pre-purchase planning, in which basic project feasibility is established and the price and amount of land determined; (2) pre-zoning approvals, in which a final statement is required about land uses, facilities, target markets, etc., for use by local authorities in deciding whether to approve land-use zoning; (3) pre-construction planning, in which detailed implementation plans and facility designs are created and approved; and (4) pre-opening planning, in which potential residents are informed and attracted to take an interest.

Ideally, therefore, the project team would vary in size over the project's life, with a small team of company staff until the detailed planning stage, and temporary staff hired from outside organizations to meet peaks in demand. Typically, however, developers object to paying a salary premium to temporary staff and prefer to create their own team, feeling that they will thereby have lower immediate cash outflows, and better control over the resources required to meet planning deadlines.

Similarly, although public sector projects often do not have to surmount equally cumbersome approval hurdles, they have the same need to obtain financing and therefore have to make a case to the Treasury or other funds source. As deadlines are often established for political reasons, the same urgency about planning is compounded by an even greater reluctance to hire specialized temporary staff, so that the creation of a large permanent project team is almost inevitable. Once formed, project teams tend to be perpetuated, regardless of project needs. Staff members often remain on the team after their key inputs have been made, adopting new roles as the project progresses. Land planners become members of the architectural control board, social program designers become administrators of community associations, and construction planners stay on to monitor the quality of construction and to develop particular programs. This pressure to maintain continuous employment for the project team is possibly even stronger among public developers, where stability of employment is the norm.

Staffing costs can be increased further by the sheer professionalism of the staff. As technical specialists they tend to be interested more in perfecting their own contribution to the planning process than in meeting the overall financial objectives of the project. Consequently, each functional specialist tends to extend and elaborate his activities—designers spend time perfecting detailed plans when only outline sketches are required and the personnel department evolves complex administrative systems without regard to the incremental contributions that these additional activities make to the project's overall success. The developer has no way of challenging the need for the extra expenditure, partly because of the specialist nature of the activities, and partly because accounting data tend to hide the real costs of a service. For example, most departmental budgets show totals for salaries, overtime, telephones, etc., without breaking these down by individual services. And who can say precisely what the services of a corporate lawyer are worth, or quantify the benefits from the company's spending on image advertising?

How can overheads be controlled? In this situation, the developer clearly needs a process for controlling overheads, both in the planning stages of a new project and in the operating phases of an existing project, to ensure that the services provided are clearly related to the development objectives. To keep staffing costs to an acceptable level, the staffing strategy for the new project must be explicitly related to the stage of the project life cycle and its particular staffing needs. In the pre-purchase decision phase, for example, there would be few permanent staff and outsiders would be used to develop the basic feasibility analyses. As the project progressed, more and more permanent staff would be used to perform detailed planning and to monitor construction progress.

Once a project is under way, the overhead control process must provide a mechanism for clearly challenging the need for each product or service provided and identifying opportunities for reducing these costs.

Overhead value analysis (OVA) helps the developer to minimize his fixed cash costs while at the same time protecting the project's marketability. These two objectives are achieved by identifying activities that make no direct contribution to short-term sales and rentals and evaluating the impact of eliminating them—balancing the financial advantages of cutting back against the potential risks and operational disadvantages.

The central feature of the process is that the task of challenging the need for services and identifying where cuts can be made is delegated to the participants in the development process who incur the costs and those who benefit from them. Top management makes the final decisions, but is guided by the combined judgements of the entire management team. By formally placing the burden of analysis on all managers, OVA brings requesters and suppliers of services together to work on what they see as a common task—thus overcoming the natural tendency to refrain from recommending changes because of the fear of being labelled a bad manager.

To ensure that recommendations are soundly based, and to guide managers as they follow through the process, a small high-level task force will be needed. Three to five task force members working full time is normally sufficient for a company with up to $75 million in overhead. In larger organizations, more team members, or possibly even multiple teams, may be required.

The OVA process has four steps, summarized below.

1. Estimate costs

The first step in the process is to identify the real cost of all current activities. Essentially this means regrouping the existing accounting information to relate the various costs of each department to the activities for which it is responsible. First, each manager lists his department's major activities, showing the number of staff involved, and the annual salary costs. He then adds in those overhead costs that can be directly attributed to that activity—e.g., telephone, transportation, insurance, etc.—to find the total cost of each activity. Figure 14.7 suggests a format for this analysis.

Department	Major Activities	Staff Per Activity	Salary Costs	Share of General Costs	Total Cost
			($000)		
Real Estate Sales	– Generate qualified prospects	15	120	40	160
		15	120	40	160
	– Close prospects				
Facility Maintenance	– Maintain common areas	13	195	98	293
	– Maintain key amenities	10	160	40	200
	– Maintain offices	7	126	38	164
Land Development	– Monitor construction	22	445	130	575
Personnel	– Maintain personnel records	12	230	80	310
	– Recruit staff				
	– Issue employee newsletter				

Figure 14.7   Activity cost worksheet

It would, of course, take months to get accurate estimates of the costs involved. At this stage, all that is required is an order-of-magnitude cost for each activity based on rough estimates of how staff deploy their time, since the purpose is merely to direct analytic effort at the most productive areas.

Having established the cost of each activity, the next phase is to estimate the contribution that each makes to the critical process of promoting short- and medium-term sales or rentals, to determine whether the activity is a direct

ILLUSTRATIVE ONLY

Department	Contributions to Sales	Impact of Total Elimination	Other Methods of Supply	Costs and Delays Rebuilding if Eliminated
Real Estate Sales	– 80% of qualified leads – 95% of sales closures	– Sales drop to 5–10% of current level, over 3 months – Bad project image	Local broker network (at 2 x commission cost)	Carrying cost of total project investment during slow sales period; $50,000 per salesman
Facility Maintenance	– Indirect: enhances project image – Negligible, except for sales office	– Sales drop to 20–30% of current rate – Residents' complaints rise 5–10x – Impact small for 3–6 months; bad image thereafter	Outside firm Lower frequency	$100 per worker $100 per worker
Land Development	– None: inventory provides 2 years' sales	– 6–9 months' lead time required prior to start of new construction	Delegate to designers/architects	About $25,000 per good project manager

Figure 14.8 Contribution worksheet

contributor, a key supporting activity, or a very indirect contributor. Many of the activities in the development process cannot be unequivocally related to the process of creating and promoting a new community, and it is these activities that will be the prime targets for elimination or reduction.

A worksheet of the form illustrated in Fig. 14.8 is helpful in defining the contribution made by each activity and evaluating the impact of eliminating it. The first column sets out the major activities performed by each department and the total cost of each activity (taken from the Activity Cost Worksheet in Fig. 14.7). The second column shows the contribution that each is expected to make to sales in the next 18 to 24 months, indicating whether this is a direct or an indirect contribution. The sales department, for example, clearly makes a direct contribution, while facility maintenance could be said to make an indirect contribution by enhancing the project image.

In the third and fourth columns, some attempt should be made to determine the impact on sales of eliminating the activity altogether and to list alternative means of obtaining the service. The conclusions reached on completing this part of the worksheet will help to refine the initial estimate of how direct a contribution each activity makes to sales. A further refinement will be achieved by completing the final column, attempting to put a figure on the cost penalties and delays of rebuilding the activity should it prove to be critical to the development and selling process.

2. Generate improvement options

Completing this checklist will indicate where the greatest potential for savings lies. Activities that make a direct contribution will usually provide less fruitful ground for further analysis than indirect contributors, but all 'big number' activities will probably warrant a second look. Several forcing mechanisms can be used in this second step to identify opportunities for reducing the costs associated with each activity. One device that has been found particularly useful is the cutback checklist illustrated in Fig. 14.9. This is based on the premise that there are six distinct ways of achieving savings from any activity: (1) to eliminate it totally, (2) to defer the introduction of new services, (3) to reduce the quality expected and hence the time involved in monitoring and in preparation, (4) to reduce the amount of paperwork involved, (5) to reduce the frequency of a regular activity, such as issuing reports, and (6) to substitute an outside supplier for some or all of the services provided.

The most effective way of listing improvement options is to make the managers responsible for supplying the services responsible also for identifying cost reduction opportunities. Only they are sufficiently acquainted with the costs and technical details of their activities to produce reasonable suggestions without the need for costly research, and as a rule they are already aware of most of the options that might be listed. But because they are not normally happy to see the demand for their services reduced, they should be encouraged to work with those within the organization who benefit from their activities, exploring with them and with the OVA task force the pros and cons of all cost reduction options.

Ways of Cutting Back	Examples
1. Eliminate totally	Discontinue newsletter to property owners Discontinue printing organization charts
2. Defer	Delay new sales literature Postpone new management training
3. Reduce quality	Permit higher error rate in reports Reduce color in promotional literature Form letters to tenants Lengthen time to respond to service requests
4. Reduce amount	Circulate summary reports, not details Use exception reports Restrict distribution of documents
5. Reduce frequency	Quarterly not monthly status reports
6. Substitute	Use outside economic advisory service, not internal experts

Figure 14.9 Cutback checklist

To ensure that a cost reduction proposal does not eliminate some critical element that would affect the continuity or fundamental quality of the development team, managers should also go through a formal process of selecting the core staff in their departments—i.e., staff with special abilities and experience or external contacts that might be essential to maintain vital political or owner/resident relationships. In identifying these staff, managers should make explicit their reasons for considering them as key members of the development team, taking into account the contribution made by the activity in question and the stage of the project's life cycle, as well as the individual's special abilities. The end product of this selection process would be a list of 'core staff' showing the activity area in which each works, the cost of retaining these people within the project team and the justification for retaining them.

3. Weigh the consequences

The total savings likely to arise from implementing any one of the various options identified will be quite small. Consequently very little time can be spent gathering data on each option and deliberating its attractiveness. Management must be content to base its decisions on available facts and judgements, but can refine these judgements by using a formal review process to gain the views of managers at different levels of the organization.

The review process operates as follows. Managers in charge of specific activities rank the cost reduction ideas they have produced, balancing the cost savings potential of each against the possible adverse consequences, their severity and the likelihood of their occurrence. The idea worksheet illustrated in Fig. 14.10 is a means

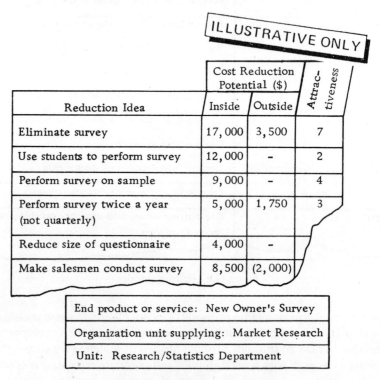

ILLUSTRATIVE ONLY

Reduction Idea	Cost Reduction Potential ($)		Attractiveness
	Inside	Outside	
Eliminate survey	17,000	3,500	7
Use students to perform survey	12,000	–	2
Perform survey on sample	9,000	–	4
Perform survey twice a year (not quarterly)	5,000	1,750	3
Reduce size of questionnaire	4,000	–	
Make salesmen conduct survey	8,500	(2,000)	

End product or service: New Owner's Survey

Organization unit supplying: Market Research

Unit: Research/Statistics Department

Figure 14.10 Idea worksheet

of systematically but rapidly evaluating opportunities for reducing costs of activities. First the magnitude of the cost savings potential is identified, broken down by savings within the activity area and savings in other activity areas. Next the possible adverse consequences are recorded, and the manager responsible then ranks the options in order of their attractiveness. This worksheet is then passed to a higher organizational level for review, both to ensure that all possibilities have been considered and to agree the priority rating of each option. Managers at higher levels may well re-rank the options in the light of their broader view of the company's priorities. For example, the head of market research may believe that his most important role is to maintain a capability to respond quickly to questions on trends in real estate. He will therefore consider national economic surveys too important to be cut back. The head of the marketing department, however, may consider it more important to identify the socioeconomic patterns of prospective buyers, and would therefore put more weight on analysing salesmen's reports on purchasers, and recommend reductions in national economic surveys.

4. Select the level of cuts required

When all departments have contributed their lists of options and these lists have been combined and ranked in order of attractiveness, some estimate of the total reduction potential can be prepared, indicating the sources of staff savings and the organizational units or programs most affected. Figure 14.11 illustrates a summary estimate

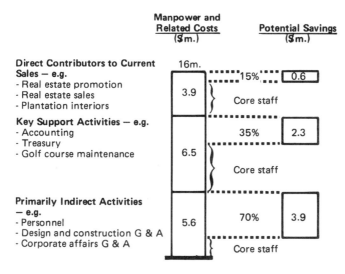

Figure 14.11 Total reduction potential

prepared by one developer, showing that savings can be made even in the key contributing activities such as real estate promotion and sales, although more savings would normally be expected to be achieved within key support activities. Obviously, however, the bulk of savings would come from indirect staff activities where the relationship between the expenditure and the direct benefits achieved is normally quite vague.

Having established the total potential, top management can then begin to select the options it will implement. Usually services would not be cut to the bone unless the project is facing severe liquidity problems. Top management will normally simply select the level it hopes to achieve against some relevant criteria. For example, it may decide that the level of savings should be equivalent to some target return on investment in the project, or enough to cover the primary debt of the project over a certain time period or reduce the operating cost burden to zero.

Once the desired level of savings has been identified, all that is needed is to review the ranked list of savings opportunities, taking a cumulative total of the potential savings and drawing a cut-off point when the required level is reached. In this way, the ranking process automatically indicates the ideas that will be implemented. However, in the interests of speedy and fair implementation a total implementation plan should be prepared, showing for each activity the change that will be made, its priority, the staff involved, timing of the change and the cumulative savings that are expected to accrue.

Changes of this type should be made as fairly, as quickly and as openly as possible. Few organizations can tolerate a series of lingering reductions that depress morale and create uncertainty for everyone in the organization. Unless staff reductions are clear cut and well planned, the organization runs the risk of losing the people who are most valuable and therefore most marketable, at a time when they are desperately needed.

Staff should also be convinced that the cuts are fairly made, and the company would probably be well advised to lay down some ground rules that are seen to be followed. For example, it should be clear that the cuts affect all levels of management and labour, that all non-contributing activities are subject to a similar level of reduction and that due consideration is given to seniority and competence.

The negative impact of these changes can be minimized by acting openly throughout. Once a reasonable reduction program has been identified, the rationale for the changes should be explained as completely as possible to the staff so that they are aware that the changes will benefit them in the long term by ensuring the company's economic viability.

Consistent use of overhead value analysis will reduce developers' fixed costs and ensure that these costs remain at an acceptable level. The process of challenging all overhead commitments makes developers more aware of the true costs of carrying staff who make a contribution only at certain stages of the project life cycle. They are therefore encouraged to make more use of outside staff to perform these tasks, rather than maintain large captive teams. One developer, using this approach, managed to reduce his overhead costs to about 40 per cent of the original level through carefully challenging the value of each of his activities, and savings between 15 and 25 per cent have been regularly realized in other projects.

Author's note: I wish to acknowledge the original contribution of Mr John Neuman in developing the approach to Overhead Value Analysis, and the assistance of Mrs Karen MacLeod in preparing this chapter.

Part IV

New directions for new communities

So far we have been concerned with community development today. This concluding section looks ahead to tomorrow.

In 'The scope for change', H. Dennis Stevenson points out a fundamental conflict in large-scale development between the enormous scale on which resource decisions have to be made and the increasing desire of citizens to be involved in decisions that affect them. The development corporation, he argues, is uniquely fitted to experiment with ways of resolving this conflict. He then turns to a theme already touched on by other contributors: the advantages of involving the private sector more closely in community development, and ways of combining public accountability with private sector initiatives.

In the final chapter, 'Looking ahead', John Griffith-Jones summarizes the main trends affecting the future course of community development throughout the world—the slackening of economic and population growth, constraints on physical and financial resources, and increasing political pressures and involvement. He forecasts the resulting new forms of development that may well displace the 'greenfield' new town as a model, and recommends ways in which development mechanisms and processes can be adapted to meet the challenge.

Chapter 15.   The scope for change

H. DENNIS STEVENSON

It is remarkable how well the original model of new town development established in 1947 has endured. Relatively unchanged, it has been consistently and successfully applied to a variety of different problems. However, it would be equally remarkable if, after 25 years of technological and institutional development, the British new town system did not show scope for change itself.

This paper discusses two aspects of British new town development where there is a need for change. First, the clash between the need to take large and complicated resource decisions on the one hand and the demands of an increasingly articulate public on the other is impairing the ability of new town development corporations to achieve their ends. In this situation the corporations must increasingly find their salvation and freedom not so much by relying on the existing system for support as in becoming their own politicians, developing new political skills and creating their own freedom of action. The apparent paradox is that the new town corporation, so often described as anti-democratic, has a potential for developing new forms of participative democracy better able to resolve these problems.

Second, the British new towns need to allow and be allowed a greater measure of the disciplines of the private sector, while still operating under public controls. I shall explore the advantages and disadvantages of both the public and private mechanisms as well as attempt to spotlight some of the problems in marrying the two.

Changes since 1947

The distinctive feature of the new town corporation as established under the 1946 New Towns Act was that central government could set up a body structured to tackle a specific problem in the most direct way possible. The performance of the British new towns since has clearly demonstrated that the original concept worked in practice. That it is now working less easily and less simply, however, there can be little doubt. New town development corporations find the negotiation and implementation of their plans more circumscribed by and more subject to political vagaries at every level. The orthodox response is to blame central government for allowing the powers and the responsibilities of the new town development corporation to be eroded. Yet, to call for pressure on central government to restore new towns to their former freedom is less than half the answer. Central government has little or no interest in deliberately weakening new towns; rather the contrary. To find the real reasons underlying the erosion of new town powers we have to look at a number of basic changes that are taking place in society.

The increasing complexity of the planning process

The first and perhaps most overlooked change is that new town development corporations no longer operate in the same conditions as they did when first established. In 1947, new town development corporations hunted a relatively empty forest. Since then, the scale of public intervention has grown substantially. Water boards, health authorities, nationalized industries, and so on, have multiplied, grown larger, and become more involved in the planning process. At the same time, the sheer concentration of resources in the postwar period has led to a more detailed and tighter system of town planning. Planning decisions are more complex and multi-dimensional. Every major land-use decision is now regarded as vital and, therefore, becomes more complicated. And the realization that the major streams of investment in, for example, roads, housing and social services are mutually interdependent has further complicated the planning process.

At the same time, changes in communications and transport have intensified the necessary links between new town plans and the plans of the authorities in the surrounding area. Because it is now practical for a much larger section of the population to live away from their work, it is wrong and irresponsible to consider investment decisions in roads, houses and factories in a new town independently of decisions in the surrounding area. One extreme solution to this (adopted, for example, in the Central Lancashire New Town) is for new towns to move away from what might be described as 'dot on the map' designations towards sub-regional designations. The problem remains, however, and indeed is magnified. Any section of land in the UK, be it a 'dot on the map' or a sub-region, is increasingly dependent on the area next to it.

The change in democratic decision-making

So far, the changes that have been described are concerned with the nature of resource decisions and the way these have changed. But there is another category of change that, although separate, bears heavily on questions of resources. This is the change that is taking place in the nature of our democracy. In current jargon, it might simply be described as the changing balance between representative and participative democracy. The traditional democratic system, whereby resource decisions were discussed and resolved by a small group of elected representatives from two or three political parties, worked effectively enough. Argument ranged hard and long in the council chamber; but at the end of the day there was a built-in mechanism for ensuring a decision; and once that decision had been taken councils could implement it secure in the knowledge that it had consensus by virtue of the democratic system. This is no longer so. Elected representatives are still elected to discuss and take major resource decisions. The fundamental change is that now the electors seek to intervene in the formation of those decisions as well as to protest at their implementation. In the age of rent strikes, squatters and factory take-overs, representative democracy no longer commands the respect and consensus that it once did.

The reasons for this are not surprising. The Butler Education Act is perhaps the first reason; the mass of the electorate are now much better educated, better able to understand the decisions affecting them and better able to express their point of view. And there is now a far greater awareness of the decisions being taken than there was in the past, largely because of the influence of the media. Any major newspaper tells daily of a myriad of key public decisions, understood and discussed by the public at large.

It would be surprising if this complex array of changes had not affected new town development corporations. In general, the effect has been that it now takes longer and is more difficult to make plans and to implement them than it was in 1947. Specifically, new town development corporations now find themselves in a rather more equal battle with other public undertakings, and will often find themselves on the losing side. They have to invest a much greater part of their time in talking to local authorities; the local authorities' view on decisions affecting the new town is now much more critical.

New town development corporations have felt the effect of the increase in participative democracy in another way, too. A count of the number of petitions, letters, and complaints addressed to the Secretary of State for the Environment about new towns would certainly show a massive increase over the last decade. In practical terms, the delays caused either through public inquiries or through ministerial intervention have increased substantially.

The need to seek political solutions

It is not surprising that men and women accustomed to preparing and implementing plans in a single-minded way—and achieving outstanding results—should resent the interference and the difficulties now besetting their jobs. It is not surprising that they should look for some measure of change in the system to enable them to return to their old freedom, and ask that the Government should help. Development corporations are creatures of government, so the argument runs; their powers have been allowed to erode. The Government must put it right.

Unfortunately, this theory has a weakness. It assumes that the Secretary of State has the power to undo the basic changes that have taken place over the past 25 years in the society within which he and the new towns operate. This is not so. The Secretary of State also operates within a far more complex and tightly interwoven institutional and political network than when new towns were first established. Development corporations should of course do everything within their power to persuade the Secretary of State to protect and support them as far as he can. But unless they recognize the basic problem limiting his freedom of action to help them and find ways of solving this problem, they are unlikely to regain any of their former freedom.

Let us restate the problem new towns face. It is no different in kind from the problem faced by most authorities in the UK. It might be said that it is a general problem found in all advanced countries: the clash between the need for complicated and large resource decisions on the one hand and an increasingly articulate and educated public on the other. The struggle is not unique to new towns. It is just as relevant to ICI, the Kremlin, or any other organization attempting to manage change. New towns are perhaps a special case in so·far as they are asked to manage and implement change very quickly (building towns in 20 years that traditionally would have taken 100 years).

Against this background the British new towns have only one course if they wish to retain their viability. To obtain support for their decisions from the Secretary of State they must so manage the complex world they live in that he finds it politically feasible to give support. They must drop the traditional passive political view of their role, which might be summed up in the statement 'we've been given a job to do—we must go straight down the middle, plan what is best for all the people and, without fear or favour, implement it. We are not politicians and indeed it would be thoroughly wrong for us to become involved in politics'. Put crudely, they must become their own politicians.

Two sets of policies

Such a change in attitude (already evident in some new towns) implies in practical terms two sets of policies. First is the need to make explicit and conscious allowance for the political dimension of planning, in every sense of the word 'political'. New towns must increasingly regard their forward planning as a process in which a huge number of political factors interact—and a process that can be more or less skilfully anticipated and managed from their point of view.

The second set of policies is what might be described as the 'education of the public' aspect. This proceeds from the recognition that the public is going to continue to be better educated and more articulate, and better able to protest for either selfish or altruistic reasons. It recognizes that in the long run cosmetic 'participation' or 'education' exercises are only stop-gaps; and that what must be developed is a different set of relationships and attitudes on the part of the people to the institutions that serve them.

From a cynical point of view, these two policies might seem antithetical. The first, so it might be argued, presupposes an élitist and manipulative view of the planning process; the second, a Utopian view where people become perfectly rational and morally ideal participants in society. In fact the apparent clash between the two is more a difference in the time scales involved. In the short term a planner must plan against a background knowledge and understanding of the political processes that exist at the time. This is not inconsistent with deliberately setting out on a course that will, more than likely, change in the long term the political processes as they currently exist. Both sets of actions are part of the long-term strategy of resolving the conflict between complicated decisions and the increasingly articulate people whom they affect.

There is one apparent paradox about what is being proposed. New towns, far from being seen as bodies experimenting with new forms of democracy in a changing society, are traditionally portrayed as anti-democratic. In a hair-splitting sense they are not anti-democratic. They are appointed by Parliament and accountable to it. The paradox lies in the fact that the very aspect of new towns that results in the criticisms (the fact that corporations are appointed and not elected) gives new town development corporations far greater potential to make genuine attempts to resolve the problem of the clash between resource decisions and people. As will become apparent, an elected local authority would find it difficult to carry through many of the actions proposed.

Planning as a political process

Let us take the first of the two policies and try to make it more specific. The new town corporation must first drop the idea that in planning its job is to produce the 'ideal' plan—the one that is in the interest of the majority of the people—independently of 'sordid' political considerations. Instead it must substitute the concept that political considerations are just as much a part of the planning process as technical considerations; and that it is legitimate for every officer involved in the formation of plans to have political skills as well as technical skills. Let us take, for example, hypothetical plans involving the demolition of old houses five or even 10 years ahead. Those involved in forming the plans should take explicitly into account the political aspects of the problem. Just as it might be conventional to outline a set of alternative land-use options, so it should be normal to establish a set of political options. To take it further, the planner, if doing his job properly, should go through the exercise of anticipating, for example, that the addition of a new department store will arouse predictable anxieties and objections from some existing traders but not others; and that by taking various pre-emptive steps, from talking to key interest groups about the proposal to publishing the anticipated traffic impact, it may be possible to win some round, leaving others still opposed. There is nothing odd or difficult about this. All it involves is recognizing that the cliché, 'planning involves people', is true and that the old-fashioned method of taking people into account—namely representative democracy—no longer works as well as it should.

The corollary of this is that it is not enough for the planners to do armchair political analysis. To make this analysis effective they must have an understanding of the people involved. In practical terms this means that planners must understand the motivations and the attitudes of the people they are planning for and with. They must be prepared to find out which *are* the key interests. For example, a planner operating in a mining community in Scotland must make it his business, as the clichés demand, **307** to get out and meet the people—for the thoroughly practical reason that he must construct for himself a framework against which to anticipate how different groups of people will react to different circumstances. In practice, this means a descriptive 'map' of the main interest groups and interests within the community, and a profile of people and personalities.

There are easy and commonsense ways of meeting people in the community—the most basic of which is through grass roots organizations. It is easiest, of course, if the planner is living in the community concerned. It is quite natural for him to go, for example, to meetings of the community association. Or he can join in simple activity clubs (no doubt there will be at least one activity to suit his taste). Unless he is quite extraordinarily gauche, the initial network of contacts he makes there will lead him further.

But if he does not live in the community (if, for example, he lives in the main town and wishes to explore the attitudes in a village outside it), there is still a host of ways of meeting the people of that village. It is normally not difficult for planners to seek invitations to speak to organizations, be they women's institutes, community associations, or political party executive committees. Another simple device is to make a point of socializing with the key representatives from that area (usually the elected representatives). Most elected representatives will take pride in showing someone who is interested around the area and introducing him to people there. In real life situations one thing leads to another. It is not very long before a variety of contacts has been created.

This is not a theoretical concept. As chairman of a development corporation, I have found it relatively easy to get access to the different shades of opinion by simple commonsense steps, such as those of getting the elected representatives of a village to talk about their problems, and asking to visit the working men's clubs. Very often the difficulty is more likely to be in the mind of the planner, if my experience is anything to go by; anxieties as to whether his own peculiarly hot-house training and education will be able to cope with modes of conversation and life styles totally different from his; or a concern as to whether he will understand things that are being talked about.

'Meeting the people' is a technique, and so personal a technique is more or less successful according to the extent one believes in it. Planning professionals tend not to regard the political aspect of their work as requiring distinctive technical skills—certainly to the extent suggested here. A major problem for an institution endeavouring to take the political dimension into account is to ensure that the planning staff themselves understand and believe in the principles of the process. Let us take, for example, the simple notion of going out into the street and talking to people whose houses are being designed or planned for in some way. Unless the professionals believe in what they are doing, it will not work. A first priority for any major resource-planning body—be it new town or other—is that of ensuring that the specialist staff it employs are aware of the political environment within which they are operating and the skills that are required of them to take it into account.

The need to view planning as a process in which you chart a course through the Scylla and Charybdis of political reaction extends further than understanding the workings of participative democracy. The effects of competing institutions (be they democratic, private enterprise, etc.) also have to be included in the planning process. This may involve quite simple skills, such as forecasting that a 'correct' planning decision to provide jobs for the unemployed may cause anxiety about wage levels among existing industrialists and thus trigger off forces counterproductive to the plans. It may involve much more subtle calculations about the 'art of the possible' in reconciling the views and perspectives of the members of several different authorities. Whatever the issue, however, one fundamental axiom remains. If professional planners are to have any chance of devising plans that are capable of implementation, they must use their skills to obtain a basic understanding of the political factors affecting those plans.

These concepts are likely to run a gauntlet of criticism from supporters of traditional forms of representative democracy. This of course is one of the reasons why it will always be more difficult for existing democratic institutions to experiment with new forms of planning. Criticism will be made that officers have no business to be indulging in political analysis; still less to be making contacts with key interest groups. The argument is not developed in this paper. Suffice for the moment to say that the notion that there is one form of democracy suitable for all forms of society and all problems must be palpable nonsense. *De facto*, if not always institutionalized and/or planned, changes in the nature of democracy have already taken place within planning authorities of one kind or another all over the country—of which new town development corporations are only a special case. What is being argued here is that new town development corporations have an unusual opportunity to do what they have always done—innovate and experiment in producing practical solutions to one of the major problems of our time.

It has already been said that the skills of anticipating and managing the planning process should be mirrored by a second set of policies involving the development of new techniques and skills of public education. So little that is genuine and constructive has been done in this way that it is difficult to be more than speculative. The paragraphs that follow describe forms of public education that take as their objective developing a new relationship between decison-taking institutions and the people they serve.

New forms of public education

The first step towards educating the public is for the institution to hire staff to work within the community at arm's length from the institution, stimulating the community to take an interest in the real issues it faces; servicing the community and enabling it so to do; and in the long run thus creating a more constructive and aware attitude. There are so many phoney experiments under this guise that it is easy to be cynical and forget that this form of operation does work, can work even better and must be applied universally. One of the major problems of course is that such activities inevitably result in strong criticism of the institution. This is once again a basic reason why it is more feasible for development corporations to experiment than for local authorities. In the new town of Aycliffe a report recently published was highly critical of the Development Corporation's provision for old people—a report stimulated and supported by the Corporation's own staff. Similarly I can remember an occasion when one of the Corporation's officers asked if he could sit on the opposite side of the table from the other officers when they were confronting a protesting group, in order to underline his position of independence.

This type of operation can be extended to larger-scale educational efforts in which the institution deliberately attempts to communicate the real resource options to people and to create conditions in which people themselves have to argue them through and see the problems. So many merely cosmetic operations have been carried out in the name of education and participation that it is easy to be cynical and overlook the fact that some real and successful attempts are being made to change the nature of the communication and understanding between resource-allocating institutions and the people they serve; and that the scope for extending these attempts is enormous. The use of television as in Germany as a means of community decision-making, and the 'Charrette' process in the US as a vehicle for more responsive planning, are all indications of what is possible.

Let us be quite clear about the likely long-term effects of such programs of education—namely, that it will change in some way the basic distribution of power. Once you admit that it is practical and feasible to educate people so that they can make a real contribution to decisions, you are effectively delegating power to them. One must return to basic principles and ask why this is so and whether it is desirable. At the moment, so the argument runs, we face an increasing problem of planning to accommodate increasingly complicated large-scale decisions on the one hand and the views, the resentment and the feedback of an increasingly articulate, involved and educated people on the other. It is not enough to yearn for the good old days when a small élite could plan in an enlightened, paternalistic way for the majority, the whole thing being reconciled through representative democracy. Those days can never return. New ways must be found of enabling people to express their feelings yet accommodate more sophisticated decisions.

Institutions such as new towns must make the blind jump of telling people things they have never been told before, involving them in planning and allowing the start of processes whose ends cannot totally be predicted. The hope is that eventually new systems will be evolved that are more appropriate to the nature of the decisions and the people affected by them.

It has been argued that the fundamental direction in which new towns can innovate and introduce change over the next few years is by experimenting with the process by which decisions are made and implemented in relation to people living in the town—a change that hits at the very principles and the 'ends' of planning and the democratic process. There are, however, other critical issues of 'means' where change and innovation are already occurring. This brings me to the second main theme of this chapter.

Private sector disciplines in new town development

In the context of the late forties, the new town model was a far more cohesive and 'total' planning tool than anything previously envisaged, even if it did not measure up

THE SCOPE FOR CHANGE

entirely to Lord Reith's ambitions. It has become increasingly clear over the years, however, that the powers of development corporations, important and comprehensive as they are, are far from complete.

For example, one dimension that runs the danger of being overlooked in the emphasis on purely physical planning is that of the *economy* of the town. New town developments tend to be seen not as economic units but rather as physical and (sometimes) social units. To give one obvious example, a corporation might not see that a supplier of a certain manufactured article could so fit into the structure of local industry as to create a dynamic value-adding situation—because his products would be bought by other industrialists, who would in turn sell products back to him. Of course, many development corporations do think that way and some may even implement schemes—though the implementation must be haphazard. But we are still far away from the concept of a total plan that aims to take advantage of the synergy of different forms of economic activity.

Again, the notion of capitalizing on the latent amenity value in a given physical situation so as to produce surplus funds to invest in other developments is relatively foreign to the new town development corporation. In the new town of Peterlee there are many beautiful sites where a far higher surplus could have been realized if different buildings had been built on them. This is not to say that the maximum gain should have been realized, but that thinking in terms of optimal levels of gain tends not to take place. Rather, thinking is in terms of physical need at one level and social need at another.

It is not surprising that the economic dimension is so little considered. The lack of market discipline in the system militates against its being considered. Sometimes, of course, the designated area simply does not correspond to the logical economic unit, which may involve a neighbouring conurbation—as for example it would for the new town of Aycliffe, with a number of conurbations within a few miles. A more fundamental reason why the economic dimension tends to be overlooked, however, lies in the way new towns are administered. They do not work like a private developer, having a limited amount of capital or gearing that is his to distribute among projects in whatever way seems optimal. They do not need to apply the discipline of finding optional ways of creating surpluses to be ploughed back into other schemes. If a development corporation creates surpluses on buildings, the surpluses when realized will usually go back to the Treasury and not be available to be ploughed back into the town.

This said, of course, the institutional problems in changing the *modus operandi* of development corporations so as to give them the motivation and the incentives to behave more like 'economic man' are horrendous, given that the development corporation is spending public money and has to be accountable for it. The Department of the Environment has over the past few years introduced management accounting systems so as to enable corporations to speculate with the same style of long-term option analysis that a private developer would use, looking at the different rates of returns, the effects of different cash flows, different investments, and so on. This is a useful discipline and marks a substantial innovation. It will, nonetheless, never enable corporations truly to act according to economic dictates while on the

311

one hand they are constrained from taking certain key risk decisions and on the other they cannot recycle profits earned.

For and against private enterprise

There is a strong argument that a public body run by a board that is not a shareholder and the rewards of which are unrelated to returns on the money it invests should not even attempt the task of operating as though in the private sector. Instead, so the argument goes, towns should be built by private companies with strong constraints and rules of the game set by the State—as is happening in America.

Analogies with other countries are dangerous, since what works in the US with one system of planning control would not necessarily work in the UK with another. However, the question of private enterprise and new towns should be free from dogma and generalization. It must be right for experiments to take place in private enterprise development of new towns in the UK, albeit with strong governmental involvement. Until such experiments take place, we cannot know the pitfalls and the difficulties. Until such experiments take place, the argument might be continued, we will be denied certain insights into the art of community development.

This said, there are some *a priori* reasons for believing that a system in which private enterprise takes the leading role in developing new towns is likely to be less successful than one led by public enterprise with a strong (and stronger than at the moment) involvement with private enterprise. One reason is the complex array of the public authorities with which any private enterprise new town developer would have to negotiate separate agreements. One would hope that the Department of the Environment would smooth the path of private developers in any way it could. No doubt it would. The reality, however, is that we have in the UK a highly complicated system of planning in particular, and municipal and governmental intervention in general, that is not best calculated to enthuse a private developer when devising long-term plans. This is not something that is likely to disappear.

Second, there is an argument against private enterprise development in the UK that involves a more political judgement. While no one can deny the increasing social responsibility of many developers, particularly in the US, and the evident imagination with which they implement their plans, their motive is that of profit. In the last analysis a private developer must worry about going bankrupt and must be prepared to compromise on otherwise desirable schemes. If we could assume that the public sector could set and enforce the rules of the game and the social conditions under which the private firm could operate, there would be no problem. But the constraints the public sector must impose are those on which there is always a come-back. For example, a public authority may insist on a certain quota of low-cost rented housing at the beginning of the development. Ten years later, when the town is a quarter built and the developer comes back and says he will go bust unless the number of low-cost houses is halved, the public authority is in an almost impossible position, with little option but to agree or take over the development.

The ideal solution of course would be for the UK new town development corporation to operate in exactly the same way as does the private developer, subject

312

to market forces in the same way, yet on behalf of the State. Thus the new town development corporations would be told that they had a limited amount of capital; certain gearing powers; certain formal methods of reporting to their holding company (the State); and certain broad objectives. The precise way in which the objectives were implemented would be a matter for the development corporation. This would contrast fairly strongly with the present system whereby at the start of a new town a master plan is agreed by the Government; and reference back to government is made for individual sums of money when the need for them arises.

Such a *modus operandi* can probably never be attained by a wholly publicly owned body. It is, however, possible to move a long way towards this model in reality—and there are signs that the British Government is doing so. Let us examine the problems. First is the objection that the State in its role of managing the economy cannot avoid interfering with the best laid plans of the development corporations (thus confounding market forces). But this also applies to the private sector. A wholly owned private developer subsidiary of a conglomerate makes its plans in relation to the commercial prospects as it sees them, and tries to get the approval of its parent. But even with that approval, it knows that, when circumstances demand, its parent may well pressure it, for example, to raise cash by the disposal of assets, and thus change its plans entirely. This is no different from the Treasury cutting back on capital expenditure or asking a development corporation to raise money by disposing of assets.

Then there is a problem already referred to of accountability. At one level the issue is that a lot of money is involved and mistakes can be made. Ministers are accountable for that money. They will wish to protect their own position by putting tight controls on the corporation's use of it. This touches on a general question of political principle and attitude—the extent to which a minister is held responsible for delegated risk decisions. The fact is that ministers now take substantial risks in granting loans of one form or another to industries that the Government is financing; against these the risks involved in the development of a new town are comparatively minor. Further down the line of personal accountability, of course, the chairmen and other senior members and officers of the development corporation are as accountable as are their opposite numbers in a private company. It may be argued that they do not own shares and so do not have a personal interest in success or failure. But neither do the vast majority of senior professional managers of large private companies. The penalty for failure will be just the same: the sack. That is a substantial constraint.

And at a more global level, there is a sense in which a deliberate attempt to simulate private sector disciplines within the public system could produce *more* and not less real accountability. At the moment new towns are controlled quite tightly on technical and financial matters. The process of administering these controls is complex and time-consuming and occupies the substantial energies of a group of extremely hard-working civil servants. It would, however, be too much to expect these same civil servants to be involved in an ongoing process of what might be called 'overall review' of corporate strategy and strategy options. If the corporation were given far greater power to decide the detail of its operations, it would probably be expected to account for them in detail too, and be subjected to a more detailed

313

analysis of its broad strategy. Far from objecting, I would welcome the idea that, together with my chief executive, I had to account once every six months for the total strategy of my corporation, and be subjected to a detailed cross-examination by people with a perspective on many other new towns on the reasoning underlying the strategy.

Working with the private sector

So far we have discussed the general principle as to whether multi-faceted urban development in the new towns in the UK is more effectively run by a public enterprise body with some private enterprise input than by a private enterprise body with some public constraint; and have suggested that, while the former model is better, it is both desirable and within 'the art of the possible' to introduce a greater measure of market discipline. There is also the more specific question as to how the private sector contribution should be made.

First, to put the question in context. The UK new towns have seen a gradual increase in the extent of private sector involvement, and also increasing innovation in the method of its participation. Examples include the use of institutional finance on a lease and lease-back basis in town centres; the use of private developers to build private housing; and the recent trend for private developers to be involved in schemes where they build estates with some facilities. At the moment some new towns are seeing their way towards even more subtle and ambitious involvement with the private sector—towards situations where 'partnerships' are formed in which the private sector deals with the multi-faceted schemes involving the provision of housing, recreational facilities, perhaps even commercial development, all in the same 'bite'.

There are a number of reasons why more ambitious involvement of private enterprise is attractive to new towns. The first is quite simply that the infusion of the best development skills in the private sector cannot be anything but good for a public sector development. It has already been argued above that new towns should try to adopt more of the private sector disciplines than they do at the moment. Currently they do not have to think in a fundamental way about cash flow. They do not face the marketing need to innovate. Certainly they do not have to think about the value-enhancing effect of different income streams one upon another. This is a very direct skill that a developer can bring to bear.

There is also a very selfish and specific interest for a new town. The very best developers will so calculate their sums as to allow for the value-enhancing effect of certain amenities on their commercial or residential property, and bear the front-end cost of investment in these amenities. If a private developer takes a total area, therefore, the town may receive certain amenities that it would otherwise have to forgo. This process can be looked at in various ways. It could uncharitably be described as a device to ensure that money is reinvested in a new town rather than returned to the Treasury. To the extent that the price the developer may have paid the new town corporation for his land is lower than market price, this has justice. But to the extent that the developer has the freedom to take deliberate investment risk

314

decisions (such as, for example, investing in squash courts or a golf course) that will lead to the extraction of greater profit from the houses or offices he is selling, this represents a net value-added that would not have happened any other way.

At a more general level, there can be nothing but good for the new town corporation in closer contact with the private sector, if only because of the cross-fertilization of ideas and techniques—for example, on methods of cost control. Private sector thinking within the framework of ongoing public sector development must have an educational effect. The education, incidentally, is likely to be two way.

There are problems, of course. One problem is very simply that the more complicated the development the greater the need for the developer's staff to work together closely with the corporation's staff. Human chemistry is involved here. When a deal is agreed, there is no way in which it can sensibly proceed unless the key implementers of it are at one with each other.

Then there are the secondary problems of control and risk. Under the present system, it is difficult, if not impossible, for the corporation to go into partnership with the developer in a major scheme. The relationship must be very much that of the planning authority controlling the developer. But when the developer asks to change a plan, for example, the corporation may have difficulty in judging whether it is justified in the light of changing market conditions, or whether it is a 'try-on'. Once the developer is well into the scheme, he is in a strong position to browbeat the corporation into changing points of principle about design and so on. It is easy but simplistic to say that if the corporation was a full partner in the scheme, picking up the check for the losses or the gains, the situation would be more straightforward. Difficult as the problems of accountability are, however, there must be a case for looking more precisely at the possibility of development corporations entering into such partnerships with developers.

This may be an appropriate thought with which to end this paper. Perhaps the fundamental characteristic of the success of the British new towns has been their consistent ability to innovate and seek new solutions to the many-sided planning problems they face. I have attempted to identify the areas in which innovation and change are already taking place, and the areas where perhaps are found the greatest challenges to the innovative forces of new towns in the future.

Chapter 16. Looking ahead

JOHN GRIFFITH-JONES

The planned community has become a widely accepted instrument for urban development in a world with strongly contrasting economic systems and institutional structures. In the UK more than 30 new towns have been started by government since the war, with the purpose of relieving urban congestion and channelling urban and regional growth. This program has been complemented by other large-scale development efforts—also sponsored mainly by the public sector—such as the expansion of existing communities under the Town Development Act. In the US, dominated by the private sector, some 70 new community projects—opinions vary as to exactly how many—are under way, ranging from second-home developments and resort projects to the Title VII new communities being implemented under Federal guarantee. Recent years have, in addition, seen a dramatic growth in the planned unit development (PUD) as a device for community development at the neighbourhood level.

In fact, ambitious programs—largely government-led—have been going ahead in many, widely differing, countries. Most European countries—particularly France, Sweden and Finland—have initiated new town projects in the last 15 years to help achieve more orderly patterns of urban growth. In Israel, new towns have been a basic tool for absorbing and distributing immigrants since the country's formation. In South America, two of the largest planned development projects in the world are now under way—Brasilia, already with a population of half a million, as a key to Brazil's strategy for developing its interior, and Ciudad Guyana, with a similar objective in Venezuela. The Soviet Union is embarking on a massive community development program to open up the plains beyond the Urals. Several developing countries, including Pakistan, Malawi and Tanzania, are in the process of relocating their capital cities in fulfilment of economic, political and physical objectives. Japan, in response to its intensive urban pressures, is now actively preparing its own new communities program.

For all the differences between national environments, community development to date—in the developed nations at least—has been founded on basic concepts that to a surprising degree are common from one country to another. The multi-use concept, providing for a wide range of housing, employment and social opportunities in close proximity, has held a widespread appeal as a new approach to urban living. Comprehensively planned and implemented, new communities have been a means for systematically addressing many current urban concerns—protecting the natural environment through the planned allocation of land, increasing accessibility to housing, jobs and community services, conserving energy through the design of efficient transportation and building layouts. At the same time, they have provided a unique laboratory for technological and social innovation, usually difficult in the established structures of existing communities. The unified organization that typifies most new community projects, often supported by special allocations of powers and resources by government, has been a means of integrating the development process on the ground and of getting results quickly.

The actual achievement, of course, has often fallen short of the promise. Ever since the inception of the new communities movement there has been heated debate about the quality of its results. While new communities in the US are alternately dismissed by the sceptics as the playthings of idealists or a paradise for speculators, Brasilia is condemned as an impersonal concrete jungle, and new towns in many countries are challenged for their visual monotony or their artificial concepts of physical and social organization.

Moreover, even in countries where substantial programs have been introduced, new communities have hardly scratched the surface of our total urban needs. For example, fewer than 10 per cent of the people who left London between 1961 and 1971 went into new town or town expansion projects, despite the prominence given to London overspill in the earlier programs. And since the war nearly three times as many houses have been built in London itself through conventional procedures as have been built under the new towns program for the entire nation. Only in Israel, where about 30 per cent of the population lives in new towns, can planned communities be said to have changed the face of a nation, and this largely because of the unique nation-building conditions prevailing in that country.

And while new communities have confronted some urban problems, they have unwittingly compounded others. The US planned communities can be seen as serving and encouraging the flight from the cities, increasing in attraction the more they are able to provide an ordered and successful alternative to existing suburban sprawl. The British new towns, despite the high degree of public intervention in the selection of people and jobs, have drawn away mobile families and skilled workers without touching to any great degree the high priority needs of the inner cities.

Whatever the faults and limitations, I believe that there is a sufficient body of successful experience to confirm community development as a device for coping with our urban needs. Indeed, in my view, it is time for community development to move from the realms of experimentation on to the centre of the stage of urban problem solving. Thus the debate should not be about whether we need new communities, but about precisely what community development should be trying to do and how it should be accomplished.

317

In this chapter I start by examining some of the key economic, social and institutional forces that will determine the development patterns of the future, and then review the kinds of community development strategy that will be needed to respond to these forces. Finally, I identify the main opportunities for adapting and improving the development machinery for translating the strategies into reality. I should add that the remainder of this discussion is confined to the experience of the developed nations—principally the UK and the US. The developing countries are at a different stage of urban evolution, have different needs and to a large extent require distinctive solutions that are beyond the scope of this chapter.

The changing development environment

Of the multitude of trends and crosscurrents in today's environment three in particular seem destined to influence the shape and direction of community development. First, a slackening in the rate of long-term population and economic growth is beginning to alter the whole context of need and demand within which community developers are operating. Second, increasing constraints on resources—finance and land—are causing complete reappraisals of how large-scale development should be conceived and carried out. Finally, political and institutional pressures are both increasing the complexity of the development process and changing the nature of its results.

Slower growth

Community development in the last quarter century has been conditioned largely by the pressures of urban growth—different in timing but similar in essence in all the developed nations. High birth rates, falling death rates and declining family size have combined to create an insatiable demand for new housing. The migration of people and jobs from the inner cities to the suburbs has been proceeding on a massive scale, whether through voluntary movement or planned relocation. In the most dynamic regions the pressures of rapid economic change have been adding to the effects of other development forces. Meanwhile, increased affluence and consequent changes in life-styles have expanded demands for living space, and led to an explosion in second-home ownership and a restless search for the 'quality' environment.

Public agencies and private developers have responded to these pressures with increasingly ambitious projects. In the UK, the new city of Milton Keynes—with an eventual population of 250,000—is a far cry from the first post-war new towns, originally intended for about 50,000–60,000 people. Meanwhile some of these early projects—such as Stevenage and Basildon—are being planned for continued expansion now that their initial targets have been reached. The nine French 'villes nouvelles', drawing on experience from the UK and elsewhere, have with only one exception been conceived at a scale of a quarter of a million people and above. During the late sixties in the US the new community of 100,000 people or more became a regular target for developer ambitions—Columbia, Irvine, Lake Havasu and others. In all these countries 'flexibility for continued growth' became an essential part of the litany of land-use planning.

On the face of it, more of the same would appear to be an appropriate prescription for the future. Population, for example, will continue to grow, by some 40 million before the end of the century in the US and by some 8 million in the UK. One study is anticipating that the land area covered by urban development will increase from 6.4 per cent of the US in 1960 to over 16 per cent in 2000. Large-scale shifts in economic activity will continue to be a development driving force. The exploitation of new energy sources in the Rocky Mountains, for example, could lead, according to one estimate, to as many as 100,000 jobs being created in the region as a result of investment decisions that have already been made.

However, for all the evidence of these continuing pressures, we are now moving in the developed nations from an era of growth to an era of consolidation. Although still considerable in absolute terms, population growth is now slackening—with an obvious and direct impact on development needs. In the UK, for example, the birth rate has already declined from over 18 births per 1,000 in the early sixties to about 14 per 1,000 now, and the country's population in the year 2000 is currently expected to be about 10 million below the estimates of 10 years ago. The birth rate in the US is now lower than at any time since records have been kept. Moreover, it also appears that the rate of new household formation is declining (although recent evidence may have been exaggerated by the current recession, which has both reduced the supply of new housing stock and restricted the ability of potential new households to afford it).

At least as significant as these demographic trends is a likelihood of a slowing-up in the pace of economic growth. In the long run the 1960s and early 1970s are likely to be seen as a period of unique and unprecedented expansion, and most forecasters are expecting growth to proceed at a more modest pace once the present worldwide recession is over.

From a community development standpoint, the most obvious consequence of these changes is that the need for marginal additions to the total development stock will be substantially reduced. 'Footloose' employment—one of the essential catalysts of large-scale development at new locations—will be less plentiful in supply. The pressure for new housing will result from mismatch between supply and demand rather than absolute shortages in the available housing stock.

This flattening of growth pressures has already led to reappraisal of some long-term urban development programs. In the UK, for example, the feasibility studies of the early 1960s for establishing several growth points for up to a million people (Severnside, Solway, Humberside, Tayside) have been quietly set aside as population projections have been revised downwards.

Equally important, the changes will raise basic questions about the relevance of existing development to emerging needs. The slackening of population growth, for example, will be accompanied by major underlying changes in demographic structure. The proportion of elderly, in particular, is likely to increase, and the proportion of children and young adults to decline. These trends will not only alter the mix of additions to the total development supply (in the US, for example, we can

319

expect increasing demand for retirement communities—and perhaps the evolution of new types of 'specialized' community to meet the needs of specific groups, such as childless couples). But also, more fundamentally, these changes will highlight the inflexibility of much of our current development stock. Most urban development in the last 25 years, especially in the suburbs, has been governed by the requirements of families with children—the family home, the garden, the school round the corner. Yet this model bears little relationship to the needs of the retired, single adults or families without children. The same could be said of the neighbour-hood concept firmly imprinted on many new communities, determined as it is by a fixed view of the relationship between homes, schools and other community facilities.

Finally, the slackening of pressures of growth will mean that relatively more development resources—money, skills and experience—will be available to cope with problems of adaptation and renewal in existing communities. In England and Wales, for example, 83 per cent of the total housing output between 1951 and 1972 was required to meet the growth in the number of households (and, to a lesser extent, the reduction of multiple occupancy in older houses). During this period, slum clearance and improvements failed to keep pace with growing obsolescence, let alone reduce the inherited backlog of worn-out housing. However, the reduced rate of household formation now anticipated will provide the scope for a much heavier future emphasis on replacement.

Increasing pressures on resources

With huge commitments required for land acquisition and infrastructure development and with the inevitable lapse of time before significant revenues are generated, community development has always been recognized as a costly investment. Nevertheless, the ultimate expectation has been of a substantial long-term payoff for the private developer, and of at least an adequate return on funds for the public authority. At the same time, this long-term perspective has often enabled developers to justify investment in innovative features, socially beneficial programs and standards of development that a shorter time horizon would rule out.

However, the worldwide combination of inflation and recession that gathered pace in 1974 both highlighted the true risks and costs of large-scale development and at the same time upset long-standing assumptions about the economics of development. The escalating cost of land in or near existing cities has long been a deterrent to all but the most intensive forms of commercial and residential development, particularly in countries such as the UK where the system of planning has limited the supply of land available. More recently, however, the problems have been increased by spiralling construction costs—labour, materials and energy—and by unprecedented fluctuations in the cost of money. One recent American estimate has determined that a community of 70,000 people now requires an outlay of about $1.5 billion—a minimum of $700 million in mortgage loans for 20,000 houses, some $400 million for capital outlays and services, and $400 million for commercial and industrial development.

320

As a result of these pressures, governments in several countries have been forced to re-evaluate programs and cut back on projects as cost estimates have escalated; in the UK, for example, limitation of funds was a significant factor in the decision not to proceed with the third London airport, and in the consequent cancellation of an associated new city project that was to have been the country's largest to date. In addition, the standards of public housing and other services are inevitably trimmed as costs move ahead faster than the ability of government to pay. A recent review of the new towns program in the House of Commons focused heavily on the need to improve the value for money of the program, to evaluate its resource implications more fully and to strengthen monitoring procedures.[1]

The most dramatic effects of inflation and the squeeze of resources have, however, been felt in the private sector. This has particularly been the case in the US, where in 1974–75 inflation, slack markets and (for a time) a tight monetary policy by the Federal Government conspired to put the real estate industry in its worst recession since the thirties—although there are signs that recovery in the industry may be under way. For example, almost all of the 14 Title VII communities ran into severe financial problems, many being at the vulnerable early stage where debts accumulated without compensating cash flows. HUD was engaged in a series of 'work-out' agreements to restructure debts and improve short-term financial viability, in several cases making emergency interest payments on behalf of the developer. One project—Riverton, New York—actually 'closed down' for three days when its main backer pulled out. Jonathan, Minnesota was up for sale, showing nothing but losses for the foreseeable future. The New York Urban Development Corporation, sponsor of three major projects in the state (Roosevelt Island, Radisson and Audubon) is itself in a critical cash position. Using its credit status as a public agency to borrow funds, but without providing formal guarantees to its investors, it has been in danger of defaulting on up to $300 million of debt as its projects are failing to generate the cash flow originally expected. In addition, several major corporations, such as Boise Cascade and Kaufman and Broad, have had to curtail sharply their commitments in the community development field.

These experiences are inevitably intensifying the already considerable debate on the role that the public sector in the US should play in key land development tasks already carried out largely by government in other countries. Whatever the results of this debate, I believe that the kind of development to be created will also be permanently affected—not only for the private developer, but also for the public authority, which although often cushioned by its government status from the full force of economic events, still has in the end to demonstrate viability and achieve a return on its assets. Already a pattern of response can be discerned in the US in a retreat from the massive new community projects of the 1960s to smaller neighbourhood-scale concepts—less ambitious, perhaps, but also less risky financially, and less vulnerable to market fluctuations. Even more than hitherto, developers will be concerned with minimizing front-end financial commitments, with avoiding dependence on single vulnerable markets and with keeping risk exposure down to a level commensurate with the scale and resources of the development enterprise. The availability of existing infrastructure is likely to become increasingly

321

important in determining the economics and content of projects, as is the need to incorporate a substantial commercial component as a means of generating early revenue.

Increasing political constraints

Financial problems have everywhere been compounded by steadily mounting complexity in the politics of community development.

One aspect of this evolution is the increasing intricacy of the structure of government, as new needs are identified and new public programs established. In the US, more than 100 separate Federal programs have a direct impact on community development projects. Approvals and clearances required now range through every aspect of development, from land-use zoning and highway provision to programs for minority groups and housing mix; moreover, they are likely to increase rather than diminish as government responds to public pressures on social and environmental issues. Meanwhile the Title VII program, which was designed in part to circumvent these procedures through a co-ordinated approach to development, has itself been widely criticized for being slow, cumbersome and bureaucratic.

In the UK, too, recent institutional changes have made the development environment more complex. The last two years have seen the division of local government into two tiers, each with a significant—but imprecisely defined—role in planning and implementing development. In addition, the creation of separate structures for water supply and health care, both involving the withdrawal of functions formerly held by local government, has if anything increased the fragmentation of government.

Apart from the increasing involvement of government, communities themselves have become more demanding and articulate. The days when it could be assumed that 'growth is good' are now past, as environmental groups and local communities confront developers with, at the very least, tough questions and stiff conditions, and often with outright opposition to new projects. In the UK the period from conception of new projects through to designation of the site and preparation of master plans has steadily lengthened under the impact of local anti-development pressures; and the new towns story contains several examples—such as Lymm and Hook—of projects abandoned as a result of local resistance.

In the US the story is similar. The Rouse Company, despite the successful Columbia precedent, was forced to scrap new communities in Maryland, Tennessee and Connecticut as a result of local opposition. Residents have also been demanding a more positive role in the development and management of their communities; at Park Forest South in Illinois, for example, residents filed suit to block proposed low-income housing, and at Irvine the residents took over the local zoning power. In addition, developers have had to combat resistance resulting from fears of social experimentation and the 'over-planned' feeling, and have been caught in the crossfire between those who demand innovation on the one hand and those who prefer the security of more conventional approaches on the other. Even where innovation has been desirable, it has not always been possible, because of restrictions in local building codes and state laws.

In the face of delays, misunderstandings and apparently irreconcilable conflicts, the community development process itself calls for adaptation—in techniques for collaboration between the many agencies in development, in devices for securing effective community participation in the development process and in procedures for circumventing current bottlenecks. At the same time, political constraints are an inevitable—and in many ways essential—feature of community development in a democratic environment. Increasingly they will need to be recognized as a fact of life in determining the form, scale and content of major projects. Whether or not it always provides the optimum solution in planning terms, a more modest, incremental approach to development is likely to prove more acceptable politically—particularly where existing communities are affected or where a multitude of government interests are involved. Integration—social, economic and physical—between new and existing development will continue to assume increasing importance, as will the survival of communities already in being.

Emerging development strategies

For all its adaptations and variations, the 'greenfield' town has remained the basic new community prototype—the self-contained community in uncrowded and attractive surroundings, leaving behind the problems and untidiness of our existing cities with fresh approaches to urban living.

However, the economic, social and political forces described above argue for a different kind of future. The core idea of the new community—meeting a complete range of human needs in one place through a comprehensive development approach—will remain a consistent theme. But concepts of the kind of development to be created—size, distribution, mix, and so on—will, I believe, need to broaden in scope and variety.

The clearest starting-point for defining these emerging concepts is the scale at which change is being conceived and implemented. Here, I distinguish the community scale from the regional scale. At the community scale, major projects—covering a neighbourhood, a local area, a town or a city—are planned and initiated. At the regional scale—embracing the interrelated settlement pattern of a whole urban region—the framework for directing and co-ordinating development is established.

Both of these, I would argue, are essential to a total community development process. Without the first, no mechanism exists for turning plans into action. Without the second, no context exists for planning in the first place.

Community scale

At the community level, the focus of development efforts has already begun to shift from problems of growth and expansion to problems of change, renewal and conservation. The stabilization of growth patterns will be reinforced by increased public pressures for the careful use of land and increased sensitivity to the problems that growth has left behind in the inner city.

At the same time, the virtues of size—the conventional wisdom of the sixties—will lose some of their allure. Many would argue that the most difficult development problems—particularly in the inner cities—are identifiable with small areas and cannot be resolved by large-scale solutions. As pressures for participation increase, the neighbourhood is becoming increasingly significant in the development process—both in planning and designing projects and in managing community programs. For the developer, too, large scale has lost some some of its earlier attraction. The recession in the US, mentioned earlier, has brought the true risks of large-scale development sharply into focus.

With these pressures in mind, I would like to suggest four prototype situations to displace the traditional 'greenfield' model, for which I consider the concepts and approaches of community development to be appropriate.

1. *Redeveloping obsolete areas.* Despite substantial programs of clearance and redevelopment, many areas in the largest cities lie derelict or under-used. As old activities have moved, or been moved, new activities have failed to take their place for a wide range of institutional and economic reasons. The publication and review of redevelopment plans has blighted large areas for years, even in countries such as the UK with strong planning machinery. The magnitude of the redevelopment task has inhibited the private entrepreneur from undertaking any but fragmented and piecemeal development. Meanwhile much of the redevelopment that has taken place, often under public initiative, has all too often been ineffective—monotonous subsidized housing creating more social problems than it solves, the local employment base eroded, essential community services left out of the development scheme.

Yet sites of 200–300 acres—of which there are many in Britain and the US, in the form of obsolete dockland, disused railway land or run-down industrial areas—provide real opportunities for injecting new life into decayed urban areas. The biggest opportunity of all is the 8,000 acres of decayed dockland area in east London. Even a 300-acre project offers the prospect of providing—at relatively high densities—for a comprehensive range of uses and services for up to 20,000 people. One or two pioneering experiments along these lines are now taking place in the US—Cedar Riverside and Roosevelt Island are examples—and, despite their current financial problems, deserve wider application.

2. *Renewing inner cities.* Even more intractable than the redevelopment situations just described are the problems of multiple deprivation in the inner city—usually long established, intensively developed communities, often quite small as identifiable areas (perhaps only a few wards or a few blocks), stubborn to survive in the face of change, but lacking effective means.

The problems of multiple deprivation have, of course, been receiving a great deal of attention and resources. But the solutions so far can be characterized largely as isolated remedies for parts of the problem—in the UK, educational priority areas, special housing action and supplementary social services; in the US, special job training and welfare programs.

However, a number of initiatives are being taken that suggest there is enormous scope for innovation and more comprehensive approaches—the Inner Area studies, for example, in the UK and some of the American community action and economic development projects. The concepts and lessons of more conventional forms of community development are highly relevant here—especially the importance of linking social, economic and physical change in a combined, integrated program, and concentrating on geographical areas as the key dimension for analysis and effort, as opposed to functions, services or individual programs.

3. *Adapting existing development.* As our total development stock increases, the potential for 'recycling' existing urban structures will become increasingly important. Pressures for the better use of resources—conservation of land, optimum use of public and private funds—could well intensify this opportunity.

One set of options arises from changing the mix of older developed areas in response to demographic and social changes. In particular, the available housing stock and physical structures of many existing suburban areas will become less relevant as needs change. One alternative would be to permit their transition—as is already happening in California and other parts of the US—to more marginal uses. However, I suggest that more constructive opportunities exist, given the necessary public intervention—for example, (1) to alter the housing mix through partial redevelopment to accommodate expanding elements in the population, such as the elderly or childless couples, for whom existing provision is inappropriate, or (2) to introduce more employment locally, and thus create some of the social and transportation advantages of the 'balanced' community.

A second set of opportunities stems from redefining the economic function of a community, and changing its concept accordingly. One example would be to convert second-home into primary-home communities. In the US many more lots are being purchased in second-home or resort projects than are ever likely to be occupied. A prime motivation has been long-term investment for the individual. But in the meantime social and physical infrastructures are being created by developers. Increasingly, the function and concept of these projects will require re-evaluation. A viable alternative—assuming that the potential exists—would be to inject a substantial employment content and thus, in effect, create a primary-home community.

A different situation arises from the release of military installations for alternative use as permanent communities. The US Department of Defense has announced plans to close 40 or more airbases in the near future; these installations occupy large tracts of land in unified ownership, are frequently located at highly accessible points in metropolitan areas, and already possess much of the required community infrastructure—streets, utilities, housing and amenities. One example of a mixed-use residential, commercial and industrial project is already in the advanced planning stage in Texas, and others may follow.

4. *Building smaller communities.* As growth pressures become less intense and market demands more selective, a smaller scale of development—the neighbour-hood project for, say, 10,000 people as opposed to the new community of 50,000 or more—becomes increasingly attractive.

This scale of development—through the planned unit development (PUD) mechanism—is already being adopted in the US for other reasons. (The PUD covers perhaps 200–400 acres and usually provides for up to about 10,000 people, with some commercial and community facilities in addition to housing provision.) The

PUD has been seen by developers who might otherwise have been tempted by grander visions as a way of spreading risk geographically through a number of projects, and also of reducing the requirement for front-end funds and thus the period required to reach cash break-even.

In addition, from the community standpoint, the PUD is large enough to reap most of the benefits of a planned approach to development. A recent study has described and, where possible, quantified these advantages—the land savings to be achieved as compared with conventional urban sprawl, and the social, environmental and energy benefits.[2]

The result of all these factors is that the number of PUDs has more than doubled in the last four years, and shows no signs of abating—while interest in initiating further full-scale new community projects has largely evaporated.

Regional scale

A regional strategy is just as vital to the achievement of change as a community strategy. Many urban policies, of course, can be clearly defined only within a co-ordinating regional framework—e.g., relocation programs between central cities and satellite communities, economic development programs, conservation of land and natural amenities. Regional economies of scale, too, are often fundamental to the provision of major urban infrastructure and services, ranging from rapid transit systems to specialized hospitals.

Moreover, the greater the diversity of community development objectives, and the greater the variety of concepts and processes for implementing them, the more essential a governing regional concept becomes. Let me take one example. Whatever the merits of the PUD as an approach for the developer and the community, their unregulated proliferation could have very undesirable regional side effects. With each PUD requiring a minimum employment content to achieve economic viability, the regional impact, unless anticipated and prevented, could be (1) a decaying central city further denuded of employment opportunities, (2) too many PUDs for the mobile employment available, or (3) a sub-optimum pattern of employment location.

A regional development strategy is likely to take one of four forms:
- *Intensive growth.* The primary emphasis would be on channelling continuing growth pressures and directing large-scale economic change. The growth strategy would be accomplished through massive continuous develop-ment—e.g., in the form of a growth corridor. However, for reasons I have already described, this is unlikely to provide a typical model for the future.
- *Selective growth.* This would be a more widely applicable model, embracing a variety of settlement patterns, including satellite communities, all linked with a comprehensive infrastructure. This pattern would both reflect a stabilization of growth pressures and recognize an increasing diversity of urban needs.
- *Revival.* Physically, this might take a form similar to the selective growth concept, with geographically discrete settlements spread throughout an urban or rural region. In this case, however, the concept would be supported by

special injections of additional infrastructure resources and industrial incentives.

● *Stable state.* In this model, the aim would be to maintain a 'holding' position, with conservation of land and existing structures a high priority, and with limited development and renewal action being taken to correct current deficiencies.

Adapting development mechanisms

While urban needs and priorities have had much in common among the developed nations, the pattern of response in community development terms has differed widely from country to country. To a large degree this has been the result of contrasting national policies and institutional frameworks. Each national approach has its special strengths and weaknesses, providing a rich body of collective experience for improvement and adaptation to new situations, as the remainder of this chapter illustrates.

The United Kingdom

The UK has a generous panoply of powers and machinery for guiding large-scale development, including the national land-use planning and control procedures administered by local government, industrial location incentives and sanctions under the control of central government, and the special machinery of the New Towns Act (Fig. 16.1). A significant expansion of these powers has just been legislated in the Community Land Act, which will eventually extend new-town-type acquisition powers to all major development.

Given the dominance of the public sector in the British system, it is not surprising that its major strength is its ability to respond to publicly determined planning needs and objectives. Perhaps this is most strikingly illustrated in the new towns program itself (Fig. 16.2). In an unbroken pattern of evolution over 30 years, the program has been adapted several times to changing national priorities. The Mark I new towns in the late forties, conceived at a time when the national population was expected to be static, were designated for the prime purpose of relieving congestion in overcrowded cities through provision for planned overspill on greenfield sites. Additionally, projects located in depressed regions were seen as instruments for economic revival, consistent with national policy for the regions. Then, following the rise in the birth rate in the fifties, the emphasis of the program shifted from redistribution towards growth, with a spate of new projects in the early sixties. More recently, as problems of restructuring and renewing Britain's existing cities assumed greater importance, new towns began to incorporate renewal objectives—most obviously reflected in Central Lancashire and in the 'partnership' towns of Peterborough, Northampton and Warrington. (No designations, however, have yet been made exclusively for the purpose of urban renewal, which has conventionally been regarded as the legitimate sphere of local government. Attempts to interfere with

327

PROCESS	PUBLIC	PRIVATE
Regional Planning	- Economic/physical plans (regional agencies) - Structure plans for sub-regions/counties (local government)	
Community planning	- Local plans for towns/local areas (local government) - Master plans for new towns (development corporations)	
Financing	- Central government loans/grants (new towns) - Local government funding with central government aid (other projects)	- Private equity/debt funding (but limited to commercial, small-scale residential)
Land assembly	- Compulsory purchase at existing use value of all development land (following Community Land Act) - Land banking for major projects	- Typically small parcels only
Land development	- All major infrastructure developed by government (usually local)	- Typically development within infrastructure provided by government
Construction (housing, commercial, community services)	- Substantial in-house construction by many authorities - Or construction out to contract under government specifications	- Builders either as sub-contractors to government or on own account for smaller projects
Management (housing, commercial, community services)	- Comprehensive role for all services and facilities (mainly local government)	- Limited commercial property role - Input to community service management by voluntary agencies
Control	- Strong planning control powers held by local government - Appeals procedure to central government	

Figure 16.1 UK development mechanisms

local autonomy have met with strong resistance—the London local authorities, for example, have been strenuous opponents of creating a development corporation to redevelop London's docklands, despite the additional resources it could bring to bear from central government.)

With this heavy government preponderance in the British experience, the need is for a more imaginative use of machinery that already exists rather than for the creation of fresh powers and institutions. In my view, two major opportunities exist for improvement. The first is to broaden the base of resources available for community development—particularly by enhancing the contribution of the private sector.

Private developers in the UK have characteristically been confined to the limited role of building and selling properties on already planned and serviced sites. In some cases, they have acted as partners to public authorities for the commercial component of large projects. But the number of instances in recent years where private developers have actually initiated projects of neighbourhood scale and above can be counted on the fingers of one hand. The reasons for this limited contribution may be several. The postwar new towns were conceived for the prime purpose of relocating the residents of overcrowded cities through provision of public housing and controlled provision of jobs. This was not a program in which the private sector appeared to have a major role to play, certainly in the political environment of the late forties, and much of this habit of mind seems to have remained. Meanwhile, the sheer weight of public machinery has, on the one hand, tended to discourage the private sector from defining a creative role for itself and, on the other hand, encouraged the public sector to assume that it has the capacity and resources for all the key community development tasks.

Whatever the reasons, large-scale development has arguably been poorer as a result. Many British new towns suffer somewhat from a lack of housing choice—an insufficient range of products to meet the subtleties and variations of the market. Much of the public housing, too, constrained by increasingly tight government design and cost yardsticks, can be visually repetitive and monotonous. Additional benefits to the community are largely forgone—including the reduction in financial burdens for the public authority and taxpayer that would result from increased private investment, and the opportunity to gain further amenities and social programs negotiated as part of a development 'package'.

There are several ways to enhance the private sector contribution without sacrificing the public authority's ability to guide the total development effort. For example, in new towns, town expansion schemes or other large public projects, one approach—already introduced successfully in France—would be for the public authority to offer developers the chance of developing large areas of land—say from 200 to 700 acres. The public body would specify the output in terms of the number of dwellings, limits on commercial space, etc., and allow the developer to plan, design, build and sell (or rent) the project from the greenfield. The suitability of the design could be assured by retaining design control, or making it the subject of competition.

Another solution could lie through the Community Land Act, despite the fact that it is widely regarded as a further blow for an already oppressed private development

329

(In Order of Designation)

NEW TOWN	POPULATION TARGET				URBAN TYPE						PLANNING OBJECTIVE				
	More than 250,000	100,000-250,000	50,000-100,000	Less than 50,000	New town-in-town	Regional city	Growth center	Freestanding community	Town expansion	Satellite community	Renew existing urban area	Direct large-scale economic change	Stimulate regional revival	Channel urban growth	Relieve urban congestion
Stevenage		×								×				×	×
Crawley			×							×				×	×
Hemel Hempstead			×							×				×	×
Harlow			×							×				×	×
Aycliffe				×			×			×			×		×
East Kilbride			×				×			×			×	×	×
Peterlee				×						×					×
Hatfield				×						×				×	×
Welwyn				×										×	×
Glenrothes		×						×					×		×
Basildon			×							×				×	×
Bracknell			×							×				×	×
Cwmbran			×				×			×			×		
Corby			×					×					×		

Cumbernauld	x	x					x						x
Skelmersdale	x	x	x				x						x
Livingston	x	x	x				x			x			x
Redditch	x	x	x			x				x		x	x
Runcorn	x	x	x	x			x					x	x
Washington	x	x	x	x			x					x	x
Craigavon	x		x	x					x	x		x	x
Antrim	x		x	x					x	x			x
Irvine	x	x	x	x		x						x	x
Milton Keynes	x	x		x	x				x				
Peterborough	x	x		x	x				x	x			x
Ballymena	x								x				
Mid Wales	x							x					
Northampton	x	x	x		x	x			x				
Warrington	x	x	x		x	x			x	x	x		
Telford	x	x	x		x	x			x				
Londonderry	x	x	x	x	x		x		x	x			
Central Lancs.	x	x	x	x	x				x			x	
Stonehouse	x	x	x			x					x		x

Figure 16.2 UK postwar new towns

industry. Well used, it could actually benefit the private developer by removing the prohibitively costly and time-consuming tasks of land assembly and acquisition. The conditions for success, of course, would be the release of sufficient land by the local authority to enable effective and timely development to be achieved.

Again, private financing sources would be tapped through use of the loan guarantee, a mechanism not yet used in the UK although it is widely used for development financing in the US and other countries. The major advantage to government of the loan guarantee is that except in the rare cases of default no public expenditure is actually required. Thus major development programs can be undertaken with relatively small cash outlays that are effectively limited to the actual risks of default and the administrative costs of the program.

After increased private sector participation, the second main opportunity I see for improvement in the UK development mechanisms is to increase local accountability. This is becoming a critical issue as national attention focuses on the problems of our existing cities and as local demands for participation in the development process become more strident. Hitherto, large-scale community development has been seen as largely anti-democratic. New towns have been expressions of national policy, implemented through corporations directly accountable to central government. Even smaller projects initiated locally have been seen as impositions on the local community, interrupting and hastening the incremental process of development that would otherwise have occurred. Thus there is a greater need for experimentation in the political structure of community development.

One approach would be to transfer ownership of development corporation assets to the local authority after the main development phases are completed. This would enable the corporation to focus on its prime development tasks, while enabling local government to take a comprehensive responsibility for the ongoing management of public services. In addition, local representation on the development corporation board could be increased, in order to improve democratic control over development. The development corporation would continue to act as a channel for the extra national development resources needed, but would be under immediate local control. (Central government would retain the same ultimate funding control as it already does in relation to rate support grants.) Local authorities could also be encouraged to establish development boards with new-town-type powers to initiate large projects crossing the geographical and functional boundaries of individual authorities. Urban renewal and new development projects could both be dealt with appropriately in this way, benefiting from the concentrated focus that a unified development organization can bring. When implemented, the Community Land Act will in any case give local authorities powers of land acquisition equivalent to those already possessed by new town development corporations.

On a smaller scale, area management techniques—community councils, area local authority offices, and so on—have already been explored as devices for implementing inner city renewal. These could well be applied more widely to other community development situations, where (1) there is a significant constituency of existing residents affected by development and (2) development is being accomplished through social and economic programs as well as by physical restructuring. Under these conditions the motivation and response of existing communities are, of course, central to the achievement of change. Appropriate mechanisms could range from a much closer than normal participation in plan making to a delegated management role for specific community programs.

The United States

The American community development system is almost the antithesis of the British one. Development, with few exceptions, has been the result of private initiatives, subject to specific government controls (Fig. 16.3). There is still a great deal of resistance to the idea, let alone the reality, of land-use planning on a comprehensive scale.

Unlike the British system, the main strengths of the American approach lie in the areas that the private developer knows best—imaginative design, careful marketing and innovative programming of community services. In the US there has been a good deal of debate as to whether new communities have really achieved a quality of development superior to the more conventional forms they were intended to displace. A recent study of 15 new communities has indicated that, despite several advantages such as better access to community facilities, reduction in automobile travel and improved environments for low-income households, new communities do not appear to differ radically from other forms of growth in terms of residents' family and social perspectives.[3] Some critics suggest that innovation has taken the form of technological gimmicks rather than substantive improvements, others that the social objectives of new communities are mere rhetoric and unlikely to be implemented. Meanwhile the recent recession has provided fuel for the sceptics, as some of the more contentious features of projects, such as low-income housing, are re-evaluated in the cold light of slack markets and financial reality.

For all these criticisms, the US new communities are beginning to achieve a greater richness and diversity than other suburban patterns (and perhaps than some of their counterparts in environments dominated by the public sector). Evidence is emerging, for instance, even in the short life of the Title VII program. Basic 'open society' goals have been much nearer to achievement in Title VII communities than elsewhere; Park Forest South, for instance, has a 19 per cent black population; Jonathan, so far, is 4 per cent black, against 3 per cent in the rest of the metropolitan area; Cedar Riverside has achieved complete integration in its first phase of 1,300 units. A number of experimental approaches and programs have been, or are being, implemented—e.g., Roosevelt Island is being designed as an automobile-free area, with electric minibuses, etc.; Jonathan has a comprehensive CATV and communications network, covering educational, medical, security and other community applications. And several innovations in government relations are being tried, apparently with some success; Newfields, for instance, is experimenting with a 'dual development' structure in which public facilities are being developed jointly by the developer and a specially created public authority; Jonathan is involved in expanding and revitalizing services for the existing community as well as for the new one.

333

PROCESS	PUBLIC	PRIVATE
Regional planning	– Plans and growth strategies (regional agencies)	
Community planning	– Master plans for city areas – Zoning ordinances (land use)	– Master plans for new communities, NTITs, etc. – Project plans for major sites
Financing	– Federal loan guarantees (Title IV and Title VII programs) – Federal grants – FMA mortgage program – Special agency funding (NYUDC)	– Equity funding by developers/ investors – Debt/mortgage funding by bankers/investors
Land assembly	– Powers of eminent domain for public projects	– Land assembly/land banking without public funding or support
Land development	– Infrastructure provision normally limited to regional/ urban transportation and utilities	– Project-scale infrastructure provided as part of development package
Construction (housing, commercial, community services)	– Very limited public role in construction process	– Builders either as sub-contractors to land developers or on own account for smaller projects
Management (housing, commercial, community services)	– Management role in some community services – e.g., education, security	– Substantial role for developers, private and voluntary agencies, community associations in providing services, supplementary public services
Control	– Weak control by local government through zoning procedures	– Design control by developers and community associations

Figure 16.3 US development mechanisms

The weaknesses of the American system begin to show when new communities are evaluated as instruments of planning policy. Even the Title VII program, which started with ambitious intentions of diversity, has in practice been fairly limited in scope—certainly as compared with the British new towns program (Fig. 16.4). Congress originally envisaged a wide range of needs being met through the program—suburban satellites to rationalize growth at the edge of metropolitan areas, new-towns-in-town to revitalize the central city, freestanding communities creating new growth points beyond the metropolitan zone, and accelerated growth centres to expand small towns in rural areas. In the event, all but three of the 14 Title VII projects fall into the satellite community category, responding to urban pressures within commuting distance of major metropolitan centres.

Two gaps in the American machinery have been critical. The first is the almost complete absence of a regional or national planning framework. Even in the Title VII program, HUD has only been in a position to react to developer initiatives. While a developer could locate a project to meet his own criteria of market potential or environmental quality, nobody—HUD, developer or anyone else—could be sure that the project made sense in terms of other public criteria such as impact on regional transportation systems, or economic growth patterns. While many regional plans are in existence, prepared under the guidance of Regional Planning Commissions, they are frequently no more than extrapolations of existing growth trends, and certainly carry no formal authority.

The second major gap is the lack of public support for key aspects of land development for major projects—land assembly, land acquisition and infrastructure development. Where the private developer has been unwilling or unable to provide the resources himself, development options have as a result been severely restricted. Land assembly either within or near existing cities is prohibitively expensive and time-consuming for large projects. Meanwhile, development beyond the hinterland of metropolitan centres is frequently constrained by the lack of available infrastructure and the shortage of existing employment on which to base early market growth and revenue generation. The same is largely true of the Title VII program, which was intended to overcome these difficulties. The Federal guarantee has removed some of the immediate risks from large-scale development, but it leaves the same requirement to achieve long-term viability as before. Moreover, the actual operation of Title VII has offset many of the alleged financial advantages. Thus developers have been required by HUD to front-end many costs of a truly public nature—e.g., relocation costs, transportation systems, social programs. In addition, successive administrations have failed to implement many of the Title VII provisions; as William Nicoson showed in chapter 2, the program of supplementary grants for activities of regional benefit has been terminated, and the special planning assistance grants were never funded.

To confront these difficulties, regional development corporations should be established at statewide or metropolitan level, responsible for developing a strategic regional plan to guide both private and public development. It is unlikely that such a plan could be made mandatory, at least in the foreseeable future; however, public financial support could be made conditional on meeting its basic land-use, economic

335

(In Order of Guarantee Commitment)

NEW COMMUNITY	PLANNING OBJECTIVE					URBAN TYPE						POPULATION TARGET			
	Relieve urban congestion	Channel urban growth	Stimulate regional revival	Direct large-scale economic change	Renew existing urban area	Satellite community	Town expansion	Freestanding community	Growth center	Regional city	New town-in-town	Less than 50,000	50,000–100,000	100,000–250,000	More than 250,000
Jonathan, Ma.		x				x			x			x			
St. Charles, Md.		x				x								x	
Park Forest South, Ill.		x				x							x		
Flower Mound, Tex.		x				x							x		
Maumelle, Ark.		x		x		x						x			
Cedar–Riverside, Ma.					x						x	x			
Riverton, NY		x				x						x			
San Antonio Ranch, Tex.		x				x							x		
Woodlands, Tex.		x				x								x	
Gananda, NY		x				x						x			
Soul City, NC		x		x				x				x			
Harbison, SC		x				x						x			
Lysander, NY		x				x						x			
Welfare Island, NY		x				x			x				x		
Shenandoah, Ga.		x				x			x			x			

Figure 16.4 US Title VII new communities

336

and social objectives. The corporation could also disseminate data and techniques that could be relevant to meeting regional needs.

A regional agency such as this could play a positive part in supporting land development by both public and private sectors, especially in or near existing cities where the need is greatest. Providing public guarantees for private financing sources is perhaps the most critical need. In this context, the creation of a nationwide Community Development Bank has already been discussed in Congress, although not yet implemented. Funds would be obtained entirely from the private sector, under Federal guarantee, to finance both renewal and new development projects. Applications would be screened for economic and financial feasibility by the bank, and for social and environmental acceptability. This scheme would increase the choice of financing mechanisms available (particularly for the earliest development stages), could reduce the risks of the Federal Government, and could perhaps shorten the funding application process compared with current Title VII procedures. However, I do not see the scheme as helping fundamentally with the most important problem—that is, subsidizing the developer to take action in areas where development could never be viable on a normal economic basis.

The regional agency, on the other hand, could engage in joint ventures with developers, picking up the front-end costs of acquisition and infrastructure, and thus in effect subsidizing the developer to undertake projects that are needed in the public interest but that are not viable commercially. It could also acquire development sites for release to developers on a subcontracted basis, at a price that would make socially beneficial projects feasible—e.g., low- and moderate-income housing.

In the longer term, regional development corporations could build up land banks for eventual development. Such a role, however, would meet with a great deal of political and public resistance, and is unlikely to be implemented for a long time to come.

The French approach to community development offers yet a third model, blending a strong government role at the regional level with a significant private sector role at the community and neighbourhood level. The French program is too new to permit conclusive judgements, but it may provide the best synthesis yet of the many dimensions of community development.

Certainly the key to success in the future will lie not only in identifying new needs and opportunities as they emerge, but also—equally important—in adopting flexible mechanisms for meeting them to marshal the resources of all the participants in the development process.

References

1. *Thirteenth Report from the Expenditure Committee, New Towns*, House of Commons, Session 1974–75.
2. *The Costs of Sprawl: Detailed Cost Analysis*, Real Estate Research Corporation; US Government Printing Office: April 1974.
3. *New Communities USA*, Center for Urban and Regional Studies, University of North Carolina at Chapel Hill, 1975.

337

Appendix:
A checklist of selected problems in community development

Throughout this book, the authors have raised issues of common concern in all community development programs. While considerable attention is being given to these in development enterprises throughout the world, relatively little of the work in progress has so far been documented.

As an aid to decision-makers and analysts who are grappling with these problems, these notes have been prepared to highlight some of the most pressing questions that need to be resolved. They are not intended to be comprehensive, nor to convey ready answers. As they are based on considerable recent experience, however, they should provide a useful checklist of 'thought starters' that developers and planners can adapt to their own situations.

The notes are grouped in four sections, addressing four basic questions:

- How can the management of community programs be improved?
- What can be done to put community development on a stronger financial footing and improve financial control?
- What role should the development corporation play vis-à-vis the local government and residents during each stage of the development process?
- How should the development corporation ensure that the overall costs and benefits are in balance?

Program management

The provision of community programs could be improved basically by making the processes for planning and managing facilities and services more rigorous and comprehensive, but this in turn raises a number of crucial questions:

How can needs and demands for community services be better identified? To ensure that programs meet the needs of residents, three main issues need to be resolved:

- Where will the new community's requirements for programs differ from those of established communities?—e.g.
  - —Communities with a high proportion of parents with growing families demand more extensive (and expensive) pre-school programs.
  - —Where there is a high proportion of young semi-skilled workers, more spare-time adult technical education is likely to be required.
- How will the pattern of demand for these programs vary over time, in contrast with traditional communities?—e.g.
  - —A drop in the demand for nursery schools as children grow up, and the population of the town as a whole moves to a more traditional age structure.
  - —More demand from groups with special needs, like the elderly, as the original population matures and a new age mix is attracted to the completed community.

- Where will the needs of the new community outstrip the resources of existing government and voluntary agencies?—e.g.
  —More social counselling and support because of the pressures of living in a new community and the lack of mature family and friendship ties.
  —Greater need for pre-school-age child care.

Can the various agencies responsible for provision be better co-ordinated? Various government, private and voluntary organizations are involved in providing community programs. To ensure that these programs do not overlap, that they are spread equitably throughout the community and that adequate opportunity is given to private enterprise to provide commercially viable facilities, there needs to be some mechanism for co-ordinating these efforts.

- Can a common focus be established to guide consultation among all groups likely to be involved in the provision of social programs?—e.g.
  —Guidelines on the basic economic and social population mix for the community.
  —An illustrative program structure defining needs, objectives, facility and service provision and proposed divisions of responsibility.
  —A handbook for representatives of institutions serving each main 'client group'—such as 'working mothers' and 'mid-teens'—that specifies planning assumptions (numbers expected in the client group), sets out the objectives of the program, and outlines the approach to be used.
- Should an overall 'community economic plan', spelling out objectives for developing the employment and commercial base, and specifying the timing, costs and incentives to be provided by local and central government, be produced to cover the activities of both public and private organizations?

Are plans for community programs specific enough to serve as a basis for action?

- Are objectives and targets adequately defined?—e.g.
  —Objectives on demographic mix and phasing that are clear and rigorous enough to provide an adequate basis for planning rather than couched in vague terms such as 'balance' that will be interpreted in numerous different ways.
  —Targets set in terms of certain standards of achievement—such as the proportion of children in special education returned to normal schools—rather than objectives left as expressions of intent.
- Do plans establish from the outset the staffing and operating expenses for a program such as health care, or do they cover only the physical provision of facilities?
- Does each agency involved know when each facility and level of provision of programs will be required to meet community needs as the population increases through the development?
- How can project organization be improved?—e.g.
  —Developer seconding skilled technical personnel to provide the local

339

authority with the resources to carry out its share of building adequate public facilities.

—Developer providing an in-house technical and administrative service to support voluntary groups.

—Processes streamlined for co-ordination among the various agencies involved to ensure that development keeps in phase—i.e., speeding up or slowing down local government activity to match the development pace.

How can program operations be made more effective?

● Should residents control the operation of selected community programs?—e.g.
  —All programs, except those that must legally remain under public authority control, under an elected resident board.
  —Services financed by developer and voluntary agencies through a resident-controlled trust fund.
● How can program efficiency be measured?—e.g.
  —Regular 'trade-off reviews' to check whether programs can be provided more economically by, for instance, spending less on daycare facilities and discounting prices on larger houses for 'foster parents'.
  —Comparative analysis of refuse collection and disposal costs with those in similar new and existing communities.
● Who should monitor program performance to ensure that programs serve their intended function?—e.g.
  —Developer reporting annually to residents and public authorites, describing progress towards agreed targets and impact of community programs
  —Annual 'audit' by *ad hoc* appointed group of local residents, academics, public figures and developers.
  —Annual review by elected resident committee.

The financial base

Since both local government and voluntary agencies will find their resources stretched in trying to provide the standard of services required by a new community before they can draw on the residents for finance and political support, timely and adequate service provision is always inhibited. The issue, then, is to discover new ways of financing these initial capital and operating expenses and of recovering the ultimate economic value to be created through development at the outset to put new communities on a stronger initial financial footing.

What financial objectives should govern new town planning and development? For example:

● Should new town economics and financing be designed to achieve a target percentage return on total investment or assets employed? If so, what measurement problems have to be resolved in this calculation?
● Should new town developments be financially self-sustaining? If so, what

requirements does this impose for phasing different types of facilities and services, each with its own economic profile?

- Should community facilities be financed solely from cash generated by land and building unit sales or rents?
- Should operating programs be financed from the same source(s)?
- Should the economic/financial structure of a 'satellite' new town be designed to sustain the amenity and service costs of its 'mother city' or neighbouring old town?

What mechanisms should be adopted to co-ordinate the financial interests of major participants in a new community development program?

- Should the 'syndicat communautaire' concept pioneered in France be adopted in other countries? What alternative mechanisms would achieve the same practical political objectives?
- Should a financial policy and review board in each development project be delegated final expenditure authority within the overall budget guidelines established by its financing sources?
- Should residents assume financial decision-making and funding responsibility for community facilities and operating programs? If so, at what point in the development cycle is it realistic for such control to pass from the development organization to a local representative body?
- Should a total 'new community budget' be developed for each project, including the sources and uses of *all* capital and operating funds, both public and private, to be employed in the project?
- Should commitments by each new town participant be enforced through a separate program budget established for each main public expenditure category—i.e., education, roads, hospitals—including operating as well as capital items?

Can local government bear the cost? Local government needs to decide whether the higher property tax yield achievable through the provision of new facilities justifies it in carrying out the initial provision and funding.

- Does it have an adequate current assessment base and management and technical capability to provide its usual services to the required standard immediately?
- Can it provide superior amenities or facilities outside conventional programs?
  —Will the cost of providing superior cultural and sports facilities be recovered within the budget cycle by the increase in property values?
- —Can it, politically and legally, provide environmental protection services in a new community superior to those elsewhere in its area?

How can the developer help? The development enterprise can assist and promote local funding efforts to support community facilities in many ways.

- Could it sponsor, initiate or join community groups to enable them to raise funds?

341

- Can it raise the capital directly at lower cost?—e.g., by building a community facility, such as a bar/restaurant/meeting hall, to be run by a community group that will repay the development loan out of profits.
- Can it provide voluntary groups with 'seed money', or other low-cost support?—e.g.
  - —Offices and secretarial support for voluntary groups meeting specific program needs.
  - —Technical advice (architects, engineers, quantity surveyors) from its own staff to help residents build churches, meeting halls, etc.

How can the value created by new amenities and facilities be identified and measured? While the most fundamental means of putting new communities on a stronger financial footing is to capture the value created by amenities and other 'social' investments, they must first be identified and measured.

- Can credible (if subjective) estimates of value created be developed?—e.g.
  - —Current prices for the residual asset value of an integral development component such as a neighbourhood centre or village.
  - —Indicators of the value created by any given facility—for example, the standard cost of community meeting rooms and their marginal contribution to total unit value.
- Do assumptions on the relative worth of development value-added hold in areas with a low discretionary income base?
- Can value created be estimated empirically from historical or comparative analysis of similar components in established communities?
- Can it be estimated experimentally?—for example, by simulating purchase decisions among a range of options to test—e.g.
  - —What premium are households at different income levels prepared to pay for an attractive physical environment?
  - —Will younger households pay more to live in a community that also attracts elderly residents to produce a balanced age distribution?

How can the value created be recovered? Value created can normally be recovered through price premiums paid on entry into a new community, through apportionments or levies and through user charges.

- What additional amenities will encourage householders to pay a price premium?—e.g.
  - —What price distribution can be developed between buyers who will pay a premium simply for the appearance of high-cost facilities, such as a country club, and those paying only for benefits that they will enjoy 'free', such as a waterside or park location?
  - —What premium can be gained for a comprehensive, locally financed health service?
  - —What premium are lower-income families willing and able to pay for basic community services—particularly where programs, such as an all-day child-care service, could over time increase family income?

- Will residents pay apportionments or levies on anything but community facilities?—e.g., Can the provision of indoor sports facilities, squash, tennis, etc., be entirely paid for by charges on all households, or must all contributions be by users?
- Does the investment in community facilities affect the amount that potential commercial or industrial residents will pay?—e.g.
  - —What marginal rent will an industrial employer be prepared to pay for a site in a community that provides extensive programs for pre-school and school-age children?
  - —What value differential can be achieved by siting industrial facilities in a landscaped industrial park?
  - —What premium can be gained from office or high-technology employers through provision of outstanding educational facilities?
- Will employers pay non-residential levies to cover facilities used by the community, only some of whom are employees?—e.g.
  - —Can firms be persuaded to contribute substantially to community facilities rather than establish private, company-financed sports and social clubs exclusively for employees?
  - —What level of community assessment (in addition to local government taxes) will commercial and industrial firms pay to recoup investment in community facilities or programs?

What methods should be used to control the development process?

- Should quantitative measures be adopted for assessing non-financial costs and benefits—e.g., scale values for 'good design', performance measures for community service program impact on residents' problems?
- Should the costs of planning and building delays be identified in new town development budgets? If so, what cost elements—i.e., interest charges, opportunities forgone, social factors—should be included?
- Should the full 'life cycle' of both operating and capital investment be considered in evaluating alternative projects? If so, what practical political, and technical problems will arise? How can they best be resolved?
- Should an integrated system linking financial and physical measures of progress and shortfalls be used?
- Should 'commitment accounting' be adopted as a planning and budgeting principle?

Developer roles

The creation of a new community inevitably requires intensive involvement by the developer in the full range of development tasks and programs, but this can take many forms and represent varying levels of commitment at different stages of the development cycle.

343

What roles should each major participant—i.e., development agency, national government, local government, private builders, residents—play in the development process?—e.g.

- Should the development agency—whether public or private—be equipped with all the powers necessary for planning, building, launching and operating the new community?
- Should the developer's direct action role be limited to site planning and development?
- Can the developer act effectively as a 'social entrepreneur', stimulating direct action and investment in community services by others but not undertaking program management himself?
- Should the residents be empowered to decide on major new facilities and investments after the start-up phase?
- Should the national government exercise any operating control during the development process if it provides the main source of finance or ensures against the major risks? If so, what balance can realistically be struck between governmental control and local residents' interests?

How can the developer help in ensuring that a desirable range of community facilities is provided? The newness of the new community presents many opportunities for innovation in providing better amenities and facilities, but these may be missed without positive developer action.

- Can traditional agencies be helped to improve the quality of their services?—e.g.
  —Acting as agent for both public authority and private enterprise providers in assembling land, and designing and building facilities to ensure that the provision is phased with the rest of the development and is as cost effective as possible.
  —Providing local government with a pool of skilled staff to ensure that it can carry out the tasks of analysing the need for new and different community services.
  Channelling finance to ensure that programs are not delayed by limitations on borrowing power.
- Can the activities of several providers be co-ordinated at the developer's initiative to eliminate duplication?—e.g.
  —Planning and co-ordinating pre-school daycare so that private, voluntary, and public agencies do not compete and thus make the best overall use of their collective resources.
  —Co-ordinating private and public agencies by, for example, providing common vehicle purchasing and servicing for local government vehicles and private passenger transport fleets.
- How can voluntary provision be encouraged?—e.g.
  —Providing finance or staff for voluntary group programs.
  —Financing or providing social development officers to establish community

voluntary groups and encourage self-help provision of programs, such as in-home care of the elderly, or day-time care for the children of working mothers.

● Should the facilities and programs be underwritten by the developer?—e.g.

—Underwriting the start-up costs of residents' associations until they are large enough to be self-supporting.

—Providing and maintaining highly profitable facilities, such as bars, to provide subsidies for less commercially attractive facilities—for example, cultural activities or minority sports.

What role can the developer usefully play in program planning and management?

● To what extent should he be involved in strategic planning and co-ordination?—e.g.

—Part of a formal group with government and resident representatives set up to advise on and control needs analysis and program planning.

—A 'clearing house' to keep providers of services and facilities in touch with the activities of others.

● Should he play a major role in managing construction and the provision of facilities?—e.g.

—Acting as project manager for all agencies involved and co-ordinating the recruitment of staff and administrative arrangements for operating programs.

—Encouraging and providing staff support for regular 'progress reviews' to resolve problems of co-ordination and provide assistance and advice on other problems.

● What role should he play in monitoring the effectiveness of community programs?—e.g.

—Sponsor a resident group to review provision, assess effectiveness and recommend changes.

—Encourage group provision of facilities and programs—public, private, and voluntary—meeting regularly to carry out 'self-assessment' of effectiveness of provision.

—Leave monitoring to normal commercial or public agency processes.

How should the developer participate in property management?

● What part should he play in organizing and co-ordinating property management?—e.g.

—Should he be responsible for maintenance throughout the marketing phase, recovering the cost from land/property sales?

—At what point can open space maintenance be shifted to a residents' association?

● How could he contribute to the property management task?—e.g.

—Providing manpower and resources.

—Collecting assessments from residents and contracting out management to a specialist firm.

345

—Establishing a property management and maintenance subsidiary, financed by a levy on all properties.

—Taking over some of the customary or statutory responsibilities of local government in this area.

● Should he be instrumental in setting up resident groups to manage the developed site—e.g.

—Establishing a resident-controlled limited company that would require residents to join as a condition of land/property sale.

—Providing facilities and administrative/secretarial support for a voluntary residents' association.

What would be the developer's role in managing the community? One role for the developer would be to fill gaps in the local government/residents' association structure. Whether this would be appropriate depends largely on resolving the following questions.

● Does the local government provide a single forum for the whole of the new community?—e.g.

—Is the local government unit coterminous with the new community?

—Is one local government unit responsible for most statutory responsibilities, or are there two or more tiers of special-purpose districts?

● Do residents' associations have the resources to act as a channel of communication?—e.g.

—Adequate finance to buy time on local television or radio, space in a local newspaper, or to issue their own newsheets.

—Sufficient skilled members to conduct a debate with the developer or with government agencies.

● Do such associations truly represent the community residents' interests?—e.g.

—Do election procedures ensure that later arrivals are represented?

—Are all significant interest groups adequately represented?

● Could the developer act as broker between the community and local government?—e.g.

—Conducting regular reviews of problems and matters of other interest with both groups.

—Inviting representatives of government and residents to participate in his own planning processes.

● Could he assist in creating strong resident groups?—e.g.

—Financing a community newspaper.

—Providing premises and staff support for a residents' council.

—Requiring residents to join and support financially a residents' association as a condition of purchase.

Community costs and benefits

The development enterprise can avoid extended political controversy by attempting as far as possible to ensure that the costs and benefits of the new community are

346

spread evenly through the existing locality and region. To do this, answers to the following questions are needed.

Can an overall assessment of the new community's 'balance sheet' be made?

- Can the impact on local government finance be calculated?—e.g.
  —Estimates of capital and revenue expenditure in the development project, obtained both privately and through published local government accounts.
  —Revenue arising directly from the new community—i.e., increased local tax base, additional state and central government subsidies attracted by the new population.
- Can the impact on central government finances be assessed?
  —Rough estimates from government and industry statistics of commercial and private tax revenue sourced from prospective residents and firms.
  —Estimates of government expenditure.
- Can assessments be made of the cost of services provided by voluntary agencies in the new town?
- Can private sector activities be assessed in financial terms—e.g., estimates of locally generated business income and expenditure?
- Can financial information be combined to provide a picture of where benefits accrue or liabilities fall?
  —Community-wide 'sources and uses of funds' statement.
  —Community cash-flow model.

How can the balance between benefits and liabilities be assessed?

- Can the developer strike a balance between local and central government contribution?—e.g.
  —Using a government 'net income statement' sheet to assist in negotiating with governments for additional resources to be channelled into the area.
  —Selling land at discount to local governments if the community places a heavy net burden on them.
- How can the developer ensure that sufficient contributions are made to community 'overheads'?—e.g.
  —A joint equity agreement with private companies whereby a 'vertical slice' or a fixed proportion of net gains over a certain figure is paid to support community facilities.
  —An arrangement whereby profitable private activities are operated for, or transferred to, the local government or a resident group for use within the community.
  —Establishment of a ceiling level of return on investment and 'effort' above which some proportion of incremental gains from development is fed back into the community accounts.
  —Subsidization of land to local government to balance the current and future development gains accruing to it or to central government.

How can the benefits of the new community be spread to the existing community/region?

● Can the developer apply across the whole region the skills and resources developed in creating the new community?—e.g.
  —Training personnel for local construction.
  —Providing a pool of staff to analyse local problems and develop new programs.
  —Setting up a joint program with the regional economic development organization to attract jobs.
● Can the layout of the project enhance the visual environment?—e.g.
  —Provision to maintain existing attractive features while removing and redeveloping unattractive areas—for example, derelict industrial sites.
  —Architectural review panel to ensure that all buildings and physical plans for the new community reach an acceptable aesthetic standard.
● Could the new community be used as a testing ground for minimizing the level of pollution typically caused by multi-use urban development?—e.g.
  —Waste disposal recycling system producing useful, or at least harmless, by-products—such as heating fuel.
  —Flood control schemes needed for water and drainage control used to provide water sports and waterside views.

How can the greatest benefit be achieved from the 'social investment' in the new community?

● How can the community facilities/services investment best reflect residents' needs and wishes?—e.g.
  —Developer funding for research into likely social welfare needs and resident attitudes to alternative types of provision.
  —Resident study groups on selected planning issues.
● How can the new community provide the greatest 'value for money' from social investment?—e.g.
  —Encouraging or providing multiple-use facilities to ensure maximum provision of facilities for a given cash input.
  —Striking a better balance between capital and operating expenses than in older communities—for example, by reducing staffing needs in housing for the elderly and the handicapped by building in simple alarm/communication devices, or reducing district heating costs by building initially to higher insulation standards.
  —Breaking down traditional boundaries between services to provide greater value from a given level of input—by, for instance, providing 'one-stop' local government offices in various neighbourhoods to deal with a range of government services, thus reducing both user and provision costs.

Experience suggests that community development will produce better results if the right questions are identified early in the planning process and comprehensively assessed against the full range of project criteria.

Notes on contributors

The Editor

MAHLON APGAR, IV is a management consultant and an authority on real estate, housing and urban planning. A principal of McKinsey & Company, he has served a wide range of business, financial and government organizations on problems of corporate strategy, public policy, community planning and operations management in North America, Europe, Japan and the Middle East. Prior to joining McKinsey he was an assistant to James W. Rouse, and a market analyst with the Columbia new city project. A graduate of Blair, Dartmouth and the Harvard Business School, he also undertook postgraduate research on British new towns and planning policies at Magdalen College, Oxford, and has been a Visiting Lecturer in City and Regional Planning at Harvard. He has contributed to four books, and his articles have appeared in leading journals, including the *Harvard Business Review, Real Estate Review* and *Journal of The Royal Town Planning Institute.* He is an Executive Group member of the Urban Land Institute's New Communities Council, and a Fellow of the Royal Society of Arts, and he received the Arthur A. May Award of the American Institute of Real Estate Appraisers for his contribution to real estate appraisal education.

The Authors

RICHARD LLEWELYN-DAVIES is senior partner of the international architectural and planning firm bearing his name. He has been responsible for the master plans of Milton Keynes new city and Washington new town, nine American new towns, and a number of major hospital and building designs, and is presently undertaking planning for one of the largest urban developments in the world in Teheran. Created a Baron in 1964 for his contributions in these fields, he is also Dean of the School of Environmental Studies in the University of London, Chairman of the UK Centre for Environmental Studies, a Fellow of the Royal Town Planning Institute and the Royal Institute of British Architects, and an honorary member of the American Institute of Architects. He has an engineering degree from Cambridge University, studied at the Beaux Arts in Paris, and later qualified as an architect.

JAMES W. ROUSE is Chairman and Chief Executive Officer of The Rouse Company. A mortgage banker and real estate developer of major regional shopping centres, he also has developed the pioneering new city at Columbia, Maryland, and applied the principles of Columbia's planning in 'The Hartford Process', a comprehensive program of private and public initiatives to revitalize the Hartford Region. He has served on the President's Advisory Committee on Housing, is an honorary member of the American Institute of Architects and the American Institute of Planners, and is on the Visiting Committees of the graduate schools of planning and design at Harvard, the Massachusetts Institute of Technology and the University of Maryland. He has a law degree from the University of Maryland.

WILLIAM NICOSON is a lawyer and consultant in Washington, DC, specializing in urban development and growth policy formulation. Appointed as the first Director of the US Office of New Communities Development, he was responsible for the administrative design of the Federal Government's Title VII new communities program. He is an Executive Group member of the Urban Land Institute's New Communities Council. Formerly with Sullivan & Cromwell in New York and Paris, he was educated at Exeter, Princeton, the Sorbonne and the Harvard Law School.

JEAN-EUDES ROULLIER is Secretary General of the Groupe Central des Villes Nouvilles, an interministerial body responsible for the French new towns program reporting to the Prime Minister. Appointed an Inspector of Finance, he began his official career as Assistant to the First Prefect of the Paris Region and later became Technical Adviser to the Ministry of Housing and Infrastructure Development. He has authored a number of papers on the administrative and financial aspects of urban development, and is a graduate of the Institut d'Etudes Politiques and the Ecole Nationale d'Administration.

H. DENNIS STEVENSON is Chairman of the Aycliffe and Peterlee Development Corporations, responsible for the planning, development and management of two new towns in the north of England. A specialist in both market and social research, he is also a partner in the Specialist Research Unit. The youngest Chairman in British new towns history, he also led a working party on the role of voluntary movements and youth appointed by the Secretary of State for the Environment in 1972, which prepared the report *Fifty Million Volunteers*, presented to the United Nations Conference on the Human Environment in Stockholm. He is currently chairman of both the National Association of Youth Clubs and an independent government body on pop festivals. He holds an MA from King's College, Cambridge.

MICHAEL D. SPEAR is General Manager for the Columbia new city project and Senior Vice-President of The Rouse Company for community development. With the degrees of Bachelor of Architecture and Master of City Planning (Harvard), he has been responsible for the full range of planning and development tasks, market research, project evaluation, land acquisition, planning, financing and marketing strategy. He has also been project director for two other planned communities and technical director for a number of planning studies. He is a member of the American Institute of Planners and other professional bodies.

350

RICHARD PHELPS is General Manager of the Central Lancashire Development Corporation, with overall responsibility for planning and developing the largest new town in Britain and expanding an existing population base of 250,000 to some 430,000. Formerly in the same position at Skelmersdale new town, he has also been a Principal in the British Treasury, an Under-Secretary in the Nigerian Ministry of Finance, and a senior administrator in the Hampshire County Council. He was educated at Merton College, Oxford, and in 1971 was awarded a Travelling Fellowship under the Churchill Memorial Trust.

RICHARD ANDERSON is a consultant specializing in development finance and management. Formerly General Manager of the Columbia new city project, he was instrumental in the design of the Columbia Economic Model and in setting up the pioneering joint venture between the Connecticut General Life Insurance Company and The Rouse Company to finance community development. He is currently serving as a Councilman of Howard County, Maryland (in which Columbia is being developed). A graduate of Clark University, he is also a Certified Public Accountant.

MORT HOPPENFELD is Dean of the School of Architecture and Planning at the University of New Mexico. He was formerly Director of Planning for The Greater Hartford Process, a landmark program to adapt the community development approach to the problems of a metropolitan region, and Vice-President and Director of Planning and Design for The Rouse Company, where he initiated and remained chief planner for the new city of Columbia. He served as Chief Urban Designer for the National Capital Planning Commission, participating in the 'Plan for the Year 2000'. He has taught both architecture and planning, lecturing and writing on design in urban and new town development. He holds a BArch. from the Massachusetts Institute of Technology and a Master of City Planning degree from the University of California at Berkeley. He is a member of the AIA and the AIP, and a Fellow of the Royal Society of Health.

PIERRE BLANCHARD is a senior consultant in the Paris office of McKinsey and a specialist in urban development and public administration, with a particular focus on management information, planning and control systems in new communities. He has worked on the implementation of the financial planning, management and control tools developed for the Groupe Central des Villes Nouvelles and the nine French new towns, and is currently responsible for supervising the implementation of new management tools in the new towns of Evry and Cergy. His prior experience includes designing an EDP system for the French navy and various consulting projects in OR and EDP for major French industrial firms. He has a degree in operations research from the Ecole National Supérieure des Arts et Métiers and holds an MBA from Carnegie-Mellon University.

JOHN GRIFFITH-JONES is a senior consultant with McKinsey and a specialist in the problems of strategy and organization in community development. He has worked extensively with national and local government agencies and construction firms in the US and Britain, analysing strategic plans and community services for both privately and publicly sponsored new communities. He has recently been managing

351

work on the planning and development of Tanzania's new capital city of Dodoma. Before joining McKinsey he was a project co-ordinator on the Warrington New Town Study for the Austin Smith/Lord Partnership. He has an MA degree in modern history from the University of Oxford, an MSc. in economics from the London School of Economics, and an MBA degree from Indiana University. He has published several articles in British journals on organization and management in local government.

R. Donnell McArthur is a consultant specializing in strategic planning, development and operations management, including the development of financial plans and programs and marketing strategies in the US and the UK. He also has extensive experience in both countries in implementing operational cost reduction programs and improving housing and facility design for development enterprises. Prior to joining McKinsey he worked for a venture capital subsidiary of Laird, Inc., and for a UK manufacturer of military radio equipment. He has a BSc. in engineering from the University of Arizona, where he was a Baird Scholar, and subsequently took an MBA degree at the Harvard Business School, graduating as a Baker Scholar with high distinction.

David Thompson is a senior associate in McKinsey's London office who specializes in the problems of real estate, community development, and local government. He has worked on problems in a range of development situations, and has been responsible for carrying out evaluations of both existing and planned new community development in the public and private sectors. In addition, he has developed an approach to evaluating the effectiveness of community programs. He holds an MA degree in history from the University of Cambridge and a Master of Science degree in business administration from the London Business School.

Charles E. Wallace, Jr is a senior consultant in the Washington, DC office of McKinsey, and specializes in community development and housing management. He has served both public and private enterprise in the fields of development planning, management information and reporting systems, including the Department of Housing and Urban Development, National Capital Housing Authority, State of Ohio, Columbia new city project and Metropolitan Atlanta Rapid Transit Authority. He is a *magna cum laude* graduate of Bucknell and also holds an MBA degree from the Wharton School of the University of Pennsylvania.

Index

Printed in Great Britain by J. W. Arrowsmith Ltd., Bristol